"This is the book I wish I could have handed to the diplomatic academies I have trained over the past decade. Dr. Kilburg has achieved something rare: a work rigorous enough for scholars and practical enough for Monday morning."

Corneliu Bjola, *Ph.D., Professor of Digital Diplomacy, University of Oxford*

"Should be required reading for any diplomat grappling with the complexity of artificial intelligence and the modern information environment."

Xander Vagg, *AI and National Security Professional; Former Defense Consultant*

"Don Kilburg gives current and future public diplomacy practitioners a much-needed guide to what is happening in AI at this moment and how to best use AI in reaching foreign publics. His examples show how AI is and can be deployed in the field, as well as the potential pitfalls if diplomats rush to automate too much, too soon and do not consider cultural context, language nuance, ethics, and the need for human oversight. The casual reader or researcher who wants to learn more about the art and science of public diplomacy will also find the vignettes a good peek into both the everyday considerations and the emergencies embassies face."

Robin Holzhauer, *Retired U.S. Foreign Service Officer and Senior Editor,* Diplomatic Diary

"Very timely. AI tools are already shaping how public diplomacy is practiced, often faster than policies, training, or institutional norms can keep up. Practitioners are experimenting in real time, while also dealing with deepfakes, synthetic media, and faster-moving narrative cycles. This book meets the field exactly where it is right now… It gives readers a practical way to think about how AI can support core public diplomacy functions (listening, messaging, monitoring, engagement, evaluation) while also being honest about the risks and tradeoffs."

Alexander Hunt, *Public Affairs Professional and Recipient of the Ameri Prize for Innovation in Public Diplomacy*

I0894170

AI Use Cases for Public Diplomacy

AI Use Cases for Public Diplomacy reveals how AI is reshaping the landscape of public diplomacy—and how it can aid diplomats in the contest for hearts and minds.

Every day, embassies monitor narratives, craft messages for divided publics, counter disinformation, respond to crises, and build coalitions across cultural and linguistic divides. These are high-stakes tasks, performed under time pressure, with imperfect information. Now, AI is transforming that challenge. Retired U.S. Foreign Service Officer Dr. Don Kilburg draws on more than two decades of frontline diplomatic experience. Through ten richly detailed chapters, a consistent narrative framework (the fictional Republic of Z), and nearly two hundred sources, he shows how AI can expand diplomatic reach, sharpen timing, and sustain credibility while confronting the ethical dilemmas head-on.

This book is essential reading for diplomats, embassy staff, politicians, and public communicators who are ready to act on the greatest lesson the AI revolution teaches us: credibility can no longer be faked, only earned.

Don Kilburg is a retired U.S. diplomat, experimental psychologist, and U.S. Army veteran with over 25 years of public service. His Foreign Service career spanned five continents, four languages, and postings from East Asia to the former Soviet Union, including service as Spokesperson for the Bureau of Energy Resources and Press Attaché at the U.S. Embassy in Beijing. A pioneer of AI adoption at the State Department, his innovations earned him multiple Superior and Meritorious Honor Awards. He is the author of *AI Use Cases for Diplomats* (Routledge 2025) and Founder & CEO of Mind Leap Institute.

AI Use Cases for Public Diplomacy

Applying AI to Public Affairs and Strategic Communication

Don Kilburg

CRC Press
Taylor & Francis Group
Boca Raton London New York

CRC Press is an imprint of the
Taylor & Francis Group, an **informa** business
A CHAPMAN & HALL BOOK

Designed cover image: Shutterstock

First edition published 2027
by CRC Press
2385 NW Executive Center Drive, Suite 320, Boca Raton FL 33431

and by CRC Press
4 Park Square, Milton Park, Abingdon, Oxon, OX14 4RN

CRC Press is an imprint of Taylor & Francis Group, LLC

British Library Cataloguing-in-Publication Data
A catalogue record for this book is available from the British Library

ISBN: 978-1-041-00938-2 (hbk)
ISBN: 978-1-041-00837-8 (pbk)
ISBN: 978-1-003-61237-7 (ebk)

DOI: 10.1201/9781003612377

Typeset in Times
by Newgen Publishing UK

Dedication

To my wife Keely, for her love, patience, and support. To my children Sonora, Vier, and Kesten, for reminding me why the future matters. And to those who practice public diplomacy and strategic communication with sincerity and good will: your work matters more now than ever before.

Lie through the machine, and you'll be the first one fooled.

Contents

Foreword

For the past 15 years, my research at Oxford has examined how digital technologies are transforming diplomatic practice. I hold what is, to my knowledge, the first professorship in digital diplomacy at any university, and I have trained diplomatic academies from London to Riyadh to Singapore. I mention this not to establish credentials but to explain why I am particularly well-positioned to assess Dr. Don Kilburg's contribution—and why I find it so necessary.

There is a persistent gap in our field. Scholars develop frameworks that often fail to reach the practitioners who could implement them. Practitioners experiment with AI tools without the benefit of systematic analysis. Staff rotate through diplomatic postings, lessons are learned and lost, and parallel conversations rarely intersect productively. When I conduct training sessions at foreign ministries, officers consistently ask the same question: "What do I actually do on Monday morning?" Too often, academic research cannot answer them. This book can.

Dr. Kilburg brings credentials rarely found in a single author. He holds a Ph.D. in experimental psychology, providing the methodological rigor that distinguishes careful analysis from speculation. He served 21 years as a U.S. Foreign Service Officer, specializing in public diplomacy and strategic communication—the very domain this book addresses. He held myriad roles ranging from Public Affairs Officer in Washington all the way to Public Affairs Officer in Kazakhstan, as well as Spokesperson for Energy Resources and Assistant Spokesperson at the U.S. Embassy in China. He trained in four languages. He has been recognized by the U.S. Department of State for innovation at the intersection of technology and diplomacy. He is not theorizing from outside; he is analyzing from within.

His earlier book, *AI Use Cases for Diplomats*, published by Routledge in 2025, provided a comprehensive survey of AI applications across diplomatic practice. This volume goes deeper, focusing specifically on public diplomacy and strategic communication—the visible face of diplomacy, where credibility is built or broken in real time. Readers familiar with the first book will find this a natural extension; those encountering Dr. Kilburg's work for the first time will find a complete and self-contained guide. Where the first book asked how diplomats might use AI across their functions, this one asks a more pointed question: how can public diplomacy practitioners use AI to build—and protect—trust?

That question of trust is what distinguishes this book from the growing literature on AI and governance. Many books focus on capabilities—what AI can do. Dr. Kilburg focuses on consequences—what AI means for credibility. His central argument is deceptively simple: credibility is cumulative, and AI accelerates both its accumulation and its erosion. Technology changes the tempo, he writes, but people decide the tone—and in public diplomacy, tone is trust. This is exactly right. The institutions that will thrive in the coming decades are those that use AI to help publics feel seen and taken seriously, not managed.

The book's structure reflects this insight. It traces a cycle of diplomatic practice—listening, messaging, monitoring, engagement, evaluation, crisis response, ethics, cultural diplomacy, coalition-building, and integration—showing how each function connects to the others. This is not a collection of isolated techniques but an interconnected system. The reader comes away understanding that listening informs messaging, monitoring enables engagement, evaluation prepares institutions for crises, and ethics sustains everything else. Break any link in this cycle, and credibility frays. Maintain it consistently, and credibility can be strengthened even under pressure.

Each chapter embodies a principle: humility, authenticity, vigilance, empathy, responsibility, readiness, stewardship, respect, resilience, continuity. These are not values invented for the AI era; they are enduring diplomatic virtues. What AI does is make them more urgent. A chatbot that provides incorrect visa information erodes trust faster than a human error might have a generation ago. A deepfake can spread globally before institutions have time to respond. A monitoring system trained on biased data can exclude the very publics diplomacy should serve. In this environment, the principles Dr. Kilburg articulates are not abstractions but operational necessities.

I should note that Dr. Kilburg engages with my own research throughout this book—on hybrid diplomacy, on the ethics of countering digital propaganda, on the distinction between digital adaptation and adoption. This familiarity allows me to assess how accurately he has understood these frameworks and how effectively he has translated them for practitioners. He has done both well. The concept of hybrid diplomacy that Ilan Manor and I developed—the fusion of human judgment with machine pattern recognition—finds its practical expression in these pages. The moral authority framework I proposed for counter-disinformation efforts is operationalized in his treatment of monitoring and crisis response. Academic concepts become actionable guidance.

This is not another book predicting AI's future impact on international relations; it is a field guide for practitioners navigating that impact today.

One of the book's most distinctive features is its narrative device. Each chapter opens with a vignette set in the fictional Republic of Z, featuring a recurring cast of embassy characters: Ambassador Grant, the Public Affairs Officer David Kim, the digital communications officer Lina Perez, the cultural affairs officer Miriam Diallo, the audience research and insights officer Aisha Rahman, and the locally employed staff member Farid Tessam. Over the course of approximately one year, readers watch this team grapple with AI implementation, make mistakes, learn from them, and grow more sophisticated. The fictional frame allows Dr. Kilburg to explore tensions that might be diplomatically sensitive if attributed to real countries, while the recurring characters create continuity and emotional investment. The Republic of Z vignettes are a masterstroke of pedagogical design. I plan to use them in my own teaching at Oxford, and I suspect diplomatic academies worldwide will do the same.

In my work with those academies—from Berlin to Addis Ababa to Jakarta—I have watched practitioners grapple with precisely the challenges this book addresses. Too often, guidance on digital diplomacy assumes Western institutional contexts and English-language information environments. Dr. Kilburg avoids this trap. His engagement with the African Union's Continental AI Strategy, ASEAN's governance frameworks, and the European Union's regulatory approach reflects genuine global thinking. He takes seriously the AU's framing of inclusivity as sovereignty and ASEAN's emphasis on contextual adaptation. This is a book that will be useful in foreign ministries worldwide, not only in Washington or London.

Yet there is a deeper temporal dimension that this book only begins to surface, and where further work is urgently needed. Ancient Greek thought distinguished between *chronos* and *kairos*: between measurable, sequential time and the opportune moment when conditions align for meaningful action. Diplomacy has long been attentive to space, to territory, regions, alliances, and institutional architectures, but it has rarely treated time itself as a critical variable. *Chronos* is the time of plans, campaigns, reporting cycles, and procedures. *Kairos* is the decisive moment when action becomes both possible and necessary. Contemporary AI systems excel at the former. They optimize workflows, accelerate drafting, and feed dashboards on a predictable schedule. They are far less capable when it comes to the latter. Recognizing when political conditions have truly matured for intervention, when fleeting alignments of actors and narratives create opportunity, or when restraint is wiser than speed remains a form of judgment that is stubbornly human. Dr. Kilburg points toward this problem in his discussions of crisis response, proportionality, and validator networks, but the profession as a whole has not yet taken kairotic judgment as seriously as it must. The challenge for readers is to treat *kairos* not as a loose metaphor about "the moment," but as a distinct object of professional training and theoretical development in its own right, one that will require as much deliberate practice and theorizing as the tools themselves.

A second structural tension that this volume inevitably touches, without setting out to resolve, concerns the growing dislocation between AI, platform power, and inherited ideas of sovereignty. For four centuries, international relations have operated within a broadly Westphalian imagination of territorially bounded states exercising authority over space. Yet the fusion of digital infrastructures with immense private capital and ideological projects is beginning to erode that settlement. Tech-libertarian visions of network states, charter cities, platform jurisdictions, and "exit over voice" are no longer abstract thought experiments. They are being prototyped in code, investment portfolios, and special regulatory zones, and they sit uneasily alongside European efforts to assert digital sovereignty and integrate defense technologies. What is striking is not only that these projects may generate concrete enclaves or regulatory clashes, but that much of international relations scholarship still treats them as marginal because they do not fit comfortably within the Westphalian frame. The moment to reflect seriously on what this means for sovereignty is now. Although this volume does not attempt to rewrite the global order, its sustained attention to AI, platforms, and credibility may prove to be precisely the stimulus needed to launch a more serious debate about how far our concepts of sovereignty and order will have to change.

In sum, the field of AI in diplomacy is evolving rapidly, and some applications discussed in these pages remain experimental. But this is precisely why Dr. Kilburg's principles-based approach is so valuable. Tools will change; the questions of credibility, proportionality, and human judgment will not. By grounding his guidance in enduring values rather than ephemeral technologies, he has written a book that will remain relevant even as the landscape shifts. Practitioners cannot wait for the academic literature to fully mature before acting. They face deepfakes, generative disinformation, and algorithmic amplification today. They need frameworks they can apply now—frameworks flexible enough to adapt as circumstances change. This book provides them.

Who should read it? Public Affairs Officers seeking practical workflows for AI integration. Foreign Service Officers navigating digital transformation in their missions. Policymakers working to translate international governance frameworks into institutional practice. Students preparing for careers in a diplomatic landscape that will look nothing like their textbooks described. Researchers seeking to bridge the gap between theory and operational reality. And the diplomatic training programs that will shape the next generation of practitioners.

This is the book I wish I could have handed to the diplomatic academies I have trained over the past decade. Dr. Kilburg has achieved something rare: a work rigorous enough for scholars and practical enough for Monday morning.

The Republic of Z awaits. Its challenges—the disinformation campaigns, the deepfakes, the algorithmic amplification, the crises that unfold faster than institutions can respond—are already unfolding in embassies and foreign ministries around the world. The question facing every practitioner is whether AI will erode their credibility or enhance it. The answer depends not on the technology itself but on the judgment, humility, and values of those who wield it.

Dr. Kilburg has provided the map. Now it is time to navigate the terrain.

Corneliu Bjola, PhD, Professor of Digital Diplomacy, University of Oxford

Preface

This book grew out of 20 years of watching technology transform diplomacy—and a growing conviction that the transformation now underway is unlike anything that came before. Each previous shift, from cables to fax to email to smart phones to social media, gave practitioners time to adapt. This one does not. Artificial intelligence is arriving at machine speed, in an environment where credibility can be destroyed faster than it can be built, and where the institutions responsible for public diplomacy are still learning what questions to ask. That gap between the speed of the technology and the readiness of the institutions is what this book is about.

But to understand why the gap matters, it helps to remember what came before. What follows is 21 years that taught me both where AI belongs in this work and where it does not.

As a newly minted PhD entering the Foreign Service in 2003, I was drawn to data and its relationship to diplomacy and technology. In 2004, I authored a cable that cross-referenced over 225,000 border apprehensions with visa records, revealing that 97% of those apprehended had never even applied for a visa. The assumption had been that migrants were trying to "game" consular officers. The data told a different story: most caught crossing illegally saw applying for a visa as futile. It was my first experiment in what we would now call a big-data approach, long before dashboards or predictive analytics existed. Today, AI-enabled audience analysis can surface patterns like these across millions of records in minutes, segmenting populations, detecting anomalies, and mapping sentiment before a policy is even announced. In 2004, I had a spreadsheet and a hypothesis. Back then, insights took weeks to produce, and by the time they reached decision-makers, the window for acting on them had often already closed.

Then came Hurricane Wilma in 2005. The storm devastated Cancun and stranded tens of thousands of Americans. Our embassy became a lifeline. For ten days, we worked around the clock, fielding 12,000 phone calls, handing out flyers in hotels and at the airport, and updating Excel spreadsheets to track evacuations. We had no social media, no apps, no AI—just rental cars, clipboards, and grit. And yet, it worked: 25,000 Americans evacuated safely, and not one life lost. It was public diplomacy in its rawest form: credibility through presence. Imagine that crisis today: chatbots fielding the panicked inquiries, dashboards tracking narrative shifts, AI translation pushing evacuation instructions into multiple languages at once. None of it would have replaced the presence that made Cancun work. It might have extended that presence, buying the human team the time and reach that clipboards alone could not. AI as amplifier, not substitute. That is the pattern the chapters ahead return to.

By 2009, the ground had shifted. I attended one of the State Department's first rounds of training on Facebook and Twitter (now X) for diplomats. At first, it seemed a curiosity—why would U.S. foreign policy care what students posted online? Within months, it was obvious: social media had become the frontline of narrative competition. Secretary Hillary Clinton's "21st Century Statecraft" initiative captured the moment. Diplomats had to meet publics where they lived and argued, or risk irrelevance. We were learning to listen at scale—but we had almost no tools for doing so. What we could hear was limited to what we could manually scan, and what we could not hear was invisible to us entirely.

The implications became undeniable in Beijing, where I served from 2010 to 2014. China's rise dominated geopolitics, but on the street, pollution and corruption consumed public debate. The U.S. Embassy's decision to install an air-quality monitor and tweet hourly readings changed everything. When one particularly bad reading was labeled "crazy bad," the phrase went viral. Millions of Chinese turned to the U.S. feed for truth. Transparency itself became public diplomacy, advancing American influence in ways that later research showed contributed to policy change and measurable health gains. It was a messaging triumph—but an accidental one. We had no way to test which framing would resonate before we published it, no system for tracking how the message mutated across platforms, no dashboard showing whether rural publics were receiving the same signal as urban elites. The chapters ahead describe what it looks like when institutions can do all of that deliberately.

But credibility was fragile. In 2012, blind Chinese activist Chen Guangcheng escaped house arrest and sought refuge in our embassy just as Secretary Clinton arrived for high-level talks. Global headlines swirled, and we had no monitoring dashboards or AI tools. We worked on instincts and long nights of drafting. What AI systems do in minutes now took us days then, and in that gap U.S. options narrowed. The crisis communication frameworks this book examines—early warning, deepfake forensics, rumor triage, validator amplification—exist precisely because institutions can no longer afford to lose days when narratives harden in minutes.

Beijing also taught me that public diplomacy is often cultural—and that culture is precisely where institutional memory is most easily lost. I helped organize a televised 9/11 vigil with floating lanterns, introduced Meryl Streep and Yo-Yo Ma at arts events, worked with Pixar animators on innovation exhibitions, and staged a baseball-themed July 4th party with Major League Baseball All-Stars. In 2013, I accompanied Ambassador Gary Locke to restive Xinjiang—the first such trip in years—where we visited mosques, museums, and universities in a sensitive region. One week I was writing speeches for Ambassador Locke; the next, ushering First Lady Michelle Obama on the Great Wall on her historic visit. Each of these moments showed America's face to foreign publics in ways no policy memo could. And yet when staff rotated, the knowledge of what had worked—which framings resonated, which audiences responded, which partnerships endured—often rotated with them. AI can help preserve that memory. What it cannot replace is the human presence that earned it.

These years coincided with China's rapid rise and the construction of its "Great Firewall," while Silicon Valley platforms began dominating global information flows. The emerging competition would pit not only Washington against Beijing, but governments against a new class of superpowers—the Big Tech firms that built the platforms, and eventually the AI systems, that structure global communication.

By 2014 I was back in Washington at the Bureau of Intelligence and Research (INR), working on the Transatlantic Trade and Investment Partnership (TTIP), the refugee crisis, and Brexit. We ran surveys and focus groups across Europe, feeding insights into briefing books for the President, the National Security Council, and

Ambassadors. I watched our data influence President Barack Obama's 2016 London warning that Britain would go to "the back of the queue" if they left the EU. For Brexit, we fused polling with Twitter trend analysis. It was the era when "big data" became a buzzword and public diplomacy entered its first evidence-driven phase: listening at scale before speaking at scale. But our evaluation was still retrospective. We could tell decision-makers what had happened; we could not tell them what was happening now, or what was likely to happen next. And looking back, none of our 2016 analysis hinted at how quickly events of the next decade would push global politics into post-truth territory. The shift from episodic snapshots to continuous, adaptive evaluation is one of the transformations this book documents.

From 2016 to 2019, I served as Public Affairs Officer in Almaty, Kazakhstan—a proving ground for narrative competition in the former Soviet Union. Russia controlled the airwaves, China expanded Belt and Road projects, and both pushed worldviews that sidelined the West. Our work, from the "Go Viral" festival to "Access English" programs, aimed to shield Kazakhstan from malign influence and help its next generation build a more balanced, pro-Western mindset. Fighting corruption was a challenge, even inside the consulate. Looking back, I have often wondered whether AI systems might have detected grant anomalies sooner than I did.

In Shymkent, I lectured on U.S. foreign policy while streaming live on Facebook, reaching thousands. In Taraz and Kazygurt, we launched Access English programs in towns with histories of radicalization. At the American Corner, my talk on disinformation literacy was viewed by 13,000 online. Public diplomacy had become hybrid: empathy on the ground, amplified in real time through cloud and mobile platforms. The empathy was the part that worked, and no tool could have manufactured it. What we lacked was the rest: shared coalition dashboards, coordinated detection across allied missions, multilateral early-warning infrastructure. When hostile narratives crossed borders, each mission fought them independently. The collaborative diplomacy frameworks this book describes did not yet exist.

Returning to Washington by 2019, I became Spokesperson for the Bureau of Energy Resources (ENR), where energy had become a strategic weapon. Russia cast the natural gas pipeline "Nord Stream 2" as commercial; we framed it as a geopolitical vulnerability. Through op-eds in the *Financial Times* and *Foreign Policy*, we spoke directly to European publics and policymakers. At the United Nations General Assembly, we launched the Energy Resource Governance Initiative (ERGI) with then Assistant Secretary Frank Fannon and Secretary Mike Pompeo, promoting diversified supply chains for critical minerals. These were narrative battles in the language of markets and energy, but the stakes were sovereignty and security.

Then came the pandemic in 2020. Oil markets collapsed, OPEC+ talks failed, and diplomacy went remote. By then, I had already been part of the small ENR Cloud Task Force that pushed our bureau into Microsoft Teams and cloud computing. When COVID hit, ENR was one of the few bureaus that could sustain productivity at almost 100% telework. What once took days of memos now happened in hours. It was the smallest version of the integration story this book tells at length: a handful of people who built digital infrastructure before the crisis demanded it, discovering that preparedness was the difference between institutional survival and collapse.

By 2023, I was helping lead the Department into the AI era through the Bureau of Global Public Affairs (GPA). I supported an "AI4PD" campaign, trained colleagues before official policies existed, and piloted AI prototypes like "StateChat" and "Northstar." Much of this work I did while teleworking from Rome, Italy, a fact that signaled how far the Department had come. From landlines and paper clippings in 2003, we had reached the point where a public diplomacy officer could run AI pilots across continents, fully cloud-enabled and location-independent. When AI tools were formally integrated into the Department's systems in 2024, it marked the shift from curiosity to infrastructure.

Today, every U.S. diplomat carries AI in their pocket. Apps can summarize media, translate instantly, flag anomalies, or draft responses in real time. On top of Teams, Zoom, and encrypted chats, diplomats can post and monitor social media on the go. The expectation is instant engagement. Publics demand it, adversaries exploit it, and credibility moves at smartphone speed.

Looking back, I see a clear arc from analog to digital, from digitization to algorithms, and now to artificial intelligence. Each stage expanded what was possible but raised the stakes of failure. Each also made one truth harder to ignore: the essence of diplomacy remains human. Whether publics trust us enough to listen has never depended on the tools in our hands.

Yet the larger picture has evolved into a three-dimensional competition. States like the United States, China, and Russia remain players, but so too are Big Tech superpowers that control platforms, data, and AI systems, alongside civil society organizations, academic institutions, and non-governmental organizations (NGOs) that increasingly shape how those systems are governed and contested. The United States and China are racing not only to develop these tools but to shape the norms of how they are used. For public diplomacy, this is no longer background context. It is *the* arena.

When I published *AI Use Cases for Diplomats* (Kilburg 2025), I described it as a field manual for a profession on the cusp of transformation. That book mapped the landscape broadly. The feedback was clear: readers valued the breadth, but they wanted a deeper dive into the area where AI's effects were sharpest—public diplomacy and strategic communication.

That is the purpose of this book.

Every challenge I have described in this preface—listening with spreadsheets, responding to crises with clipboards, messaging without feedback, monitoring without dashboards, evaluating after the fact, defending against narratives alone, preserving cultural memory across rotations, and building digital infrastructure before anyone demanded it—is addressed in the chapters ahead. Not as theory, but as practice: with case studies from institutions that have deployed these tools, workflows that practitioners can adapt, and honest accounting of what works, what fails, and what remains at risk.

If the last two decades taught me anything, it is that technology magnifies choices, but it does not make them. In public diplomacy, that distinction is the difference between earning trust and performing it. The chapters ahead are about using new tools, including AI, to do the first. They are also about the work where no tool, however capable, should be allowed to do it for us.

Acknowledgments

No book is written alone, and this one benefited from the insight and generosity of many.

I am grateful to the colleagues who reviewed early drafts and offered critical feedback: Robin Holzhauer, Alexander Hunt, Kelly McCarthy, and Xander Vagg. Their practical experience and sharp questions strengthened every chapter. Alexander Hunt deserves particular thanks for his pioneering work applying AI to public diplomacy in the field.

The scholars whose research underpins this work—Corneliu Bjola, Ilan Manor, Nicholas Cull, Joseph Nye, Claire Wardle, Kate Crawford, and many others cited throughout—have shaped how an entire generation of practitioners thinks about diplomacy in the digital age. I have not met most of them in person, but I have learned from all of them.

To my colleagues across the U.S. Foreign Service who pioneered AI adoption before policies existed, trained others when no playbook was available, and continue to experiment with integrity: Thank you.

Any errors, omissions, or shortcomings in this book remain entirely my own.

Acknowledgments

Statement on AI Use in Writing This Book

In writing this book about AI use cases for diplomats, I made a deliberate choice to "practice what I preach" and thereby embrace various AI tools throughout my writing process, including: ChatGPT (version 5.2), Claude (versions Sonnet 4.6 and Opus 4.6), Gemini (version 3), and Perplexity. Using AI helped me to expand my thinking about the subject matter and to write the book quickly, in hopes of forging new knowledge at a pace that could keep up with AI advancement. I recognize that there is currently lively debate over the extent to which writers should use AI in their writing process, including for diplomacy.

I would therefore like to be specific about how AI assisted in creating this book, as I believe transparency about AI use in writing can help advance an important discussion in my field. I used AI tools as my thought partners and editorial assistants. The tools helped me to brainstorm ideas, organize research, create structured outlines, improve clarity, and ensure consistent formatting. Throughout my AI-assisted writing process, I found myself reflecting on how such collaborative approaches might benefit diplomatic work. My experience came with careful consideration about where to draw the lines, particularly in balancing innovation with tradition, efficiency with deliberation, and technological capability with my own human judgment. Did I always succeed? Probably not.

Nevertheless, I have come to see AI-assisted writing on a spectrum, with different tools and approaches being appropriate for different tasks and contexts, rather than a simple yes/no choice for authors. Some aspects of writing and diplomacy (or any field) may benefit greatly from a degree of AI assistance, while others may require more traditional human-centered approaches. As AI tools continue to evolve, I believe authors, diplomats, and professionals should share their experiences openly and engage in constructive dialogue about best practices. I make no apology for openly using AI as a writing assistant—if anything, avoiding AI while writing a book on conscientious AI adoption would be disingenuous.

While I am confident in the value this human-AI collaboration has brought to the project, I also recognize that we are all walking unique paths as these technologies evolve. I invite you to engage critically with the ideas presented here, drawing on your own experiences and perspectives. My hope is that by being transparent about my own approach, while remaining open to diverse viewpoints, we can collectively develop thoughtful frameworks for integrating AI tools into diplomatic practice. The future of diplomacy will likely be neither purely human nor predominantly automated, but rather a careful synthesis of human wisdom and technological capability. I look forward to exploring this path forward together!

Introduction

Opening Vignette and Framing the Stakes

It began with a shaky video posted after dark. In the clip, the U.S. ambassador in the Republic of Z appears to make a dismissive remark about the host country's religious customs. Within minutes, the clip ricochets across TikTok and WhatsApp; by morning, talk radio is in full outrage and a crowd has formed outside the embassy gates. In the public affairs section upstairs, screens glow with contradictory signals: one dashboard shows anger cresting, another suggests the spike is starting to ebb. A generative tool has drafted a holding statement in two languages. A chatbot is handling routine questions, escalating the most sensitive ones—but its replies sound clipped and cold. The ambassador's media adviser asks a simple question no tool can answer: what do people actually believe?

A careful check reveals what the team suspected: the video is a deepfake. The subtleties are easy to miss—lip-sync just slightly off, metadata incomplete, no provenance tag—but real enough to feel plausible. The embassy pushes a short, clear correction through verified channels, and validators—local journalists, alumni, respected community figures—amplify it. When the ambassador appears live on television to reiterate respect for the country's traditions, the temperature begins to drop. The damage is not permanent, but the lesson is unmistakable: artificial intelligence now sits in the middle of diplomatic communication—both the problem set and the toolkit.

FRAMING THE BOOK

What happened that morning in the Republic of Z—the scramble to verify, the race to respond, the fragile line between credibility preserved and credibility lost—is no longer exceptional. It is the new normal. Public affairs teams across the globe now navigate the same essential tension: AI tools that promise unprecedented awareness alongside risks that move faster than human judgment can follow.

What makes this moment especially consequential is a dangerous convergence. AI is arriving precisely when democratic institutions are most fragile, when truth itself is openly contested, and when technology corporations wield influence over information systems that rivals nation-states. Authoritarian actors and profit-driven platforms operate at machine speed, flooding information spaces with content designed to overwhelm, fragment, and disengage. Democratic institutions, constrained by deliberation and accountability, cannot match that tempo through human effort alone. AI has become one of the few tools capable of operating at the scale of this information environment.

This book is about that tension and what to do with it. It is about the daily work of listening to foreign publics, speaking with clarity, monitoring how narratives mutate, engaging at scale, evaluating whether efforts work, responding in crisis, acting with ethics, representing culture and education authentically, coordinating with partners—and, finally, integrating all of this so it functions as a coherent practice rather than a pile of disconnected pilots.

Public diplomacy is where these pressures are felt first because it unfolds in the open. Unlike quiet negotiations between states, the relationship between an embassy and a society is tested in real time: in comment threads and call-in shows, on sidewalks and in alumni networks. Tools that can read the room at scale—sentiment analysis, translation, anomaly detection—promise a level of awareness no press office has ever had. The same tools can misread sarcasm, miss dialects, or give the appearance of certainty where there is none. What counts in that space is not technical novelty but credibility. The institutions that endure will be the ones that use AI to help people feel seen and taken seriously, not managed.

The point is not that technology is destiny; it is that choices about technology now shape diplomatic outcomes. Officers can deploy a chatbot that answers in local idioms and hands off gracefully to a human when nuance is needed—or one that frustrates, alienates, and embarrasses. They can use dashboards to guide judgment, or they can outsource judgment to dashboards. They can invest in systems that include rural voices and minority languages, or they can rely on data pipelines that flatten a society into what is easiest to scrape. The same capacity that lets a mission understand more can also make it overlook more.

This book takes those choices seriously. It is not a celebration of tools, nor is it a warning siren. It is a field-ready guide to applying AI responsibly to public diplomacy, public affairs, and strategic communication.

UNPACKING THE TITLE—WHAT THIS BOOK IS ABOUT

To understand what this book offers, we need to pause and unpack its title: *AI Use Cases for Public Diplomacy: Applying AI to Public Affairs and Strategic Communication.*

Artificial Intelligence (AI) Here the term refers to applied systems that process language, images, and patterns at machine scale: machine translation, natural language processing, sentiment analysis, anomaly detection, and generative models. These tools do not "think" like humans, but they collapse time and scale. They can produce a draft speech in seconds, flag an emerging rumor before it trends, or translate an article into dozens of languages.

Diplomacy At its core, diplomacy is how states and institutions manage relationships with each other and with societies abroad. Once conducted through controlled media and private negotiation, diplomacy now unfolds in public, in real time, on platforms where narratives are shaped as much by algorithms as by official statements.

Public Diplomacy This is a broad branch of diplomacy that focuses on engaging directly with foreign publics, not only governments. It includes exchanges, cultural programming, media outreach, alumni networks, and digital engagement. Its purpose is to build mutual understanding and long-term trust.

Public Affairs and Strategic Communication These overlapping terms describe the outward-facing functions and offices of government and institutions. Public affairs is about clear, accurate explanation of what an institution is doing and why. Strategic communication or "StratComm" widens the lens, describing the deliberate use of communication to shape outcomes. Both are integral to modern public diplomacy. At a typical embassy, there is often a public affairs section and sometimes within that a "StratComm" team.

This book sits precisely at the intersection of these domains. It asks: how can AI support, challenge, and transform the way diplomats listen to, speak with, and build trust among foreign publics? And equally: what are the risks if these tools are misused or misunderstood?

Part of a Series, Built to Stand Alone

It is also part of a series. My earlier book, *AI Use Cases for Diplomats: Applying Artificial Intelligence to Diplomacy* (Kilburg 2025), was the first book-length exploration of AI across diplomacy broadly. That volume sketched the landscape: negotiation, security, crisis management, cultural exchange, and more. Public diplomacy appeared there in a single chapter (Chapter 7), identified as one of the areas most immediately transformed by AI. Complementary essays on AI's role in diplomatic engagement and the State Department's emerging AI toolkit further developed these themes (Kilburg 2025a, 2025b). This book narrows the lens, offering a sustained exploration of public diplomacy, public affairs, and strategic communication across ten dedicated chapters.

That said, this volume is designed to stand on its own. Readers need not have read the first volume to benefit. This book defines its terms, explains its contexts, and provides workflows and cases throughout, so it can serve as both a stand-alone primer and a deeper dive for those already familiar with the subject.

WHY AI MATTERS FOR PUBLIC DIPLOMACY

Artificial intelligence matters for diplomacy because it has reshaped the environment in which information circulates. A rumor that once took days to spread can now reach millions in minutes; a translation that once required a team of experts can be produced instantly; a synthetic video that would once have demanded a professional studio can now be created on a laptop. Public diplomacy, which engages directly with foreign publics, is one of the first areas of diplomacy to feel this impact.

The opportunities are clear. AI extends scale: dashboards can scan millions of posts across multiple languages, identifying trends and anomalies invisible to human readers. It accelerates speed: detection systems can flag deepfakes or spikes in disinformation before they dominate a news cycle. And it enhances responsiveness: chatbots can handle routine queries, freeing officers to focus on sensitive cases, while alumni mapping tools can identify which networks are most active.

The risks are equally stark. Systems trained primarily on elite or Western data risk marginalizing minority voices and rural publics—concerns the African Union (2024) frames in terms of unequally sourced data, widening gaps in access to AI, and threats to Indigenous knowledge and cultural heritage. Left unchecked, these dynamics could amount to a form of "AI colonialism" or "AI neo-feudalism," in which outside actors shape how less powerful publics are represented and governed (see Hao 2022). Monitoring can be perceived as surveillance, even when lawful. Personalization can slip into manipulation, undermining transparency. And fragile infrastructures can fail if adversaries poison inputs with synthetic content. As Kissinger, Schmidt, and Huttenlocher (2021) warn, AI produces correlations without understanding—a critical limitation in contexts where meaning matters most.

Real-world experience underscores both sides. During COVID-19, the WHO's Early AI-supported Response with Social Listening (EARS) platform helped governments understand and respond to the infodemic early (WHO 2021c). The EU's East StratCom Task Force has combined structured monitoring, analytical tools, and human expertise to document hostile information manipulation campaigns. Ukraine's rapid exposure of a deepfake of President Zelenskyy succeeded not because the fake was technically sophisticated but because validators across civil society and partner governments amplified the debunking quickly and consistently (Cull 2023).

The central reason AI matters for public diplomacy is not that it makes communication faster or broader, but that it changes the conditions under which credibility is earned. Public diplomacy has always depended on publics granting institutions the benefit of the doubt. AI can help earn that trust by making institutions more responsive, inclusive, and accurate. It can also squander it if publics perceive surveillance, exclusion, or manipulation. The stakes are higher because the margin for error is smaller.

THE GAP IN KNOWLEDGE

Artificial intelligence dominates headlines and policy reports, but systematic analysis of its application to diplomacy remains scarce. Commentators warn of disinformation, deepfakes, and bots; ethicists debate regulation and governance. What is missing is a grounded treatment of how AI tools are being used—and should be used—in the day-to-day practice of public diplomacy and strategic communication.

Part of the gap is disciplinary. International relations tends to focus on statecraft and security; communication studies on media and publics. Public diplomacy lies between these fields, and is often sidelined. AI forces the overlap into focus. Narratives shaped by algorithms, publics networked across borders, and adversaries wielding generative content make it impossible to separate diplomacy from communication.

The gap is also practical. Embassies and ministries experiment with AI, but pilots are scattered, undocumented, and often forgotten as staff rotate. Lessons learned in one mission rarely become enduring institutional knowledge. This book captures those lessons, systematizes them, and presents them in usable form.

And the gap is educational. Students encounter AI in everyday life but rarely learn how it intersects with diplomacy. Universities lag behind in preparing graduates for this reality. This book fills that need, offering definitions, use cases, and frameworks for classroom and professional use alike.

Finally, there is a gap in synthesis. Research often examines things like NATO's simulations, the EU's task forces, WHO's rumor monitoring, or AU strategies in isolation. Practitioners need integrated lessons that cut across regions, institutions, and contexts. This book provides that synthesis.

HOW THIS BOOK WORKS—STRUCTURE AND NARRATIVE ARC

The Cycle of Practice

The book is structured in three parts that together form a complete cycle of public diplomacy practice. Part I establishes the core functions—listening, messaging, monitoring, and engaging—that define daily diplomatic work in the information age. Part II addresses how to strengthen these practices through evaluation, crisis preparedness, and ethical frameworks. Part III expands the lens to cultural diplomacy, multilateral coordination, and institutional integration.

This structure reflects both the logic of diplomatic practice and the reality of AI adoption. Diplomacy has always moved in cycles: listening before speaking, monitoring to stay informed, engaging to build relationships, evaluating to improve. AI adoption similarly progresses from experimentation to institutionalization. The book's three-part arc mirrors both journeys, moving from foundational practices to resilience under pressure to sustainable transformation.

How the Ten Chapters Map to the Three-Part Structure

The book is organized into three parts, each building on the previous to create a complete system for AI-enabled public diplomacy.

PART I: The Core Cycle (Chapters 1–4)
Public diplomacy begins with understanding audiences, crafting messages that resonate, protecting the information environment, and building genuine engagement. These four chapters explore how artificial intelligence transforms each stage of this daily cycle—from listening at scale to engaging authentically—while showing why human judgment and cultural sensitivity remain essential to credibility.

Chapter 1: Strategic Audience Insight: AI for Knowing and Reaching the Right People
Examines how AI enables listening at scale through sentiment analysis, audience segmentation, and narrative intelligence. Shows both the power of machine-scale awareness and the risks of algorithmic misreading.

Chapter 2: Crafting Impactful Messaging with AI
Explores AI-assisted content creation, from generative writing tools to cultural adaptation and multilingual translation. Balances efficiency gains against authenticity concerns.

Chapter 3: Media Monitoring, Disinformation, and Narrative Intelligence
Investigates AI tools for detecting disinformation, tracking narrative evolution, and distinguishing authentic discourse from manipulation. Addresses deepfakes, provenance systems, and coordinated inauthentic behavior.

Chapter 4: Engaging Audiences through Smart Digital Diplomacy
Demonstrates how AI can extend digital engagement through chatbots, virtual assistants, alumni mapping, and participatory platforms. Emphasizes the balance between automation and authentic human connection.

PART II: Strengthening Practice (Chapters 5–7)
Once the core functions are in place, diplomats must measure what works, respond rapidly when crises strike, and ensure that every AI deployment upholds democratic values. These chapters examine how to optimize programs through continuous evaluation, maintain credibility under pressure, and embed ethical safeguards that turn responsible practice into strategic advantage.

Chapter 5: Monitoring, Evaluation, and Program Optimization with AI
Shows how AI transforms program evaluation, impact assessment, and predictive analytics. Addresses the challenge of measuring what matters rather than what is easily quantifiable.

Chapter 6: Crisis Communication in the Age of AI
Addresses AI's role in rapid response, early warning systems, real-time translation during emergencies, and maintaining credibility under pressure. Shows how speed must be balanced with accuracy.

Chapter 7: Ethics, Trust, and Responsible AI in Public Diplomacy
Establishes ethical frameworks for responsible AI deployment, drawing on UNESCO, OECD, EU, African Union, and ASEAN guidelines. Argues that ethics is not a constraint on innovation but the foundation of credibility.

PART III: Expanding Impact (Chapters 8–10)
The final challenge is making AI serve diplomacy's longest horizons and broadest coalitions. These chapters address cultural and educational exchange across generations, coordination among multilateral partners, and the institutional transformation required to move from scattered pilots to sustainable systems that enhance credibility, inclusivity, and resilience.

Chapter 8: AI for Cultural and Educational Diplomacy
Explores AI applications in cultural heritage preservation, exchange program selection, accessibility enhancement, and authentic cultural representation. Warns against automation that erodes cultural authenticity.

Chapter 9: Collaborative Diplomacy: AI for Multilateral Campaigns
Examines how AI can support coalition coordination, joint messaging campaigns, narrative alignment, and federated learning across partner nations. Shows both opportunities for scale and risks of manipulation.

Chapter 10: From Innovation to Integration: A Roadmap for AI-Ready Public Diplomacy
Provides a roadmap for moving from experimental pilots to institutional integration. Addresses change management, capacity building, governance structures, and the creation of AI-ready diplomatic institutions.

The Republic of Z: A Recurring Narrative Device

Throughout the book, each chapter opens with a vignette set in the fictional Republic of Z, a middle-income country navigating democratic transition, digital transformation, and complex regional dynamics. These vignettes feature a recurring cast of characters from the U.S. Embassy:

- *Ambassador Daniel Grant*—Strategic leader balancing innovation with values
- *David Kim (PAO)*—Public Affairs Officer managing AI implementation
- *Lina Perez*—Digital Communications Officer, tech-savvy but learning diplomatic nuance
- *Miriam Diallo*—Cultural Affairs Officer focused on authentic exchange
- *Aisha Rahman*—Audience Research and Insights Officer bringing technical expertise
- *Farid Tessam*—Locally Employed Staff member providing essential cultural context
- And supporting characters, including Maria Santos (Consular Officer), who appear in specific chapters

The Republic of Z vignettes serve multiple purposes. They dramatize each chapter's core concept in action, showing both AI's capabilities and its limitations. They reveal how human judgment remains essential even as technology accelerates decision-making. They provide continuity across chapters, with characters learning from earlier experiences and technology implementations evolving over time. And they make abstract concepts concrete, helping readers see how the frameworks and tools discussed would actually function in diplomatic practice.

The vignettes are not meant to be prescriptive templates but rather illustrative scenarios that help bridge theory and practice. The Republic of Z is also an open invitation: readers are encouraged to imagine their own embassy, consulate, or mission in its place. By grounding these scenarios in a fictional country rather than a real one, the book allows practitioners to engage with the situations more directly—without the distraction of specific bilateral politics or regional sensitivities that might otherwise get in the way of the broader lessons. Different missions will face different challenges, but the core tensions—between speed and accuracy, efficiency and authenticity, innovation and values—remain constant. To complement these fictional scenarios, each chapter also includes a "Synthetic Narratives in Action" call-out box documenting a real-world case from 2022 to 2025, ensuring that readers see both how challenges might unfold and how they already have.

Chapter Structure and Design

Each chapter follows a rhythm designed to serve different reader needs:

Vignette Opens with a Republic of Z scenario demonstrating the chapter's focus
Synthetic Narratives in Action A call-out box highlighting a real-world case from 2022–2025, grounding the chapter's themes in documented events
Framing Establishes why this function matters and where it fits in the cycle
Research and Policy Foundations Grounds the chapter in scholarly literature and governance frameworks
AI Capabilities Explains the relevant technologies and what they can do

Real-World Applications Presents case studies from multiple regions showing AI in practice
Practical Guidance Offers workflows, prompts, or tools practitioners can adapt
Ethical Considerations Addresses risks, limitations, and responsible deployment
Advanced/Future Applications Explores emerging capabilities and future directions
Reflection and Strategic Questions Prompts readers to consider application to their own contexts
Conclusion Synthesizes key insights and connects to broader themes

This structure ensures accessibility for different readers: students seeking definitions and context, practitioners seeking workflows and tools, policymakers seeking governance frameworks and compliance guidance. The fictional Republic of Z vignettes and the real-world "Synthetic Narratives in Action" cases work in tandem—one illustrating how challenges unfold in practice, the other demonstrating that these challenges are already here. Chapters can stand alone but also build sequentially into a full roadmap for AI-enabled public diplomacy.

WHO THIS BOOK IS FOR—AUDIENCES AND USES

This book is written for multiple audiences.

For **students**, it is a primer: it explains diplomacy, public diplomacy, and AI clearly, illustrating practice with case studies and workflows.

For **practitioners**, it is a guide: it offers adaptable workflows for listening, messaging, monitoring, evaluation, and crisis communication, designed to be scaled to different missions.

For **policymakers**, it is a bridge: it shows how high-level governance frameworks from UNESCO, the EU, the AU, ASEAN, and OECD translate into daily practice.

For **multi-stakeholder actors**—journalists, NGOs, civil society, and technology firms—it is a reminder that legitimacy is co-produced. States do not control narratives alone; credibility now depends on validators, platforms, and partners.

And for **general readers**, it is an entry point: it explains how AI shapes the information space that touches everyone, from health rumors to climate commitments.

Different readers may use the book differently: as a textbook, a manual, a policy guide, or a primer. Its structure is designed to accommodate all.

THE PROMISE TO THE READER

By the end of this book, you will have a vocabulary and a toolkit for understanding how AI intersects with public diplomacy and strategic communication. You will know what it means to listen at scale, to message authentically, to monitor narratives vigilantly, to engage empathetically, to evaluate responsibly, to respond in crises with readiness, to embed ethics into practice, to represent culture and education authentically, to coordinate coalitions, and to integrate innovations sustainably.

You will also be able to distinguish between what AI can and cannot do. Machines can scan data, generate drafts, or flag anomalies, but they cannot provide judgment or meaning. Those remain human tasks. This book will help you see where AI adds value, where it creates risk, and how to apply it in ways that reinforce credibility.

Most importantly, you will leave with perspective. AI is not a magic solution or an inevitable threat. It is a set of tools that magnify human choices. The question is whether those choices will build trust or erode it. This book equips you to make them responsibly.

Diplomacy has always rested on credibility. In the age of AI, that truth has not changed; it has only become more urgent.

PART I

The Core Cycle

Public diplomacy begins with understanding audiences, crafting messages that resonate, protecting the information environment, and building genuine engagement. These four chapters explore how artificial intelligence transforms each stage of this daily cycle—from listening at scale to engaging authentically—while showing why human judgment and cultural sensitivity remain essential to credibility.

DOI: 10.1201/9781003612377-1

1 Strategic Audience Insight

AI for Knowing and Reaching the Right People

"Soft power is the ability to obtain preferred outcomes by attraction rather than coercion or payment."

—Joseph S. Nye, "Soft Power: The Origins and Political Progress of a Concept" (2017)

"Diplomacy in the digital age depends on how diplomats understand and transform online influence into tangible offline diplomatic influence."

—Corneliu Bjola, "Diplomacy in the Digital Age" (2018)

"Integrating AI into our workflows has elevated our efforts, shifting focus from rote tasks to the real work of diplomacy."

—Alexander Hunt, quoted in Farakh Khan, "AI in Action" (2024)

Opening Vignette: When the Dashboard Misreads the Crowd

It began with what looked like a breakthrough. Overnight, the embassy's narrative intelligence dashboard had detected a surge of activity across more than two hundred accounts in Zorani-language social media. The posts clustered around a new U.S.-funded education initiative in the eastern provinces—memes, short videos, and commentary that the system's sentiment classifier tagged as overwhelmingly positive. By the time staff arrived for the morning briefing, the dashboard's charts told what appeared to be a clear story: grassroots enthusiasm was building in rural areas, and the program was gaining organic traction.

Aisha Rahman, the mission's audience research and insights officer, pulled the overnight summary for David Kim, the public affairs officer, before the morning meeting. "Two hundred twelve accounts, most active between midnight and four a.m. local time," she said. "Sentiment scores are running above eighty percent positive. The system flagged it as a significant uptick." David studied the clusters. "That's a strong signal. If rural audiences are picking this up on their own, we should think about amplifying." Farid Tessam, a

DOI: 10.1201/9781003612377-2

locally employed cultural affairs assistant who had grown up in the eastern provinces, was scanning the same posts on his phone. He looked up. "These are not endorsements." The room went quiet. "The memes are jokes," Farid said. "They are making fun of the logo. This phrase here"—he pointed to a line of Zorani script—"is a pun. It sounds like the word for 'empty gift.' And this one references a saying about outsiders who arrive with promises and leave with photographs. The algorithm is reading the words correctly. It is missing what the words mean." Aisha pulled up the original posts and compared them against the sentiment classifications. Farid was right.

The system had processed the language accurately but had no framework for interpreting irony, sarcasm, or the particular strain of dry humor common in rural Zorani dialects. What the dashboard called enthusiasm was, in context, skepticism dressed in wit. David set aside the amplification plan. "What do we actually know about how the program is landing out there?" Farid contacted alumni and teachers in the region who had served as trusted validators in the past. Their conversations confirmed what the memes suggested: beneath the humor lay real frustration about past promises that had not materialized. The sentiment was not hostile, but it was far from the grassroots endorsement the dashboard had advertised. The embassy adjusted its approach. Instead of amplifying, the public affairs team shifted to engagement—preparing outreach that acknowledged concerns directly and invited dialogue rather than celebrating momentum that did not exist.

At the debrief, Aisha added the episode to the mission's misread log, a record of moments when the dashboard's categories had failed to capture what was actually happening. "The system did what it was built to do," she said. "It detected a real signal across two hundred accounts that none of us would have caught manually. But detection is not interpretation." David nodded. "The machine saw the conversation. Farid understood it. We need both."

FRAMING THE CHAPTER

Listening has always been the foundation of diplomacy. Before an embassy can persuade, it must first understand. What publics think, how they feel, and the stories they tell about themselves and others form the ground on which credibility is built. In the past, diplomats relied on public opinion polls, media clippings, or carefully assembled focus groups to get a sense of these dynamics. These methods, though valuable, were often slow, geographically narrow, and ill-suited to capturing the fragmented, fast-moving conversations that define today's digital public sphere. Artificial intelligence changes that equation.

The arrival of AI-enabled narrative intelligence tools gives diplomats a kind of radar screen for the information environment. Natural language processing can scan millions of posts across multiple platforms and languages, clustering them into themes and detecting anomalies before they crest into headlines. Dashboards can show how a message travels, which influencers amplify it, and where counter-narratives take root. Properly used, these tools are not merely descriptive but anticipatory. They offer early warning of reputational risks and help policymakers sense emerging currents of opinion in real time.

RESEARCH AND POLICY FOUNDATIONS

For all its promise, the ability to listen at scale comes with new vulnerabilities. Scholars have warned that AI often produces what Henry Kissinger, Eric Schmidt, and Daniel Huttenlocher describe as a widening "gap between human knowledge and human understanding" (Kissinger, Schmidt, and Huttenlocher 2021). Dashboards can show that a rumor is spreading rapidly, or that sentiment around a policy announcement appears positive, but they cannot explain why publics are reacting as they are. Without context, signals are easily mistaken for truths.

The danger is overconfidence: assuming that a clean visualization captures lived reality when it may conceal as much as it reveals. This caution has a methodological corollary. When missions move from listening to segmentation—grouping publics in order to reach them—the temptation is to sort audiences by demographic markers or by inferred personality traits. Both shortcuts mislead. Demographic categories correlate only loosely with the behaviors diplomats actually care about, and personality-based profiling risks what psychologists call the fundamental attribution error: over-explaining behavior through disposition while discounting circumstance. NATO analysts studying AI-assisted audience work recommend a corrective drawn from behavioral science, the COM-B model, which holds that behavior depends on Capability, Opportunity, and Motivation together—so that the channels an audience trusts and the constraints it faces weigh as heavily as who its members are (Bergmanis-Korāts et al. 2024). For public diplomacy, the discipline is to segment around behavior and situation, not stereotype, and to treat any profile as a hypothesis to be tested rather than a verdict.

This is why some researchers frame AI-assisted listening as a form of anticipatory intelligence rather than definitive knowledge. Corneliu Bjola and Ilan Manor (2025) argue that AI allows diplomacy to shift "from hindsight to foresight," helping practitioners detect weak signals before they harden into crises. Their concept of "hybrid diplomacy" emphasizes precisely this: the fusion of human judgment with machine pattern recognition. Yet they also caution that foresight without accountability can become reckless, especially if diplomatic missions treat early warnings as certainties rather than prompts for deeper investigation. The application of AI to public affairs functions more broadly—including media monitoring, messaging, and stakeholder engagement—is examined in detail in Kilburg (2025).

THE EVOLUTION OF STRATEGIC LISTENING

AI-enabled listening is more than a technical upgrade. It changes how governments understand public opinion. Traditional public diplomacy relied on what might be called "episodic listening"—periodic polls, occasional focus groups, and reactive media monitoring. These methods produced useful insights, but they operated on a timeline ill-suited to the velocity of digital discourse. By the time a poll was fielded, analyzed, and reported, the narrative landscape had often shifted.

Contemporary narrative intelligence systems enable what scholars increasingly call "continuous listening" (Bjola and Manor 2024). Rather than snapshots, these systems provide ongoing streams of data that reveal not just static sentiment but dynamic narrative trajectories. Diplomats can observe how a rumor emerges, gains velocity, bifurcates across different communities, and either fades or hardens into accepted belief. Tracking how narratives evolve in near real time meaningfully changes what diplomats can do.

The geographic dimension matters equally. Traditional listening often reflected the geographic distribution of diplomatic posts: strong in capitals and major cities, weak in rural provinces or border regions. AI systems can theoretically overcome this limitation, monitoring discourse wherever digital connectivity exists. Yet here too, the promise comes with caveats. Rural communities often communicate through platforms, languages, or formats—community radio, SMS, vernacular social media—that mainstream monitoring systems overlook. The African Union's (AU) critique of what has been called "AI colonialism" speaks directly to this gap: systems designed by and for urban elites risk systematically excluding the voices most peripheral to power (African Union 2024, Hao 2022).

For diplomats, the imperative is clear. Listening at scale requires not just sophisticated algorithms but also deliberate design choices that prioritize equity and inclusion. This means investing in multilingual models, incorporating low-bandwidth channels, and validating digital signals against offline engagement. Without these safeguards, AI-enabled listening risks becoming what might be called "elite surveillance": a capacity to hear the loudest voices while missing those most in need of being heard.

The broader lesson is that AI-enabled listening is never merely technical. It is embedded in questions of power, legitimacy, and representation. Diplomats who approach narrative intelligence as simply a better version of media monitoring miss this deeper dimension. Responsible practice requires not just deploying capable systems but also engaging publics about why listening matters, how it is conducted, and what safeguards protect against abuse. As Nicholas Cull (2019) argues, credibility in public diplomacy depends not on information dominance but on "reputational security"—the sense that institutions listen not to manipulate but to understand. AI makes that distinction harder to hold, and more important.

Historical Precedents: Lessons from Earlier Information Revolutions

The arrival of AI-enabled narrative intelligence is not the first time diplomats have confronted information technologies that fundamentally altered the landscape of communication. Each previous information revolution—the telegraph, radio, television, and the internet—forced diplomatic institutions to adapt their practices of listening, messaging, and engagement. Understanding how earlier transitions unfolded can illuminate both the opportunities and the risks that AI presents today.

The telegraph, introduced in the mid-19th century, collapsed the temporal distance between events and their diplomatic consequences. Before the telegraph, ambassadors operated with substantial autonomy; instructions from capitals could take weeks to arrive, by which time circumstances had often changed. The telegraph tethered diplomats more tightly to their home governments, enabling near real-time coordination but also reducing local discretion. Listening, in this era, remained largely manual: embassies relied on local newspapers, personal networks, and periodic reports. The lesson of the telegraph era is that speed can centralize control, sometimes at the expense of contextual judgment.

Radio, emerging in the early 20th century and reaching its apex during World War II and the Cold War, introduced the capacity for governments to broadcast directly to foreign publics. Voice of America, BBC World Service, and Radio Free Europe/Radio Liberty exemplified this shift. Listening in the radio era still depended on human analysts monitoring broadcasts, reading newspapers, and conducting interviews. What changed was the scale of messaging: for the first time, governments could bypass local gatekeepers and speak directly to mass audiences. Yet this also meant that listening became more critical. Broadcasters needed feedback mechanisms—listener letters, defector interviews, local informants—to gauge whether messages were resonating or backfiring. The radio era underscored a principle that remains relevant today: the capacity to broadcast at scale is worthless without mechanisms to listen at equivalent scale.

Television, dominant from the 1960s through the 1990s, introduced visual storytelling into diplomatic communication. Embassies began producing cultural documentaries, educational programs, and news segments designed for foreign broadcast. Listening, however, remained largely analog: opinion polls, focus groups, and media content analysis. The challenge of the television era was that imagery could be misinterpreted across cultural contexts. A documentary celebrating national (e.g., American) innovation might be read as arrogance in societies wary of foreign influence. The lesson here is that medium matters: what works in one format may fail in another, and listening must be sophisticated enough to detect these nuances.

The internet, arriving in the 1990s and accelerating through the 2000s, shattered the one-to-many broadcast model. Social media platforms enabled many-to-many communication, where publics no longer passively received messages but actively debated, remixed, and countered them. This shift forced diplomatic missions to develop new listening capacities. Early efforts were crude: keyword searches on forums, manual monitoring of influential bloggers. By the 2010s, some missions had adopted rudimentary sentiment analysis tools, precursors to today's narrative intelligence systems. The internet era revealed a paradox: publics now spoke loudly and constantly, yet understanding what they were saying grew exponentially harder. Volume became noise, and discerning signal from noise demanded new analytical capacities.

AI-enabled narrative intelligence is the latest phase in this evolution. It promises to address the signal-noise problem by automating pattern detection, multilingual analysis, and anomaly flagging. Yet history suggests caution. Each previous technology was hailed as transformative, and each introduced unintended consequences. The telegraph centralized control but reduced local nuance. Radio enabled mass messaging but required new feedback loops. Television added visual power but introduced cross-cultural misinterpretation risks. The internet democratized voice but created information overload.

What lessons, then, should guide the AI era? First, speed must not override judgment. The telegraph's lesson applies: real-time capability is only valuable if diplomats retain the authority and expertise to interpret signals contextually. Second, scale requires new listening capacities. Radio and television taught that broadcasting without listening produces noise, not dialogue. AI systems can listen at unprecedented scale, but only if designed with equity, validation, and humility. Third, medium matters. Just as television imagery could be misinterpreted, AI-generated insights can mislead if they lack cultural grounding. Finally, each technology embeds power dynamics. The internet's promise of democratization was undermined by platform monopolies and algorithmic manipulation. AI systems risk similar capture if diplomats do not insist on transparency, accountability, and pluralism in their design and deployment.

The historical arc is clear: technologies that extend diplomatic reach also expose new vulnerabilities. Narrative intelligence is powerful precisely because it operates at machine speed across machine scale. But power without judgment can be reckless. The challenge for today's diplomats is to learn from earlier transitions, adopting AI's capabilities while guarding against the overconfidence, centralization, and exclusion that have plagued previous information revolutions.

TECHNICAL CAPABILITIES

For practitioners to deploy narrative intelligence responsibly, they must understand not only what these systems can do but how they do it. This technical literacy need not extend to coding or algorithm design, but it should encompass the core capabilities that enable AI to process, analyze, and surface patterns in discourse at scale. Four interrelated technical functions—sentiment analysis, discourse clustering, narrative mapping, and anomaly detection—form the foundation of contemporary narrative intelligence systems.

Sentiment Analysis and Affective Computing

Sentiment analysis is the easiest place to start with AI-enabled listening. At its simplest, sentiment analysis categorizes text as positive, negative, or neutral based on linguistic cues. Early systems relied on lexicons: predetermined lists of words associated with particular emotions (e.g., "excellent" signals positive sentiment, "terrible" signals negative). Contemporary approaches use machine learning models trained on large corpora of labeled examples, enabling them to detect sentiment even when explicit emotional language is absent.

The value for diplomacy lies in tracking how sentiment evolves over time and varies across communities. A sudden shift from neutral to negative sentiment around a policy announcement might signal emerging resistance worth investigating. Comparative analysis can reveal whether urban and rural populations respond differently to the same message, or whether youth cohorts express sentiments distinct from older demographics. Tools like World Health Organization's (WHO) EARS (Early AI-supported Response with Social listening platform) employed sentiment analysis to categorize COVID-19 discourse, helping identify regions where vaccine hesitancy was intensifying (Purnat et al. 2021).

Yet sentiment analysis remains blunt. It struggles with sarcasm, cultural context, and implicit meaning. A post stating "Great, another foreign aid program we don't need" expresses negativity through sarcasm, but crude sentiment models might misclassify it as positive based on the word "great." This limitation explains why human validation remains essential: AI provides the first pass, but cultural interpreters must refine the analysis.

Discourse Analysis and Thematic Clustering

Beyond sentiment lies discourse analysis: the identification of themes, topics, and frames within large text corpora. Natural language processing techniques such as topic modeling (e.g., Latent Dirichlet Allocation) can automatically cluster documents into thematic categories without prior labeling. A system monitoring social media during an election, for example, might identify clusters around themes like "economic policy," "immigration," "healthcare," and "corruption," even if users never explicitly label their posts with these categories.

For diplomats, discourse clustering provides situational awareness about what publics are discussing and how prominently different issues register. If a diplomatic initiative launches but generates minimal online discussion, that silence itself is meaningful—it may signal indifference or lack of awareness. Conversely, if a routine embassy announcement unexpectedly generates intense discourse, that anomaly warrants investigation. The EU's EDMO system employed discourse analysis to track how election-related narratives evolved across member states, revealing when local issues suddenly gained cross-border traction (European Commission 2025b).

Discourse analysis also enables frame detection: identifying how issues are conceptualized. Is foreign aid framed primarily as "generosity" or "interference"? Is climate action discussed as "opportunity" or "burden"? These frames shape how publics interpret policies and predict how they will respond to messaging. By tracking frame prevalence, diplomats can calibrate communication strategies to align with dominant frames or strategically challenge them.

Narrative Mapping and Network Analysis

Narrative intelligence extends beyond individual posts to map how stories propagate across networks. Network analysis techniques visualize how content spreads: who shares it, who amplifies it, and through which pathways it reaches broader audiences. This capability is critical for distinguishing organic discourse from coordinated manipulation. A rumor that spreads through diverse, unconnected users likely reflects genuine concern. A rumor amplified primarily through tightly clustered accounts posting in synchronized patterns suggests coordinated inauthentic behavior—bots or troll farms manufacturing the appearance of grassroots sentiment.

Canada's Rapid Response Mechanism employed network analysis to expose "Spamouflage" campaigns. By mapping how content flowed across accounts, analysts identified coordination patterns invisible in individual posts: accounts created simultaneously, posting at identical intervals, and amplifying content within seconds of each other. These behavioral signatures, more than content alone, revealed manipulation (Global Affairs Canada 2025; Chenrose and Rizzuto 2025).

Narrative mapping also identifies influencers: individuals or entities whose posts disproportionately shape discourse. Not all influencers are celebrities or officials; sometimes, local activists, respected journalists, or community leaders wield significant narrative power within specific audiences. For diplomats, identifying these validators enables more strategic engagement. Rather than broadcasting messages indiscriminately, missions can engage validators whose endorsement carries credibility within target communities.

Anomaly Detection and Early Warning Systems

Anomaly detection lies at the heart of early warning. These systems establish baseline patterns—typical levels of activity around particular topics, normal sentiment distributions, expected network structures—and flag deviations. A sudden spike in mentions of a diplomatic initiative, an abrupt shift from positive to negative sentiment, or the emergence of new amplifier networks all constitute anomalies worth investigating.

The sophistication lies in distinguishing meaningful anomalies from noise. Social media exhibits constant fluctuation; not every spike matters. Advanced systems employ statistical thresholds and contextual filters to prioritize anomalies likely to have real-world consequences. WHO EARS, for example, categorized anomalies by severity: low-level rumors confined to small networks triggered monitoring but not response, while high-velocity falsehoods with broad reach prompted immediate corrective action (Purnat et al. 2021).

Temporal analysis adds another dimension. Anomalies that persist over days signal durable shifts in discourse; ephemeral spikes that fade within hours often require no response. By tracking rumor velocity (how fast content spreads) and rumor half-life (how long it persists after correction), diplomats can calibrate interventions proportionately. Rapid, sustained spread demands urgent attention; slow, fading anomalies may resolve organically.

Integration and Human Oversight

These four capabilities—sentiment analysis, discourse clustering, narrative mapping, and anomaly detection—rarely operate in isolation. Contemporary narrative intelligence platforms integrate them into dashboards that provide multidimensional views of the information environment. A single interface might show (1) sentiment trends over time, (2) thematic clusters ranked by volume and growth, (3) network visualizations revealing amplification pathways, and (4) flagged anomalies prioritized by severity.

Yet even the most sophisticated dashboard is only as valuable as the human judgment applied to its outputs. The EEAS FIMI reports exemplify this principle: algorithmic detection identified suspicious patterns, but human analysts determined whether those patterns constituted foreign interference, considered attribution questions, and assessed policy implications (EEAS 2025). The lesson for practitioners is clear: technical literacy enables better questions, not automatic answers. Understanding how systems generate insights allows diplomats to probe their limitations, demand transparency about methodologies, and resist automation bias—the tendency to defer uncritically to machine outputs.

As narrative intelligence systems grow more powerful, the temptation to treat them as oracles will intensify. Resisting that temptation requires not only ethical commitment but also technical understanding. Diplomats who comprehend how sentiment analysis struggles with irony, how discourse clustering reflects training data biases, how network analysis can misidentify grassroots movements as manipulation, and how anomaly detection amplifies noise as well as signal will be better equipped to deploy these tools responsibly. When machine speed and scale amplify both insight and error, that discernment is what protects credibility.

REAL-WORLD APPLICATIONS

The cases that follow show both what AI-enabled narrative intelligence can do and what it cannot. Across health emergencies, electoral integrity, and democratic defense, governments and international organizations have deployed systems that illustrate what works, what fails, and what remains contested. These cases demonstrate that narrative intelligence is most valuable not when it replaces human judgment but when it augments situational awareness, enabling faster triage and more inclusive monitoring.

WHO EARS—Multilingual Pandemic Narrative Tracking at Global Scale

When the World Health Organization launched its *Early AI-supported Response with Social listening* (EARS) platform in January 2021, it confronted an unprecedented information challenge. The COVID-19 pandemic had generated not only a global health crisis but also what WHO Director-General Tedros Adhanom Ghebreyesus called an "infodemic"—a flood of misinformation, rumors, and conspiracy theories that threatened to undermine public health responses worldwide (WHO 2021b). Traditional media monitoring could not keep pace with the velocity and volume of COVID-related discourse spreading across dozens of languages and hundreds of digital platforms.

EARS was designed to address this temporal and linguistic mismatch. The system employed natural language processing to monitor social media posts, news articles, and online forums in multiple languages, clustering content into thematic categories such as vaccine hesitancy, prevention measures, treatment rumors, and conspiracy theories. By analyzing patterns in real-time, EARS could flag emerging "hot spots" of harmful misinformation before they hardened into widespread beliefs. Peer-reviewed research confirmed the platform's value for situational awareness: Purnat and colleagues (2021) documented how EARS enabled WHO country offices to adapt communication strategies more rapidly by identifying which rumors were gaining traction in specific regions.

The platform's architecture combined automated detection with structured human oversight. Machine learning models performed the initial classification, but WHO analysts reviewed flagged content to verify accuracy and assess severity. This hybrid approach proved essential. The peer-reviewed analysis revealed that cultural nuance frequently eluded the algorithms. Sarcasm, slang, and context-dependent meanings—especially prevalent in informal social media discourse—often resulted in misclassification. A satirical post mocking vaccine skepticism might be categorized as vaccine-hesitant content, while a serious expression of concern could be missed if phrased indirectly. WHO's *Infodemic Management Annual Report* (2023) emphasized this limitation explicitly, noting that human analysts remained essential for interpretation and that no automated system could replace local cultural expertise.

The quantitative impact was nonetheless significant. During critical phases of vaccine rollout in 2021–2022, EARS processed millions of posts across regions with varying levels of digital infrastructure and linguistic diversity. The system enabled WHO to issue targeted guidance to member states about emerging rumors before they crystallized into widespread hesitancy. In several documented cases, early detection allowed public health communicators to preempt harmful narratives through validator outreach—engaging trusted local voices to correct misinformation before it gained velocity. The "rumor half-life" metric, adapted from epidemiology, showed that rumors addressed within 24 hours of EARS detection faded significantly faster than those left unchecked (Purnat et al. 2021).

Yet EARS also exposed the ethical and operational challenges of listening at scale. Privacy concerns emerged immediately. Although the platform monitored only publicly available posts, civil society organizations in some countries raised alarms about potential surveillance, particularly in contexts with histories of government monitoring of dissent. WHO responded by publishing methodologies and emphasizing that EARS was designed to inform communication, not to identify individuals or suppress speech. The transparency effort helped, but tensions persisted. In societies where governments had weaponized health surveillance during earlier epidemics, even well-intentioned listening could trigger suspicion.

A second challenge involved inclusivity. EARS performed best in languages with robust training data—English, Spanish, Mandarin—but struggled with lower-resource languages and vernacular dialects. This meant that rural communities or linguistic minorities were often underrepresented in the system's outputs, creating blind spots precisely where misinformation could flourish unchecked. WHO acknowledged this limitation and invested in expanding linguistic coverage, but the experience underscored a broader truth: AI listening systems inherit the biases embedded in their training data. Without deliberate efforts to include marginalized voices, they risk amplifying existing inequalities.

For diplomatic practitioners, the distinctive lesson of EARS is one of positioning: by publishing its methodology and engaging civil society openly, WHO framed listening at scale as a public service rather than surveillance. The difference lay not in the technology but in the disclosure.

EDMO and EEAS—Coordinated Election Monitoring Across Europe

The European Union's experience with AI-enabled narrative intelligence during the 2024 European Parliament elections illustrates how multilateral institutions can deploy monitoring at continental scale while navigating intense political sensitivities. The European Digital Media Observatory (EDMO), established in 2020, and the European External Action Service (EEAS) collaborated to provide member states with real-time situational awareness of disinformation campaigns targeting electoral integrity. The effort combined technological sophistication with diplomatic coordination, yielding insights about both the capabilities and the constraints of AI in democratic defense.

EDMO's mandate centered on election monitoring. During the June 2024 European Parliament elections, the observatory's network of fact-checkers and researchers across 27 member states produced daily bulletins synthesizing emerging disinformation narratives. These bulletins drew on natural language processing systems that monitored social media platforms, news websites, and messaging apps in all 24 official EU languages plus additional regional languages. The scale was unprecedented: millions of posts analyzed daily, anomalies flagged within hours, and patterns visualized in dashboards accessible to national authorities and media outlets. The European Commission's *EU Elections 2024 Monitoring Report* documented how this coordination enabled rapid identification of cross-border manipulation efforts, including coordinated campaigns that recycled identical narratives across multiple languages (European Commission 2025b).

The EEAS complemented EDMO's election-specific work with broader threat assessment. Its *Foreign Information Manipulation and Interference* (FIMI) reports, issued quarterly, provided systematic documentation of hostile information operations targeting European democracies. The third FIMI report, released in March 2025, marked a significant evolution. For the first time, the report included detailed analysis of synthetic media—AI-generated text, images, and videos—used in manipulation campaigns. The EEAS documented cases where deepfake audio recordings of European officials were circulated to sow confusion, and where large language models were employed to generate bulk disinformation content at scale (EEAS 2025). The report's findings were widely covered in European media, with *The Guardian* (2024) highlighting how synthetic content had become a "force multiplier" for adversaries seeking to destabilize democratic discourse.

The technological architecture underlying these efforts combined multiple AI capabilities. Anomaly detection algorithms flagged sudden spikes in activity around particular hashtags or narratives, helping analysts identify coordinated inauthentic behavior—networks of fake accounts amplifying content in synchronized patterns. Natural language processing enabled semantic analysis: the systems could identify when seemingly different messages across languages conveyed identical underlying narratives, suggesting centralized coordination. Network analysis tools mapped how content spread across platforms and borders, revealing amplification patterns that distinguished organic viral spread from manufactured campaigns.

Yet the political and ethical complexities were formidable. Labeling content as "manipulation" or "interference" is inherently contestable. Critics, including some civil society organizations and opposition politicians, argued that EDMO and EEAS risked becoming arbiters of truth, potentially silencing legitimate dissent by categorizing it as disinformation. The charge of over-reach was particularly acute regarding content that criticized EU policies or institutions. Who decides, these critics asked, when critique becomes manipulation? The EU's response emphasized procedural safeguards: content was flagged based on behavioral indicators (coordination, inauthenticity) rather than ideological stance, and final assessments required human review by diverse teams of analysts.

Transparency proved both a strength and a vulnerability. By publishing detailed reports and methodologies, the EU demonstrated accountability and invited scrutiny. This openness helped build trust among member states and civil society. But it also provided adversaries with intelligence about detection capabilities. Once manipulation tactics were documented publicly, hostile actors could adapt. The EEAS acknowledged this trade-off explicitly, arguing that democratic legitimacy required transparency even at the cost of operational surprise.

For diplomatic missions, the distinctive lesson of the EDMO/EEAS experience is that multilateral coordination amplifies capacity: no single member state could have monitored discourse across 24 languages and 27 jurisdictions, but pooled resources and shared intelligence made continental situational awareness possible.

The 2024 elections and the March 2025 FIMI report also highlighted an emerging frontier: the convergence of foreign interference and synthetic media. As adversaries gain access to increasingly capable generative AI tools, the boundary between authentic and fabricated content grows more porous. This evolution demands not only better detection technologies but also new forms of media literacy among publics and new norms of provenance and verification among platforms. The EU's experience suggests that narrative intelligence, while valuable, is insufficient on its own. It must be paired with policy interventions—platform regulation, content provenance standards, and public education—that address the structural conditions enabling manipulation at scale.

Canada's Rapid Response Mechanism

Canada offers another instructive example through its Rapid Response Mechanism (RRM), created with G7 partners but particularly visible in its public advisories. In October 2023, RRM reported on a "Spamouflage" campaign targeting Members of

Parliament, and in March 2025 it exposed another campaign directed at Chinese-language journalists in Canada. By using AI-enabled anomaly detection and network analysis, the mechanism identified coordinated inauthentic behavior that might otherwise have passed unnoticed (Global Affairs Canada 2023; Global Affairs Canada 2025; Chenrose and Rizzuto 2025). What set RRM apart was its decision to publish its findings. By making disinformation threats visible, the Canadian government signaled transparency and bolstered trust, even as questions of attribution—who exactly was behind the campaigns—remained difficult to answer.

U.S. Department of Defense and Primer

The U.S. Department of Defense has approached narrative intelligence from a different angle, piloting systems designed not for diplomacy but for military information operations. In 2020, the Pentagon funded the private company Primer to train neural networks capable of classifying and ranking the "credibility" of online content. Reporting from *Defense One* and *Nextgov* described the effort as an attempt to filter disinformation more efficiently (Tucker 2020; Nextgov 2020; PR Newswire 2020). While technically ambitious, the pilot raised immediate ethical red flags. Allowing AI to score the credibility of information risks politicizing truth itself, a prospect that may be tolerable in closed military settings but is untenable in open diplomacy. For public diplomacy practitioners, the Primer case is a cautionary tale: algorithms can help prioritize attention, but credibility must remain a human judgment.

PRACTITIONER GUIDANCE

For practitioners, adopting AI is as much about mindset as technology. Effective strategic listening depends not only on what AI can detect, but on how diplomats interpret, validate, and act on those signals. The principles that follow provide a practical foundation for using AI to strengthen, rather than undermine, diplomatic credibility.

The AI Mindset for Strategic Listening

If listening is the foundation of diplomacy, then mindset determines whether AI strengthens or undermines that foundation. To use AI responsibly in listening, diplomats must adopt a mindset shaped by humility, vigilance, inclusivity, and restraint.

The first principle is to treat dashboards as radar, not autopilot. A radar screen shows turbulence ahead, but it is the pilot who interprets the signal and decides how to steer. Likewise, narrative intelligence tools can surface spikes in online chatter, but only diplomats—drawing on cultural context and institutional priorities—can determine whether those anomalies matter. Without this distinction, practitioners risk abdicating responsibility to the machine.

Synthetic Narratives in Action: Moldova's AI Election Operations (2025)

In the autumn of 2025, Moldova became the focus of international concern when its parliamentary elections were accompanied by a wave of disinformation powered by artificial intelligence. Journalists and Moldovan officials documented networks of websites and articles that looked like legitimate news outlets but were, in fact, generated by AI. These sites produced persuasive stories portraying pro-European parties as corrupt and unstable, while promoting pro-Russian positions. The material was stylistically polished, grammatically fluent, and difficult for ordinary readers to distinguish from mainstream journalism. What made this campaign especially troubling was its precision. The false stories were not generic propaganda; they were tuned to Moldova's social divisions over whether to align with the European Union or remain in Russia's orbit.

This is a reminder that generative tools are not only about scale but also about targeting. By simulating journalistic authority and speaking directly to local anxieties, the campaign blurred the line between legitimate media and manipulation. The Moldovan case highlights the challenge of information saturation. Fact-checkers and independent outlets tried to expose the synthetic sites, but the volume of content outpaced their efforts. For outside observers, the episode revealed both the fragility of small democracies and the global stakes of synthetic media. If AI can cheaply produce convincing false narratives, then the question is not whether audiences believe every story, but whether they become so overwhelmed that they no longer know which voices to trust (Associated Press 2025; Calmis, Olari, and Gigitashvili 2024; McGrath 2025; McGrath and Ghirda 2024).

Closely related is the need for epistemic humility. AI excels at revealing correlations, but it cannot explain causation. A model may show that posts mentioning "scholarships" are trending positively, but it cannot discern whether the tone reflects gratitude, sarcasm, or frustration. As Henry Kissinger, Eric Schmidt, and Daniel Huttenlocher consistently warn, AI often produces knowledge without understanding (Kissinger, Schmidt, and Huttenlocher 2021). Practitioners must resist the temptation to treat elegant visualizations as conclusive. At best, they are signals pointing to deeper questions that demand human interpretation.

The third principle is vigilance against manipulation. Information environments are contested spaces, and adversaries understand the weaknesses of AI. Coordinated inauthentic networks can flood hashtags, seed rumors, or mimic grassroots voices in ways that distort the very inputs on which dashboards rely. If left unchecked, such poisoning can lead institutions to chase shadows or amplify disinformation inadvertently. Canada's Rapid Response Mechanism illustrates one way forward, combining

AI anomaly detection with human analysis to expose inauthentic campaigns rather than mistake them for organic sentiment (Global Affairs Canada 2023; 2025). Strategic listening requires this constant skepticism: not every spike is what it seems.

Equity by design forms the fourth principle. Listening systems often privilege the voices easiest to capture—urban, digitally fluent, and majority-language users—while excluding rural communities, minority languages, or publics who rely on radio and SMS. As the AU has warned, such exclusion is more than a technical gap; it is a question of sovereignty and legitimacy. Publics who feel unseen in official listening efforts are unlikely to trust subsequent engagement. Designing inclusivity into systems from the start is therefore not optional but essential.

Finally, strategic patience is necessary in deciding when to act. AI can dramatize anomalies, creating pressure to respond quickly to fringe rumors or ephemeral spikes. Yet overreaction can amplify those narratives, giving them more visibility than they would have achieved on their own. WHO's EARS system addressed this challenge by categorizing rumors by severity, allowing proportionate responses that focused on the most harmful narratives (Purnat et al. 2021). The lesson for diplomacy is that restraint is often the most strategic choice. Not every anomaly requires intervention, and sometimes silence is the wiser course.

Together, these principles define an AI mindset for strategic listening that is less about technology than about judgment. AI can accelerate the detection of patterns, but only humans—guided by humility, vigilance, inclusivity, and restraint—can preserve the credibility that diplomacy depends on.

Narrative Intelligence Workflows

Mindset provides the compass, but workflows determine whether that compass can guide action under pressure. In the fast-moving world of digital narratives, listening cannot be treated as a sporadic exercise. It must become a disciplined routine, embedded into daily embassy life. Artificial intelligence can scan and classify at scale, but only structured workflows ensure that its signals are validated, contextualized, and acted upon responsibly.

The process begins with intake and coverage. Missions that rely solely on mainstream platforms risk mistaking elite or urban voices for the broader public. Effective listening therefore requires a deliberate effort to capture diverse inputs, from major social media networks to vernacular messaging apps, community radio transcripts, and local news outlets. This breadth helps counter "AI colonialism," the tendency of systems trained on dominant languages to overlook marginalized publics (African Union 2024, Hao 2022). To operationalize inclusivity, some missions conduct regular "equity audits," verifying whether minority languages or rural communities are represented in their listening streams.

Once data is collected, it must be pre-processed and translated. Duplicate posts are removed, languages are identified, and machine translation systems such as eTranslation, eLUNa, or ITU Translate are used to generate working versions across multiple languages. Here again, human validation remains essential. Locally employed staff play a crucial role in refining translations, adding idioms to glossaries, and noting when sarcasm or double meanings could distort interpretation. These small interventions, often invisible in dashboards, prevent repeated errors and preserve cultural nuance.

Detection comes next, as AI systems cluster topics, flag velocity spikes, and highlight anomalies across networks. They can reveal, for example, that a rumor about vaccine safety is spreading unusually quickly among youth in one province, or that a hashtag linked to migration has suddenly gained traction across multiple platforms. But the raw signals are not enough. Without human validation, they risk being misleading. This is why many missions establish "misread logs," documenting when the system classifies satire as support, or treats coordinated bot activity as authentic sentiment. By capturing these errors, missions both improve their interpretation and build institutional memory.

Human validation and cultural interpretation are the heart of the workflow. Locally employed staff review anomalies and provide contextual analysis, while validator networks—trusted journalists, exchange alumni, or civil society partners —offer external perspectives on whether online signals reflect offline sentiment. Together, these checks ensure that AI outputs are cross-referenced against real-world experience. A rumor that looks alarming on X (formerly Twitter) may in fact be confined to a small circle of activists; a meme that appears positive may actually be mocking. By triangulating across sources, diplomats prevent missteps that could damage credibility.

The next stage is triage and prioritization. Not every anomaly warrants attention, and overreaction can amplify fringe content. Structured rubrics help missions assess whether to ignore, monitor quietly, engage validators, issue corrections, or attempt prebunking. WHO's EARS platform offers one model, categorizing rumors by severity to ensure proportionate responses (Purnat et al. 2021). In practice, this means that a low-level rumor with limited reach may be allowed to fade, while a high-velocity falsehood linked to public safety is corrected quickly through trusted validators and official channels.

Finally, reporting and briefing close the loop. Many missions now produce daily narrative briefs that highlight top anomalies, note cultural interpretations, and recommend actions. Weekly narrative reviews bring together locally employed staff—host-country nationals hired by the embassy who provide essential cultural and linguistic expertise—and section leads to synthesize trends, assess validator feedback, and refine strategies. Change logs document what was flagged, how it was interpreted, and what action was taken. These records are invaluable during staff rotations, preventing the loss of institutional memory that has long plagued diplomatic missions.

These workflows turn AI listening from a technical exercise into a practice of disciplined judgment. They ensure that anomalies are contextualized, decisions are proportionate, and publics are treated with respect. The speed of narrative spread means that workflow discipline is not optional. When synthetic narratives gain traction rapidly—a dynamic examined in depth in Chapter 3—improvisation is dangerous.

Structured routines ensure that AI serves as radar rather than autopilot, providing foresight without surrendering control.

Risks, Ethics, and Compliance

Reach cuts both ways. The narrative-intelligence tools that let diplomats hear public conversations at an unprecedented scale also expose a mission to new failure modes—surveillance perceptions, the communities the tools quietly overlook, and the temptation to act on signals no one fully understands. Understanding these vulnerabilities is crucial, not only to avoid missteps but also to reassure publics that AI is being used responsibly. Five risks, in particular, demand attention: surveillance perceptions, exclusion, politicization, amplification, and governance gaps.

The first and most immediate risk is the perception of surveillance. Even when social listening draws only on publicly available data, many publics interpret large-scale monitoring as invasive. In societies with histories of censorship or repression, the line between "listening" and "spying" can feel especially thin. During the COVID-19 pandemic, for example, some health agencies faced backlash when publics suspected that online rumor tracking was being used to silence dissent rather than to inform communication. For diplomatic missions, transparency becomes the safeguard. Publishing methodologies, clarifying what types of data are included, and explaining how insights are used can help reframe narrative intelligence as a service to publics, rather than an intrusion. UNESCO's *Recommendation on the Ethics of Artificial Intelligence* (2021) underscores this point, emphasizing proportionality and accountability as core principles.

A second risk is bias and exclusion. AI listening systems often privilege the voices that are easiest to capture: urban residents with reliable internet connections, speakers of dominant languages, or users of mainstream platforms. Meanwhile, rural communities, minority-language speakers, and publics who rely on radio or low-bandwidth channels can be overlooked—producing a distorted picture of sentiment that reinforces existing inequalities. The solution lies in designing systems that actively include marginalized voices and validating digital insights with offline engagement.

The third risk lies in politicization, what some have called the "truth problem." Narrative intelligence tools can drift from detecting anomalies to adjudicating truth itself. This is particularly fraught in the realm of counter-disinformation, where algorithms may be asked to label content as "false" or "manipulated." The U.S. Department of Defense's 2020 Primer pilot, which experimented with AI-based "credibility scoring," illustrates both the ambition and the danger. While such scoring might help prioritize information in military contexts, it risks politicization if adopted in civilian diplomacy, where publics expect openness and debate. The EU's *AI Act* (2024) addresses this by requiring explainability in high-risk systems, reminding practitioners that credibility must remain a human judgment, not a machine output.

Amplification presents a fourth risk. AI dashboards can dramatize anomalies, creating pressure for missions to respond quickly to spikes that may, in fact, be ephemeral. Overreaction can inadvertently give fringe narratives greater visibility—a dynamic often referred to as the "paradox of amplification." WHO's EARS platform sought to mitigate this by categorizing rumors by severity, ensuring that only those with real potential for harm triggered public responses (Purnat et al. 2021). For diplomats, adopting triage protocols and practicing strategic patience is essential. Not every anomaly deserves attention; sometimes restraint protects credibility more effectively than rapid reaction.

Finally, there is the broader challenge of governance and compliance. Narrative intelligence systems rely on sensitive data pipelines and carry high stakes for democratic legitimacy. Weak governance—whether in data security, retention policies, or provenance tracking—can leave missions vulnerable to reputational or legal challenges. This is why international frameworks matter. The OECD's updated *AI Principles* (2024) stress fairness and inclusivity; UNESCO insists on transparency and proportionality; the EU mandates provenance labeling for synthetic media; and the African Union emphasizes multilingualism and sovereignty. At the U.S. national level, the U.S. Department of State's Enterprise Data and Artificial Intelligence Strategy (2025) identifies audience insight and narrative monitoring as priority applications for AI across the diplomatic enterprise. Adhering to these frameworks is not just bureaucratic compliance; it is a visible demonstration of values. By aligning with global norms, diplomats can show publics that their listening practices are grounded in accountability and respect.

Metrics and Evaluation

For narrative intelligence to matter, it must produce insights that improve strategy, not just attractive dashboards. Too often, monitoring systems are judged by the volume of data they process—how many posts were scraped, how many anomalies flagged, how many charts generated. These outputs are easy to count, but they are a poor proxy for credibility. What truly matters is whether publics feel understood and whether institutions adapt in ways that reflect those voices. Evaluating narrative intelligence therefore requires a shift from counting activity to assessing outcomes.

One of the most useful measures developed in recent years is the idea of the "rumor half-life." Adapted from epidemiology, the term describes how long it takes for a piece of misinformation to fade after being corrected. WHO's EARS system demonstrated the utility of this approach during COVID-19, showing that rumors corrected quickly and amplified by trusted validators lost traction far faster than those left unaddressed (Purnat et al. 2021). For diplomats, measuring rumor half-life can reveal whether corrections are resonating or whether publics remain unconvinced. A shortening half-life suggests growing resilience, while persistence signals the need to adjust strategy.

Another valuable metric is the uptake of corrections themselves. Counting how many times an embassy's correction is shared relative to the rumor can indicate whether publics find official information credible. But numbers alone cannot tell the full story. Qualitative analysis—such as whether validators echo corrections in their own words—adds depth. When trusted local journalists or alumni restate an embassy's message, it demonstrates that the correction has been absorbed into the narrative landscape rather than simply repeated as foreign propaganda.

The role of validators points to a third measure: amplification. Which validators are picking up embassy messages, and how effectively do they carry them into their networks? In an age of declining trust in institutions, publics often find messages more believable when they come from familiar figures rather than official channels. Tracking validator amplification rates can therefore help missions identify which relationships are most valuable and where new ones need to be cultivated.

AI systems themselves also need to be evaluated. False positives—cases where dashboards misclassify satire as support or sarcasm as hostility—should be recorded in "misread logs." By documenting these errors, missions can quantify the system's weaknesses and build safeguards against overreliance. Related to this is the metric of "time to human validation": how quickly can anomalies flagged by AI be reviewed by trained staff? Shorter validation times increase agility while preserving judgment.

Finally, inclusivity must be treated as a metric in its own right. Equity audits can track how well listening systems reflect diverse publics by measuring the share of coverage across languages, regions, and demographics. A dashboard that analyzes millions of posts but ignores minority dialects or underserved communities cannot claim to represent public sentiment. Evaluating inclusivity ensures that narrative intelligence strengthens credibility rather than distorting it.

These measures connect directly to the broader cycle of diplomacy. As Chapter 5 will argue, evaluation is not a box to be checked but a feedback loop that enables learning. For narrative intelligence, the principle is simple but profound: measure not only what the system sees but whether publics feel heard. Credibility is earned when publics recognize that their voices have shaped the response. The real measure of success is not how much data is collected but how much trust is preserved.

Practical Tools and Implementation Guidance

Beyond mindset and workflow, practitioners benefit from concrete tools that operationalize responsible listening. These tools are not software products but rather frameworks, checklists, and practices that embassy teams can adopt immediately.

The Anomaly Assessment Matrix provides structured triage. When an AI system flags an anomaly, this matrix guides the response decision:

Velocity How quickly is content spreading? (Low/Medium/High)
Reach What proportion of target audiences are exposed? (<1% / 1–10% / >10%)
Severity Does content pose immediate harm? (Low/Medium/High)
Authenticity Is spread organic or coordinated? (Organic/Suspicious/Confirmed inauthentic)

Low velocity, low reach, low severity anomalies typically warrant monitoring only. High scores on multiple dimensions trigger immediate validator engagement and potential correction. The matrix prevents both overreaction and neglect, calibrating responses to actual threat levels.

The Cultural Validation Protocol ensures human oversight catches what algorithms miss. Before acting on AI-flagged content, missions should

1. Have at least two locally employed staff review the content independently
2. Check interpretation against the mission's "cultural glossary" (documented idioms, sarcasm markers, local humor)
3. Consult external validators if disagreement persists
4. Document the case in the mission's "misread log" if AI classification was incorrect

This protocol has prevented costly errors in missions using narrative intelligence. One embassy discovered that its system consistently misclassified posts using a particular slang phrase. Only after validator consultation did staff learn that the phrase had undergone semantic shift: what once meant enthusiasm now conveyed skepticism. The cultural glossary was updated, preventing future misreads.

The Inclusivity Audit Framework makes equity measurable. Monthly or quarterly, missions should assess

- *Language coverage* What percentage of local languages are monitored? (Target: >80% of languages spoken by >5% of population)
- *Geographic balance* Are rural and urban areas proportionally represented?
- *Platform diversity* Are low-bandwidth channels (SMS, radio transcripts, community forums) included?
- *Demographic gaps* Are youth, elderly, and marginalized communities visible in data streams?

Missions that score below 70% on inclusivity metrics should pause expansion of listening systems until equity gaps are addressed. This prevents the institutionalization of biased data collection.

Validator Relationship Management recognizes that AI listening depends on human networks. Successful missions maintain structured validator relationships:

- *Tier 1 Validators (10–15 individuals)* Trusted local voices consulted for high-stakes anomalies. Includes respected journalists, alumni leaders, civil society figures.
- *Tier 2 Validators (30–50 individuals)* Broader network providing periodic feedback on trends and cultural interpretation.
- *Validator Engagement Protocol* Regular check-ins (monthly for Tier 1, quarterly for Tier 2), transparent about how their insights are used, compensated for time when appropriate.

These relationships cannot be built reactively. Missions invest in validator networks during calm periods so that when crises emerge, trusted channels already exist.

Reflection and Strategic Questions

For reflection, practitioners might ask themselves several questions. How can listening be conducted at scale without triggering surveillance fears among publics, especially in societies with histories of repression? What systems are in place to capture and learn from misclassifications, and who is responsible for maintaining cultural glossaries that prevent repeated errors? Where should diplomats draw the line between benign personalization and manipulative microtargeting, and how can missions avoid sliding from anomaly detection into attempts to define truth itself? Which publics are most likely to be excluded from digital listening, and what steps can be taken to ensure their voices are heard? Finally, in moments of crisis, how should missions balance the need for speed with the responsibility for accuracy?

FRONTIER AND NEAR-TERM PILOTS

The most mature applications of narrative intelligence today are clustered around public health, electoral integrity, and disinformation defense. WHO's EARS platform, the EU's election monitoring, and Canada's Rapid Response Mechanism have already shown how AI can surface early warnings and strengthen resilience. Yet researchers and practitioners are already looking ahead to the next generation of tools. These frontier applications remain largely experimental, but they point toward how narrative intelligence could evolve in the latter half of this decade.

One area of growing interest is stakeholder and influence mapping. Rather than focusing solely on the content of narratives, these approaches attempt to map the networks that carry them. By tracing who shares, reposts, or amplifies particular themes, AI can reveal clusters of influence that are not always visible through traditional monitoring. Analysts at the Atlantic Council's Digital Forensic Research Lab, for example, have used similar techniques to expose coordinated inauthentic behavior. For diplomats, such tools could help identify validators whose voices carry disproportionate weight in local discourse, enabling more targeted engagement. But the risks are clear as well. Misidentifying grassroots activity as manipulation could alienate publics, stigmatize communities, and erode credibility.

A second frontier lies in proactive narrative testing. Borrowing techniques from marketing, diplomats could use AI to experiment with alternative framings of a message before releasing it widely. One version might emphasize partnership, another stability, and a third prosperity. AI-assisted surveys and sentiment analysis could help predict which framing is most likely to resonate with different publics. The promise here is obvious: clearer, more effective communication that avoids costly missteps. Yet the ethical pitfalls are equally stark. If publics discover that their reactions were tested without disclosure, they may feel manipulated. Particularly in sensitive contexts such as security or identity politics, the backlash could outweigh any communicative gain. Transparency and restraint would be essential if such practices were ever adopted in diplomacy.

Finally, some scholars and think tanks are exploring narrative wargaming and simulation. RAND and Carnegie reports have suggested that AI simulations could be used to anticipate how adversaries might distort a message or weaponize a rumor.

Militaries have begun experimenting with such models to prepare counter-narratives in advance. In principle, this could allow diplomats to anticipate disinformation campaigns before they emerge, shifting from reaction to prevention. But scenario modeling carries its own dangers. Simulations are only as good as their training data, and biased assumptions can produce false confidence. Worse, overreliance on simulated foresight could narrow imaginative horizons, blinding institutions to unanticipated developments.

What unites these frontier applications is a shift from descriptive listening—cataloguing what publics are already saying—to anticipatory strategy: predicting what they might say, how adversaries might respond, and where narratives are likely to evolve. This is where narrative intelligence intersects with strategic forecasting and defense, one of the six deployment categories identified in this book. Yet it is also where the ethical stakes are highest. Publics will generally accept efforts to correct misinformation once it appears, but they may view undisclosed testing or anticipatory modeling with suspicion. For this reason, the frontier of narrative intelligence will require not only technical innovation but also new forms of transparency, proportionality, and human oversight.

CONCLUSION

By now you've seen how diplomatic listening has shifted from episodic snapshots to continuous, machine-scale awareness.

The central lesson to carry forward is this: detection is not interpretation. Every prior information revolution—the telegraph, radio, television, the internet—extended diplomatic reach while exposing new vulnerabilities, and AI-enabled listening is the latest chapter in that arc. Humility about its limitations is the surest guard against repeating earlier mistakes.

Listening, however, is only the beginning of the cycle. The insights you now have—what publics care about, what language carries historical weight, which communities feel seen and which feel overlooked—must eventually become the words you put into the world. The next chapter takes up that craft: how artificial intelligence is reshaping diplomatic messaging, and why the speed of production means nothing if the message itself fails to honor the cultural realities that listening has revealed.

2 Crafting Impactful Messaging with AI

"When we think about this technology, we need to put human dignity, human well-being—human jobs—in the center of consideration."

—Fei-Fei Li, "Stanford's Fei-Fei Li on Human-Centered AI" (2023)

"We have to move beyond sort of the simple prompts and start understanding what we're asking for."

—Chris Gee, quoted in Sean Devlin, "The Prompt Engineering Guide for Comms Pros" (2025)

"As has been said, translation is always a shift, not between two languages but between two cultures – or two encyclopaedias. A translator must take into account rules that are not strictly linguistic but, broadly speaking, cultural."

—Umberto Eco, Mouse or Rat?: Translation as Negotiation (2003)

Opening Vignette: When One Word Changes the Message

The trade agreement had taken months to negotiate, and the embassy in the Republic of Z was ready to make the most of it. David Kim, the public affairs officer, had worked with Washington to develop a coordinated rollout—a press release in English, French, and Zorani, timed to coincide with a joint appearance by the ambassador and the Zorani trade minister. The messaging framework emphasized economic partnership, shared prosperity, and long-term investment in Zorani infrastructure. It was the kind of proactive campaign that public affairs sections rarely had time to plan properly, and David wanted it done right. Lina Perez, the embassy's digital communications officer, ran the English draft through the mission's neural machine translation system. Within two hours, she had polished versions in all three languages—work that would have taken a contracted translator the better part of a week. The outputs were fluent, grammatically precise, and tonally consistent with the policy guidance. She circulated them for final review.

DOI: 10.1201/9781003612377-3

Miriam Diallo, the cultural affairs officer, was reading through the Zorani version when she paused. "This word," she said, pointing to a term the system had selected for "modernization." "I would not use it." David looked over her shoulder. "It is the direct translation." "It is the correct translation," Miriam said. "But in the eastern provinces, this word is not heard the way it reads. The forced agricultural reforms of the 1970s were called modernization. For a generation of rural Zorani families, the word still carries the memory of displacement. If we publish this, we are not announcing a trade agreement. We are reopening a wound." Farid Tessam, a locally employed cultural affairs assistant with deep ties to rural communities, confirmed Miriam's concern within the hour. Two contacts in the eastern provinces said the same thing independently: the word would land badly, regardless of the intention behind it. Lina replaced "modernization" with "renewal"—a term that preserved the forward-looking spirit of the message while carrying none of the historical weight. The rest of the translation stood.

The press release went out on schedule, was well received, and generated the kind of constructive coverage the embassy had planned for. No crisis had been averted. No scandal had erupted. But a single word, flagged by a cultural affairs officer who understood what the algorithm could not, had made the difference between a message that resonated and one that would have alienated the very communities the agreement was meant to benefit. At the debrief, David noted what the episode revealed about the team's workflow. "The AI gave us speed we could not have achieved on our own," he said. "Three languages in two hours. But speed without cultural review is a liability. The system translated the words. Miriam translated the meaning."

FRAMING THE CHAPTER

If listening is the foundation of diplomacy, messaging is the moment when that foundation is tested. It is the first point of contact where publics encounter a state's intentions, whether through a press release, a speech, a social media post, or even the words of a chatbot. Messages shape impressions instantly: they can build trust when phrased with clarity and respect, or they can spark skepticism and backlash when tone-deaf or poorly adapted. In the digital age, where a phrase can be clipped, remixed, and circulated worldwide in minutes, the stakes of diplomatic messaging have never been higher.

Artificial intelligence has already begun to alter how these messages are crafted and delivered. Machine translation systems now allow embassies to release announcements simultaneously in dozens of languages, reducing the lag that once left smaller publics waiting days for updates. Generative models can produce multiple drafts of speeches or press releases in seconds, offering alternative framings and tones for diplomats to refine. Government AI co-pilots—large language model assistants embedded directly into staff workflows—promise to relieve overburdened staff by handling boilerplate drafting and summarization, with early deployments visible in offices from Ottawa to London. And in times of crisis, chatbots can provide instant responses to public queries, ensuring that vital information circulates faster than rumor. AI, in short, has turned messaging from a slow, resource-intensive process into one characterized by abundance and speed.

RESEARCH AND POLICY FOUNDATIONS

For much of the twentieth century, the challenge of messaging was one of scarcity. Drafting took time, translation was labor-intensive, and distribution was limited to the speed of print and broadcast. What AI has introduced is not incremental improvement but a reversal of conditions: diplomacy now faces an abundance of outputs generated at unprecedented speed.

Recognizing these dilemmas, global governance frameworks have begun to set boundaries for responsible use. UNESCO's *Recommendation on the Ethics of Artificial Intelligence* (2021) insists on transparency, inclusivity, and accountability, reminding practitioners that publics have a right to know when AI shapes the information they receive. The European Union's *AI Act* (2024) codifies these expectations, banning manipulative design practices and requiring labeling of AI-generated content in sensitive domains. The African Union's (AU) Continental AI Strategy (2024) reframes inclusivity as a matter of sovereignty, stressing that AI systems must reflect Africa's linguistic and cultural diversity rather than reproducing Western corpora. Similarly, ASEAN's *Expanded Guide on AI Governance and Ethics* (2025) highlights contextual adaptation, warning that literal translation without cultural nuance risks widening trust gaps. The OECD's updated *AI Principles* (2024) add another layer, emphasizing fairness and purpose-driven design.

Taken together, scholarship and governance converge on a paradox: AI has multiplied the tools available for messaging, but it has also raised the risks of inconsistency, manipulation, and mistrust. The task for diplomats is not simply to adopt new systems but to embed them in workflows and norms that preserve authenticity. AI can accelerate communication and expand reach, but credibility depends on whether publics recognize the human intent behind the words.

TECHNICAL CAPABILITIES

Generative Drafting Tools

Generative models can produce drafts in seconds, offering multiple versions of the same announcement in different tones or rhetorical styles. Neural machine translation enables institutions like the European Union to publish in all of its official languages simultaneously, reducing delays that once signaled hierarchy among publics. Government pilots with large language model "co-pilots" show that routine drafting, once a drain on staff resources, can now be completed in minutes, freeing officers to focus on strategy. In principle, this abundance expands creativity and responsiveness.

Reid Hoffman (2023) has described generative AI as a "superagent," multiplying the options available and allowing human users to select the framing that best fits the moment.

Neural Machine Translation

But abundance comes with risks. Mustafa Suleyman (2023) warns that systems which produce more content than humans can meaningfully review create fragility. With multiple variants available at once, the challenge shifts from creation to discernment: which version feels authentic, which resonates across audiences, and which risks contradiction? Abundance also opens space for adversaries to exploit confusion, remixing official messages into parodies or circulating contradictory outputs to portray institutions as incoherent. Karen Sutherland (2025) has noted that publics are quick to detect when communication feels artificial or generic, especially in political or cultural contexts where authenticity is prized. In such cases, efficiency without empathy may accelerate not trust but alienation.

Multilingual Publication Workflows

The stakes are high because credibility in messaging rests on more than accuracy. As Marguerite Sullivan argued two decades ago in A Responsible Press Office, effective communication depends on clarity, consistency, and respect (Sullivan 2001). These principles remain constant, but the speed and volume introduced by AI magnify the costs of error. A mistranslated term, a tone-deaf phrase, or a poorly disclosed chatbot response can reverberate across networks faster than corrections can catch up. In this sense, AI intensifies rather than replaces the core dilemmas of diplomatic messaging. The broader application of AI to diplomatic communication functions—including how messaging intersects with monitoring, engagement, and crisis response—is examined across the companion volume to this book (Kilburg 2025).

REAL-WORLD APPLICATIONS

Although much of the debate around AI in diplomacy imagines what might be possible, a number of deployed systems already demonstrate how artificial intelligence is reshaping the practice of messaging. These cases span multilingual translation, crisis communication, and internal government drafting support, and together they show both the opportunities and the vulnerabilities of using machines to craft words intended for publics.

EU eTranslation—Eight Years of Linguistic Parity at Continental Scale

The European Union's *eTranslation* platform represents perhaps the most sustained and comprehensive deployment of AI-enabled translation in diplomatic practice. Launched in November 2017, the system emerged from a recognition that linguistic parity was not merely a technical challenge but a political imperative. For an institution representing 450 million citizens across 27 member states, the inability to communicate simultaneously in all 24 official EU languages risked creating hierarchies of information access—where English, French, or German speakers received updates days before speakers of Maltese, Irish, or Croatian.

eTranslation employs neural machine translation, a deep learning approach that processes entire sentences rather than word-by-word substitution. This enables more natural phrasing and better handling of context-dependent meanings. The system was designed from the outset to be secure, processing documents within EU infrastructure rather than relying on external cloud services—a critical consideration for diplomatic and administrative texts that often contain sensitive policy deliberations. By 2025, eight years into operation, eTranslation had processed hundreds of millions of words annually, supporting not only EU institutions but also member state administrations, small and medium enterprises, and non-governmental organizations (European Commission 2017; 2018; 2025a).

The operational impact has been transformative. Translation turnaround times that once required days of human effort can now be measured in hours or even minutes. This speed enables the EU to present a unified public face across languages during crises or major policy announcements—a capacity that proved especially valuable during the COVID-19 pandemic, when health guidance needed to reach all member state publics simultaneously. The system also democratizes access: smaller language communities, which historically received translated materials last, now receive them at the same pace as larger ones, reinforcing the EU's commitment to multilingual equality.

Yet eTranslation's 8-year track record also illuminates the enduring limitations of automated translation. Research on machine translation has documented that while systems achieve high accuracy for straightforward administrative texts, they struggle with nuanced political discourse, cultural idioms, and context-dependent terminology. Human post-editing remains indispensable—not as a luxury but as a necessity. EU translators review machine outputs, correcting errors, refining tone, and ensuring that cultural resonances are preserved. A literal translation may be technically accurate but politically tone-deaf; only human judgment can distinguish between them.

The European Commission has been remarkably transparent about these trade-offs. Official reports acknowledge that eTranslation is most effective for routine documents with stable vocabularies—budget reports, procedural guidelines, technical specifications. For politically sensitive communications—statements on foreign policy crises, negotiations with partner countries, messaging during electoral periods—human translation remains the standard, with eTranslation used primarily to generate first drafts that accelerate the process. This tiered approach reflects a mature understanding of AI's role: it can enhance productivity without replacing expertise.

For diplomatic practitioners beyond the EU, the distinctive lesson of eTranslation is that linguistic parity at scale is achievable — but only as a sustained institutional commitment, not a one-time purchase. The system required years of development, and its continued effectiveness depends on continuous retraining with updated corpora and feedback from human translators as language and political contexts evolve.

UN and ITU Translation Systems—Multilateral Communication Infrastructure at Global Scale

While the European Union's eTranslation operates at continental scale, the United Nations and its specialized agencies face an even more complex challenge: maintaining linguistic consistency across six official languages (Arabic, Chinese, English, French, Russian, and Spanish) for an organization that encompasses 193 member states. The UN's approach, developed over decades and enhanced with AI capabilities since 2015, offers a complementary model—one that emphasizes translation memory and terminological precision alongside machine learning.

The UN's *eLUNa* (e-Library of United Nations Library and Archives) system, developed by the Department for General Assembly and Conference Management (DGACM), represents a hybrid approach to translation. Rather than relying solely on neural machine translation, eLUNa integrates computer-assisted translation (CAT) tools with translation memory—essentially a database of previously translated UN documents that can be searched and reused (DGACM 2015; United Nations 2022). When a translator encounters a phrase that appears in past resolutions, statements, or reports, eLUNa surfaces the accepted translation, ensuring consistency across decades of diplomatic discourse.

This emphasis on consistency reflects the UN's unique requirements. Unlike the EU, where policy debates occur in real-time across multiple languages, UN documents often reference past resolutions, legal precedents, and established terminology that must remain stable across translations. A Security Council resolution from 1998 must use the same French terminology as one from 2024; deviations could create legal ambiguities or political disputes. eLUNa's translation memory ensures this continuity, preventing the "semantic drift" that can occur when different translators render the same concept differently over time.

The system has been in continuous use since 2015, processing everything from General Assembly speeches to committee reports to Secretary-General statements. The quantitative impact is significant: human translators working with eLUNa can process documents 20–30% faster than without assistance, allowing the UN to meet the demanding timelines of multilateral diplomacy without compromising on quality (United Nations 2022). During major international summits or emergency Security Council sessions, this acceleration matters enormously—the difference between publics worldwide receiving information in their language within hours rather than days.

The International Telecommunication Union (ITU), a UN specialized agency focused on global telecommunications standards, has developed its own variant: *ITU Translate*. Operational since approximately 2019–2020 and refined continuously through 2024, this system addresses a particularly challenging niche—the translation of highly technical telecommunications vocabulary across the six official UN languages (ITU 2022; 2023; 2024). Terms like "spectral efficiency," "latency tolerance," or "network slicing" have no established equivalents in many languages, requiring ITU to develop specialized glossaries and train models on telecommunication-specific corpora.

ITU Translate exemplifies how specialized AI translation can serve diplomatic functions even in technical domains. The Union's work on global telecommunications standards affects billions of people, yet the standards themselves are often impenetrable to non-experts. By ensuring that technical documentation is available in all official languages, ITU democratizes access to global governance decisions that shape internet connectivity, mobile networks, and satellite communications. The political dimension is clear: if standards were only published in English or French, developing countries with limited capacity in those languages would be systematically disadvantaged in shaping rules that govern their digital futures.

Both eLUNa and ITU Translate highlight a broader truth about AI in multilateral diplomacy: translation is not merely a technical service but a form of infrastructure that enables participation. When smaller member states can access documents in their official language at the same time as larger powers, it levels the playing field of international negotiations. When technical standards are linguistically accessible, it reduces information asymmetries that have historically favored wealthy, English-dominant countries.

Yet these systems also reveal persistent challenges. Both eLUNa and ITU Translate require extensive human oversight. UN translators review machine outputs, correct errors, and flag cases where literal translation misses political nuance. During contentious Security Council debates, for instance, every word is scrutinized for implied positions; machine translation that accurately captures denotation but misses connotation can create diplomatic incidents. The human cost is also noteworthy: translators report that post-editing machine output can be cognitively taxing, requiring constant vigilance for subtle errors that might slip past cursory review.

Security and confidentiality present another layer of complexity. UN documents often contain sensitive diplomatic communications, negotiating positions, or information about ongoing peacekeeping operations. Processing such materials through external commercial translation services would be unacceptable; like the EU's eTranslation, both eLUNa and ITU Translate operate on secure UN infrastructure. This sovereignty over translation infrastructure is a prerequisite for trust—member states must be confident that sensitive texts are not being processed, stored, or potentially accessed by third parties.

For diplomatic practitioners, the UN and ITU examples offer distinct lessons from the EU case. Where eTranslation prioritizes speed and simultaneous publication, eLUNa and ITU Translate emphasize consistency and terminological precision. This reflects different institutional priorities: the EU's challenge is real-time communication across a political union; the UN's challenge is maintaining a stable linguistic foundation for international law and technical standards over decades. Both approaches work, but they require different technical architectures and different human workflows.

UK Government Co-Pilots—Quantifying Productivity While Managing Risk

Between September and December 2024, the United Kingdom conducted one of the most systematic evaluations of generative AI in government communication to date. The Government Digital Service (GDS) piloted Microsoft Copilot across approximately 20,000 civil servants, including substantial participation from communicators in the Government Communication Service (GCS). The trial aimed to answer a straightforward question with profound implications: can large language models deliver measurable productivity gains in government work without compromising accuracy, security, or public trust?

The results were striking. Evaluation reports documented an average time saving of 26 minutes per user per day—approximately 5% of an 8-hour workday (GDS 2025b). Extrapolated across the civil service, this translated to thousands of staff-hours recovered annually, time that could be redirected from routine drafting and summarization to strategic communication planning, stakeholder engagement, and policy development. For press officers juggling multiple briefings, social media managers drafting rapid responses, and policy communicators synthesizing complex documents, the productivity impact was transformative. Tasks that previously consumed hours—drafting routine statements, summarizing lengthy reports, generating alternative message framings—could now be completed in minutes (GDS 2025a).

The Government Digital Service's detailed evaluation revealed how Copilot was being used in practice. The most common applications included: drafting first versions of press releases, ministerial statements, and social media posts; summarizing briefing documents and consultation responses; generating multiple variants of messages for different audiences; and creating meeting agendas and follow-up notes. In each case, the AI functioned as a drafting assistant rather than a final author. Human staff reviewed, edited, and often substantially revised the outputs before any external dissemination. The productivity gain came not from eliminating human work but from accelerating the initial drafting phase, allowing communicators to spend more time on refinement and strategic judgment.

Yet the UK trials also exposed significant risks that tempered the enthusiasm. First, hallucinations—instances where Copilot generated plausible but false information—occurred with concerning frequency. In several documented cases, drafts included fabricated statistics, misattributed quotations, or invented policy details that looked credible on first glance but were factually incorrect. Under deadline pressure, there was a documented temptation among some staff to accept AI outputs without adequate verification. The National Audit Office's 2024 report on AI in government specifically flagged this "automation bias"—the tendency to trust machine outputs uncritically—as a systemic risk requiring explicit countermeasures (NAO 2024).

Second, data confidentiality emerged as a major concern. Microsoft Copilot, as a commercial product, processes inputs through Microsoft's infrastructure. While the company provides assurances about data handling, the UK government remained uncomfortable with the prospect of sensitive policy drafts, ministerial communications, or confidential briefing materials being processed by external commercial systems. The risk was not necessarily that Microsoft would misuse the data, but that any external processing created potential attack vectors for sophisticated cyber adversaries or introduced uncertainties about data sovereignty that were unacceptable for government communication.

This security concern prompted parallel development of a domestic alternative. The Government Communication Service, working with the Government Digital Service, developed its own secure AI drafting tool, initially piloted under various names and formally rebranded as *GCS Assist* in May 2025 (GCS 2024). Built on open-source large language models hosted on UK government infrastructure, GCS Assist provides similar drafting and summarization capabilities to Copilot but ensures that all data processing occurs within sovereign government systems. The tool was specifically designed for government communicators, trained on appropriate corpora, and integrated with existing workflow tools used across departments.

The UK's approach—piloting commercial tools while simultaneously developing sovereign alternatives—reflects a mature institutional strategy. Commercial AI products offer immediate capability and continuous updates from large R&D investments. Sovereign systems offer security, customization, and independence from vendor decisions about features, pricing, or continued service. By maintaining both pathways, the UK government gains flexibility: commercial tools for routine, non-sensitive work; sovereign systems for classified or policy-sensitive communication.

The evaluation also revealed uneven adoption patterns that offer lessons for any institution deploying AI co-pilots. Younger staff and those with prior experience using AI tools adapted quickly, integrating Copilot into daily workflows. More senior staff and those in roles requiring deep subject-matter expertise were more skeptical, often finding that the AI's outputs required such extensive revision that the time savings disappeared. The lesson: AI co-pilots work best for routine, structured tasks with clear formatting requirements. They struggle with nuanced policy communication, culturally sensitive messaging, or contexts where subtle word choice carries political weight.

The UK government's decision to publish detailed evaluations—including candid discussion of failures, risks, and limitations—also exemplifies best practice in AI deployment transparency. By acknowledging what does not work alongside what does, the Government Digital Service has provided other governments with an evidence base for informed decision-making. This transparency itself builds trust: publics and civil servants alike can see that AI adoption is being approached thoughtfully rather than recklessly.

Taiwan's *Central Epidemic Command Center* chatbot shows how AI can serve publics in moments of acute crisis. Launched in May 2020 at the height of the COVID-19 pandemic, the bilingual chatbot provided information in Chinese and English through Google Assistant, answering common questions and directing users to official resources (Taiwan CDC 2020; *Taipei Times* 2020). By reducing pressure on hotlines and ensuring that foreign residents received timely updates, the system helped to counter rumor and panic. Yet it also revealed the fragility of crisis communication: the chatbot required daily updates to remain accurate, and complex or sensitive queries had to be escalated to human staff. The lesson was clear—AI can extend reach in emergencies, but without constant human oversight, it risks spreading outdated or incomplete information.

Together, these cases reveal a spectrum of practice. eTranslation and eLUNa demonstrate how AI supports linguistic parity in multinational institutions, while ITU Translate shows its potential in highly technical domains. The UK co-pilot pilots reveal both productivity gains and significant risks—hallucinations, security concerns, and the irreplaceable need for human judgment. Taiwan's crisis chatbot illustrates both the speed and fragility of AI-enabled engagement.

Synthetic Narratives in Action: Imran Khan's AI Speeches (2023–24)

When Pakistan's former Prime Minister Imran Khan was jailed in 2023, his political party faced an extraordinary problem: how to keep their leader's presence alive without his physical participation. The solution came through synthetic voice technology. Supporters took Khan's written statements and processed them through an AI system that could replicate his distinctive speaking style. The resulting audio was played at rallies and shared widely on social media, where many listeners accepted it as an authentic extension of his leadership.

This use of AI raises questions that strike at the heart of modern political communication. On one level, the words were his, reflecting his authorship and political agenda. On another, the delivery was artificial, generated by a machine rather than spoken from a podium. For supporters, this did not diminish the speeches' legitimacy. Indeed, the very act of "hearing" Khan while he was barred from public life may have deepened loyalty. Critics, however, warned that the technique blurred important boundaries between authentic presence and synthetic simulation. The case illustrates both the promise and peril of generative technologies in diplomacy and politics. AI can bridge gaps in communication, making messages more accessible across space, time, and language. Yet it also creates a credibility gap: once audiences grow accustomed to synthetic delivery, it becomes harder to know when a leader's voice truly represents their intent. For future international communicators, this tension between accessibility and authenticity is likely to become a recurring challenge (Goldstein and Lohn 2024; Reuters 2023).

CULTURAL LOCALIZATION BEYOND TRANSLATION

Machine translation has advanced dramatically, enabling embassies to publish in dozens of languages simultaneously. Yet diplomatic communication requires more than linguistic accuracy—it demands cultural resonance. A press release that is grammatically perfect but culturally tone-deaf can alienate the very publics it aims to reach. This section explores how AI can assist with cultural localization, while highlighting why human cultural expertise remains irreplaceable.

The Limits of Literal Translation

Effective diplomatic messaging goes far beyond converting words from one language to another. It requires understanding how concepts, values, and rhetorical styles resonate across cultural contexts. A message framed around "individual rights" may be compelling in societies with strong traditions of liberal individualism but may feel alien or even threatening in communities that prioritize collective harmony and family obligations. Similarly, direct, assertive language that signals confidence in one culture can be perceived as arrogant or disrespectful in another.

Machine translation systems, even sophisticated neural models, typically operate at the sentence or paragraph level. They can capture denotative meaning—what words literally say—but struggle with connotative meaning—what words culturally imply. An AI system translating a U.S. embassy statement about "modernization" into a language where that term evokes traumatic historical experiences (as illustrated in this chapter's opening vignette) may produce a technically accurate but diplomatically disastrous translation. The algorithm lacks access to the historical memory, emotional associations, and political context that determine how publics will actually receive the message.

This limitation extends beyond individual words to encompass rhetorical structures. Some cultures favor indirect communication, where meaning is conveyed through implication and context. Others value directness and explicit statement. A diplomatic message structured for one style may feel inappropriate when mechanically translated into another. The gap between intended meaning and received meaning is not merely theoretical. In February 2025, an AI-generated video depicting a luxury "Trump Gaza" resort—complete with a golden Trump statue, imagery of wealth, and scenes widely perceived as culturally demeaning—circulated internationally in the context of U.S. proposals regarding Gaza reconstruction. Originally produced as satire by Israeli-American filmmakers, the video reached a much wider audience than its creators anticipated, with Arab governments, the United Nations, and Palestinian leaders condemning it as deeply offensive (Goggin 2025; McCammon and Al-Shalchi 2025). The case illustrates a principle that applies equally to diplomatic communication: AI-generated content carries no built-in cultural intelligence. What reads as aspirational or humorous in one cultural context can register as contemptuous or provocative in another. For diplomatic missions, this underscores why cultural validation cannot be skipped—not only for content produced internally, but for third-party content that official channels might amplify or appear to endorse. The EU's eTranslation system has documented this challenge: while it excels at translating EU administrative texts with stable, formal vocabularies, it struggles with political speeches where rhetorical nuance, metaphor, and allusion carry substantial meaning (Gaspari et al. 2014).

AI-Assisted Cultural Adaptation Strategies

Despite these limitations, AI can assist with certain dimensions of cultural localization when deployed thoughtfully. Large language models trained on diverse international corpora can flag phrases that may carry problematic connotations in target cultures. By analyzing how similar messages have been received across different contexts, these systems can suggest alternative framings that preserve core meaning while adapting rhetorical style.

For instance, an embassy preparing a statement on a bilateral trade agreement might use AI to generate variants emphasizing different values: one version highlighting economic growth and prosperity (appealing to audiences focused on development), another emphasizing partnership and mutual respect (resonating with publics sensitive to historical power imbalances), a third stressing environmental sustainability and social equity (connecting with younger, value-driven audiences). The AI provides options; human judgment selects which framing best fits the political and cultural moment.

Some advanced systems incorporate cultural knowledge bases—structured databases of cultural norms, taboos, historical sensitivities, and communication preferences. When generating or reviewing messaging, these systems can surface warnings: "In this cultural context, direct criticism of government institutions may be viewed as disrespectful. Consider framing suggestions as 'opportunities for collaboration' rather than 'problems requiring reform.'" Such guardrails do not make cultural decisions, but they prompt human communicators to consider dimensions they might otherwise overlook.

Sentiment analysis tools can also assist by previewing how messages might be emotionally received. By analyzing responses to similar messages in the past, these systems can estimate whether a proposed framing is likely to generate positive, negative, or mixed reactions across different demographic or cultural groups. A message that tests well with urban youth might generate skepticism among rural elders; an approach that resonates in one province might fall flat in another. Again, the AI provides foresight; humans decide whether and how to adapt.

The Irreplaceable Role of Cultural Validators

Yet all these AI-assisted approaches remain fundamentally limited because culture is not reducible to rules or patterns that machines can learn. Culture is lived experience, shaped by history, identity, power dynamics, and constantly evolving social norms. Only humans immersed in that experience can reliably judge whether a message will resonate or alienate.

This is why locally employed staff and cultural validators are indispensable. A press officer who grew up in the host country, speaks the local language natively, and maintains deep community ties can detect nuances that no algorithm can match. They know which historical references carry emotional weight, which phrases have recently acquired new connotations, which metaphors feel natural versus forced, which rhetorical styles align with current political discourse. Their expertise is tacit knowledge—often difficult to articulate but immediately recognizable when absent.

Effective diplomatic missions institutionalize this expertise through cultural validation protocols. Before any significant message is released, it undergoes review by locally employed staff who assess not only linguistic accuracy but cultural appropriateness. They ask: Does this phrasing respect local communication norms? Are there historical references that might be misunderstood? Does the tone match the gravity of the situation? Would local publics perceive this message as authentic or as foreign imposition?

This validation extends to visual communication as well. Images, colors, gestures, and even typography carry cultural meanings. An embassy social media post featuring an image that seems innocuous in one culture might inadvertently include symbols, poses, or settings that carry problematic associations in another. AI image analysis tools can flag some obvious issues—detecting religious symbols, political imagery, or culturally specific gestures—but they cannot replicate the comprehensive cultural literacy that humans provide.

Building Institutional Cultural Memory

One practical application of AI in cultural localization is helping missions build and maintain cultural glossaries and style guides. These living documents capture institutional learning: which phrases have worked well in the past, which have failed, which metaphors resonate, which historical references to avoid, how different audiences prefer to be addressed. AI can help organize this knowledge, surface relevant precedents when new messages are being drafted, and flag when proposed language conflicts with established best practices.

For instance, an embassy's cultural glossary might document that in the host country, the term "partnership" should always be paired with language emphasizing equality and mutual benefit, never presented as a unilateral offer. The glossary might note that references to "youth" should acknowledge intergenerational respect rather than implying youth should replace older generations. It might flag that certain economic terms carry colonial connotations and suggest alternative vocabulary. When AI drafting tools generate messages, they can be configured to check against this glossary and alert human reviewers to potential issues.

Such systems work best when they facilitate rather than replace human judgment. The goal is not to automate cultural sensitivity but to ensure that hard-won cultural insights are not lost when staff rotate, and that new communicators can benefit from institutional memory. The AI serves as a knowledge management tool, helping humans access relevant cultural context at the moment of drafting.

Strategic Implications for Diplomatic Messaging

The distinction between translation and localization has profound strategic implications. Embassies that treat AI translation as sufficient for diplomatic communication risk systematically alienating the publics they aim to engage. Messages that are linguistically correct but culturally oblivious signal disrespect, even when unintentional. Over time, this corrodes credibility and reinforces perceptions that foreign governments do not genuinely understand or value local culture.

Conversely, missions that invest in cultural localization—combining AI tools with robust human cultural expertise—can achieve genuine resonance. Messages that reflect cultural sensitivity, acknowledge local values, and demonstrate authentic engagement build trust. Publics recognize when communication has been crafted with care, and that recognition itself becomes a diplomatic asset.

The African Union's *Continental AI Strategy* (2024) emphasizes this point forcefully, arguing that linguistic inclusion without cultural adaptation amounts to a new form of digital colonialism, or AI colonialism (Hao 2022). Simply translating Western-designed messages into African languages does nothing to address whether those messages resonate with African values, histories, or communication traditions. True equity requires not just multilingual access but culturally grounded communication that reflects diverse worldviews.

PRACTITIONER GUIDANCE

For diplomats, the challenge of AI-assisted messaging is not simply technical; it is strategic and ethical. The tools now available—translation engines, drafting co-pilots, and chatbots—can dramatically reduce workloads and expand reach. But unless embedded in thoughtful practice, they risk producing communication that is fast, polished, and hollow. The key is to ensure that speed does not outpace judgment, and that publics continue to feel spoken to rather than spoken at.

The most effective practice begins with validation. AI drafts, no matter how fluent, must be reviewed by humans who understand the local cultural and political context. Locally employed staff are essential here, not as proofreaders but as cultural interpreters, able to detect when a technically correct phrase might carry unintended connotations. Maintaining records of these interventions—what the system produced, how it was revised, and why—helps missions build an institutional memory that prevents repeating mistakes.

Transparency is another pillar of effective practice. Publics are increasingly aware of AI and sensitive to the ways it can be used in communication. When institutions acknowledge that a chatbot is AI-assisted, or that a draft was machine-generated but human-reviewed, they signal accountability. Concealment, by contrast, can backfire if automation is later exposed. In diplomacy, where legitimacy often rests on credibility, openness about methods can become a strategic asset rather than a liability.

Personalization demands particular care. Tailoring messages for different audiences can make them more relatable, but the line between adaptation and manipulation is thin. Practitioners must ensure that personalized messages emphasize different facets of a consistent policy, rather than constructing divergent or contradictory realities. Disclosure also matters here: publics are more likely to trust personalization when they know why they are receiving a message. The ethical test is straightforward—does personalization clarify intent, or does it obscure it?

Finally, proportionate response remains as important in messaging as it is in listening. AI can flood missions with drafts and variants, but not all deserve release. Diplomatic communication is not a numbers game; more is not always better. Careful editorial judgment, applied through structured clearance protocols, ensures that abundance does not fragment narratives or create confusion.

The AI Mindset for Messaging

A press statement drafted in thirty seconds is not automatically a better press statement. The tools now available for drafting, translating, and tailoring diplomatic messages are genuinely powerful, but their worth is set entirely by the choices practitioners make about when, and whether, to use them. A message that is fast but inauthentic can erode trust, while a slower one that resonates with cultural nuance can build lasting credibility. To use AI responsibly in messaging, practitioners must approach it with a mindset shaped by authenticity, transparency, restraint, and humility.

The first principle is *human-in-the-loop authenticity*. AI can generate words, but it cannot create meaning in the diplomatic sense. Messages succeed not when they are grammatically correct but when they feel credible and human. Locally employed staff are indispensable here, providing cultural validation that no algorithm can replicate. The Republic of Z vignette illustrates the point: only human review could detect that "modernization" carried traumatic connotations in rural dialects. Without that correction, efficiency would have been purchased at the cost of legitimacy.

Closely tied to authenticity is *transparency*, which is increasingly becoming an advantage rather than a liability. Studies have shown that publics are more likely to trust institutions that acknowledge the use of AI than those that conceal it (Bjola and Kornprobst 2023). When governments disclose that a chatbot is AI-assisted, or that a draft was produced with machine support but reviewed by staff, they signal honesty and accountability. Concealment, by contrast, risks greater reputational harm if automation is later exposed. This matters because AI does not inherently undermine authentic voice—but it can, if practitioners treat machine outputs as finished products rather than starting points. The distinctive tone, judgment, and cultural attunement that make a diplomat's communication credible cannot be generated by an algorithm; they must be preserved through deliberate human review at every stage of the drafting process.

The third principle concerns *personalization and manipulation*. AI enables extraordinary levels of tailoring, allowing embassies to frame messages differently for youth, journalists, NGOs, or diaspora communities. When done responsibly, this can enhance clarity by addressing publics in terms that resonate with their experience. But personalization carries risks if different audiences receive contradictory framings of the same policy. In an age of networked communication, publics will quickly detect inconsistency, and once discovered, manipulation can corrode credibility across the board. The ethical boundary lies in ensuring that personalized messages emphasize complementary aspects of the same truth rather than constructing divergent realities.

Responsiveness is the fourth mindset. In a world where rumors can spread in minutes, delay can cause greater harm than a message that is accurate but not perfectly polished. AI can help missions respond quickly, drafting initial statements and allowing staff to refine them before release. WHO's experience with rumor surveillance during COVID-19 showed that publics valued timely corrections, even when the information was partial, more than silence while agencies waited for certainty (WHO 2023). The balance lies in using AI to accelerate response while preserving accuracy through structured review.

Finally, *epistemic humility* remains essential. Generative models produce outputs that can sound authoritative even when incorrect. Hallucinations—fabricated statistics, invented quotations, or plausible but false claims—are well-documented risks. The UK's Copilot trials raised concerns that under deadline pressure, staff risked accepting AI-generated content without adequate verification—a tendency the National Audit Office identified as "automation bias" requiring explicit countermeasures (NAO 2024). Practitioners must resist automation bias and maintain skepticism about machine outputs, treating them as drafts requiring validation rather than finished products.

Together, these principles define an AI mindset for messaging that balances speed with judgment, efficiency with authenticity, and personalization with consistency. AI can multiply options and accelerate drafting, but credibility depends on the human decisions about which words to use, how to frame them, and when to hold back.

Messaging Workflows

To integrate AI responsibly into diplomatic messaging, missions need structured processes that ensure authenticity, accuracy, and cultural resonance at every stage—from initial drafting through final dissemination. These workflows should be designed not to eliminate human judgment but to channel it where it matters most.

The process typically begins with *briefing and framing*. Before any AI tool is used, communications staff must clarify the message's purpose, target audiences, and core policy intent. This briefing stage is critical because AI drafting tools can only work with the instructions they are given. Vague prompts produce generic outputs; clear, detailed briefs generate more useful drafts. A well-constructed brief specifies tone (formal, conversational, empathetic), audiences (general public, journalists, specific communities), and any cultural sensitivities to consider.

Next comes *AI-assisted drafting*. Using generative tools such as large language model co-pilots, staff can produce initial versions of press releases, social media posts, speeches, or other materials. The UK's Copilot trials showed that AI excels at routine formats—announcements, summaries, agendas—but struggles with nuanced political messaging (GDS 2025b). The goal at this stage is speed and volume: generating multiple options allows human communicators to compare framings and select the most promising direction. Some missions now use AI to produce variants emphasizing different themes (economic benefits, security cooperation, cultural exchange), then choose the framing that best aligns with strategic goals.

Cultural validation comes next. Locally employed staff review drafts for linguistic accuracy, cultural appropriateness, and historical sensitivity. They check whether terminology carries unintended connotations, whether metaphors resonate or confuse, and whether the tone matches local communication norms. This validation cannot be rushed; it is where the Republic of Z "modernization" error would have been caught. Missions that skip or shortcut this stage risk alienating publics with tone-deaf messaging, no matter how polished the prose.

Following cultural validation, *policy and legal clearance* ensures that the message aligns with official positions and meets any regulatory requirements. In some contexts, this includes checking against EU AI Act requirements for transparency, verifying that personalization does not violate privacy norms, or ensuring compliance with host country communications laws. This stage also involves senior review: do the words accurately reflect policy intent? Are there unintended implications or contradictions with previous statements?

Translation and localization occur next for multilingual outputs. AI translation systems such as eTranslation, eLUNa, or ITU Translate can rapidly produce versions in multiple languages. But as the previous section emphasized, literal translation is insufficient. Each language version requires human post-editing to ensure cultural resonance, idiomatic correctness, and alignment with local communication styles. For politically sensitive messages, some missions use back-translation—having a different translator convert the translated version back into the original language to check whether meaning has been preserved.

Before final release, *quality assurance and testing* provide a last safeguard. This may include fact-checking (verifying that any statistics, quotes, or references are accurate), consistency checks (ensuring alignment with previous messaging), and sometimes pre-testing with small validator groups to gauge likely reception. The UK's experience with hallucinations in AI-generated drafts underscores why this step cannot be automated: humans must verify every factual claim, not just assume machine outputs are correct (NAO 2024).

Finally, *dissemination and monitoring* complete the cycle. Once approved, the message is released through appropriate channels—press releases, social media, official websites, validator networks. But the workflow does not end with publication. Missions should monitor how messages are received, whether they are being shared or remixed, and whether any corrections or clarifications are needed. This feedback loops back into future messaging, refining institutional understanding of what works.

Throughout this workflow, documentation matters. Recording which AI tools were used, what instructions were provided, how outputs were revised, and what validation revealed creates institutional memory. When staff rotate, this documentation ensures continuity. When errors occur, it enables after-action review to prevent repetition. UNESCO's ethics recommendation emphasizes that accountability requires traceability: missions should be able to explain how any AI-assisted message was produced and reviewed (UNESCO 2021).

The workflow described here may seem elaborate, but its purpose is to embed judgment at every stage where it matters. AI accelerates drafting and translation; humans provide cultural validation, policy alignment, and final quality control. The result is messaging that combines machine efficiency with human authenticity—fast enough to be responsive, careful enough to be credible.

Risks, Ethics, and Compliance

The efficiencies that make AI attractive for messaging are exactly what make it hazardous. A tool that drafts and translates in seconds can, with the same ease, push an off-key phrase or an unreviewed translation into the world before any human has weighed in. Understanding these vulnerabilities is crucial for diplomats, not only to avoid technical errors but also to preserve the trust that sustains public diplomacy.

One of the most pressing risks is the potential for manipulation through personalization. Generative systems can now tailor messages for particular audiences with extraordinary precision, framing the same policy in ways designed to appeal to different groups. When handled ethically, this can make communication more relevant and accessible. But if publics discover that they are receiving contradictory framings, trust can collapse. What was intended as empathy can be perceived as deception. The European Union's *AI Act* (2024) explicitly bans manipulative "dark patterns" and requires transparency about personalization criteria, reflecting the concern that targeted messaging can too easily blur into covert persuasion.

The risks of AI-generated messaging are not hypothetical. Beginning in 2025, the Trump administration's sustained use of AI-generated imagery across White House and agency social media accounts—depicting the president as a king, a medieval crusader, and a muscular hero, among other figures—provided one of the first documented cases of a major government deploying synthetic content as a routine foreign policy communication tool. Analysts described the pattern as "memetic warfare," noting that AI imagery was used deliberately to project dominance and shape international perceptions (Tuquero 2025; Goggin 2025).

The Greenland case in January 2026 illustrated the diplomatic consequences directly: AI-generated images posted to official accounts—including a doctored map showing Greenland as U.S. territory—prompted emergency European Union consultations, market reactions, and retaliatory tariff discussions (Newsweek 2026). For diplomatic practitioners, this pattern offers a dual lesson. First, AI-generated content used without transparency or restraint can produce measurable damage to alliance relationships and diplomatic credibility, even when the intent is strategic rather than accidental. Second, missions must be prepared to operate in an information environment where adversaries—and allies—may use synthetic imagery as a deliberate communication instrument, requiring new frameworks for detection, response, and counter-messaging.

A second risk comes from hallucinations and automation bias. Large language models sometimes generate plausible but inaccurate content, from misattributed quotations to fabricated statistics. Under deadline pressure, there is a temptation to trust machine outputs without sufficient review. The UK's Copilot trials found measurable productivity gains but also instances where drafts included factual errors, reminding staff that oversight could not be automated away (GDS 2025b). UNESCO's Recommendation on the Ethics of Artificial Intelligence (2021) emphasizes that human validation is essential in high-stakes communication, and diplomatic messaging is nothing if not high stakes.

Authenticity represents a third area of vulnerability. Messages that sound generic or "machine-written" risk alienating publics, especially in contexts where credibility rests on perceived sincerity. Communication scholars have documented that publics are quick to detect "synthetic empathy," the polished but hollow tone sometimes produced by generative models (Moore and Hübscher 2021). In diplomacy, where authenticity is closely tied to legitimacy, this can be damaging. The OECD's *AI Principles* (2024) stress purpose-driven design for exactly this reason: messaging should always be rooted in human intent, not algorithmic convenience.

Surveillance perceptions present another danger. Personalization often requires analyzing data about audience behavior, and even when the data is drawn from public sources, the line between attentive listening and intrusive monitoring can feel thin. Publics in societies with histories of state surveillance may be especially sensitive to such practices. The African Union's *Continental AI Strategy* (2024) cautions that if publics perceive themselves as objects of hidden monitoring rather than participants in open dialogue, trust will erode quickly. Transparency about how data is used, and what boundaries are respected, is therefore essential.

Finally, the abundance of outputs that AI enables can itself become a risk. When multiple versions of a message are produced, there is a danger of narrative fragmentation. Different teams might release slightly divergent drafts, or publics might compare versions across platforms and detect inconsistency. This incoherence can be exploited by adversaries eager to portray governments as confused or dishonest.

ASEAN's *Expanded Guide on AI Governance and Ethics* (2025) warns that while contextual adaptation is important, consistency of core messages must be preserved across audiences.

Taken together, these risks show why ethics and compliance are not bureaucratic afterthoughts but strategic necessities. In diplomacy, where publics weigh every word for sincerity, the guardrails are not constraints on effectiveness; they are the foundation of it.

Metrics and Evaluation

For AI-assisted messaging to be meaningful, it must be judged not by how many drafts are generated or how many languages are covered, but by whether the communication resonates with publics and reinforces credibility. Traditional performance indicators—such as the number of press releases issued or the volume of social media impressions—are increasingly inadequate. They capture activity but not trust. What matters is whether messages are understood, whether they feel authentic, and whether they influence public perceptions in ways that support diplomatic goals.

Translation accuracy is one obvious area for evaluation. Systems like the EU's *eTranslation* or the UN's *eLUNa* can process immense volumes of text, but literal translations are not enough. Embassies must track error rates and, more importantly, assess whether translations preserve the intended meaning and tone. Local validators can provide critical feedback here, pointing out when a phrase feels awkward, tone-deaf, or culturally insensitive. By institutionalizing these feedback loops, missions ensure that efficiency does not come at the cost of resonance.

Another important measure is authenticity of tone. Messages may be factually correct yet fail if they sound mechanical or generic. Publics quickly detect when language feels artificial, and in diplomacy, that perception can undermine legitimacy. Surveys, focus groups, and informal validator debriefs can help missions determine whether AI-assisted messages sound credible and human, or whether they fall into what some scholars call "synthetic empathy"—polished but hollow communication that fails to build trust.

For public-facing systems such as chatbots, trust in accuracy becomes a metric of its own. Taiwan's COVID-19 chatbot was judged successful not only because it answered questions, but because users considered its responses reliable. Tracking satisfaction, error rates per query, and the proportion of queries escalated to human staff all provide insight into whether AI tools are serving publics effectively. Here again, credibility rests less on speed than on publics' perception that they can depend on the information provided.

Efficiency metrics, while secondary, are not irrelevant. The UK's Copilot trials demonstrated quantifiable productivity gains—the specific figures are examined in Chapter 5's discussion of program evaluation. For overstretched missions, such time savings matter. But efficiency gains must always be weighed against accuracy and trust. A message produced quickly but corrected later at the cost of credibility is no success at all.

Finally, consistency across platforms deserves attention. AI makes it easy to generate multiple versions of the same message, but inconsistency can fracture narratives. Missions can evaluate coherence by tracking how messages appear across press releases, social media posts, and chatbot interactions. The goal is not uniformity of style but unity of intent. Publics should recognize that they are receiving different formats of the same message, not divergent stories.

In all of this, transparency functions as a cross-cutting measure. How openly do missions acknowledge AI use? How well do they explain personalization? Transparency builds trust, and trust is the ultimate metric of successful diplomatic messaging. Publics may forgive imperfect translation or occasional delays, but they rarely forgive deception. The measure of AI-assisted messaging is whether it strengthens the credibility diplomacy depends on.

Reflection and Strategic Questions

Practitioners reflecting on these issues might ask themselves difficult questions. How can missions maintain authenticity when automation becomes part of the process? Where should the line be drawn between personalization and persuasion? Should embassies always disclose when AI has been used in drafting, or does context matter? How can provenance standards be applied practically to reassure publics about the authenticity of images, video, and text? And in crises, when time is short, is it better to release a message that is "good enough" quickly or to risk delay in pursuit of perfection?

FRONTIER AND NEAR-TERM PILOTS

The most mature applications of AI in messaging today center on translation, drafting assistance, and crisis chatbots. But practitioners and researchers are already exploring what comes next. These frontier applications remain experimental, yet they point toward how messaging might evolve in the latter half of this decade—and the ethical dilemmas that evolution will create.

One emerging frontier is AI-assisted cultural framing. Current translation systems convert words across languages; future systems might adapt entire messages to resonate with cultural norms, values, and communication styles. A message framed for one audience could be reframed—not just translated—for another, adjusting metaphors, examples, and rhetorical structure to maximize cultural resonance. The promise is obvious: diplomacy that speaks to publics in their own cultural idioms. The risk is equally clear: if such adaptation crosses the line into constructing divergent realities for different audiences, it becomes manipulation. Transparency will be essential if such tools are deployed. Publics have a right to know when messages are being culturally adapted, not merely translated.

A second area involves predictive testing. Some researchers have proposed using AI to simulate how audiences might respond to different message framings before they are released. These "narrative simulations" could act as early-warning systems, flagging phrasing that may backfire or identifying metaphors that are likely to be misinterpreted. The potential benefits are obvious: institutions could refine their communication before mistakes reach the public stage. Yet simulations carry the same dangers as all predictive analytics—they are only as good as their training data. Biased datasets may produce skewed forecasts, and misplaced confidence in a simulated outcome can blind practitioners to the complexity of real-world reactions.

Finally, some have proposed creating "narrative laboratories," collaborative spaces where diplomats, academics, and civil society actors test messages together using AI tools. Unlike covert testing, these labs would emphasize openness and consent, framing message design as a participatory process. While politically difficult to implement in highly sensitive areas, such initiatives could make messaging more inclusive and trustworthy by involving publics directly in the process of communication design.

These frontier applications all push messaging toward anticipatory design: narratives tested and refined before they enter circulation, not after publics raise concerns. This represents both an opportunity and a dilemma. On the one hand, AI could make diplomacy more responsive, reducing the lag between intent and resonance. On the other, the line between anticipation and manipulation is perilously thin. The future of AI-assisted messaging will depend not only on technological advances but also on the ethical choices diplomats make about disclosure, restraint, and respect for publics as partners in dialogue rather than objects of experimentation.

CONCLUSION

By now you've seen how artificial intelligence is transforming diplomatic messaging from a challenge of scarcity into one of abundance—and why that transformation creates fragilities as consequential as the efficiencies it delivers.

The central distinction to carry forward is this: translation is not the same as communication, and efficiency is not the same as credibility. The opening vignette showed it at the level of a single word in a press release. Recent events have shown it at the level of alliance relationships.

Messages, however, do not remain under your control once released. They enter an information environment where adversaries can distort them, algorithms can amplify them, and publics can remix them into meanings far from those you originally intended. The next chapter turns to that contested landscape—examining how AI reshapes the defensive dimension of diplomatic communication through media monitoring, disinformation detection, and narrative intelligence, and why the speed that makes messaging possible also makes vigilance essential.

3 Media Monitoring, Disinformation, and Narrative Intelligence

"If you make it trend, you make it true."

—Renée DiResta, *Invisible Rulers* (2024)

"To abandon facts is to abandon freedom. If nothing is true, then no one can criticize power, because there is no basis upon which to do so."

—Timothy Snyder, *On Tyranny* (2017)

"Just as attention is under-appreciated as a resource for social movements, distractions and ignorance are under-appreciated as methods of repression through denial of attention."

—Zeynep Tufekci, *Twitter and Tear Gas* (2017)

Opening Vignette: When the Signal Appeared in the Noise

It started as a routine Monday morning. Aisha Rahman, the mission's audience research and insights officer, was scrolling through the embassy's overnight dashboard clusters when a small anomaly caught her eye: a group of accounts in Zorani, most created within the past six weeks, were all posting variations of the same claim. A U.S.-funded agricultural program in the eastern provinces had contaminated local water supplies. Fewer than two hundred interactions—but the accounts were not talking to each other. They were seeding the same narrative into separate communities simultaneously, like stones dropped in different parts of a pond.

She flagged it for David Kim, the public affairs officer, before the morning staff meeting. "How confident are you?" David asked. "Confident enough to take it seriously," Aisha said. "The account creation dates cluster around the same two-week window. The posting patterns are almost identical—same cadence, similar phrasing, overlapping keyword clusters—across accounts with no apparent connection to each other. And the narrative is designed to

DOI: 10.1201/9781003612377-4

travel—short, emotional, tied to something people already worry about." "Could be organic," David said. "Could be. That's why I'm flagging it, not declaring it."

Lina Perez, the embassy's digital communications officer, had already drafted a rebuttal post—a sharp, factual correction citing program water safety data. She slid it across to David for approval. He set it aside. "Not yet." "The narrative is spreading," Lina said. "Every hour we wait, it gets more traction." "And if we respond publicly to two hundred posts, we turn it into two thousand. We need to know what we're dealing with before we amplify it."

The next call was to Farid Tessam, a locally employed cultural affairs assistant with deep ties to communities in the eastern provinces. Within two hours, he had spoken with three community leaders and a regional journalist. None of them had heard the water contamination story from real people. It was circulating online but had not entered the oral networks—the tea houses, the markets, the evening gatherings where Zorani communities processed news that actually mattered to them. "It hasn't landed yet," Farid reported. "But if it does, it will be hard to dislodge. Water fears in that region go back a long way."

At the afternoon briefing, Ambassador Grant listened and asked the question that cut to the heart of it: "Do we know who is behind this?" "Not yet," Aisha said. "The pattern is consistent with influence operations we have seen before, but pattern is not proof." "Then we do not accuse. We prepare." Rather than issuing a public rebuttal, the embassy activated its validator network quietly. Trusted journalists received background briefings. Community leaders were contacted directly. Alumni with agricultural expertise shared factual information through their own channels. The embassy's social media posted a routine program update—not a rebuttal, but fresh accurate content that would rank alongside the false narrative in search results.

By the end of the week, the story had not disappeared—but it had not broken into mainstream coverage either. No public rebuttal had been necessary. At the Friday debrief, Lina acknowledged it had been a difficult call. "I still think we waited too long," she said. "We waited the right amount of time," Farid replied. "In the eastern provinces, a denial from the embassy would have been seen as confirmation. What we did instead was give people they trusted the information to make up their own minds." Aisha added the episode to the mission's monitoring log—not as a success exactly, but as a case study in disciplined restraint. The AI system had surfaced a signal that human eyes would have missed. But the decisions that followed—when to act, how to act, who to involve, and above all what not to do—had been entirely human.

FRAMING THE CHAPTER

If listening is how diplomats detect the mood of publics, and messaging is how they respond, then monitoring is where those two functions collide with the unpredictable energy of the digital information environment. Messages rarely travel in a straight line. They are received, remixed, contested, and sometimes deliberately distorted. For diplomats, credibility now depends not only on what they say but also on how effectively they monitor what happens after their words enter circulation. In a world where hostile actors use artificial intelligence to fabricate videos, amplify rumors, and manipulate algorithms, monitoring has become both a defensive shield and a source of foresight.

Artificial intelligence magnifies this function by scanning vast flows of data and detecting patterns that humans alone could never track in real time. Dashboards can show how narratives mutate as they cross platforms, whether a falsehood is gaining traction, and which communities are amplifying or resisting it. Properly designed, these systems offer early warning and help practitioners respond before disinformation spirals into crisis. Yet AI also complicates monitoring by producing its own distortions. Algorithms may mistake satire for disinformation, misclassify dissent as manipulation, or overlook conversations happening in underrepresented languages and spaces. The very tools meant to protect credibility can, if misapplied, undermine it.

Once messages are released, their fate is no longer in the hands of diplomats alone. They enter a dynamic ecosystem where adversaries can seed synthetic media, bots can flood hashtags, and publics can remix official statements into satire or outrage. Monitoring is therefore not a passive function of observation but an active process of defense, interpretation, and proportionate response.

This new public diplomacy environment can involve what I describe as *synthetic statecraft*: the normalization of AI-generated or AI-altered media as a tool of official state communication, where governments use synthetic images, video, audio, avatars, or automated narratives to signal policy, shape perception, fabricate events, or wage information warfare — often without disclosure — thereby turning the state itself into a producer of deepfakes and weakening public trust in reality.

The shift is not principally about adversaries acquiring new technical capabilities, though that has occurred. It is about the broader information environment in which states now address foreign publics — an environment in which AI generates content, mediates the channels through which content reaches audiences, and increasingly shapes the verification tools audiences use to assess what they encounter. In such an environment, monitoring is not merely defense against external manipulation; it is the practice through which states maintain their footing in an information landscape that no actor fully controls.

I introduced this framing in March of 2026 with the explosion of state-sponsored AI-generated imagery on official social media accounts, originating from the United States and Iran (Kilburg 2026a). I also delivered it in May of 2026 before the U.S. Advisory Commission on Public Diplomacy (Kilburg 2026b).

This chapter develops that framing in three ways. Conceptually, it examines how AI reshapes the dynamics of disinformation and narrative competition. Practically, it describes how missions can embed monitoring workflows that detect anomalies, validate signals, and calibrate responses without amplifying fringe content. Strategically, it considers the ethical boundaries of monitoring—how to protect publics from manipulation without sliding into censorship, and how to preserve legitimacy in an environment where surveillance perceptions are acute. Together, these perspectives situate monitoring not as a technical add-on but as a new core function of public diplomacy in the age of AI.

RESEARCH AND POLICY FOUNDATIONS

Monitoring has always been central to diplomacy, but the stakes are higher in an era when adversaries can manufacture narratives as quickly as publics can consume them. Machine learning systems can now detect anomalous spikes in narratives long before humans notice them, making monitoring a frontline defense against manipulation—but the same systems introduce new vulnerabilities.

Scholars caution that AI systems, while powerful, are fragile. Henry Kissinger, Eric Schmidt, and Daniel Huttenlocher (2021) describe the problem as one of "knowledge without understanding." An AI model can show that a rumor is spreading across platforms, but it cannot explain why it resonates. Left unexamined, dashboards risk being treated as authoritative when they are, in fact, incomplete. Mustafa Suleyman (2023) has gone further, warning that AI infrastructures are vulnerable to poisoning: adversaries can flood systems with false inputs, distorting outputs and creating illusions of consensus or outrage where none exists. For monitoring to serve diplomacy responsibly, it must be designed with resilience in mind—using anomalies as prompts for human judgment rather than machine verdicts.

At the same time, scholars of digital diplomacy emphasize that credibility in monitoring depends as much on restraint as on detection. Corneliu Bjola and Ilan Manor (2024) argue that in contested environments, the danger lies not only in failing to identify falsehoods but also in overreacting to them. Amplification, they note, can give fringe narratives greater visibility, especially when governments draw attention to disinformation that publics might otherwise have ignored. Proportionate response, informed by cultural context and validator input, is therefore as important as speed.

Global governance frameworks reinforce this balance. UNESCO's Recommendation on the Ethics of Artificial Intelligence (2021) stresses proportionality and accountability, principles that directly apply to monitoring: not every anomaly should trigger a response, and institutions must be clear about the methods they use. This challenge is not only technical but institutional—as Kilburg (2025a, 2025b) has documented, diplomatic missions that have begun deploying AI monitoring tools consistently report that human judgment remains the decisive variable in determining when and how to act on machine-generated alerts. The European Union's *AI Act* (2024) sets more specific obligations, requiring labeling of synthetic media and explainability in high-risk systems, a recognition that authenticity verification is now a matter of democratic security. The OECD's updated *AI Principles* (2024) emphasize fairness and inclusivity, reminding practitioners that choices about which languages, platforms, and communities to monitor are inherently political. The African Union's *Continental AI Strategy* (2024) warns that monitoring systems built on Western data sources risk silencing African voices. And the G7's *Hiroshima Code of Conduct* (2023) calls for democratic alignment in the use of AI, including commitments to transparency in counter-disinformation efforts.

These frameworks highlight a recurring paradox. AI monitoring can provide governments with unparalleled situational awareness, but it can also generate suspicion among publics who interpret it as surveillance or censorship. Decisions about what to flag, label, or counter are never purely technical—they are acts of power that shape what is seen as legitimate speech and what is not. Kate Crawford (2021) reminds us that AI systems are always embedded in political and social contexts, and nowhere is this clearer than in disinformation monitoring. For diplomats, the challenge is not simply to detect falsehoods but to do so in ways that protect credibility, preserve openness, and sustain trust.

TECHNICAL CAPABILITIES – HOW AI DETECTS MANIPULATION AND DISINFORMATION

For practitioners to deploy monitoring systems responsibly, they must understand not just what these systems can do but how they do it. This technical literacy enables better questions, more realistic expectations, and more effective human oversight. Four interrelated capabilities form the foundation of AI-enabled counter-disinformation: authenticity verification, coordinated behavior detection, content provenance analysis, and narrative propagation tracking.

Authenticity Verification and Deepfake Detection

The challenge of verifying whether visual or audio content is authentic has become central to diplomatic monitoring. Deepfake technology—AI-generated synthetic media that convincingly mimics real people—has advanced dramatically in recent years. Detection systems employ several complementary approaches to identify manipulated content.

Forensic analysis tools examine media artifacts that betray synthetic generation. In video, these include inconsistencies in facial lighting (shadows that don't match ambient light sources), unnatural eye blink patterns (humans blink at predictable frequencies; early deepfakes often failed to replicate this), and temporal inconsistencies between frames. Audio deepfakes may exhibit spectral anomalies—subtle distortions in frequency patterns that human ears cannot detect but which algorithms can identify. The EEAS FIMI Report #3 documented how adversaries are adapting to these detection methods, employing adversarial training to generate content that passes forensic tests (EEAS 2025).

Metadata analysis provides another detection layer. Legitimate media typically carries metadata indicating when and where it was captured, what device was used, and whether it has been edited. Synthetic content often lacks this metadata or contains inconsistencies—a video purportedly captured on a smartphone may have metadata suggesting professional video editing software. However, metadata can also be stripped or fabricated, so it functions as corroborating evidence rather than definitive proof.

Content provenance systems represent an emerging approach. The Coalition for Content Provenance and Authenticity (C2PA) has developed an open technical standard that creates cryptographic signatures when media is captured, establishing a verifiable chain of custody. If content is edited, the signature breaks, alerting viewers that the media has been modified. Early adopters include major camera manufacturers, news organizations, and social platforms. The EU AI Act (2024) includes provisions encouraging provenance standards, and some diplomatic missions have begun exploring provenance tools in the field—the U.S. Embassy in Conakry, Guinea, piloted Digimarc's provenance tagging system for official imagery, an early example of embassy-level implementation. Global adoption remains uneven, but the infrastructure for authenticated media is advancing rapidly.

Importantly, detection is inherently reactive. Each new generation of synthetic media tools requires updated detection algorithms. The arms race between generation and detection means that no system provides permanent protection. Diplomatic missions should treat detection tools as probabilistic aids—flagging suspicious content for human review—rather than infallible arbiters of authenticity.

The technical asymmetry between generation and detection has begun to produce a perceptual consequence on the audience side. I call this condition the *authenticity threshold* — the point at which authentic and synthetic content have become structurally indistinguishable for substantial fractions of the public (Kilburg 2026b). The threshold is not a property of any particular piece of content but of the audience's epistemic environment. When the cost of producing convincing synthetic content collapses while authoritative verification remains slow and reaches narrower audiences, default skepticism extends to all content. Verification that arrives after the original has circulated reaches a fraction of the audience the original reached.

Empirical evidence suggests that this threshold has measurable consequences in identifiable conflict environments. During the first weeks of the 2026 war involving the United States, Israel, and Iran, *The New York Times* identified more than 110 unique AI-generated images and videos circulating online about the conflict. These fakes falsely depicted active fighting, war preparations, destruction, crying soldiers, missile strikes, attacks on U.S. military vessels, and other scenes of wartime devastation; collectively, they reached millions of users across platforms such as X, TikTok, and Facebook, as well as private messaging apps (Thompson and Cardia 2026). The reporting also found that much of this content advanced pro-Iranian narratives by exaggerating Iran's military effectiveness and the scale of destruction inflicted on U.S. and Israeli targets. At rates of synthetic production approaching this scale, verification systems that depend primarily on human review are structurally disadvantaged: even when individual fakes can be identified, the volume and velocity of generation can outpace the capacity to authenticate, contextualize, and correct them in real time.

The audience-side consequence runs in both directions. Authentic content is rejected as synthetic; fabricated claims are accepted as exposing concealment. In March 2026, as rumors circulated online that Israeli Prime Minister Benjamin Netanyahu had been killed or injured in an Iranian strike, social media users treated authentic "proof of life" footage as suspect. After Netanyahu's March 12 video press briefing, users claimed the footage was AI-generated because his hand appeared to have six fingers; PolitiFact found the claim unfounded, concluding that he had five fingers on both hands and that nothing indicated the briefing had been AI-generated or altered (Tuquero 2026). Within days, the inverse fabrication appeared: a photocard circulated claiming that Netanyahu had in fact been killed, that Yariv Levin had been appointed prime minister, and that the U.S. and Israeli governments were using AI to fake Netanyahu's survival to maintain military morale (Ayon and Hosen 2026).

The two moves together — authentic content rejected, fabricated content accepted as exposing the lie — are what Chesney and Citron (2019) termed the "liar's dividend," now in mature form. For diplomatic monitoring, the implication is structural: detection operates on the artifact, but the authenticity threshold sits with the audience. Catching the fake does not restore the audience's ability to recognize what is real.

Coordinated Behavior Detection and Bot Network Identification

Disinformation campaigns often rely not on fabricated content but on artificial amplification—using bot networks or coordinated human operators to make fringe narratives appear mainstream. Detecting this coordinated inauthentic behavior requires analyzing patterns across accounts rather than examining individual posts.

Network analysis algorithms map how accounts interact—who follows whom, who shares whose content, who replies to or quotes whom. Legitimate communities exhibit organic network structures with varied connection patterns. Bot networks often display telltale signatures: accounts created in batches (identical registration timestamps), symmetric follower/following ratios (bots typically follow each other reciprocally), and clustered interactions (bots primarily engage with other bots rather than genuine users). Canada's RRM has extensively documented these patterns in its Spamouflage advisories (Global Affairs Canada 2023; 2025).

Temporal analysis examines posting patterns over time. Human accounts exhibit circadian rhythms—less activity during typical sleep hours, more during waking hours. Bot accounts may post at constant intervals regardless of time zone, or multiple bot accounts may post simultaneously down to the second, indicating centralized control. The U.S. Department of Defense's experimental credibility-scoring system with Primer (discussed later as a frontier case) employed neural networks to identify these temporal anomalies at scale (Tucker 2020).

Linguistic analysis detects unnatural language patterns. Automated accounts may use template-based posting, resulting in repeated phrases or grammatical structures. Machine-translated content may lack idiomatic fluency. Large language model–generated content sometimes exhibits distinctive markers—excessive politeness, verbose explanations, or unnatural transitions—though these signatures evolve as models improve.

Behavioral amplification analysis tracks how content spreads. Organic viral spread typically follows a diffusion pattern: content gains traction gradually, amplified by accounts with diverse follower bases and varied interests. Artificial amplification often exhibits coordinated spikes: dozens or hundreds of accounts share identical content within narrow time windows, frequently using identical text. Network analysis reveals that these amplifying accounts may have few genuine followers, low engagement on their own posts, and shallow posting histories.

These detection approaches work best in combination. An individual signal—a suspicious temporal pattern or a linguistic quirk—may be innocuous. Multiple signals converging raise confidence that behavior is coordinated and inauthentic. The Atlantic Council's DFRLab has refined methodologies that assess coordinated behavior probabilistically, providing confidence scores rather than binary authentic/inauthentic labels (Chenrose and Rizzuto 2025).

Content Provenance and Source Verification

Beyond detecting synthetic media, monitoring systems must help practitioners assess whether content comes from credible sources. Source verification has become more challenging as adversaries create entire ecosystems of fake news sites, fictitious journalists, and fabricated credentials designed to appear legitimate.

Domain analysis examines website infrastructure. Legitimate news organizations typically have established domains registered years earlier, professional web design, contact information, and transparent ownership. Disinformation sites often use recently registered domains, lack clear ownership information, and may employ design templates mimicking legitimate outlets. WHOIS database searches can reveal when domains were registered and who registered them, though privacy protections sometimes obscure this information.

Content consistency analysis compares a source's current output against its historical record. Legitimate outlets maintain editorial consistency—voice, formatting, coverage patterns. Compromised or fabricated sources may exhibit abrupt shifts. For instance, a website that spent years covering local community events suddenly publishing exclusively political content in a different stylistic register may indicate the site has been hijacked or repurposed for disinformation.

Cross-platform verification checks whether content appears across multiple independent sources. If a claim appears only on obscure websites with no mainstream media pickup, it warrants skepticism. Conversely, if reputable outlets in multiple countries report similar information independently, credibility increases. However, this heuristic has limits: adversaries sometimes coordinate across multiple fake outlets to create an illusion of independent confirmation.

Journalist and source authentication systems attempt to create verified credentials. Some platforms offer verification badges indicating an account belongs to a real journalist or organization. Yet verification systems themselves can be compromised—accounts can be hijacked, badges can be faked, and verification criteria may be inconsistently applied. The EEAS has called for standardized verification and provenance systems across platforms, though implementation remains uneven (EEAS 2025).

Narrative Propagation Tracking and Mutation Analysis

Understanding how narratives spread, mutate, and evolve as they cross platforms and communities provides situational awareness crucial for proportionate response.

Narrative propagation analysis maps these dynamics. At the U.S. Department of State, the Northstar platform has been developed to provide exactly this capability at an institutional scale—tracking how narratives relevant to U.S. foreign policy interests evolve across languages and platforms, and surfacing patterns that individual missions cannot detect on their own (Alder 2024). For embassies operating in contested information environments, tools of this kind represent a significant force multiplier, connecting mission-level monitoring to a broader analytical picture.

Semantic clustering identifies when different posts or articles express the same underlying narrative despite varied wording. Natural language processing can recognize that "foreign aid is corruption" and "international assistance enables graft" convey the same core message. By clustering semantically similar content, systems reveal how widely a narrative has spread even when exact phrases vary.

Mutation tracking monitors how narratives evolve. A story that begins as "diplomatic discussions ongoing" may mutate through social media sharing into "secret agreements confirmed" and eventually "sovereignty sold out." Tracking these mutations helps practitioners understand which versions of a narrative are gaining traction and where interventions might be most effective.

Platform migration analysis follows narratives as they move across digital spaces. Content may originate on fringe forums, gain traction on social media, and eventually reach mainstream media. Understanding these migration pathways helps identify where narratives are most vulnerable to correction—often at transition points between platforms, where gatekeepers (journalists, moderators, fact-checkers) can intervene.

Amplification source analysis determines who is spreading narratives and whether amplification appears organic or manufactured. A narrative amplified primarily by accounts with few followers and little engagement may be artificially boosted. A narrative spreading through accounts with large, engaged follower bases and varied interests likely reflects genuine public interest. This distinction helps prioritize response: artificial amplification may not require counter-messaging, while organic spread demands serious engagement.

Integration and Limitations

These technical capabilities work best when integrated into comprehensive monitoring systems that combine algorithmic detection with human analysis. The algorithms surface anomalies—potential deepfakes, suspicious coordination patterns, rapid narrative mutation. Human analysts assess whether these anomalies actually constitute threats, whether responses are warranted, and what form responses should take.

Critical limitations must be acknowledged. Detection systems struggle with sophisticated adversaries who understand detection methods and design campaigns to evade them. Cultural and linguistic diversity challenges systems trained primarily on Western data. The arms race between generation and detection means yesterday's tools may miss tomorrow's threats. And all detection methods produce both false positives (flagging legitimate content as suspicious) and false negatives (missing actual manipulation).

For diplomatic practitioners, technical literacy means understanding these capabilities not to operate the systems but to ask the right questions: What confidence level does the system assign to this detection? What happens when the system encounters content it hasn't been trained on? Who can audit the system's decision-making? What biases might be embedded in training data? This critical engagement ensures that AI serves human judgment rather than replacing it.

REAL-WORLD APPLICATIONS

Although much of the conversation about disinformation feels speculative, several high-profile initiatives already demonstrate how AI is being used to monitor hostile narratives and defend credibility in real time. These cases show both the possibilities of technology and the limits of machine detection, underscoring the need for human oversight and political judgment.

Canada's Rapid Response Mechanism – Transparency as Democratic Defense

Canada's Rapid Response Mechanism (RRM), established with G7 partners in 2018, has emerged as one of the most transparent government efforts to detect and expose foreign information manipulation. Unlike many counter-disinformation programs that operate behind closed doors, RRM has made a strategic choice to publish public advisories when it identifies coordinated campaigns—a decision that transforms detection into a form of democratic defense. The mechanism's experiences, particularly its October 2023 and March 2025 advisories on "Spamouflage" operations, illustrate both the power and the complexity of AI-enabled monitoring in diplomatic contexts.

The October 2023 advisory marked a turning point. RRM identified a coordinated network of inauthentic accounts spreading disinformation targeting Canadian Members of Parliament. The campaign employed classic bot network tactics: accounts created in batches, posting at synchronized intervals, amplifying identical content across multiple platforms. What made the operation particularly insidious was its targeting strategy—the false narratives were designed to inflame existing political divisions, making them more likely to be organically shared by genuine users who saw the content as validating their views (Global Affairs Canada 2023).

RRM's detection relied on AI-enabled network analysis. Algorithms mapped how content flowed across social media, identifying patterns invisible to human observers. Accounts that appeared independent were revealed to be tightly coordinated based on behavioral signatures: identical posting times down to the second, linguistic patterns suggesting automated translation, metadata anomalies indicating use of virtual private networks to mask origins. The Atlantic Council's Digital Forensic Research Lab (DFRLab) independently analyzed the campaign, confirming RRM's findings and documenting how the network had operated across multiple countries, not just Canada (Chenrose and Rizzuto 2025).

The decision to publish the advisory publicly was deliberate and controversial. Some within government argued that exposure would simply alert adversaries to detection methods, allowing them to adapt tactics. Others worried about attribution—while the behavioral evidence was clear, definitively identifying state sponsors remained difficult. RRM proceeded nonetheless, reasoning that transparency itself was a form of resilience. By making the threat visible, the advisory educated publics about coordinated inauthentic behavior, inoculated journalists against manipulation, and demonstrated governmental accountability.

The strategy appeared to work. Canadian media covered the advisory extensively, and fact-checkers began scrutinizing similar content more carefully. The campaign's effectiveness diminished as awareness spread. Critically, the advisory became evidence in Canada's public inquiry into foreign interference, demonstrating how RRM's work connected to broader democratic security concerns. The transparency approach transformed what might have been a classified intelligence finding into a public education moment about information manipulation.

The March 2025 Advisory: Evolving Threats and Refined Responses

The March 6, 2025 advisory revealed how adversaries had adapted. This time, the "Spamouflage" network targeted Chinese-language journalists in Canada, employing more sophisticated tactics than the 2023 campaign. Rather than obvious bot networks, the operation used a mix of hijacked legitimate accounts, newly created personas with developed posting histories, and strategic amplification by influencers who may not have known they were participating in a coordinated campaign (Global Affairs Canada 2025).

The targeting was strategic: Chinese-language journalists serve as crucial information bridges between Mandarin-speaking communities in Canada and broader Canadian society. By flooding their social media with harassment, false accusations, and manufactured controversies, the campaign aimed to silence critical voices and create self-censorship. The sophistication extended to timing—attacks intensified whenever journalists published content critical of certain foreign government policies, creating a chilling effect where cause and effect were difficult to prove but easy to feel.

RRM's detection of this campaign showcased advances in AI monitoring capabilities. The system employed natural language processing trained on Mandarin to identify coordinated messaging despite variations in phrasing. Network analysis revealed amplification patterns where seemingly unrelated accounts boosted the same content within narrow time windows. Sentiment analysis flagged the abrupt shift in tone when legitimate accounts were hijacked—a journalist's account that had posted about community events suddenly began sharing inflammatory political content in a different linguistic register.

The 2025 advisory was more detailed than its 2023 predecessor, reflecting RRM's institutional learning. It included specific examples of manipulated content, explained detection methodologies in lay terms, and provided guidance for journalists and community members about recognizing coordinated campaigns. Importantly, it also acknowledged limitations: RRM could document the campaign's existence and patterns but could not access communications platforms end-to-end to fully map the operation's scale or definitively attribute state sponsorship.

The advisory sparked intense discussion about the appropriate balance between security and free expression. Some community advocates worried that highlighting Chinese-language disinformation could fuel anti-Chinese sentiment or be weaponized to dismiss legitimate political discourse within diaspora communities. RRM's response emphasized that the advisory targeted coordinated inauthentic behavior, not content or viewpoints. The distinction mattered: monitoring focused on how content spread (coordinated amplification, hijacked accounts) rather than what it said (political opinions, policy critiques).

That same behavioral focus also solved RRM's other hard problem: attribution. AI can identify coordinated campaigns with high confidence from behavioral patterns, but tracing them to specific state actors requires intelligence beyond what monitoring systems provide. By publishing advisories about behavior without waiting for definitive attribution, RRM could act credibly even when state sponsorship remained uncertain.

Lessons for Diplomatic Monitoring

The Canadian experience offers several critical lessons for diplomatic missions considering AI-enabled monitoring. First, transparency can be a strategic asset rather than a liability. While exposing detection methods does risk alerting adversaries, it also builds public resilience, educates media gatekeepers, and demonstrates institutional accountability. In democratic contexts, publics may be more willing to trust monitoring systems they can see and understand than opaque intelligence operations.

Second, attribution remains the enduring challenge. AI can identify coordinated campaigns with high confidence based on behavioral patterns, but tracing those campaigns back to specific state actors requires additional intelligence beyond what monitoring systems provide. RRM navigated this by focusing advisories on behavior (coordinated inauthentic activity) rather than attribution (which state sponsored it), allowing publication even when full attribution was uncertain.

Third, evolving threats demand continuous technical and analytical adaptation. The shift from crude bot networks (2023) to sophisticated account hijacking and influencer amplification (2025) shows how quickly adversaries learn. AI systems that detect yesterday's tactics may miss today's. This requires sustained investment in training data, algorithm refinement, and analyst expertise—counter-disinformation is not a problem that gets "solved" but an ongoing contest requiring constant vigilance.

Fourth, community context is essential. RRM's 2025 advisory could have backfired if it failed to account for the political and cultural dynamics within Chinese-Canadian communities. By engaging community leaders, explaining the distinction between content and behavior, and acknowledging legitimate concerns about stigmatization, RRM maintained credibility even when addressing sensitive topics.

EEAS FIMI Report #3 – Synthetic Media as Force Multiplier

In March 2025, the European External Action Service (EEAS) released the third installment of its *Foreign Information Manipulation and Interference* (FIMI) threat reports, marking a significant evolution in how European institutions understand and communicate about information threats. Unlike previous FIMI reports that focused primarily on identifying narratives and tracking amplification networks, Report #3 centered on a new dimension: the role of AI-generated synthetic media—text, images, audio, and video—as a force multiplier in foreign interference campaigns.

The report emerged from unprecedented coordination across European institutions. EEAS worked with the European Digital Media Observatory (EDMO), national cyber defense units, and platform transparency teams to compile a comprehensive picture of how adversaries were deploying generative AI tools. The findings were sobering: synthetic media was no longer experimental or niche but had become a routine component of information operations targeting European democracies (EEAS 2025).

The technical analysis revealed how dramatically AI tools have lowered barriers to producing convincing fake content. Where deepfake video production once required specialized expertise and computing resources, Report #3 documented campaigns using freely available or low-cost AI tools to generate synthetic content at industrial scale. One documented operation had produced hundreds of fake "local news" articles complete with AI-generated photographs of fictitious journalists, all designed to appear as grassroots reporting critical of European Union policies (EEAS 2025). The articles were written in multiple languages with culturally appropriate idioms, shared through networks designed to mimic organic news distribution, and optimized to evade platform detection systems.

Audio deepfakes represented another concerning trend. The report documented cases of synthetic audio recordings purporting to be leaked phone calls between European officials, discussing policies in ways designed to create scandal or controversy. The audio quality was sophisticated enough that casual listeners found them credible, though forensic analysis revealed telltale artifacts of AI generation. What made these particularly dangerous was their distribution strategy: rather than seeking mass viral spread, the campaigns targeted specific influencers, journalists, and political figures likely to share the content with their trusted networks, leveraging credibility by association.

Perhaps most concerning were campaigns that blended authentic and synthetic content. Adversaries would take genuine video footage of a European official's speech, then use AI to alter a few key phrases—changing "we should consider" to "we have decided," or "potential cooperation" to "confirmed alliance." These micro-alterations were nearly impossible to detect without frame-by-frame forensic analysis, yet they fundamentally changed meaning. When called out, perpetrators could point to the predominantly authentic content and frame accusations of manipulation as overreaction or censorship.

The EEAS report also documented defensive innovations. Several member states had begun deploying AI-powered detection systems that analyzed content for synthetic artifacts—inconsistencies in lighting, unnatural facial micro-expressions, audio spectral anomalies. Yet the report acknowledged an escalating arms race: as detection improved, generation techniques evolved. By the time Report #3 was published, adversaries were already using "adversarial training"—techniques that specifically optimize synthetic content to evade detection systems.

Critically, Report #3 addressed the political and ethical dimensions beyond technical detection. The report noted that not all synthetic media constitutes disinformation—satire, clearly labeled parody, and artistic expression use similar tools legitimately. The challenge is distinguishing malicious deception from protected expression. EEAS emphasized that responses must be proportionate and respect fundamental rights, even as they defend democratic processes from manipulation.

The report's policy recommendations reflected this complexity. It called for mandatory provenance labeling for synthetic content shared on major platforms, transparency requirements for AI tools capable of generating realistic fake content, and investment in media literacy programs teaching publics to evaluate content critically. Notably, it stopped short of recommending platform removal of synthetic content, instead emphasizing labeling and context as preferable to censorship in democratic contexts.

The timing of Report #3's release was strategic. Published in March 2025, it provided member states with situational awareness ahead of multiple national elections scheduled throughout the year. By documenting specific tactics and techniques, the report enabled governments, journalists, and civil society to anticipate and prepare for similar operations targeting their own information environments. Several European media organizations published guides for journalists on verifying content, citing FIMI Report #3 as the authoritative reference.

For diplomatic missions beyond Europe, the report's most portable lesson lies in its restraint: labeling over removal. Pressing host governments or platforms to take down synthetic content invites perceptions of censorship; working to label it and supply context preserves publics' agency to judge for themselves—a posture missions can adopt in almost any political environment.

In Europe, the *EU vs Disinfo* project of the East StratCom Task Force has become one of the most prominent efforts to monitor disinformation at scale. Created in 2015 in response to Russian influence operations, it has evolved into a multilingual database cataloging thousands of false narratives. During the 2024 European Parliament elections, this work was reinforced by the European Digital Media Observatory (EDMO) and the European External Action Service (EEAS), which used AI-enabled tools to issue daily bulletins on election disinformation (European Commission 2025b). These initiatives illustrate how institutions can use AI to identify cross-border narratives, but they also raise questions of legitimacy. Labeling a narrative as "manipulation" can reassure some publics while alienating others, who may see it as an attempt to police legitimate dissent.

NATO's Strategic Communications Centre of Excellence in Riga has approached the problem from another angle: simulation. Its exercises illustrate how quickly hostile narratives can dominate an information space if left unchecked, especially during the critical first minutes of a crisis (NATO StratCom COE 2024, n.d.). These simulations underscore the importance of early detection, but they also reveal the tension between speed and accuracy. Responding too quickly risks acting on false positives, while waiting too long risks ceding the narrative. For NATO and its partners, AI-assisted monitoring is therefore a tool not of certainty but of preparedness, helping communicators rehearse proportionate responses under pressure.

WHO's EARS (Early AI-supported Response with Social listening) platform, introduced in Chapter 1, extended this monitoring logic to public health: rumors addressed quickly lost traction faster than those left unchecked, though cultural and linguistic limits required human interpretation throughout (Purnat et al. 2021; WHO 2021b; WHO 2023).

Ukraine's experience during the early months of Russia's 2022 invasion offers perhaps the most vivid illustration of AI monitoring in practice. When a deepfake video appeared purporting to show President Volodymyr Zelenskyy urging troops to surrender, it was quickly identified as synthetic. AI tools helped detect inconsistencies in the video's production, but the real success came from how quickly validators—journalists, civil society groups, and foreign governments—amplified the debunk. The episode revealed that detection alone is insufficient; credibility depends on mobilizing trusted voices to repeat corrections before disinformation takes hold.

Together, these cases reveal a spectrum of practice. Canada and the EEAS show how transparency and institutional coordination can build resilience; the EU and NATO demonstrate how institutions can coordinate monitoring across borders; WHO illustrates how early warning can protect publics in health crises; Ukraine demonstrates that detection must be paired with rapid validator amplification.

The Israel-Iran Conflict: AI Disinformation at Industrial Scale

If the Zelenskyy deepfake of 2022 was a prototype, the Israel-Iran conflict of 2025–2026 became the full production run. Researchers at the Carnegie Endowment for International Peace, the Atlantic Council's Digital Forensic Research Lab, and the European Digital Media Observatory have described the conflict as the first major war in which AI-generated content played a central role in shaping public perception on all sides.

During the 12-day war between Israel and Iran in June 2025, Iranian state television broadcast AI-generated images of Israeli F-35 fighter jets allegedly shot down over Iranian territory. The images contained telltale signs of synthetic generation—a misplaced Star of David, untouched grass around the crash site, and unrealistic proportions—yet they circulated for weeks before being quietly retracted, reframed not as a correction but as evidence of a "Zionist psychological operation" (EDMO 2025). Simultaneously, AI-generated videos of missile strikes on Tel Aviv, some bearing watermarks from commercial AI tools, spread across social media. Pro-Israel networks circulated synthetic footage of pro-Israel protests in Tehran, falsely depicting popular dissent against the Iranian regime. The University of Toronto's Citizen Lab documented a coordinated Israeli-backed campaign called PRISONBREAK that used AI-generated imagery and video, mimicked real news outlets, and deployed deepfakes during active hostilities to encourage the overthrow of the Iranian government (Carnegie Endowment for International Peace 2025).

When the conflict resumed in March 2026 under Operation Epic Fury, the pattern intensified. AI-generated images of the USS Abraham Lincoln aircraft carrier engulfed in flames reached eight million views on X before U.S. Central Command issued an explicit denial. NewsGuard identified at least eighteen false war-related claims by Iranian outlets in a single week, many incorporating AI-generated imagery or recycled footage relabeled as current events. Perhaps most troubling was the role of AI verification tools themselves: researchers at the Digital Forensic Research Lab documented over three hundred instances in which X's integrated AI chatbot, Grok, gave wildly inconsistent verdicts on the same viral war footage—sometimes calling it "likely real," sometimes "likely not authentic," often within minutes of each other (NPR 2025; Anlen and Alimardani 2026).

Iran's campaign also extended beyond realistic deepfakes to openly stylized AI-generated content targeting Western audiences in their own visual idioms. AI-generated Lego-style videos depicting U.S. President Donald Trump and Israeli Prime Minister Benjamin Netanyahu as Lego minifigures circulated widely across X, TikTok, Instagram, and Bluesky, reaching audiences in the millions; Iranian state media outlets praised the "speed of production" and described the campaign as a "victory in the soft war" (Llana 2026). Unlike realistic deepfakes, this content was not designed to deceive but to spread political messaging through emotional engagement and cultural fluency—a mode of synthetic statecraft that operates beyond questions of authenticity.

For public diplomacy practitioners, the conflict exposed three uncomfortable realities. First, AI-generated disinformation now operates at a speed and volume that outpaces institutional response, regardless of how sophisticated detection tools become. Second, all sides—not only adversaries—deploy synthetic content to shape narratives, complicating any claim of moral authority in counter-disinformation. Third, the very tools publics turn to for verification can themselves become vectors of confusion, eroding the baseline trust on which all monitoring depends.

Synthetic Narratives in Action: Zelenskyy's Deepfake Surrender (2022)

In March 2022, during the early weeks of Russia's full-scale invasion of Ukraine, a video appeared online that seemed to show President Volodymyr Zelenskyy calling on his troops to surrender. The clip was quickly identified as a deepfake: his face and voice had been digitally manipulated, and the production quality was unconvincing by professional standards. Still, the fact that it circulated at all—however briefly—signaled a new frontier in the information war. The purpose of the video was less about convincing Ukrainians to actually lay down their arms than about injecting doubt. Even a short-lived synthetic message can force officials to divert resources into rebuttals, distract media outlets, and seed suspicion in online communities.

Scholars of disinformation note that confusion, not persuasion, is often the true objective of deepfakes. In this sense, the Zelenskyy video was successful: it showed that no leader's words could be taken entirely for granted in the digital age. For global audiences, the incident was a wake-up call. If a head of state under invasion could be digitally impersonated, then any leader, diplomat, or activist might face the same risk. The Zelenskyy deepfake was a prototype, but its symbolic effect was outsized. It demonstrated that synthetic media is not only a domestic problem but a tool with direct consequences for international security and crisis stability (Allyn 2022; Lewis 2019).

ETHICAL FRAMEWORKS AND TRUST-BUILDING IN COUNTER-DISINFORMATION

The technical capacity to detect disinformation at scale creates profound ethical responsibilities. Monitoring systems touch fundamental questions about free expression, privacy, the boundaries of legitimate discourse, and the role of governments in shaping information environments. For diplomatic practitioners, these ethical questions are essential to the legitimacy that makes counter-disinformation credible rather than counterproductive.

The Free Expression Paradox

Democratic governments face an inherent tension: they must defend information spaces from manipulation while preserving the openness that defines democracy. Authoritarian regimes face no such constraint; they can surveil, censor, and control with impunity. Democracies must find ways to protect publics from coordinated deception without becoming the arbiters of truth themselves.

This paradox manifests most acutely in decisions about content moderation and labeling. When should governments recommend that platforms remove content versus simply labeling it as disputed? Removal carries the risk of censorship—suppressing speech that, while false or manipulative, may represent someone's sincerely held belief. Labeling preserves access while providing context, but it still involves governmental or platform judgment about veracity, which can be contested.

The EEAS approach, articulated in FIMI Report #3, offers one framework: focus interventions on behavior (coordinated inauthenticity, synthetic media, platform manipulation) rather than content (political positions, policy critiques). A bot network amplifying a false narrative can be removed based on violating platform policies against inauthenticity, not because the narrative itself is false. This behavioral focus preserves broader free expression while defending against manipulation (EEAS 2025).

Yet even behavioral approaches face complications. Legitimate grassroots movements can exhibit coordinated behavior—activists organizing to amplify a message, citizens sharing identical talking points from advocacy organizations. The line between authentic coordination and inauthentic manipulation is not always clear. Monitoring systems must incorporate human judgment about intent, context, and proportionality—judgments that algorithms alone cannot make.

Privacy and Surveillance Concerns

Effective monitoring requires analyzing vast quantities of data about how information flows through societies—who shares what, who influences whom, how narratives propagate across networks. This analytical capacity, essential for detecting manipulation, creates surveillance risks that democratic institutions must carefully manage.

The privacy concern operates on multiple levels. At the individual level, monitoring systems that track user behavior to identify bot networks or coordinated campaigns may inadvertently collect data about ordinary citizens' reading habits, social connections, and political views. Even when analysis focuses on aggregate patterns rather than individual users, the potential for surveillance exists.

At the community level, monitoring that identifies vulnerable or marginalized groups as targets of disinformation can inadvertently stigmatize those communities. For instance, RRM's March 2025 advisory about campaigns targeting Chinese-language journalists required careful communication to avoid suggesting that Chinese-Canadian communities were themselves sources of disinformation (Global Affairs Canada 2025).

Best practices emerging from operational experience include several safeguards. First, minimize data collection—monitor only what is necessary for detection, not everything that is possible. Second, anonymize and aggregate data wherever feasible, focusing on patterns rather than individuals. Third, establish clear data retention and deletion policies—information collected for specific investigations should not be retained indefinitely for other purposes. Fourth, provide transparency about monitoring methods, allowing publics and oversight bodies to assess whether practices respect privacy norms.

UNESCO's AI ethics recommendation emphasizes that surveillance risks are particularly acute in contexts with histories of government monitoring and repression. Diplomatic missions operating in such contexts must be especially sensitive to how their monitoring activities might be perceived. What might be seen as democratic defense in one society could be viewed as threatening surveillance in another (UNESCO 2021).

Accountability and Oversight Mechanisms

Trust in monitoring systems depends partly on the existence of meaningful accountability mechanisms—ways to ensure that detection capabilities are used responsibly and that errors or abuses can be identified and corrected.

Internal oversight typically includes protocols requiring human review before any public attribution of disinformation. The Canada RRM model, where advisories undergo multiple levels of review and legal vetting before publication, exemplifies this approach. Such protocols prevent impulsive or politically motivated attributions and ensure that claims can withstand scrutiny.

External oversight might include legislative review, ombudsperson investigations, or civil society audit. Some democracies have established parliamentary committees with security clearances that can review classified monitoring activities, providing accountability without compromising operational security. Others have created independent bodies—hybrid organizations combining government officials, academics, and civil society representatives—that evaluate monitoring practices against human rights standards.

Transparency reporting represents another accountability mechanism. Governments or platforms periodically publish statistics about monitoring activities: how many accounts were removed for coordinated inauthentic behavior, how many pieces of content were labeled as disputed, what criteria were applied. These reports allow publics to assess whether monitoring is proportionate or whether it has drifted toward excessive control.

Critically, accountability mechanisms must have teeth—ability to compel changes in practice, not merely to recommend them. Without enforcement capacity, oversight becomes performative rather than substantive. The EU AI Act's provisions for regulatory oversight of high-risk AI systems, including those used in counter-disinformation, exemplify binding accountability (European Commission 2024).

Cultural Sensitivity and Inclusive Monitoring

Monitoring systems designed in one cultural context may function poorly or unjustly in others. A system trained predominantly on English-language data may systematically misinterpret content in other languages, mistaking cultural communication styles for suspicious patterns. Humor, satire, indirect communication, and linguistic code-switching—all common in human discourse—may be flagged as anomalous by systems lacking cultural sophistication.

The African Union's Continental AI Strategy (2024) frames this as a sovereignty concern: monitoring systems that reflect only Western data and norms risk digital colonialism, imposing external standards on African discourse. Inclusive monitoring requires several practices. First, train systems on diverse datasets representing multiple languages, cultures, and communication styles. Second, employ culturally diverse teams of analysts who can interpret alerts with appropriate context. Third, engage local civil society in designing monitoring approaches, ensuring that definitions of manipulation align with local understandings rather than being imposed externally.

Case example: A monitoring system trained primarily on North American political discourse might flag certain rhetorical styles common in Global South activism—dramatic language, calls for systemic change, criticism of international institutions—as suspicious or extreme. Yet these styles may be entirely mainstream and legitimate within their cultural contexts. Only human analysts with deep cultural knowledge can distinguish legitimate dissent from actual manipulation.

The Trust Deficit Challenge

Perhaps the most fundamental ethical challenge is that counter-disinformation efforts operate in environments where institutional trust is often already low. Publics who distrust governments are unlikely to trust governmental determinations about what is or is not disinformation. This creates a legitimacy problem: the more aggressively governments counter disinformation, the more they risk being perceived as censors, which further erodes trust, which makes counter-disinformation less effective—a vicious cycle.

Breaking this cycle requires approaches that build rather than assume trust. Transparency about methods, external oversight, partnerships with independent fact-checkers, and validator networks that include voices from outside government all help establish legitimacy. The goal is to create systems where publics can assess for themselves whether disinformation claims are credible, rather than requiring blind trust in governmental determinations.

Canada's RRM has attempted this by publishing detailed methodologies alongside advisories, allowing media and civil society to independently verify claims. While not perfect, this approach has generated more trust than opaque intelligence-style attributions would have (Global Affairs Canada 2023; 2025). Similarly, the EEAS's practice of documenting specific examples and techniques in FIMI reports enables independent verification by researchers and journalists (EEAS 2025).

Proportionality and the Amplification Dilemma

A final ethical consideration is proportionality: ensuring that responses to disinformation do not themselves cause more harm than the disinformation. The amplification dilemma—that calling attention to false narratives can give them greater reach—creates ethical complexity. A fringe conspiracy theory seen by hundreds may be amplified to millions through governmental debunking efforts. The challenge is compounded when governments themselves contribute to the information environment's instability. The Trump administration's sustained use of AI-generated imagery across White House and agency social media accounts throughout 2025—depicting the president in fantastical scenarios and deploying synthetic content as routine political communication—offered diplomatic missions worldwide an unsettling lesson: when major governments normalize unlabeled synthetic media, the information environment that all diplomats must operate within becomes measurably harder to defend. Missions attempting to counter disinformation abroad must now account for the possibility that allies as well as adversaries are contributing to the erosion of content authenticity norms (Tuquero 2025).

Proportionate response requires structured decision-making: What is the reach and velocity of the disinformation? What publics are likely to be exposed? What harm might result if left unchecked versus corrected? Often, the most ethical response is strategic silence—allowing fringe content to fade naturally rather than elevating it through attention.

When response is warranted, proportionality also applies to method. Quiet validator outreach may suffice for content with limited reach. Public correction may be necessary for viral falsehoods. Legal action should be reserved for the most egregious cases—persistent, harmful, and demonstrably false. Escalating responses beyond what threats warrant risks creating martyrs, triggering backlash, and undermining the very credibility counter-disinformation aims to protect.

These ethical frameworks are not abstract philosophy; they are operational necessities. Counter-disinformation efforts that violate free expression norms, ignore privacy concerns, lack accountability, demonstrate cultural insensitivity, or respond disproportionately will fail—not because the technology is inadequate but because legitimacy has been forfeited. For diplomatic practitioners, technical capability alone is not enough; ethics is what turns detection into credible defense.

PRACTITIONER GUIDANCE

For diplomats, counter-disinformation is ultimately about preserving the conditions for credible communication. AI tools can surface threats, but only thoughtful practice ensures that defensive measures strengthen rather than undermine trust. Several principles guide effective practice.

First, maintain proportionality. Not every false narrative warrants response, and overreaction can be more damaging than the original disinformation. Structured triage helps ensure that limited resources focus on threats that genuinely matter—those with significant reach, velocity, and potential harm. Fringe content with limited exposure often fades naturally; calling attention to it may amplify more than correct.

Second, prioritize validator networks over institutional voice. Publics often trust familiar community voices more than official channels. When validators—journalists, civil society leaders, alumni—echo corrections, messages carry greater credibility than when governments speak alone. Building these relationships before crises arrive enables rapid mobilization when they do.

Third, transparency builds legitimacy. Explaining why monitoring occurs, what safeguards protect privacy, and how findings inform action helps publics see counter-disinformation as defense rather than censorship. The more opaque the process, the more suspicious publics become. Canada's RRM advisories exemplify how transparency can transform potential suspicion into trust (Global Affairs Canada 2023; 2025).

Fourth, acknowledge uncertainty and error. No detection system is infallible, and false positives are inevitable. When mistakes occur—legitimate content wrongly flagged, attributions later proven incorrect—institutional willingness to acknowledge and correct errors protects long-term credibility. Defensiveness corrodes trust; humility sustains it.

Fifth, invest in cultural and linguistic capacity. Technical sophistication without cultural knowledge produces monitoring systems that systematically misunderstand the societies they aim to protect. Locally employed staff, cultural validators, and diverse analytical teams ensure that alerts are interpreted with appropriate context rather than through algorithmic simplification.

The AI Mindset for Monitoring

Every monitoring dashboard poses the same two questions the moment it lights up: is this signal real, and does it matter? Software raises the alert in seconds; answering those questions under time pressure, with incomplete information, is where the actual work of monitoring begins. The mindset practitioners bring to monitoring often makes the difference between strengthening credibility and eroding it. Four principles are particularly important: vigilance, speed balanced with accuracy, collaboration, and transparency.

The first principle is vigilance. In contested information environments, adversaries are always adapting. They know that governments rely on dashboards, and they design campaigns to exploit those systems. Coordinated networks can flood hashtags, synthetic personas can mimic grassroots voices, and manipulated content can be seeded in ways that look organic. AI systems can help spot these patterns, but they are also vulnerable to being gamed. Practitioners must therefore treat anomalies with skepticism, cross-checking signals across multiple platforms and validating them with local sources. Vigilance means recognizing that what looks like a groundswell may be an engineered mirage.

Closely linked to vigilance is the principle of balancing speed with accuracy. As the NATO StratCom simulations discussed earlier make clear, the pressure to move fast is real—but speed without validation is its own form of risk. Overreacting to an anomaly risks amplifying falsehoods or mislabeling legitimate debate as manipulation. The mindset required is one of disciplined agility: move quickly to investigate and prepare, but act publicly only when the evidence is clear and the response is proportionate.

Collaboration forms the third principle. No single mission or institution can monitor the information environment comprehensively. Narratives cross borders, mutate across languages, and travel through platforms beyond the reach of any one actor. Effective monitoring therefore depends on partnerships—with other embassies, with multilateral institutions like the EU or NATO, with civil society validators, and with journalists who can amplify corrections. Ukraine's experience with deepfake exposure showed how critical these partnerships are. AI tools identified the manipulation, but credibility was restored only because validators repeated the debunk quickly and consistently. Monitoring is strongest when it is shared.

Finally, transparency is essential. Publics are often wary of monitoring systems, fearing surveillance or censorship. When governments explain why they monitor, what safeguards are in place, and how findings are used, suspicion can be transformed into trust. Canada's decision to publish RRM advisories exemplifies this principle: by making threats visible, transparency itself becomes a form of defense. Conversely, opaque monitoring risks backlash if later exposed. The AI mindset for monitoring thus requires not only technical capability but also ethical courage—the willingness to operate in the open and accept scrutiny.

Monitoring Workflows

Mindset and ethics provide the compass, but workflows provide the operational map. Effective counter-disinformation monitoring requires structured processes that balance speed with validation, technical detection with human judgment, and defensive vigilance with proportionate response.

The workflow begins with continuous scanning. AI systems monitor designated platforms, languages, and topics, clustering content into themes and flagging anomalies. This scanning is not indiscriminate—missions define parameters based on their strategic priorities, available resources, and ethical constraints. A mission might monitor content related to specific policy areas (bilateral relations, security cooperation, trade agreements) while deliberately excluding broader political discourse that falls outside diplomatic purview.

When anomalies are detected—sudden narrative spikes, suspicious coordination patterns, potential synthetic media—the system triggers alerts for human review. This triage stage is critical: not every alert warrants investigation. Analysts assess several factors: velocity (how quickly is the content spreading?), reach (what proportion of target audiences are exposed?), potential harm (could this content damage interests or endanger people?), and authenticity signals (do preliminary checks suggest manipulation?).

For alerts that clear the triage threshold, deeper investigation begins. This may involve forensic analysis of suspicious media, network mapping to identify coordination patterns, cross-platform tracking to understand propagation, and validator consultation to assess cultural context and local significance. Throughout investigation, documentation is essential: what was detected, what methods were used, what findings emerged, what confidence level is assigned. This creates institutional memory and accountability.

Based on investigation findings, missions calibrate responses on a spectrum from monitoring without action (for low-threat content) to active counter-messaging (for high-threat, high-confidence cases). Response options include: validator outreach (engaging trusted voices to provide organic corrections), platform engagement (requesting content review under platform policies), public attribution (issuing statements or advisories), media engagement (providing background to journalists), and legal action (in extreme cases of targeted harassment or criminal threats).

After response, monitoring continues to assess effectiveness. Did the correction gain traction? Did narrative velocity decrease? Are new mutations emerging? This feedback loop informs future responses, building institutional learning about what works in specific contexts. It also guards against overconfidence—sometimes the best response is recognizing that a chosen strategy failed and pivoting to alternatives.

Throughout, coordination mechanisms ensure that different parts of the mission work cohesively. Public affairs officers, political officers, consular sections, and security personnel may all have relevant insights or equities. Regular coordination meetings prevent duplicated effort and ensure that responses align with broader mission strategy.

Risks, Ethics, and Compliance

In monitoring, AI's defensive value and its liabilities are tightly bound together. Four vulnerabilities in particular demand attention: surveillance perceptions, false positives, adversarial exploitation, and the trust problem.

Surveillance perceptions are perhaps the most immediate reputational risk. Even when monitoring draws only on publicly available data and focuses on aggregate patterns rather than individuals, publics may interpret large-scale information analysis as invasive. In societies with histories of government surveillance, this perception can be especially acute. Diplomatic missions must therefore be proactive about explaining monitoring purposes, methods, and safeguards. Transparency functions as both ethical imperative and strategic necessity.

False positives—incorrectly flagging legitimate content as disinformation—present another danger. Algorithms trained to detect coordination may misidentify grassroots advocacy. Systems designed to spot synthetic media may flag creative satire. Linguistic analysis may mistake dialectical variations for suspicious patterns. False positives can alienate communities, stifle legitimate discourse, and corrode credibility. This is why human validation is non-negotiable: no algorithmic detection should trigger public response without human review confirming both the finding and the appropriateness of acting on it.

Adversarial exploitation represents a sophisticated threat. Hostile actors study counter-disinformation methods and design campaigns specifically to evade or manipulate detection systems. They may deliberately trigger false positives, overwhelming analysts with spurious alerts to mask genuine operations. They may employ adversarial training to generate synthetic content designed to pass authenticity tests. They may even weaponize counter-disinformation infrastructure itself, falsely accusing opponents of manipulation to censor their voices. Defensive monitoring systems must therefore incorporate resilience against manipulation, including anomaly detection for the detection systems themselves.

The trust problem is perhaps most fundamental. Counter-disinformation efforts presume some baseline institutional credibility—that publics will believe governmental assessments about what is or is not manipulation. Yet in environments of deep distrust, such presumption is unwarranted. Aggressive counter-disinformation in low-trust contexts may backfire, being perceived as censorship rather than defense. Building trust may require starting not with counter-disinformation but with transparency, consultation, and demonstrable respect for free expression even when it includes criticism of government.

Compliance with international frameworks provides both legal protection and ethical grounding. UNESCO's AI ethics principles, the OECD's AI governance standards, the EU AI Act's requirements for transparency and accountability, and regional frameworks like the African Union's AI strategy and ASEAN's ethics guide all establish expectations for responsible monitoring. Aligning practices with these frameworks demonstrates that counter-disinformation is being conducted according to internationally recognized norms, not arbitrary governmental preferences.

Metrics and Evaluation

Evaluating counter-disinformation effectiveness is complex because success often appears as the absence of crisis—threats detected and neutralized before they escalate. Traditional metrics like "narratives debunked" or "accounts removed" capture activity but not impact. What matters is whether monitoring strengthened credibility, protected publics, and maintained trust.

One valuable measure is threat velocity reduction. When disinformation is detected early and countered effectively, its spread should decelerate. Tracking narrative velocity before and after intervention—how quickly content is being shared, how broadly it is reaching new audiences—provides evidence of impact. WHO's EARS system demonstrated this during COVID-19: rumors addressed quickly lost traction faster than those left unchecked (Purnat et al. 2021).

Validator amplification rates offer another metric. When corrections are echoed by trusted independent voices, credibility is reinforced. Tracking how many validators repeat a correction, and how effectively their networks amplify it, indicates whether counter-disinformation is leveraging trusted intermediaries or isolated to governmental sources.

False positive rates must also be monitored. What percentage of alerts flagged by AI systems turn out, upon human investigation, to be misidentifications? High false positive rates waste analyst time and, if exposed, damage credibility. Tracking this rate enables continuous refinement of detection algorithms and validation protocols.

Transparency scores assess whether monitoring practices are sufficiently open. Are methodologies publicly documented? Are advisories detailed enough for independent verification? Is oversight robust? These process metrics indicate whether counter-disinformation is being conducted in ways that build rather than erode trust.

Finally, trust surveys directly assess whether monitoring efforts enhance or undermine public confidence. Do citizens believe their government is protecting them from manipulation or censoring dissent? Do they trust governmental assessments about disinformation? Regular survey data provides feedback about whether operational practices align with democratic legitimacy imperatives.

Reflection and Strategic Questions

Practitioners might reflect on several questions. How can missions balance the urgency of rapid response with the responsibility of accurate attribution? What thresholds should trigger public action versus quiet monitoring? How can monitoring respect free expression while defending against manipulation? What role should diplomatic missions play in counter-disinformation versus deferring to host country authorities or civil society? And perhaps most fundamentally: how can institutions remain vigilant against external threats without becoming threats themselves—surveillance apparatuses rather than defenders of open discourse?

FRONTIER AND NEAR-TERM PILOTS

While established systems like Canada's RRM and the EEAS's FIMI reports represent current best practice, several frontier applications point toward how counter-disinformation may evolve—and the ethical challenges this evolution will create.

U.S. Department of Defense Neural Network Credibility Scoring

In 2020, the U.S. Department of Defense funded an experimental program with the private AI company Primer aimed at addressing a specific military challenge: how to rapidly triage vast quantities of online information during operations, identifying credible intelligence sources while filtering out disinformation designed to mislead. The program, involving both the Air Force and Special Operations Command, represented an ambitious attempt to automate credibility assessment using neural networks trained on millions of examples of verified and debunked content.

The technical approach combined multiple AI capabilities. Natural language processing analyzed textual content for linguistic markers associated with credibility or deception—precise vs. vague claims, verifiable vs. unverifiable assertions, logical consistency vs. internal contradictions. Network analysis examined source characteristics—established vs. newly created accounts, diverse vs. homogenous follower bases, transparent vs. opaque ownership. Content provenance systems tracked whether information originated from known credible sources or appeared first on suspect platforms.

The neural network synthesized these inputs into credibility scores, ranking content on a scale from highly reliable to highly suspect. In principle, this would allow military analysts to prioritize attention on credible intelligence while filtering out noise and active deception. During the reported pilot phases, the system processed content at scales impossible for human analysts—millions of posts analyzed, ranked, and flagged for further review (Tucker 2020; Nextgov 2020).

Yet the program also exposed profound limitations and ethical concerns that make its applicability to civilian diplomacy highly questionable. First, credibility is inherently contextual and domain-specific. A source credible about military movements may not be credible about political negotiations or cultural developments. Neural networks trained on one domain may produce unreliable judgments in others, yet the system's complexity made it difficult for operators to understand why particular scores were assigned—the classic "black box" problem of advanced AI.

Second, adversaries aware of the system could conduct adversarial poisoning—deliberately producing content designed to game credibility metrics. If the system rewards certain linguistic patterns or source characteristics, hostile actors can mimic those patterns while embedding false information. The arms race between scoring and deception would be relentless, with no guarantee that scoring would stay ahead.

Third, and most troubling for diplomatic contexts, automating credibility judgments risks politicizing truth itself. In military operations, where information is used primarily for tactical decision-making, credibility scoring might be defensible as operational triage—a way to prioritize analyst attention, not to definitively declare truth. But in public diplomacy, where legitimacy depends on transparent reasoning and respect for contested perspectives, algorithmic credibility scoring would be profoundly corrosive.

Imagine a diplomatic mission deploying similar technology: content critical of mission policies receives low credibility scores, while supportive content scores highly. Even if the scoring reflects genuine quality differences, the perception of politically motivated filtering would be unavoidable. Publics would see the system as censorship infrastructure disguised as quality control, and credibility would collapse. The tool designed to defend against disinformation would itself become a disinformation vector.

The Primer case thus functions as a cautionary tale rather than a model. It demonstrates that some technically feasible AI applications should not be deployed in diplomatic contexts because their deployment would violate the democratic norms diplomacy aims to uphold. Credibility assessment must remain fundamentally human—analysts drawing on expertise, cultural knowledge, and political judgment to evaluate information. AI can assist by flagging anomalies, detecting coordination, and verifying authenticity, but the moment machines begin scoring truth itself, legitimacy erodes.

For practitioners, the lesson is to maintain clear boundaries about what AI should and should not do in counter-disinformation. Detection: yes. Alerting: yes. Forensic analysis: yes. Automated credibility judgments: no. The line may seem arbitrary, but it reflects a deep understanding that in democratic contexts, legitimacy depends on preserving human agency in assessments that touch fundamental questions of truth, trust, and authority.

Beyond credibility scoring, other frontier applications include predictive disinformation forecasting (using AI to anticipate what false narratives adversaries might deploy before they appear), automated counter-narrative generation (AI systems drafting prebunks based on anticipated disinformation), and cross-platform synthetic identity tracking (following single actors who operate multiple personas across platforms). Each promises enhanced capability but also raises ethical questions about surveillance, manipulation, and the appropriate scope of governmental information intervention.

The common thread across these frontier applications is a shift from reactive defense—responding to disinformation after it appears—to anticipatory action—predicting and preempting information threats before they materialize. This shift magnifies both power and risk. Anticipation could enable more effective defense, but it also creates temptations toward excessive control, prophylactic censorship, and overreach. The future of diplomatic counter-disinformation will depend less on technical innovation than on whether institutions develop the ethical sophistication to wield anticipatory capabilities without betraying the democratic values they aim to protect.

CONCLUSION

This chapter has examined the defensive dimension of diplomatic communication: the work of monitoring information environments, detecting manipulation, and protecting institutional credibility in an era when adversaries can fabricate, amplify, and weaponize narratives at machine speed. By now you have seen an escalating sequence of cases, from Canada's transparent RRM advisories to the Israel-Iran conflict's industrial-scale deployment of AI-generated content on all sides. One tension runs through all of them: the paradox of democratic defense, the need to protect the information environment without compromising the openness that democracies represent.

The chapter's most actionable ethical insight—focusing interventions on behavior rather than content, on how narratives spread rather than what they say—offers one path through that paradox. The Primer experiment marks the boundary: AI can flag anomalies, detect coordination, and verify authenticity, but the moment machines begin scoring truth itself, legitimacy erodes. Detection yes, automated credibility judgments no, because democratic credibility depends on keeping human judgment at the center of questions that touch trust and authority.

Monitoring, however, reveals more than threats. The same analytical capabilities that expose manipulation also illuminate where publics are engaged, what questions they are asking, and which communities feel included or overlooked. That intelligence creates the conditions for the next stage of the cycle: direct, interactive engagement with the publics whose trust monitoring is meant to protect. The next chapter takes up that engagement—through chatbots, participatory platforms, alumni networks, and digital outreach—and asks why the measure of success is not the volume of interactions but whether publics feel genuinely heard.

4 Engaging Audiences through Smart Digital Diplomacy

"When we change the way we communicate, we change society."

—Clay Shirky, *Here Comes Everybody* (2008)

"Face-to-face conversation is the most human—and humanizing—thing we do. Fully present to one another, we learn to listen. It's where we develop the capacity for empathy. It's where we experience the joy of being heard, of being understood."

—Sherry Turkle, *Reclaiming Conversation* (2015)

"I believe in a world that will have an abundance of artificial intelligence, but what will be scarce is real intelligence and human qualities, like empathy."

—Satya Nadella, quoted in Andy Trotman, "AI Must Be Built with Empathy" (2017)

Opening Vignette: When the Chatbot Gets It Wrong

At first, the numbers looked like a victory. The embassy's new AI-powered chatbot, launched to handle the surge of questions about student visas in the Republic of Z, had logged tens of thousands of interactions in its first three months. Response times dropped from days to seconds. Call volume to the consular section fell by nearly 40%. Students in the capital praised the convenience of getting answers at midnight rather than waiting on hold for hours. Lina Perez, the digital communications officer who had championed the pilot, tracked the metrics closely. "Engagement is up, complaints are down, and the consular section is finally able to focus on complex cases," she reported at a staff meeting. David Kim, the public affairs officer, approved a short feature on the embassy's social media channels highlighting the chatbot as an example of innovation in public service.

Then came the misstep. A parent, worried about her child's health coverage while studying abroad, typed a question into the chatbot late one evening.

DOI: 10.1201/9781003612377-5

The system, drawing on its retrieval-augmented knowledge base, provided a response that seemed confident but was wrong. It assured her that the student would automatically receive full health coverage—something that was true in certain systems but not under Zorani law. The parent posted the chatbot's answer on a community Facebook group, where it spread rapidly. By morning, dozens of families were citing the chatbot's words as official policy.

Maria Santos, the consular officer, was the first to feel the impact. Families arrived at the consular window quoting the chatbot, frustrated and distrustful when told the information was incorrect. "They are not angry at a machine," Maria told David. "They are angry at us. As far as they are concerned, the embassy told them something that was not true." Local media picked up the story within days, framing it as an example of foreign technology dismissing Zorani realities. What had begun as a tool to build accessibility had become a credibility problem that no dashboard metric had anticipated.

David convened the team. Lina corrected the chatbot's knowledge base, rebuilt its intent-classification logic, and added a routing layer that escalated sensitive queries—health coverage, legal rights, financial obligations—to human officers. The consular section issued a public clarification. Alumni of U.S. exchange programs, enlisted as validators, posted explanations in community forums to help rebuild trust. What she did not anticipate was how much of her daily work would shift from content creation to what the team came to call agent wrangling—monitoring the system's outputs, catching drift in its responses, and retraining it when policy guidance changed faster than the model could absorb.

The crisis faded, but the episode left a mark. At the debrief, Lina was candid. "I built the launch around speed and volume," she said. "I measured how many questions the system could answer. I should have been measuring how many it could answer correctly—and what would happen when it got one wrong." David nodded. "The chatbot earned trust one interaction at a time over three months. It lost that trust in a single night. That is the math we have to keep in mind. Automation scales access, but it also scales errors. And when it fails, publics do not blame the algorithm. They blame the flag on the building."

FRAMING THE CHAPTER

Engagement has always been the most visible face of public diplomacy. If listening is how diplomats understand publics, and messaging is how they articulate intent, engagement is where relationships are tested in real time. It is the moment when publics reach back—through questions, participation in programs, or direct interaction—and measure whether institutions are attentive, accessible, and trustworthy. In the analog era, this meant cultural events, exchanges, press interviews, and community outreach. In the digital age, engagement unfolds across platforms, often mediated by algorithms and, increasingly, by artificial intelligence.

AI alters this dynamic by making institutions more interactive and responsive at scale. Chatbots now answer routine questions, alumni networks are mapped and mobilized through AI-assisted analysis, and youth engagement platforms like UNICEF's U-Report allow millions of young people to participate in dialogues that were once limited to a handful. Governments experiment with co-pilot tools that suggest responses for public affairs officers, while multilateral organizations deploy multilingual assistants to make resources accessible across diverse publics. What was once constrained by staff time and geographic reach can now be scaled across countries, languages, and time zones.

Listening (Chapter 1) shows what publics are saying, messaging (Chapter 2) demonstrates what institutions wish to convey, and monitoring (Chapter 3) tracks how those narratives circulate. *Engagement* is where the cycle becomes reciprocal: it is no longer a matter of broadcasting or observing but of participating. In these exchanges, publics evaluate institutions not only by the information they provide but by the tone, empathy, and accessibility with which they provide it.

This chapter develops the practice of AI-enabled engagement in three ways. Conceptually, it explores how digital tools expand interactivity but risk depersonalization if publics feel they are speaking to machines rather than people. Practically, it outlines how missions can design workflows that integrate AI chatbots, alumni mapping, and participatory platforms while ensuring transparency and escalation to human staff when nuance is required. Strategically, it highlights the ethical challenges of inclusion, disclosure, and manipulation, asking how institutions can embrace efficiency without eroding authenticity. In diplomacy, engagement has always been about relationships. AI changes the scale and speed of those relationships, but the measure of success remains the same: whether publics feel that their voices matter.

RESEARCH AND POLICY FOUNDATIONS

Scholars of diplomacy have long emphasized that publics evaluate institutions not only on the information they provide but also on whether those institutions appear attentive and respectful (Cull 2008).Artificial intelligence adds a new layer to that relational test, creating opportunities for unprecedented responsiveness but also raising questions about authenticity, inclusivity, and ethics.

Research on digital diplomacy has shown that publics are quick to perceive when communication feels impersonal. Studies of AI-enabled chatbots in customer service and government contexts, for example, reveal that users value speed and convenience but also expect empathy and clarity (Sutherland 2025). If a chatbot provides answers that are technically correct but emotionally tone-deaf, publics may leave the interaction feeling dismissed rather than supported. This tension between efficiency and empathy sits at the core of AI-enabled engagement. The lesson from scholarship is clear: institutions must design digital interfaces not simply for accuracy but for relational credibility.

Public trust also hinges on inclusivity. Corneliu Bjola and Ilan Manor (2024) argue that digital diplomacy often overrepresents connected elites while neglecting rural or marginalized voices. AI tools can exacerbate this bias if they rely on datasets dominated by urban or majority-language users. The African Union's *Continental AI Strategy* (2024) frames this as a question of sovereignty, asserting that systems which exclude minority languages or rural populations are not neutral but actively exclusionary. The European Union's *AI Act* (2024) codifies this principle as a requirement, mandating that public-facing AI systems be accessible across diverse groups. UNESCO's *Recommendation on the Ethics of Artificial Intelligence* (2021) extends the argument further, insisting that AI systems must be designed not just for efficiency but for dignity and respect.

These frameworks converge on a shared insight: engagement is inherently relational, and technology cannot substitute for relationships. ASEAN's *Expanded Guide on AI Governance and Ethics* (2025) reinforces this view by emphasizing contextual adaptation, noting that engagement practices must reflect local norms rather than impose external standards. The OECD's updated *AI Principles* (2024) add that fairness and transparency must be built into systems from the start, not retrofitted after deployment. For diplomatic practitioners, these documents offer more than compliance checklists; they provide strategic guidance on how to maintain credibility in an age of automation.

At the same time, scholarship reminds us that engagement is not only about avoiding harm but also about seizing opportunities. UNICEF's global *U-Report* platform demonstrates how AI-powered chatbots can create participatory spaces where millions of young people contribute to policy discussions (UNICEF 2022). This illustrates that digital engagement can empower publics who were previously excluded from elite conversations, provided the platforms are designed with accessibility in mind.

The convergence of research and policy suggests a central paradox. AI can make diplomacy more inclusive by lowering barriers to participation, but it can also entrench exclusion if publics perceive interactions as manipulative, inauthentic, or inaccessible. Governance frameworks now require disclosure, inclusivity, and fairness, but compliance alone will not guarantee trust. For engagement to be credible, it must be designed as a relationship, not simply a transaction. AI can expand that relationship at scale, but only if diplomats use it with humility and transparency.

TECHNICAL CAPABILITIES

The technical foundation of AI-enabled engagement rests on three interconnected capabilities: natural language understanding, dialogue management, and response generation. Each plays a distinct role in making digital interactions feel responsive and intelligent, yet each also carries limitations that practitioners must understand to avoid the pitfalls illustrated in the Republic of Z vignette.

Natural Language Understanding and Intent Classification

At the heart of any conversational AI system lies natural language understanding (NLP), the capacity to parse human language and extract meaning from it. Early chatbot systems relied on pattern-matching—recognizing specific keywords or phrases and triggering pre-programmed responses. Such systems could handle simple, predictable queries but collapsed when faced with ambiguity, slang, or cultural idiom. Modern approaches use machine learning to classify user intent, identifying not just what words appear but what the user is trying to accomplish. A query like "How do I renew my visa?" might be classified as intent: visa renewal, while "My visa expired last week" could trigger intent: visa emergency.

This shift from pattern-matching to intent-based classification represents a significant advance, but it also introduces new complexities. Machine learning models require large datasets to train on, and those datasets determine what the system learns to recognize. If a chatbot is trained primarily on English-language queries from urban users, it may struggle to interpret questions phrased in rural dialects or posed in languages with limited training data. UNICEF's U-Report platform, which operates in 102 countries, has encountered this challenge repeatedly. In some regions, the system performs well because training data is abundant; in others, particularly for minority languages, accuracy declines sharply (UNICEF 2025). The lesson for diplomats is that technical capability is never culturally neutral—it reflects the populations and contexts from which its training data were drawn.

Intent classification also struggles with multi-intent queries. A user might ask, "Can I renew my visa if I lost my passport?" This single question contains at least two intents: visa renewal and passport replacement. Some systems can parse such queries and route them appropriately; others default to recognizing only the first intent or failing entirely. Singapore's Virtual Intelligent Chat Assistant (VICA) addresses this by prompting users to break complex questions into steps, a design choice that improves accuracy but requires users to adapt their behavior (GovTech Singapore 2023; Government Technology Agency of Singapore 2025). The trade-off between system simplicity and user flexibility is one that every mission must navigate.

Dialogue Management and Contextual Memory

Once a system understands what a user is asking, it must manage the conversation over multiple turns. Dialogue management refers to the system's ability to track context, remember previous exchanges, and maintain coherence across interactions. In simple implementations, each user query is treated as independent, with no memory of earlier turns. This works for one-off questions but breaks down in scenarios where users expect continuity. If a user asks, "What are the visa requirements?" and then follows up with "How long does it take?" a system without contextual memory will not know that "it" refers to the visa process.

Advanced systems maintain session memory, storing the history of a conversation and using it to interpret follow-up questions. This allows for more natural, human-like exchanges. However, session memory introduces privacy concerns: how long should data be retained, who has access to it, and what safeguards prevent misuse? These are not merely technical questions but ethical and legal ones, particularly when conversations involve sensitive topics like asylum claims or medical conditions. The European Union's AI Act (2024) requires that systems processing personal data disclose how long information is stored and allows users to request deletion, a standard that diplomatic missions should adopt even when not legally required.

Dialogue management also determines when a conversation should be escalated to a human. Well-designed systems recognize their limits and transfer control gracefully. Singapore's VICA, for example, flags queries that involve legal interpretation, policy exceptions, or emotional distress and routes them to human officers (GovTech Singapore 2023). This escalation logic must be carefully calibrated: set the threshold too high, and users become frustrated when simple questions are unnecessarily handed off; set it too low, and the system handles cases it should not, as occurred in the Republic of Z scenario. The art of engagement lies not in automation alone but in knowing when automation should yield to human judgment.

Response Generation and Personalization

The final technical capability is response generation: how systems produce answers to user queries. In template-based systems, responses are pre-written by humans and retrieved based on the recognized intent. This ensures accuracy and consistency but limits flexibility. Modern generative models, by contrast, use large language models (LLMs) to compose responses dynamically, drawing on vast corpora of text to generate answers that feel tailored and contextually appropriate. Generative approaches can handle a wider range of queries and adapt tone or style to match the user, but they also introduce the risk of "hallucination"—confidently stated answers that are factually incorrect.

The Republic of Z vignette exemplifies this risk. The embassy's chatbot assured a parent that students would receive automatic health coverage, a claim that was plausible enough to sound authoritative but wrong in the specific legal context. Generative models excel at producing fluent, coherent text, but fluency is not the same as accuracy. For diplomatic missions, this distinction is critical. A chatbot that provides incorrect visa information or misrepresents policy can cause real harm, eroding trust in ways that are difficult to repair.

Personalization adds another layer of complexity. AI systems can tailor responses based on user demographics, previous interactions, or inferred preferences. In theory, this makes engagement feel more attentive and relevant. In practice, it risks manipulation if publics perceive that they are being "played" by algorithms designed to trigger specific reactions. Bjola and Manor (2024) warn that micro-targeting in digital diplomacy, when taken too far, can undermine the very authenticity that engagement is meant to build. The ethical line is whether personalization clarifies intent or obscures it—whether it helps publics understand policy or nudges them toward pre-determined conclusions.

Together, these three capabilities—natural language understanding, dialogue management, and response generation—define what AI-enabled engagement can accomplish. They also reveal its limits. Systems can scale interactions, provide instant responses, and handle routine queries efficiently, but they cannot replicate human empathy, cultural fluency, or ethical judgment. The challenge for diplomats is to harness these capabilities while recognizing that credibility ultimately rests on relationships, not algorithms.

REAL-WORLD APPLICATIONS

Several high-profile deployments already illustrate how AI is transforming diplomatic engagement. These cases demonstrate both the opportunities for scale and the risks to credibility when publics feel they are engaging with machines rather than people.

UNICEF U-Report: Youth Engagement at Unprecedented Scale

Among the most ambitious experiments in AI-enabled engagement is UNICEF's U-Report platform, a global system that has engaged 37 million young people across 102 countries as of mid-2025 (UNICEF 2025). Launched in 2011 in Uganda, U-Report began as a modest SMS-based polling tool to gather youth perspectives on health and education. Over the subsequent 14 years, it evolved into a comprehensive engagement platform using chatbots, natural language processing, and social media integration to create what UNICEF describes as "the world's largest youth participation network" (UNICEF 2022).

Deployment and Scaling

The platform's scale is remarkable not just in user numbers but in geographic and linguistic diversity. U-Report operates through multiple channels—SMS, WhatsApp, Facebook Messenger, Viber, and Telegram—allowing youth to participate regardless of internet access. This multi-channel approach proved critical during the COVID-19 pandemic, when U-Report scaled rapidly from 40 countries in 2020 to over 90 by 2022 (UNICEF 2022). The system uses AI chatbots to pose questions, collect responses, and provide information, with natural language processing helping to categorize open-ended feedback. Polls on topics ranging from climate change to mental health generate millions of responses, which UNICEF aggregates and shares with policymakers.

What makes U-Report distinctive is its commitment to two-way engagement. The platform does not simply extract data from young people; it feeds insights back to them. After a poll closes, users receive summaries of how their peers responded, creating a sense of collective voice. UNICEF also highlights how poll results have influenced policy—for example, youth feedback on vaccine hesitancy informed COVID-19 messaging strategies in multiple countries (UNICEF 2022). This feedback loop transforms participants from passive data sources into active contributors to policy dialogue.

Results and Impact

By 2025, U-Report had become one of the world's largest youth engagement platforms, with 37 million registered users (UNICEF 2025). During the pandemic, the platform fielded polls on COVID-19 misinformation, economic anxiety, and vaccine attitudes, providing real-time insights that traditional surveys could not match. In one notable example, U-Report data revealed that youth economic anxieties were often higher than health concerns, prompting UNICEF to advocate for economic support packages alongside public health measures (UNICEF 2022). The platform's reach extends beyond data collection: U-Report users have participated in campaigns to combat child marriage, improve education access, and address mental health stigma.

Yet scale also brings challenges. The most significant is the digital divide. While U-Report's multi-channel design helps bridge connectivity gaps, participation remains skewed toward urban youth with reliable access to mobile networks. Rural populations and marginalized groups—precisely those whose voices are often excluded from policy conversations—are underrepresented. UNICEF acknowledges this limitation and has invested in SMS-based participation to reach lower-connectivity areas, but the fundamental challenge remains: AI-enabled engagement reflects the populations who can access it, not necessarily those who most need to be heard (UNICEF 2025).

Data Privacy and Safeguarding

Engaging millions of minors across 102 countries raises profound ethical questions. How is personal data protected? What happens if a young person discloses abuse or self-harm through a chatbot? UNICEF has developed safeguarding protocols that flag concerning responses and route them to human moderators, but the scale of the platform makes comprehensive monitoring difficult. The tension between collecting feedback at scale and ensuring individual safety is one that U-Report navigates continually, with no perfect solution. The lesson for diplomats is that engagement platforms designed for efficiency must also be designed for dignity, particularly when vulnerable populations are involved.

Authenticity and Expectations Management

Perhaps the most subtle challenge is managing expectations. When millions of young people participate in polls, they expect their voices to matter. If they perceive that their input is collected but ignored, participation can backfire, reinforcing cynicism rather than dialogue. UNICEF addresses this by publishing impact reports and showcasing policy changes influenced by U-Report data, but the platform cannot guarantee that every poll will lead to action. The credibility of participatory platforms depends not just on technical functionality but on institutional follow-through—proof that engagement is genuine, not performative.

Implications for Diplomatic Engagement

U-Report offers a powerful model for diplomatic missions seeking to engage youth at scale. Alumni networks, exchange program participants, and diaspora communities could be organized using similar platforms, allowing missions to gather feedback, share information, and demonstrate responsiveness. Yet the UNICEF experience also underscores the risks. Scale without inclusivity can deepen existing inequalities. Participation without follow-through can breed distrust. And automation without human oversight can miss the nuances that define credibility in public diplomacy. U-Report succeeds not because of AI alone but because UNICEF has invested in the human infrastructure—moderators, policy advocates, safeguarding teams—that makes digital engagement meaningful.

Taiwan CECC Chatbot: Crisis Engagement under Pressure

While U-Report demonstrates sustained engagement over years, Taiwan's Central Epidemic Command Center (CECC) chatbot offers a contrasting case: rapid deployment during a crisis. Launched in May 2020 as COVID-19 spread globally, the bilingual chatbot (Chinese and English) provided real-time answers to pandemic-related questions through Google Assistant (Taiwan CDC 2020). Its purpose was to provide timely official information, answer common questions about COVID-19, and improve access to public health guidance for both Chinese- and English-speaking users.

Deployment Context

Taiwan's response to COVID-19 was widely praised for its speed and effectiveness, but communicating rapidly with both Mandarin- and English-speaking audiences remained a continuing challenge as guidance evolved.. The CECC held daily press briefings, but these were conducted primarily in Mandarin Chinese, leaving English-speaking residents dependent on delayed translations or secondhand summaries. The chatbot addressed this gap by providing instant, bilingual responses to common queries: testing locations, quarantine requirements, mask policies, and travel restrictions. It was designed not to replace human communication but to complement it, handling routine questions so that human staff could focus on complex cases requiring judgment or empathy.

Technical Design and Human Oversight

The chatbot used natural language processing to interpret queries and retrieve answers from a regularly updated knowledge base maintained by CECC staff. Unlike generative models that compose responses dynamically, this system relied on pre-written, human-verified answers to ensure accuracy. Public health officials regularly updated the chatbot's content to reflect evolving public health guidance and policy changes. to reflect the latest policy changes, a labor-intensive process that ensured the chatbot never provided outdated information. This human-in-the-loop design was critical to the system's credibility: it offered the speed of automation with the accuracy of human oversight.

The chatbot was designed to answer routine questions while directing users to official resources for additional assistance when needed. This reflected an important principle of crisis communication: automation can rapidly disseminate information, but complex situations still require human judgment and support. Queries that involved individual medical circumstances, legal exceptions, or emotional distress were flagged and referred to hotline staff. This design choice recognized a fundamental truth about crisis communication: automation can provide information, but humans must provide reassurance. When a user asked, "I have symptoms—should I get tested?" the chatbot directed them to testing centers but also provided a hotline number for medical advice. The lesson is that even in emergencies, engagement must balance efficiency with empathy.

Results and Lessons

The chatbot handled thousands of queries during the height of the pandemic, reducing call volumes to overburdened hotlines and providing non-Mandarin speakers with timely information (*Taipei Times* 2020). Anecdotal evidence suggests it reduced panic by offering clear, consistent answers to common questions. Yet the system was retired as the acute phase of the pandemic subsided, a reminder that crisis tools are not always suited for long-term engagement. The CECC chatbot succeeded because it was narrowtained, and explicitly framed as a complement to—not a replacement for—human communication. Its distinctive crisis lesson is maintenance discipline: emergency chatbots must be updated daily, even hourly, because stale information erodes trust precisely when credibility is most needed.

Singapore's VICA: Service-Oriented Engagement

Singapore's *Virtual Intelligent Chat Assistant*, or VICA, is one of the most advanced examples of AI-enabled public service communication. Operating in English, Mandarin, Malay, Tamil, and even Singlish, the system handles more than 800,000 interactions each month (GovTech Singapore 2023). It allows citizens to ask questions about everything from passport renewals to tax inquiries, with instant responses at any hour. For government communicators, VICA reduces the burden of routine queries, allowing staff to focus on complex cases. Yet the platform also reveals the risks of depersonalization. Users sometimes complain that the chatbot sounds "cold" or unempathetic, a reminder that speed does not always translate into satisfaction. The lesson for diplomats is that efficiency must be paired with escalation paths to human staff when nuance or empathy is required.

Learning from UK Government Co-Pilots

As discussed in Chapter 2, the United Kingdom's deployment of large language model co-pilots offers parallel lessons for engagement. The UK government tested Microsoft Copilot with 20,000 civil servants in late 2024, reporting an average time savings of 26 minutes per user per day (GDS 2025b). While the primary application was internal drafting and summarization, the pilot revealed challenges directly relevant to public-facing engagement systems. Staff reported instances where AI-generated drafts contained subtle factual errors that required careful review—errors similar to the health coverage mistake in the Republic of Z vignette (GDS 2025b).

The UK experience reinforced the importance of staff training. Civil servants needed to learn not just how to use AI tools but how to critically evaluate their outputs. This training imperative applies equally to diplomatic missions deploying chatbots or engagement platforms: staff must understand both the capabilities and the failure modes of the systems they oversee. The UK also developed GCS Assist, a secure alternative to commercial LLMs, recognizing that data sovereignty concerns preclude using external platforms for sensitive government communications (GCS 2025). For diplomatic missions, this lesson is critical: engagement tools that handle visa applications, policy queries, or consular issues must protect data and maintain institutional control.

The UK pilot also highlighted the risk of over-reliance on AI-generated content. When staff became accustomed to accepting AI drafts with minimal editing, quality declined. The solution was not to abandon AI but to establish clearer editorial guardrails: AI assists, humans decide. This principle applies directly to engagement: chatbots can provide information, but humans must judge whether that information is appropriate, accurate, and empathetic.

Together, these cases reveal the spectrum of AI-assisted engagement. Singapore demonstrates efficiency in multilingual service delivery, UNICEF shows how platforms can empower publics to participate, and Taiwan highlights the stakes of engagement under crisis conditions.

Synthetic Narratives in Action: India's AI Election Campaigns (2024)

India's 2024 general elections offered one of the most striking examples of how synthetic media can be woven into democratic communication at scale. Political parties across the spectrum embraced AI-powered tools to reach voters in new ways. Unlike the Imran Khan case discussed in Chapter 2—where AI preserved a single leader's voice while he was silenced—India's campaigns used synthetic media to multiply voices across dozens of languages simultaneously, prioritizing reach over fidelity.

Campaign speeches were dubbed into dozens of India's regional languages, allowing candidates' messages to reach constituencies that would otherwise have been linguistically excluded. In some cases, AI was even used to "revive" deceased political leaders, creating synthetic endorsements that played on nostalgia and cultural attachment. For many voters, these tactics felt innovative and inclusive. Hearing a candidate speak directly in their local language created a sense of accessibility and personal attention.

Yet the same techniques also blurred ethical boundaries. Was a "resurrected" leader truly speaking, or was the party simply borrowing the credibility of the dead? And if a message can be infinitely adapted for every audience, does it risk losing the authenticity of direct communication? The Indian case illustrates how synthetic media can act as a double-edged sword. On the one hand, it lowers barriers of access and makes democratic communication more inclusive. On the other, it introduces new risks of manipulation and depersonalization, where the mechanics of AI overshadow the genuine voice of political figures. For students of international relations, it shows how digital diplomacy tools that seem benign in one context can carry profound cultural and political consequences when deployed in another (Al Jazeera 2024a; Christopher and Bansal 2024).

PRACTITIONER GUIDANCE

For diplomats, AI-enabled engagement presents both an opportunity and a temptation. The opportunity is to make institutions more accessible, more inclusive, and more responsive than ever before. The temptation is to mistake scale for impact—to measure success by the number of chatbot interactions rather than by the depth of trust they generate. As Kilburg (2025) observes, the most effective AI deployments in diplomatic contexts are those designed around relationship outcomes rather than efficiency metrics alone.

The most effective practice begins with clarity about roles. Chatbots and conversational agents are well suited to handling routine queries, but they must never present themselves as final arbiters of complex or sensitive issues. Missions that design escalation pathways—where AI seamlessly hands queries over to human officers—signal both efficiency and humility. The Republic of Z vignette in this chapter showed what happens when this line blurs: publics attributed the chatbot's error to the institution itself, eroding trust. In engagement, the burden of credibility always rests on human shoulders.

Transparency is equally important. Publics are increasingly sophisticated about AI and quick to detect when interactions feel automated. Concealment is rarely sustainable, and when it fails, the damage to credibility can be severe. Disclosure, by contrast, can strengthen trust. Labeling a system as "AI-assisted, supervised by staff" makes clear that efficiency and oversight coexist. UNESCO's *Recommendation on the Ethics of Artificial Intelligence* (2021) and the EU's *AI Act* (2024) both make this principle explicit, but in practice it is not only a matter of compliance—it is also a matter of respect.

Inclusivity should also guide practice. Platforms that draw disproportionally on urban, digitally fluent publics risk excluding rural communities or minority-language speakers. Equity audits, designed to check who is being reached and who is not, help ensure that engagement reflects society rather than a privileged subset of it. UNICEF's U-Report demonstrates both the potential and the limitation: it has given millions of young people a voice, but only those with access to mobile networks. For diplomacy, inclusivity is not just a technical consideration but a strategic one. Publics who feel excluded are less likely to grant credibility when it matters most.

Finally, practitioners should reflect critically on the ethics of personalization. Tailoring messages to different publics can make them more relatable, but it can also appear manipulative if groups discover they are receiving contradictory framings. The ethical test is straightforward: does personalization clarify policy intent, or does it obscure it? In polarized contexts, even the perception of manipulation can undo years of relationship-building.

The AI Mindset for Engagement

Diplomatic engagement rests on relationships, and it always will. What AI changes is their physics: the scale and speed at which relationships now form, mediated through chatbots, alumni platforms, and participatory apps that reach millions at once. Chatbots, alumni platforms, and participatory apps can connect institutions with millions of people across languages and time zones, but whether those publics feel genuinely heard depends less on the technology itself than on the mindset of those deploying it. Four principles are especially important: accessibility, empathy, transparency, and inclusivity.

The first principle is *accessibility*. AI has the potential to lower barriers that once limited engagement to those living in capital cities or near consulates. A well-designed chatbot or mobile platform can provide instant access to information for publics in rural areas, in minority languages, or outside regular office hours. Singapore's VICA demonstrates how multilingual chatbots can reduce friction and make services available across diverse communities (GovTech Singapore 2023). Yet accessibility is not only about providing an entry point. It is also about designing interactions so that users feel they can ask questions without fear of being ignored or dismissed. AI can open the door, but diplomats must ensure that walking through it feels worthwhile.

Empathy is the second principle, and here AI faces its sharpest limitations. Machines can mimic politeness, but they cannot understand emotion. Publics sense this quickly. A chatbot that delivers technically correct answers in a flat tone may leave users feeling frustrated or devalued. As Karen Sutherland (2025) notes, communication in digital diplomacy is judged as much by warmth and attentiveness as by accuracy. The Republic of Z vignette in this chapter underscores the stakes: when a chatbot mishandled a parent's concern about health coverage, the technical error became a perceived failure of care. Speed of reply is easy to automate; the sense of being understood is not. Missions must therefore design systems with clear escalation paths to human officers when queries demand emotional intelligence.

Transparency is the third principle and perhaps the most straightforward. Publics are increasingly aware that they may be interacting with AI, and concealment creates unnecessary risk. Studies show that users trust institutions more when AI assistance is disclosed than when it is hidden and later revealed (Bjola and Kornprobst 2023). The EU's *AI Act* (2024) codifies this principle by requiring disclosure when people are engaging with AI systems. A label stating, "You are speaking with the Embassy's AI assistant, supervised by staff," may seem modest, but it signals honesty and accountability. Transparency turns what could be suspicion into legitimacy.

Finally, *inclusivity* must guide every decision about AI-enabled engagement. Tools that rely only on dominant languages or urban datasets risk reinforcing inequalities, leaving rural and marginalized communities outside the conversation. The African Union's *Continental AI Strategy* (2024) describes inclusivity as sovereignty, reminding us that publics who feel excluded are unlikely to see institutions as credible. UNICEF's U-Report offers a positive example: by using multiple channels, including SMS, it has brought millions of young voices into dialogue who might otherwise have been absent (UNICEF 2025). Inclusivity in engagement is not a matter of fairness alone; it is a matter of strategic credibility.

The European Union's AI Act (2024) mandates that public-facing AI systems disclose their nature, but compliance should not be the only motivation for transparency.

Disclosure is also a form of democratic accountability. When publics know they are interacting with an AI system, they can adjust their expectations and hold institutions accountable for the system's performance. When disclosure is absent, publics may attribute AI errors to deliberate deception rather than technical limitations. The Republic of Z episode illustrates this: families accused the embassy not just of providing wrong information but of misleading the public. Transparency could have mitigated that perception, framing the error as a system limitation rather than institutional duplicity.

Inclusion also demands continuous auditing. The African Union's *Continental AI Strategy* (2024) warns against "AI colonialism"—the imposition of systems designed for Western contexts onto societies with different needs, languages, and infrastructures. Engagement platforms that work well in capital cities may fail in rural areas. Chatbots trained on standard dialects may misunderstand regional variants. Systems optimized for smartphone users may exclude those relying on basic mobile phones. Inclusivity audits—regular assessments of who is using the system and who is not—help ensure that engagement reflects society rather than a privileged subset of it.

Taken together, these principles define the mindset required for AI-assisted engagement. AI can provide scale, but only this mindset can ensure that scale strengthens rather than weakens relationships.

Backend System Integration and Human Oversight

Authentic engagement also requires robust backend integration. Chatbots and engagement platforms cannot function in isolation; they must connect to the same knowledge bases, policy systems, and case management tools that human staff use. When systems are siloed, inconsistencies emerge. A chatbot might provide one answer while a human officer provides another, confusing publics and eroding trust. The UK government's co-pilot trials revealed this challenge: AI tools that lack access to current internal databases risk generating responses based on incomplete or outdated information, a challenge the UK trial highlighted when discussing data management practices across departments (GDS 2025b). For diplomatic missions, backend integration is not a technical detail but a strategic imperative. Engagement systems must reflect the institution's authoritative knowledge, not approximate it.

Many missions treat human oversight of AI systems as a fallback—something to invoke when automation fails. The UK experience and UNICEF's U-Report model suggest a different approach: human oversight should be strategic, not reactive. Staff should not merely correct AI errors after they occur but should actively shape how systems operate. This means reviewing conversation logs to identify recurring issues, updating knowledge bases proactively, refining escalation logic, and ensuring that the system learns from mistakes. Oversight is not surveillance; it is stewardship.

Engagement Workflows

Mindset provides the compass, but workflows ensure that the compass can be followed under real-world conditions. Engagement at scale is not just a matter of launching a chatbot or setting up a platform; it requires disciplined routines that integrate automation with human oversight. AI can lower barriers and extend access, but without structured workflows, it risks producing confusion or alienation rather than trust.

The first workflow centers on conversational agents. Chatbots are increasingly used to answer routine questions—from visa inquiries to cultural programming schedules—but they must be carefully managed. Effective practice requires tiered interaction: AI can handle predictable, low-sensitivity questions, but complex or sensitive issues should be escalated seamlessly to human staff. Taiwan's COVID-19 chatbot illustrated this principle. It relieved pressure on hotlines by handling common queries in real time, but when questions touched on urgent health risks, the system redirected users to human operators. The workflow lesson is clear: automation should never present itself as final authority when human empathy and judgment are required.

Alumni engagement provides a second workflow. Many embassies maintain extensive networks of exchange program alumni, but historically these networks have been underutilized. AI tools now make it possible to map which alumni are most active online, which issues they discuss, and where they exert influence in their communities. Used responsibly, this enables missions to tailor outreach and mobilize validators who can amplify credible messages. Yet this workflow also requires guardrails: alumni are partners, not instruments, and data-driven analysis must respect privacy and avoid reducing people to metrics of utility. Transparency with alumni about how AI is being used strengthens trust in these networks and ensures that engagement remains a relationship rather than a transaction.

Participatory platforms represent a third workflow. UNICEF's U-Report demonstrates how AI-driven chat systems can be used not only to answer questions but to collect feedback from millions of young people across dozens of countries. This participatory design transforms publics from passive recipients of information into active contributors to policy dialogue. Missions adopting similar platforms must design feedback loops that ensure participants see their contributions reflected in action. Without evidence that their voices matter, publics may quickly disengage. In diplomacy, participation must feel consequential, not symbolic.

Finally, continuous improvement forms the backbone of all engagement workflows. Chatbots should log errors and user complaints, alumni mapping should be reviewed with input from the participants themselves, and participatory platforms should track not only volume of responses but the diversity of voices engaged. Error logs, validator feedback, and inclusivity audits create a cycle of learning that refines AI tools over time. Singapore's VICA illustrates the importance of this approach. The system has evolved through multiple iterations, adding languages and refining responses based on user feedback, ensuring that engagement improves rather than stagnates.

Together, these workflows turn AI engagement from a technical experiment into a credible practice. By embedding escalation paths, treating alumni as partners, designing meaningful participation, and institutionalizing learning, missions can use AI to extend their reach without sacrificing authenticity. Engagement at scale, in this model, is not about replacing human interaction but about making it more accessible, inclusive, and sustainable.

Risks, Ethics, and Compliance

The appeal of AI in engagement is simple: reach millions of people at once. The danger is just as simple: publics do not distinguish the tool from the institution behind it, so every clumsy chatbot reply or excluded language group lands as a verdict on the mission itself. When a chatbot gives an unhelpful answer, or when a platform excludes certain groups, citizens do not blame the algorithm—they blame the embassy, the ministry, or the government itself. This makes the ethical design of AI engagement systems not a peripheral concern but central to the credibility of diplomacy.

The most immediate risk is depersonalization. Chatbots and automated platforms are efficient, but they lack the warmth of human interaction. Research shows that publics expect not only correct information but also empathy in official communication (Sutherland 2025). A technically accurate but emotionally flat response can leave users feeling dismissed or undervalued. This is particularly damaging in moments of crisis, when reassurance matters as much as facts. Missions must therefore design systems with escalation pathways, ensuring that publics can always reach a human when nuance or compassion is required.

A second risk is exclusion. Digital engagement platforms often reflect the biases of their underlying datasets, overrepresenting urban, connected, majority-language users while neglecting rural communities and minority voices. UNICEF's U-Report has faced this challenge, with participation skewed toward young people with access to mobile networks, leaving the most marginalized less likely to be heard. The African Union's *Continental AI Strategy* (2024) observes, publics excluded from engagement may perceive themselves as invisible to institutions, undermining trust.

Transparency presents a third risk. If publics discover after the fact that they were speaking to a chatbot without disclosure, they may feel deceived. The European Union's *AI Act* (2024) explicitly requires that users be informed when they are interacting with an AI system, reflecting the recognition that concealment corrodes legitimacy. UNESCO's *Recommendation on the Ethics of Artificial Intelligence* (2021) reinforces this, urging disclosure in public-facing applications.

Trust erosion is a fourth concern, especially when errors occur. Taiwan's CECC chatbot showed how quickly publics can lose confidence if answers are outdated or misleading. Once misinformation is attributed to an official source, even inadvertently, correcting it becomes far harder than preventing it in the first place. This dynamic is amplified online, where screenshots and posts can outlive corrections. Continuous updating, error logging, and proactive clarification are therefore essential safeguards.

Finally, AI engagement raises the risk of manipulation. The ability to tailor messages to different publics can make communication more relevant, but it can also be perceived as covert persuasion if different groups receive contradictory framings. In polarized societies, adversaries are quick to highlight such inconsistencies to portray governments as dishonest. The January 2026 circulation of an AI-generated map depicting the United States as including Greenland, Canada, and Venezuela—shared from official White House channels—illustrated how AI-assisted content can blur the line between aspirational messaging and territorial assertion, generating international alarm disproportionate to any diplomatic statement (Newsweek 2026). OECD's AI Principles (2024) and ASEAN's Expanded Guide on AI Governance and Ethics (2025) both stress the importance of fairness and contextual adaptation, underscoring that personalization must clarify rather than distort.

These risks reveal the paradox of AI-enabled engagement: the very features that make it powerful—scale, speed, personalization—are also those that make it fragile. Without transparency, inclusivity, and human oversight, automation can depersonalize, exclude, and erode trust. But when guided by ethical principles, the same tools can make institutions more open, more accessible, and more credible. In diplomacy, where publics weigh not only what is said but how it is said, credibility depends on ensuring that AI extends human attentiveness rather than replacing it.

Metrics and Evaluation

Evaluating engagement has always been a challenge in public diplomacy. In earlier decades, officers measured success by attendance at events, the number of media stories secured, or the size of exchange program cohorts. These were easy to count but often poor indicators of trust or influence. AI-enabled engagement platforms risk repeating this mistake if evaluation is reduced to usage statistics—how many queries a chatbot answered, how many users logged into a platform, or how many polls were completed. The more meaningful question is whether publics leave these interactions feeling heard, respected, and better informed.

User trust is perhaps the most important metric. In Singapore, VICA's high volume of interactions demonstrates its utility, but surveys and focus groups reveal that some users perceive the system as impersonal. Tracking satisfaction requires going beyond numbers to qualitative measures, asking not only whether users received an answer but whether they felt reassured in the process. Taiwan's COVID-19 chatbot provides a similar lesson. Its value lay not in the number of queries answered but in whether publics trusted its responses. When errors emerged, credibility faltered, showing that trust is fragile and must be constantly reinforced through accuracy and escalation.

Inclusivity is a second vital measure. UNICEF's U-Report shows how AI platforms can engage millions of young people, but participation is skewed toward those with mobile access. Evaluating inclusivity means asking whose voices are represented and whose are absent. Equity audits that assess the distribution of participation across languages, regions, and demographics can prevent engagement from reproducing existing inequalities. A platform that reaches millions but excludes rural or minority communities risks deepening distrust rather than building legitimacy.

Escalation rates also provide insight. Effective chatbots are not those that answer every question themselves, but those that know when to hand queries over to humans. Monitoring how often and under what circumstances users escalate to staff can reveal both the strengths and limits of AI systems. High escalation rates may point to design flaws, but they can also signal healthy transparency if users feel confident that their concerns will reach human ears.

Finally, longitudinal evaluation matters. Engagement should not be measured only in one-off interactions but in whether publics return to the platform, whether alumni networks remain active, and whether validator voices amplify institutional messages over time. Repeat engagement is a proxy for trust: publics return when they believe their voices matter.

In short, evaluation must move beyond counting activity to assessing outcomes. The central question is not how many people used the platform but whether engagement strengthened credibility. Did publics feel included, respected, and taken seriously? Did the interaction foster trust rather than suspicion? AI can scale participation, but only careful evaluation can determine whether that scale translates into legitimacy.

Reflection and Strategic Questions

These practices raise questions that every mission must answer for itself. How much should publics be told about the role of AI in their interactions? What criteria determine when an AI query should be escalated to a human? Which publics are being heard most clearly, and which remain at the margins? And how should diplomats draw the line between adaptation and manipulation in tailoring their engagement?

FRONTIER AND NEAR-TERM PILOTS

While current deployments of AI in engagement focus on service chatbots, participatory platforms, and translation systems, a new set of experiments is beginning to suggest where the next frontier may lie. These pilots are uneven and often small in scale, but they offer a glimpse of how digital diplomacy could evolve if managed responsibly.

One emerging area is alumni network mapping. Embassies have long maintained databases of participants in exchange programs, but AI can now analyze digital traces to identify which alumni are most active, which issues they discuss, and where they carry influence in their communities. Used carefully, this could allow missions to re-engage alumni in targeted ways, amplifying voices that already carry credibility in local contexts. Yet the ethical stakes are high. Alumni are partners, not instruments, and data-driven outreach risks feeling manipulative if publics suspect they are being ranked or categorized for utility. Transparency in how such systems are used will be critical if alumni engagement is to strengthen trust rather than diminish it.

A second frontier involves participatory platforms that extend beyond simple polling. Taiwan's *vTaiwan* project and UNICEF's U-Report already hint at this model, where publics contribute not just opinions but ideas and proposals, often in real time. AI can make such platforms scalable, moderating conversations, summarizing inputs, and highlighting consensus. In theory, this transforms publics from passive recipients into active collaborators in shaping diplomacy. Yet participatory platforms face the same risks of digital divides and manipulation as other tools. If publics feel their input is collected but ignored, participation can backfire, reinforcing cynicism instead of dialogue.

A third area of experimentation lies in cultural adaptation. AI systems are increasingly capable of analyzing which formats, tones, or metaphors resonate most in particular contexts. Instead of translating a campaign literally, they can suggest whether to frame it as a story, an infographic, or a video, or whether to use humor, solemnity, or appeals to tradition. Early pilots in marketing have shown promise, and governments are beginning to explore similar approaches. The opportunity is clear: campaigns that feel culturally fluent are more likely to be trusted. But so are the risks. Over-adaptation may slide into pandering, or worse, manipulation, if publics feel they are being "played" by algorithms designed to trigger emotional reactions.

Together, these frontiers point toward a future where AI helps diplomats not only respond to publics but co-create with them. Alumni networks become more active, participatory platforms become more inclusive, and campaigns become more resonant. Yet they also highlight the need for humility. AI can suggest patterns and preferences, but only humans can decide how to balance responsiveness with respect. The most promising future for AI-enabled engagement lies not in making machines more human, but in making institutions more attentive, transparent, and accountable.

CONCLUSION

This chapter has examined the stage of the diplomatic cycle where institutions stop broadcasting and start participating—the direct, interactive exchanges through which publics evaluate whether governments are accessible, responsive, and worth trusting. By now you have seen what scale offers and where it falters, from U-Report's 37 million young voices to India's AI-dubbed campaigns and synthetic "resurrections" of deceased leaders. The central tension running through all of these cases is the asymmetry between building and losing trust.

What the Republic of Z vignette dramatized is the arithmetic every mission deploying engagement tools must internalize: automation scales access, but it also scales errors, and when it fails, publics do not blame the algorithm; they blame the flag on the building. A chatbot can earn credibility one interaction at a time over three months and lose it in a single night. The vignette also surfaced what the team came to call "agent wrangling"—the ongoing stewardship of monitoring outputs, catching drift, and deciding when automation should yield to human judgment.

The chapter's guiding principle is empathy: publics measure engagement not by the speed of the response but by whether the interaction left them feeling valued.

Underlying all of them is the chapter's guiding principle: empathy. Publics measure engagement not by the speed of the response but by whether the interaction left them feeling valued. When a worried parent types a question late at night, what is at stake is not response time but whether the answer honors the concern behind the question.

Engagement at scale, however, raises a question the chapter has touched but not resolved: how do you know whether any of this is working? Chatbot interactions can be counted, platform registrations tracked, and alumni networks mapped—but volume is not the same as impact, and the voices that appear most prominently in dashboards may not represent the full range of communities your mission is meant to serve. The next chapter takes up that challenge, examining how artificial intelligence is transforming the evaluation of public diplomacy programs—and why the most important question is not what the data shows but whose voices the data includes.

PART II

Strengthening Practice

Once the core functions are in place, diplomats must measure what works, respond rapidly when crises strike, and ensure that every AI deployment upholds democratic values. These chapters examine how to optimize programs through continuous evaluation, maintain credibility under pressure, and embed ethical safeguards that turn responsible practice into strategic advantage.

DOI: 10.1201/9781003612377-6

5 Monitoring, Evaluation, and Program Optimization with AI

"Algorithms don't make things fair if you just blithely, blindly apply algorithms. They don't make things fair. They repeat our past practices, our patterns. They automate the status quo."

—Cathy O'Neil, "The Era of Blind Faith in Big Data Must End," TED Talk (2017)

"When automated decision-making tools are not built to explicitly dismantle structural inequities, their speed and scale intensify them."

—Virginia Eubanks, *Automating Inequality* (2018)

"If we aren't clear about what we want and the trade-offs that are involved, simply opening up data can – and often does – reify existing inequities and structural problems in society."

—danah boyd, "Data, Algorithms, Fairness, Accountability" (2016)

Opening Vignette: When the Numbers Told Half the Story

The embassy in the Republic of Z was proud of its flagship scholarship program. Each year, dozens of Zorani students traveled to the United States for graduate study, and the mission regularly highlighted the program as one of its most successful initiatives. When headquarters requested an evaluation, David Kim, the public affairs officer, asked Aisha Rahman to lead the analysis. Aisha, the mission's audience research and insights officer, had spent weeks building an AI-driven evaluation dashboard. By scraping alumni social media profiles and clustering posts with topic modeling and sentiment analysis, the system generated a detailed picture of how alumni talked about their experiences. The results were striking: references to "opportunity," "growth," and "innovation" dominated the analysis. Sentiment scores ran consistently high. She had spent weeks tuning the system—adjusting the topic models, filtering out

DOI: 10.1201/9781003612377-7

bot-generated noise, retraining the classifier when it confused Zorani idioms with English cognates. The dashboard looked effortless. The work behind it was not.

Aisha presented the findings at the weekly staff meeting. "Alumni engagement is strong across every metric we track," she said. "The data supports recommending expansion." Farid Tessam, a locally employed cultural affairs assistant who had maintained relationships with alumni across the country for years, studied the charts quietly. Then he spoke. "Which alumni are these?" Aisha pointed to the sample size. "Over three hundred profiles analyzed. It is a robust dataset." "It is a large dataset," Farid said. "That is not the same thing. The alumni I stay in contact with in the eastern provinces—most of them are not posting online about their experiences. Some do not have reliable internet access. Others came home to discover that their degrees did not open the doors they expected. They are not writing about growth and opportunity. They are looking for work."

Aisha's first instinct was to defend the methodology. The system had done what it was designed to do—aggregate publicly available data and identify patterns. The sample was large. The sentiment scores were consistent. "The methodology is sound," she said. "The data reflects what people are actually saying." "It reflects what some people are saying in the places where your system can hear them," Farid replied. "The alumni who are struggling are not posting on platforms your dashboard monitors. They are having conversations in living rooms and tea houses. Their silence in your data does not mean satisfaction. It means invisibility." Aisha remembered the education-initiative dashboard that had mistaken mockery for enthusiasm. This was the same lesson wearing different numbers.

The room was uncomfortable. David let the exchange settle before asking Aisha to run a supplementary analysis—offline interviews with alumni in underrepresented regions, conducted through Farid's network of community contacts. The results changed the picture. Rural alumni reported limited career pathways, frustration with follow-up support, and a sense of being forgotten once they returned home. The dashboard had not lied—the online voices were genuinely positive. But it had amplified the voices most visible in the digital record while rendering the rest invisible. David revised the report. The final version sent to Washington included both the successes and the gaps, recommending targeted follow-up with underrepresented groups alongside the case for expansion.

At the debrief, Aisha was quiet for a moment. "I built a system that measured what was easy to measure," she said. "And I defended it because the numbers were clean. But clean numbers are not the same as a complete picture. What gets measured reflects choices about whose voices count—and I did not question those choices until Farid forced me to."

FRAMING THE CHAPTER

Evaluation has always been one of the hardest parts of public diplomacy. Listening, messaging, and engagement all generate activity, but assessing whether those efforts actually change perceptions, build trust, or influence behavior is far more difficult. Traditional evaluation methods—surveys, interviews, and focus groups—provide important insights but are often expensive, slow, and retrospective. They tell practitioners what worked months or even years after the fact, when the opportunity to adapt has already passed. Artificial intelligence is beginning to change that equation by making evaluation more continuous, more data-rich, and potentially more adaptive.

Within the framework of this book, evaluation belongs to the strategic domain of *program optimization.* It closes the feedback loop in the cycle of public diplomacy. Listening (Chapter 1) provides insights into what publics think, messaging (Chapter 2) communicates intent, monitoring (Chapter 3) detects distortions, and engagement (Chapter 4) opens channels for dialogue. Evaluation draws these threads together, asking the central question: *Did it work?* Of the six categories of real-world deployment, evaluation aligns most directly with internal government AI co-pilots and multilingual communication and knowledge management, since it often relies on large-scale data synthesis and institutional learning.

AI expands the scope of what can be measured. Dashboards can track the spread of narratives in real time, analyze sentiment across languages, and quantify how quickly rumors decay after a correction. They can reveal which publics are amplifying a message, which validators are most influential, and which communities are absent from the conversation altogether. Properly designed, these systems allow diplomats to shift from static assessments to continuous optimization, adjusting strategies while programs are still unfolding.

But evaluation is not only a technical exercise. It is also a matter of ethics and legitimacy. Which publics are measured, which voices are counted, and which indicators are prioritized all reflect political choices. As the vignette in this chapter showed, AI systems can easily overrepresent connected elites while overlooking marginalized groups, producing optimistic metrics that mislead policymakers. Frameworks like UNESCO's Recommendation on the Ethics of *Artificial Intelligence* (2021) and Canada's Directive on Automated Decision-Making exist precisely to keep automated evaluation from embedding bias into governance.

This chapter explores how AI is reshaping the practice of evaluation in diplomacy. Conceptually, it examines how measurement is shifting from retrospective to real-time. Practically, it describes how missions can integrate AI dashboards into workflows while ensuring validation and inclusivity. Strategically, it highlights the risks of quantification bias, privacy concerns, and overreliance on machine outputs. Above all, it argues that credibility in evaluation depends not on the volume of data collected but on whether publics feel their experiences and concerns are accurately represented. AI can optimize programs, but legitimacy still requires human judgment.

RESEARCH AND POLICY FOUNDATIONS

For decades, public diplomacy practitioners have struggled with the problem of evaluation. Unlike advertising or commercial marketing, where consumer behavior provides immediate feedback, the effects of diplomacy are diffuse and long term. Exchange programs may influence participants years later; communication campaigns may shift perceptions subtly across entire societies. Scholars such as Zaharna (2010) have argued that success in public diplomacy is relational rather than transactional, making it difficult to measure with conventional metrics. Yet policymakers often demand evidence of impact, and practitioners have searched for tools that can capture effectiveness without reducing diplomacy to numbers.

Artificial intelligence offers new possibilities by enabling evaluation to move from episodic to continuous. Machine learning systems can process vast datasets in real time, identifying trends and anomalies that once required months of analysis. The World Health Organization's *EARS* platform, for example, applied natural language processing to track the "half-life" of COVID-19 rumors, measuring how quickly misinformation lost traction once corrected (Purnat et al. 2021). This approach reframed evaluation from retrospective surveys to dynamic monitoring, providing practitioners with immediate insight into whether their interventions were working.

At the same time, scholars caution against an overreliance on quantification. Bjola and Holmes (2015) note that data-driven diplomacy risks privileging what can be measured—social media shares, impressions, sentiment scores—over what matters most, such as credibility and trust. Numbers may show reach but cannot capture resonance. AI intensifies this tension by producing outputs that appear objective but often conceal the biases of their training data. Without careful validation, evaluation dashboards may mislead rather than inform.

Policy frameworks increasingly recognize these risks. Canada has been a pioneer, introducing its Directive on Automated Decision-Making (2019) and requiring algorithmic impact assessments for federal systems that use AI in governance. This approach emphasizes transparency, accountability, and the need to test for unintended bias before deployment. The OECD's updated AI Principles (2024) similarly stress fairness and inclusivity, reminding governments that evaluation should serve the public good, not just institutional efficiency. The European Union's AI Act (2024) requires explainability for high-risk applications, ensuring that AI systems used in sensitive domains such as democratic governance can be audited. UNESCO's Recommendation on the Ethics of Artificial Intelligence (2021) adds a global normative layer, calling for proportionality, human oversight, and respect for cultural diversity. At the practitioner level, the U.S. Department of State's AI Strategy (2025) identifies program evaluation as one of the core functions where AI can strengthen diplomatic effectiveness, emphasizing that automated tools must be paired with human review to ensure accountability.

These frameworks converge on a central principle: evaluation is not neutral. What gets measured reflects choices about whose voices count and whose experiences are valued. The African Union's *Continental AI Strategy* (2024) warns against evaluation systems trained on Western data that ignore African contexts. For public diplomacy, this means that evaluation must not only track effectiveness but also signal respect. Publics who feel unseen in evaluation processes are unlikely to believe that programs serve their interests.

The research and policy foundations therefore set both opportunity and caution. AI can make evaluation more timely and evidence-based, but it can also deepen existing inequities if poorly designed. The challenge for diplomats is to embrace the analytical power of AI while ensuring that evaluation remains relational, inclusive, and accountable. As Kilburg (2025) argues, the credibility of AI-assisted programs depends not on technical sophistication but on whether practitioners maintain human judgment at every stage of the evaluation cycle. In diplomacy, legitimacy comes not from the sophistication of dashboards but from publics' recognition that their experiences are understood and matter.

TECHNICAL CAPABILITIES

Real-Time Sentiment Tracking and Narrative Decay Metrics

One promising approach is to track the "rumor half-life," a measure of how long falsehoods persist before fading once corrected. Developed in the context of the WHO's *EARS* platform, the metric reframes evaluation from static reach numbers to dynamic decay rates (Purnat et al. 2021). In public diplomacy, the same concept can be applied to hostile narratives, asking not how widely they spread but how quickly they lose traction once validators amplify corrections. A shorter half-life signals resilience; a longer one suggests that publics are unconvinced or that corrections lack credibility.

Validator Amplification Mapping

Another valuable metric is resonance, often captured through validator amplification. When trusted voices—alumni, journalists, or civil society actors—pick up a message and restate it in their own words, the communication has moved beyond mere transmission to relational uptake. AI can track which validators amplify embassy content, how widely their networks carry it, and whether their language aligns with the institution's intent. These signals provide more insight into credibility than simple counts of clicks or likes.

Predictive Impact Modeling

One of AI's most promising applications in evaluation is impact forecasting—the ability to predict how programs or policy announcements might resonate before they are fully deployed. Drawing on historical data, social media trends, and cultural sentiment analysis, AI systems can model potential outcomes and identify risks or opportunities that practitioners might miss. For example, before announcing a new visa policy, a mission could use AI to forecast how different demographic groups might respond, which media outlets might amplify criticism, and where validator networks could provide support.

The U.S. Department of Defense has experimented with such approaches through programs like Primer, which uses neural networks to analyze large-scale narrative patterns and identify emerging trends (Tucker 2020). While these pilots have been limited to intelligence contexts, the methods could be adapted for civilian diplomacy. The European Union's research programs have explored scenario modeling for climate communication, testing how different framings—emphasizing economic opportunity versus environmental urgency—might perform across member states before messages are released (Mazarr et al. 2019).

Yet forecasting carries epistemic risks. Models are only as good as their training data, and biased inputs produce biased predictions. A forecast based primarily on urban, English-language social media may miss how rural or non-English-speaking communities will respond. Moreover, forecasts can become self-fulfilling: if a model predicts negative reactions to a policy, practitioners may abandon it even if the model was wrong. The Canadian government's approach offers a safeguard: requiring algorithmic impact assessments that explicitly test for bias and overconfidence before forecasting systems influence decisions (Government of Canada 2019).

MEL Frameworks for AI Programs

As AI becomes integral to diplomatic operations, missions must develop systematic frameworks for evaluating AI systems themselves—not just using AI to evaluate traditional programs. This creates a recursive challenge: how do practitioners measure the effectiveness, fairness, and impact of the very tools they use to measure other initiatives? The answer lies in adapting monitoring, evaluation, and learning (MEL) frameworks to account for AI's unique characteristics.

Adapting these frameworks also means being honest about how hard strategic communication is to assess. A NATO capability study puts the difficulty plainly: influence and advocacy work is notoriously resistant to clean measurement, and routine campaign follow-ups do not amount to a genuine assessment of capability (Pamment 2022). Its guidance is worth importing. First, separate three levels of indicator that are easily conflated—organizational capacity (staff, budget, training), communication output (reach, evaluations, case studies), and response capability (the ability to actually shift perception or behavior against a live threat). Second, where an existing planning model such as the UK Government Communication Service's OASIS is already in use, evaluation metrics may be embedded in it and can be repurposed. Third, complement outcome metrics with risk-based assessment—stress-testing how communication would hold up under a shock such as an infodemic, and rehearsing the judgment calls of when, how, and whether to respond through tabletop exercises (Pamment 2022).

Stakeholder Mapping for Attribution

For instance, AI can identify which validators amplified a message, which secondary networks picked it up, and how quickly it reached critical mass. By comparing campaigns with and without AI assistance, missions can begin to isolate AI's specific contribution. Singapore's evaluation of VICA showed this approach in practice: by tracking which queries the chatbot handled versus which required human escalation, the government could attribute efficiency gains specifically to automation while identifying where human judgment remained essential (GovTech Singapore 2023).

Yet attribution remains imperfect. Diplomatic outcomes are shaped by countless confounding variables—geopolitical events, domestic politics, economic trends—that AI cannot fully account for. The risk is that institutions overattribute success to AI interventions while ignoring broader context. Responsible evaluation requires pairing AI attribution analysis with qualitative case studies that capture what numbers cannot: the lived experiences of publics and the subtle shifts in credibility that define diplomatic success.

Adaptive Learning and Continuous Improvement

The most valuable MEL frameworks treat evaluation not as a final report but as a continuous loop. AI makes this adaptive learning possible by providing real-time feedback that allows programs to evolve while they are still active. The WHO's EARS platform demonstrated this by adjusting communication strategies based on rumor half-life metrics, shortening response times from weeks to days (Purnat et al. 2021). UNICEF's U-Report similarly uses participation data to identify underrepresented groups and expand outreach to them, turning evaluation into program refinement (UNICEF 2022).

For diplomatic missions, adaptive learning means institutionalizing feedback loops. Chatbots should log errors and escalations, dashboards should flag inclusivity gaps, and sentiment analysis should be compared against validator feedback and offline conversations. Quarterly reviews should ask not just whether programs are working but whether evaluation itself is improving. Are errors declining over time? Are underrepresented groups gaining voice? Are staff learning to interpret AI outputs more critically?

The UK government's trials of Microsoft Copilot offer a model. Rather than treating the pilot as a one-time experiment, the Government Digital Service established continuous monitoring of user satisfaction, error rates, and time savings, adjusting training and guardrails as lessons emerged (GDS 2025b). This approach transformed evaluation from a compliance exercise into a learning system—exactly what diplomatic missions need if AI is to enhance rather than undermine credibility.

REAL-WORLD APPLICATIONS

Several governments and institutions have already begun experimenting with AI-driven evaluation, offering early lessons in both the possibilities and the pitfalls of the technology. These cases show how machine learning can accelerate assessment while also underscoring the need for human oversight, transparency, and inclusivity.

Canada has been at the forefront of integrating AI into evaluation frameworks. Its *Directive on Automated Decision-Making* requires all federal agencies using AI systems to complete algorithmic impact assessments before deployment. These assessments score systems based on criteria such as transparency, fairness, and privacy, and higher-risk applications must undergo external review (Government of Canada 2019). For Global Affairs Canada, this has meant embedding evaluation dashboards that track disinformation campaigns and foreign interference, while simultaneously subjecting those dashboards to scrutiny about potential bias or overreach. The Canadian experience illustrates how evaluation can serve not only as a technical tool but also as a form of accountability, signaling to publics that AI is being deployed responsibly.

Singapore's *Virtual Intelligent Chat Assistant* (VICA), which handles hundreds of thousands of queries each month, has also generated a rich dataset for evaluation. By analyzing which questions are most common, which answers are escalated to human staff, and where users express dissatisfaction, the government has been able to refine both the chatbot and its broader communication strategies. Here, AI is not just a tool for engagement but a source of continuous program feedback. Yet the risks are visible as well: satisfaction scores may reflect only digitally fluent users, leaving rural or elderly populations less well represented. This highlights the need to treat AI-derived metrics as one input among many rather than a comprehensive picture of public sentiment.

WHO EARS: Dynamic Evaluation through Rumor Half-Life

The World Health Organization's *Early AI-supported Response with Social Listening* (EARS) platform offers one of the most sophisticated examples of AI-enabled real-time evaluation. Launched in January 2021 during the COVID-19 pandemic, EARS was designed to monitor misinformation and rumors across multiple languages and platforms, providing situational awareness to public health communicators (WHO 2021b). What distinguished EARS from traditional monitoring was its introduction of "rumor half-life" as an evaluative metric—the time it takes for a piece of misinformation to lose traction after correction efforts begin (Purnat et al. 2021).

This dynamic approach shifted evaluation from retrospective reporting to continuous adaptation. Rather than asking months later whether a communication campaign succeeded, EARS allowed WHO to assess interventions in near real-time. If a rumor about vaccine side effects persisted despite corrections, communicators could identify which channels, languages, or validators were failing to penetrate. If a correction worked quickly, the approach could be replicated for other narratives. By 2023, WHO's *Infodemic Management Annual Report* documented how rumor half-life had become a standard metric across multiple health crises, enabling faster response and more targeted resource allocation (WHO 2023).

Yet EARS also revealed the limits of automated evaluation. Natural language processing struggled with sarcasm, irony, and cultural nuance, sometimes misclassifying satirical posts as genuine misinformation or failing to detect coded language used by anti-vaccine groups. Human analysts were essential to contextualize what the algorithms detected, a reminder that even sophisticated AI systems require judgment to interpret their outputs. For diplomatic practitioners, the lesson is clear: dynamic metrics like rumor half-life can make evaluation more adaptive, but only when paired with human insight that understands local context and cultural subtlety.

UNICEF U-Report: Evaluating Participation at Scale

UNICEF's U-Report platform, discussed in Chapter 4 as a model of youth engagement, also provides valuable lessons for evaluation. With 37 million registered users across 102 countries as of 2025, U-Report generates unprecedented volumes of data on youth perspectives (UNICEF 2025). The platform's evaluation approach goes beyond counting participants to assessing the quality and representativeness of engagement. UNICEF tracks demographic reach—which age groups, genders, and regions are participating—and compares this against national population data to identify gaps (UNICEF 2022).

This inclusivity-focused evaluation reveals both successes and challenges. In countries with high mobile phone penetration, U-Report reaches diverse youth populations. In others, participation skews urban and middle-class, leaving rural and economically marginalized youth underrepresented. UNICEF's response has been to pilot SMS-based participation in lower-connectivity areas and to weight feedback to account for demographic imbalances. These adjustments demonstrate how evaluation can become a tool for equity, ensuring that scale does not come at the expense of inclusivity.

U-Report's evaluation framework also tracks impact: whether youth feedback influences policy decisions and whether participants feel their voices are heard. Annual reports document instances where U-Report data informed government responses to COVID-19, education policy, and climate initiatives (UNICEF 2022). Yet sustaining this credibility requires continuous transparency. If young people participate but see no evidence that their input matters, engagement can decline or become cynical. The platform's success as an evaluation tool depends not just on data collection but on institutional follow-through—proof that participation leads to action.

For diplomatic missions considering similar participatory platforms, U-Report offers a model: evaluation must measure not only volume but also diversity, influence, and participant satisfaction. Metrics that celebrate scale without examining who is excluded or whether engagement translates into impact risk becoming exercises in self-justification rather than genuine accountability.

Academic institutions have also begun testing AI for evaluation. The USC Center on Public Diplomacy piloted projects using natural language processing to analyze alumni survey responses, identifying patterns that traditional coding would have missed. One study uncovered gender disparities in exchange experiences, insights that were not visible in aggregate statistics but emerged when machine learning clustered responses by theme. These pilots suggest that AI can illuminate hidden patterns, but they also show that interpretation still requires human sensitivity. Algorithms may reveal differences, but it takes practitioners to understand their significance and decide how to act on them.

Finally, the African Union's Continental AI Strategy treats inclusivity itself as an evaluative criterion. An AI system that produces detailed dashboards but neglects minority languages is not successful by AU standards; it is incomplete—a reminder that evaluation is a normative act as much as a technical one.

Taken together, these cases demonstrate a spectrum of practice. Canada shows how evaluation can be tied to governance and accountability, Singapore illustrates the potential of engagement analytics, WHO highlights dynamic measures of impact, UNICEF demonstrates scale with inclusivity audits, USC demonstrates how AI can surface hidden patterns, and the AU makes inclusivity itself a criterion of success.

Measuring AI's Return on Investment: The UK Copilot Trials

While much of AI evaluation in diplomacy focuses on program outcomes—did the campaign work, did the exchange program build networks—missions also need to evaluate AI systems themselves. One of the most rigorous examples comes from the United Kingdom's large-scale trials of AI co-pilots in government communication.

Deployment and Scale

The UK's Copilot pilot with some 20,000 civil servants, examined in Chapters 2 and 4, matters here for a different reason: it produced the richest quantitative dataset yet on how to evaluate an AI deployment itself. The results, published in early 2025, provided rare quantitative data on AI's impact in government contexts (GDS 2025b).

The headline finding was striking: on average, users saved 26 minutes per day when using Copilot for tasks that previously required manual effort. Across 20,000 users, this translated to approximately 8,700 hours saved daily—time that could be redirected toward higher-order strategic work. The GCS reported that communicators found the tool especially valuable for drafting initial versions of press releases, summarizing lengthy reports, and retrieving precedent documents from institutional knowledge bases (GCS 2024).

Evaluation Methodology and Findings

User satisfaction surveys assessing whether staff felt Copilot improved work quality, not just speed

Error logging documenting instances where AI-generated content contained inaccuracies or required substantial revision

Productivity metrics comparing output volume and quality before and after adoption

Equity audits checking whether benefits were distributed evenly across seniority levels, departments, and roles

The findings were nuanced. While time savings were consistent, user satisfaction varied. Junior staff appreciated the tool's ability to generate first drafts, reducing the anxiety of starting with a blank page. Senior staff were more ambivalent, noting that AI-generated content sometimes required as much time to edit as it saved in drafting. Error rates were low but not zero: evaluations noted that some drafts contained subtle factual errors or tone mismatches that could have caused problems if not caught (GDS 2025b; Department for Business and Trade 2025).

The National Audit Office's 2024 report on *AI in UK Government* highlighted additional lessons. Training was essential: staff who received guidance on prompt engineering and critical review performed better than those who used the tool without preparation. Data governance proved critical: some departments hesitated to use commercial AI tools with sensitive information, leading the GCS to develop GCS Assist, a secure alternative hosted on government infrastructure (NAO 2024; GCS 2025).

Implications for Diplomatic Evaluation

For diplomatic missions evaluating their own AI deployments, the UK trials yield two key lessons that go beyond the findings themselves:

First, quantify efficiency gains, but contextualize them: time savings are meaningful only if the time is redirected toward strategic work rather than more low-value tasks, so missions should track not just minutes saved but what staff do with those minutes.

Second, track error rates, not just success rates: a system that works 95% of the time can still cause serious problems if the 5% of errors involve high-stakes communications, which makes error logging—with regular reviews to identify patterns—standard practice.

The UK Copilot trials demonstrate that rigorous evaluation of AI systems is both possible and necessary. By measuring not just speed but quality, not just adoption but equity, and not just benefits but risks, missions can ensure that AI becomes a genuine asset rather than a source of new vulnerabilities. As discussed in Chapter 2, the lessons extend beyond drafting: any AI tool used in diplomacy—from chatbots to translation systems to sentiment dashboards—deserves the same level of scrutiny.

Synthetic Narratives in Action: The Pentagon Explosion Fake (2023)

In May 2023, U.S. markets briefly shuddered after an image began circulating on Twitter (now X) showing a massive plume of smoke near the Pentagon. The photo looked like evidence of a terrorist attack or military strike, and it was picked up by a handful of accounts associated with Russian-aligned influence networks. Within minutes, trading algorithms and human investors responded with sell-offs, causing a dip in major indices before the image was debunked by journalists and the Pentagon itself.

The incident illustrates how synthetic media can have measurable consequences even when it fails to convince people for long. The image was quickly exposed as AI-generated—the geometry of the building was subtly wrong, and the smoke cloud looked unnatural—but the damage had already been done. Markets are hypersensitive to signals of risk, and even a short-lived fake can create volatility worth billions of dollars.

For public diplomacy and strategic communication, the Pentagon case underscores the importance of *evaluation*. The impact of a narrative is not only in whether it persuades but also in how it reverberates through interconnected systems—markets, media, and policymaking. Measuring those ripples, and anticipating them, is part of the emerging practice of AI-informed monitoring. If narratives can trigger economic or diplomatic consequences within minutes, then institutions need tools to evaluate not just truth, but resonance and reach (Marcelo 2023; Oremus, Harwell, and Armus 2023).

THE ATTRIBUTION CHALLENGE: MEASURING WHAT AI REALLY CONTRIBUTES

One of the hardest problems in AI evaluation is attribution: determining what outcomes can be credibly linked to AI interventions versus what would have happened anyway. This challenge is endemic to public diplomacy, where outcomes are shaped by countless factors beyond any single program. AI both complicates and clarifies this problem—complicates it by introducing new variables, clarifies it by providing data that was previously invisible.

Why Attribution Matters in AI Evaluation

Attribution matters because institutions need to justify investments in AI and ensure that resources are directed toward interventions that work. If a mission deploys an AI-powered chatbot and public sentiment improves, can the chatbot claim credit? Or was sentiment already trending positive due to geopolitical developments, economic conditions, or other diplomatic efforts? Without clear attribution, evaluation risks becoming a narrative exercise where institutions selectively claim credit for successes while blaming external factors for failures.

The problem intensifies with AI because these systems often work alongside traditional methods. A messaging campaign might use AI for audience segmentation (Chapter 1), human creativity for content development (Chapter 2), AI for distribution optimization (Chapter 4), and traditional surveys for evaluation. Isolating AI's specific contribution becomes analytically complex. The risk is twofold: overattributing success to AI when it played a minor role, or under attributing impact when AI's contributions are invisible but essential.

How AI Makes Attribution Both Easier and Harder

Validator tracking AI can map which influencers amplified a message, revealing pathways of influence that surveys would miss

Temporal analysis Real-time monitoring shows when attitudes shifted, allowing practitioners to correlate changes with specific interventions

Counterfactual modeling AI can simulate "what if" scenarios, comparing actual outcomes against projected baselines

A/B testing Digital platforms allow controlled experiments where AI-assisted and non-AI-assisted approaches can be compared directly

The WHO's EARS platform demonstrated this by tracking rumor half-life before and after corrections, providing evidence of intervention impact that retrospective surveys could not capture (Purnat et al. 2021). Similarly, UNICEF's U-Report can compare participation rates in countries with and without AI-enhanced chatbots, isolating the technology's contribution to engagement (UNICEF 2025).

Yet AI also makes attribution harder by introducing complexity:

Black box problem Machine learning systems often work in ways practitioners cannot fully explain, making it unclear what drove outcomes

Confounding variables AI interventions rarely occur in isolation, making it hard to separate their effects from simultaneous changes

Delayed impacts Diplomatic outcomes unfold over years, while AI systems are evaluated in months, creating temporal mismatches

Measurement bias If AI shapes both the intervention and the evaluation, it may systematically overstate its own effectiveness

The Republic of Z vignette illustrated this: the embassy's AI dashboard amplified urban alumni voices, creating an illusion of success that masked rural dissatisfaction. Attribution failed not because the AI was technically flawed but because it measured the wrong things.

Strategies for Responsible Attribution

Responsible attribution requires combining AI's analytical power with human judgment and mixed methods:

Triangulation Compare AI-derived metrics with traditional surveys, focus groups, and qualitative case studies. If dashboard sentiment improves but interviews reveal skepticism, something is being missed.

Temporal tracking Monitor trends before, during, and after AI deployment, checking whether changes align with intervention timing or reflect broader patterns.

Comparative analysis Where possible, compare outcomes in contexts with and without AI assistance. If two missions run similar programs but only one uses AI, differences in outcomes may suggest attribution.

Validator verification Ask trusted local voices—alumni, journalists, civil society—whether they perceive that AI interventions made a difference. Publics' own assessments of credibility offer ground truth that algorithms cannot replicate.

Error analysis Track where AI systems fail, not just where they succeed. A chatbot that escalates 30% of queries to humans is doing something—either the AI is weak, or the questions are appropriately complex—but attribution requires understanding which.

Humility in claims Acknowledge uncertainty openly. Rather than claiming "AI increased satisfaction by 15%," report "satisfaction increased 15% during the period when AI was deployed, though multiple factors likely contributed."

The Canadian approach to algorithmic impact assessments provides a model. By requiring institutions to document not just outcomes but also assumptions, limitations, and alternative explanations, Canada ensures that attribution claims remain honest (Government of Canada 2019). For diplomatic missions, this means treating evaluation as a hypothesis to test rather than a conclusion to defend.

PRACTITIONER GUIDANCE

The AI Mindset for Evaluation

Every evaluation makes a quiet political statement about whose voices count and which outcomes matter. AI sharpens the stakes: a model that decides what to measure has, in effect, already decided what will count as success. Dashboards can generate endless charts, sentiment scores, and keyword clusters, but unless practitioners adopt the right mindset, those numbers risk becoming an illusion of precision. To evaluate credibly, diplomats must approach AI not as an oracle that delivers answers, but as a tool that supports learning, humility, and inclusivity.

The first mindset shift is humility. AI can process data at speeds far beyond human capacity, but it cannot determine meaning on its own. A sentiment analysis might show that a campaign is "trending positive," but without context, such conclusions are fragile. Are publics genuinely supportive, or are they mocking the campaign with irony? Do the signals reflect broad sentiment, or only the most digitally visible communities? AI excels at counting, but it cannot interpret without human judgment. Evaluation therefore requires practitioners to treat dashboards as provisional, testing their claims against local knowledge and offline evidence.

A second principle is inclusivity. AI systems, if left unchecked, tend to amplify the voices already loudest: urban users, majority-language speakers, and digitally connected elites. The vignette in this chapter illustrated how alumni in the capital city dominated an embassy's evaluation metrics, while rural participants barely registered. An inclusive mindset demands deliberate correction. Equity audits that track who is represented—and who is missing—are not just technical safeguards but ethical imperatives. Inclusivity in evaluation is therefore not a luxury but a strategic necessity.

Transparency forms a third principle. Publics are increasingly aware that institutions use AI to measure their attitudes, and concealment breeds suspicion. When evaluation systems operate behind closed doors, publics may question whether they are being assessed fairly or manipulated. UNESCO's *Recommendation on the Ethics of Artificial Intelligence* (2021) and the EU's *AI Act* (2024) both call for transparency in public-facing AI applications. For evaluation, this means disclosing not only how data is collected but also how it is used to inform decisions. When missions explain openly that dashboards guide program adjustments, publics are more likely to see evaluation as stewardship rather than surveillance.

Finally, resilience underpins credible evaluation. AI systems are fragile in ways that traditional methods are not. They can be gamed by bots, manipulated by coordinated campaigns, or distorted by sudden platform changes. An evaluation based on social media sentiment, for example, may be skewed if adversaries flood channels with fake positive or negative responses, skewing results, and misleading decision-makers. The European Union's *AI Act* (2024) recognizes this danger by requiring explainability and provenance in high-risk applications. For diplomats, resilience means designing evaluation systems that account for manipulation, whether through anomaly detection, validator cross-checks, or safeguards against tampering.

Together, these principles—humility, inclusivity, transparency, and resilience—define the mindset required for AI-assisted evaluation. They ensure that measurement serves diplomacy's relational goals rather than becoming an end in itself. Without this mindset, dashboards risk becoming performance theater: impressive to look at but disconnected from the lived experiences of publics. With it, evaluation becomes what it should be: a tool for learning, adaptation, and accountability.

Risks, Ethics, and Compliance

Evaluation is where AI's risks are easiest to miss, precisely because the outputs look so authoritative. A page of sentiment scores and completion rates carries the weight of objectivity, yet the publics who never see the model still judge the institution by the decisions those numbers drive. When evaluation systems produce biased metrics, or when they exclude certain groups, citizens do not blame the algorithm—they blame the embassy, the ministry, or the government itself. This makes the ethical design of AI evaluation systems not a peripheral concern but central to the credibility of diplomacy.

The most immediate risk is depersonalization. Evaluation can become reductive when complex human experiences are translated into numerical scores. A dashboard showing "75% positive sentiment" may obscure the 25% who feel marginalized, dismissed, or excluded. Research shows that publics expect not only technical accuracy but also recognition that their lived experiences matter (Sutherland 2025). An evaluation system that reduces people to data points, no matter how elegant its visualizations, risks appearing indifferent.

A second risk is exclusion. Digital evaluation platforms often reflect the biases of their underlying datasets, overrepresenting urban, connected, majority-language users while neglecting rural communities and minority voices—the pattern U-Report's demographic audits revealed earlier in this chapter. The African Union's *Continental AI Strategy* (2024) treats such exclusion as a failure of the evaluation itself, not a rounding error.

Privacy presents a third risk. Evaluation requires collecting data about publics, and AI intensifies both the volume and sensitivity of this data. Alumni surveys may reveal career struggles, sentiment analysis may expose political views, and engagement platforms may track participation patterns. If publics discover that their data is being used in ways they did not consent to, or if data breaches occur, credibility can collapse. UNESCO's *Recommendation on the Ethics of Artificial Intelligence* (2021) requires that data collection be proportional to purpose, transparent about use, and protective of individual privacy. The EU's *AI Act* (2024) adds enforcement mechanisms, requiring explainability and accountability for high-risk evaluation systems.

Trust erosion is a fourth concern, especially when errors occur. As the Republic of Z vignette showed, evaluation systems that produce misleading results can cause institutions to make poor decisions, undermining both programs and reputations. Once evaluation is perceived as biased or inaccurate, publics may discount future assessments, even when they are valid. Continuous validation, error logging, and proactive transparency are therefore essential safeguards.

Finally, AI evaluation raises the risk of manipulation. Adversaries aware that institutions rely on social media metrics may flood platforms with fake positive or negative responses, skewing results and misleading decision-makers. The European Union's *AI Act* (2024) recognizes this danger by requiring explainability and provenance in high-risk applications.

These risks underscore why compliance with governance frameworks is not a box-ticking exercise but a strategic necessity. UNESCO, the OECD, the EU, and the African Union all stress transparency, inclusivity, and proportionality as essential guardrails. Adhering to these standards signals to publics that evaluation is conducted not as surveillance or institutional self-justification but as a practice of accountability.

Metrics for Credible Evaluation

If evaluation is to move beyond activity counts, it must focus on indicators that capture credibility, resonance, and resilience. Artificial intelligence can help generate these indicators, but the challenge lies in ensuring that they measure what matters rather than what is easiest to quantify. The risk, as scholars of digital diplomacy caution, is that metrics become ends in themselves, detached from the deeper relational outcomes that public diplomacy seeks to build (Bjola and Holmes 2015).

Inclusivity offers a third evaluative lens. AI systems can monitor the distribution of participation across languages, regions, and demographics, revealing whether engagement platforms are reaching marginalized communities or only the digitally privileged. Equity audits that compare online participation with national demographic data help identify who is absent from the conversation. As the African Union reminds us, inclusivity is not just a moral imperative but a measure of sovereignty and legitimacy (African Union 2024). A program that excludes significant portions of the public cannot claim success, no matter how impressive its dashboards appear.

Efficiency metrics also matter, though they must be contextualized. Time savings, such as the 26 minutes per day reported during the UK's Copilot trials (GDS 2025b), indicate that AI can reduce administrative burdens. But efficiency should not overshadow impact. A program that saves staff time but fails to build trust is not a success. Efficiency is best treated as a secondary metric—valuable when it enables staff to redirect effort toward higher-order relational work.

Finally, evaluation must track learning itself. Are missions adapting programs based on AI insights? Are error logs and misread records being reviewed to refine future strategies? AI makes continuous optimization possible, but without institutional learning, the data risks becoming decorative rather than transformative. Measuring adaptation—whether strategies shift in response to feedback—is perhaps the most important sign that evaluation is doing its job.

Reflection and Strategic Questions

Practitioners might ask themselves hard questions. Which of our metrics measure meaning, and which merely measure volume? When a dashboard flatters the mission, who is empowered to challenge it? Which publics does our evaluation hear clearly, and which remain statistically invisible? And is our evaluation designed to impress with numbers, or to build credibility through honest reflection?

FRONTIER AND NEAR-TERM PILOTS

While AI has already begun to reshape evaluation, the next wave of experiments suggests how the practice may evolve further. These frontier initiatives are still tentative, but they point toward a future in which optimization is not a retrospective exercise but a continuous, predictive process.

Predictive Modeling

One area of innovation is predictive modeling. By combining historical data with current social media trends, AI systems are being developed to forecast how publics are likely to respond to specific programs or policy announcements. In principle, this allows diplomats to anticipate outcomes before they occur, adjusting strategies proactively. A public diplomacy campaign on climate change, for example, could be modeled against past reactions to similar initiatives, predicting where resistance might emerge and where narratives are likely to resonate. The promise is foresight; the risk is overconfidence. Predictive models are only as good as their training data, and biased inputs can produce misleading forecasts. Used responsibly, predictive modeling can sharpen strategic awareness, but it must always be paired with humility about what cannot be foreseen.

Narrative Testing for Optimization

A second frontier involves narrative testing for optimization. Borrowing methods from marketing, some governments are experimenting with A/B testing of policy messages on small sample audiences, using AI to analyze which framings are most effective. For example, a message about sanctions might be tested in variants emphasizing fairness, security, or partnership, with real-time sentiment analysis guiding refinements before the message is released more broadly. The potential benefits are clear: greater clarity, fewer missteps, and more resonance across diverse publics. Yet the ethical stakes are high. If publics discover they were unknowingly subjected to narrative experiments, trust could erode. As Chapter 2 noted, transparency and restraint are essential if such testing is to enhance rather than undermine credibility.

Cross-Program Dashboards

A third emerging practice is the development of cross-program dashboards that integrate evaluation across multiple initiatives. Instead of measuring exchange programs, media campaigns, and cultural events separately, AI could consolidate their metrics into a single system, allowing missions to see how efforts reinforce—or sometimes contradict—each other. Early pilots suggest that such dashboards can reveal synergies, such as how alumni engagement amplifies messaging campaigns, or how cultural events influence online discourse. But integration also raises risks: reducing complex programs to comparable metrics may encourage a false sense of equivalence, obscuring the unique relational value of different forms of diplomacy.

Participatory Evaluation

Finally, frontier pilots are beginning to explore how evaluation itself can be made participatory. Platforms modeled on UNICEF's U-Report envision publics not only as subjects of evaluation but as co-creators of it, contributing feedback that shapes how success is defined. AI can help analyze this input at scale, clustering themes and identifying priorities. If scaled responsibly, such participatory evaluation could transform legitimacy, showing publics that their voices matter not only in programs but in the very metrics by which those programs are judged.

These frontiers illustrate both opportunity and danger. Predictive modeling, narrative testing, cross-program dashboards, and participatory evaluation could make diplomacy more adaptive, inclusive, and resilient. Yet they also carry the risk of overreach, manipulation, or reductionism. The challenge for practitioners will be to embrace experimentation while maintaining transparency, proportionality, and humility. In evaluation, as in every other stage of diplomacy, AI can expand capacity, but only ethical practice can sustain credibility.

CONCLUSION

By now you have walked through the stage of the diplomatic cycle where institutions face the hardest question: *did any of it work, and for whom?* AI is transforming that inquiry from expensive, retrospective surveys into continuous, adaptive learning—but the transformation carries risks as consequential as the efficiencies it delivers.

The thread running through every case study: evaluation is not a neutral act but a choice about whose voices count. The opening vignette gave you the distinction that defines the chapter—between a large dataset and a robust one. Silence in the data did not mean satisfaction; it meant invisibility. The trap is measuring what is easy to measure and defending it because the numbers are clean. The Pentagon explosion fake extended the point: narratives that fail to persuade for long can still reverberate through interconnected systems fast enough to do real damage.

You also now have a framework for the chapter's hardest analytical problem—attribution, the problem of determining what outcomes can be credibly linked to AI interventions when diplomatic results are shaped by countless confounding variables. Triangulation, temporal tracking, validator verification, and humility in claims give you a way to assess honestly rather than self-justify. The guiding principle is that dashboards are provisional instruments, not authoritative verdicts. Treat every metric as a hypothesis to test rather than a conclusion to defend.

These tools work in the steady state. The next chapter asks what happens when the time you have for assessment and response collapses from weeks into minutes. The missions that survive narrative crises are the ones that invested in preparedness, validator networks, and disciplined judgment before the emergency arrived—and that is the discipline Chapter 6 takes up.

6 Crisis Communication in the Age of AI

"The result of a consistent and total substitution of lies for factual truth is not that the lies will now be accepted as truth, and the truth be defamed as lies, but that the sense by which we take our bearings in the real world—and the category of truth vs. falsehood is among the mental means to this end—is being destroyed."

—Hannah Arendt, "Truth and Politics" (1967)

"We are increasingly seeing the weaponisation of context."

—Claire Wardle, "Understanding Information Disorder" (2019)

"By using viral campaigns, we make sure that factual humor spreads faster than rumor."

—Audrey Tang, "The Key to Taiwan's Pandemic Success: Fast, Fair … and Fun" (2020)

Opening Vignette: When the Clock Is Already Running

David Kim, the public affairs officer, had been in crisis mode before, but never quite like this. The video had appeared overnight—ninety seconds, apparently showing Ambassador Grant at a private reception, telling a small group that the Republic of Z's coalition government was "too fragile to last the year." By the time David arrived at 6:45, it had been shared 40,000 times across Telegram, Facebook, and TikTok. Two television stations had requested comment. Washington had sent a query marked urgent. It was not the first synthetic video to target the mission. The earlier fakes had unraveled under a careful check. This one would take real forensics, and forensics took hours the crisis would not give them.

Aisha Rahman, the mission's audience research and insights officer, was already at her workstation. "File timestamps don't match the upload date. Audio compression artifacts. Lip sync degrades in the second half." She turned the monitor toward David. "Forensic signals are consistent with synthetic generation—likely

DOI: 10.1201/9781003612377-8

a face swap using a generative adversarial network trained on publicly available footage. But full confirmation is 4 to 6 hours minimum." David looked at the dashboard. The mention spike was still climbing. "We don't have 4 hours."

Three months earlier, when a low-volume water contamination narrative had appeared in the eastern provinces, the team had waited, validated quietly, and let the story fade before it hardened. That playbook had worked because they had time—the narrative had not yet reached mainstream audiences. This was different. The crisis had arrived first. Lina Perez, the digital communications officer, appeared in the doorway. "The opposition party just called for the ambassador's expulsion. It's on the wire."

Ambassador Grant joined them 10 minutes later, calm in the way experienced diplomats are calm when the situation is genuinely serious. "Walk me through what we know and what we don't." Aisha laid it out. Forensic indicators suggested synthetic origin but were unconfirmed. The video had appeared simultaneously on three unrelated accounts—coordinated seeding, not organic spread. The reception setting matched an event the ambassador had attended six weeks earlier.

Ambassador Grant turned to Farid Tessam, a locally employed cultural affairs assistant with deep community ties across the country. "How is this landing?" Farid had already spoken with two contacts and a journalist. "Credible to people who already distrust the mission. Skeptical reception from those who trust us. The question is which group is louder today."

The decision took under 20 minutes. The ambassador would not wait for full forensic confirmation—silence was too costly. But a categorical denial risked looking defensive if anything in the video proved ambiguous. Instead: a calm public appearance speaking to what he actually believed about the coalition government, letting that statement do the work of contrast. Simultaneously, Aisha would brief two independent digital rights analysts and ask them to publish their own forensic assessments. Farid would contact the journalist network directly, providing technical background without attribution.

"We are not the most credible voice on our own credibility," Ambassador Grant said before leaving for the camera. "We never are. Our job is to give the people who are credible the information they need."

The ambassador spoke for 4 minutes at noon—reaffirming respect for Zorani democratic institutions, no mention of the video. By mid-afternoon, two independent analysts had published forensic assessments raising serious doubts about its authenticity. Three journalists led with the technical questions rather than the political accusation. By evening the dominant narrative had shifted from "ambassador caught speaking privately" to "fabricated video targets U.S. mission." Some publics remained unconvinced. But the center had held.

At the debrief, Lina reflected on what had changed since the water contamination episode. "Three months ago I wanted to respond to 200 posts immediately. Today I understood why we couldn't wait. Crisis communication isn't one playbook—it's knowing which one applies." David nodded. "The AI gave us the early warning and the forensic signals. The judgment calls—when to go public, what to say, who to trust to carry the message—none of that came from the dashboard."

FRAMING THE CHAPTER

Crisis has always been the harshest test of diplomacy. Unlike routine communication, where messages can be refined through deliberation and engagement can be scaled over time, crisis communication unfolds under intense pressure. Publics are anxious, narratives evolve by the minute, and adversaries exploit the fog of uncertainty. In such moments, credibility is fragile, and even small missteps can cascade into lasting reputational damage. What makes crisis communication distinctive is not only the urgency of speed but the impossibility of certainty. Decisions must be made before all the facts are known, and publics will judge institutions as much by how they respond as by what they say.

Artificial intelligence has transformed the possibilities of crisis response. Machine learning systems can detect anomalous spikes in conversation, flag potential disinformation, and help draft or translate rapid rebuttals. Provenance tools can signal when a video is likely manipulated, while chatbots can handle surges of public inquiries when phone lines collapse under demand. Properly deployed, these systems can give diplomats the precious minutes they need to act before rumors solidify into belief. Yet AI also magnifies the risks. Automated systems may produce false positives, spreading confusion if institutions deny an event that later proves real. Dashboards can pressure missions into overreacting, amplifying fringe content that might otherwise have faded. In a crisis, speed is essential, but so is restraint.

Within the framework of this book, crisis communication belongs to the strategic domain of *narrative defense under extreme conditions*. Of the six categories of real-world deployment, it intersects most directly with *counter-disinformation and authenticity verification*, while also drawing on *narrative intelligence and early warning*. What sets it apart from the earlier chapters is the compression of time. Listening, messaging, monitoring, and engagement unfold in cycles that allow for adjustment; crisis communication unfolds in minutes, with little margin for error.

This chapter builds on the tools introduced earlier but situates them in the most demanding environment. Listening provides early warning, messaging articulates intent, monitoring tracks distortion, and engagement builds trust through interaction. In a crisis, all of these functions are called upon simultaneously, compressed into a narrow window where decisions must be made under uncertainty. The central question is whether AI can help diplomats act fast enough to be credible without acting so fast that they sacrifice accuracy or empathy.

This chapter develops that dilemma in three ways. Conceptually, it examines how AI changes the dynamics of rumor, panic, and adversarial manipulation during crises. Practically, it outlines workflows for integrating AI tools into detection, validation, and rapid response while avoiding overreaction. Strategically, it addresses the ethical boundaries of crisis communication, asking how institutions can remain transparent and proportional when publics are fearful and disinformation is rampant. In short, it argues that while AI can accelerate crisis response, credibility will always rest on human presence and judgment.

RESEARCH AND POLICY FOUNDATIONS

Crisis communication has always been a central concern of diplomacy. In moments of sudden upheaval—whether political violence, natural disaster, or pandemic—institutions are judged not only on what they say but on how quickly and credibly they say it. Scholars of crisis management note that publics evaluate responses less on the precision of facts delivered than on the perception of transparency, empathy, and timeliness (Coombs 2014). In the digital age, this challenge has intensified. Rumors spread globally within minutes, synthetic media blur the boundary between true and false, and adversaries exploit confusion to undermine trust. The imperative to respond swiftly collides with the risk of making mistakes.

The fragility of digital rumor has been highlighted repeatedly in research. Studies of misinformation show that falsehoods often spread faster and deeper than corrections, particularly in moments of uncertainty (Vosoughi, Roy, and Aral 2018). Bjola and Manor (2022) emphasize that disinformation thrives in the gaps between events and institutional responses, weaponizing delay. NATO StratCom's "golden quarter-hour" simulations, introduced in Chapter 3, reinforce the point: hostile narratives can dominate an uncontested information space within minutes (NATO StratCom COE 2024, n.d.). AI can help detect these narratives quickly (Juršėnas et al. 2022), but institutions must be prepared to act proportionately within this compressed window.

Global governance frameworks reflect growing recognition of the risks. UNESCO's *Recommendation on the Ethics of Artificial Intelligence* (2021) stresses proportionality and accountability, principles especially important in emergencies where mistakes carry heightened costs. The European Union's *AI Act* (2024) mandates provenance labeling for synthetic media, a safeguard directly relevant to the problem of deepfakes in crises. The OECD's updated *AI Principles* (2024) call for fairness and explainability, reminding policymakers that the speed of AI outputs cannot excuse the need for justification. The G7's *Hiroshima Code of Conduct* (2023) commits democratic states to transparency in the deployment of AI, including in crisis communication, signaling that legitimacy depends not only on content but on process.

These foundations underscore a paradox at the heart of AI-enabled crisis response. On one hand, AI provides unprecedented speed and scale, allowing diplomats to detect and respond to narratives before they metastasize. On the other, crises magnify the risks of error, overreaction, and mistrust. Credibility in such contexts depends not only on what AI reveals but on how institutions choose to act on those revelations—with humility, empathy, and proportionality.

TECHNICAL CAPABILITIES

AI-Enabled Early Warning and Anomaly Detection

Artificial intelligence has transformed the tempo of this equation. Natural language processing can flag spikes in rumor activity, clustering narratives that signal emerging crises. Image and video forensics can detect anomalies suggestive of deepfakes, providing early warning that manipulation is underway. Generative systems can draft initial statements in multiple languages, allowing missions to communicate faster than ever before. In principle, these tools allow diplomats to keep pace with the velocity of digital crises. Yet scholars caution that technological speed is not the same as communicative credibility. Henry Kissinger, Eric Schmidt, and Daniel Huttenlocher (2021) argue that AI produces "knowledge without understanding," a liability in crises where empathy and cultural nuance matter as much as accuracy.

REAL-WORLD APPLICATIONS

Several real-world cases already demonstrate how AI is reshaping the practice of crisis communication. These examples show both the promise of technology in moments of high pressure and its limits when publics demand clarity, empathy, and trust.

Ukraine's Zelenskyy Deepfake: Detection and Validator Amplification

Ukraine's experience during the Russian invasion in 2022 offered one of the earliest glimpses into the role of AI in countering synthetic media. When a deepfake video appeared showing President Volodymyr Zelenskyy allegedly urging Ukrainian troops to surrender, the clip spread quickly across Telegram and fringe outlets. AI-enabled forensics flagged the anomalies—lip movements out of sync, audio mismatches, metadata inconsistencies—but detection alone was insufficient. The crisis was contained because Ukrainian officials, validators in civil society, and allied governments moved quickly to amplify the debunk. The lesson was stark: AI can identify manipulation, but only trusted human voices can neutralize it in real time.

Taiwan's CECC Chatbot

Among the most instructive examples of AI in crisis communication is Taiwan's *Central Epidemic Command Center* (CECC) chatbot, deployed in May 2020 during the COVID-19 pandemic. As the virus spread globally and information ecosystems fractured into competing narratives, Taiwan faced a particular challenge: how to provide accurate, timely information to a diverse public that included both Mandarin-speaking citizens and a significant population of English-speaking foreign residents, all while managing unprecedented demand for official guidance.

Deployment Context and Technical Design

The CECC chatbot was launched on Google Assistant as a bilingual (Chinese and English) crisis communication tool designed to answer frequently asked questions about testing locations, quarantine requirements, mask policies, and travel restrictions (Taiwan CDC 2020). Unlike generative AI systems that compose responses dynamically, the chatbot relied on a curated knowledge base maintained and updated daily by public health officials. This design choice prioritized accuracy over flexibility: every answer was pre-written and human-verified, reducing the risk of hallucinations or outdated information that could have fueled panic.

The system was intentionally scoped to handle routine queries, with built-in escalation logic to direct users to hotlines when questions involved individual medical circumstances, legal exceptions, or emotional distress. Here too, the design turned on a simple division of labor: the system delivered information at speed, while the reassurance that steadies a frightened public came only from people. The chatbot did not replace CECC's daily press briefings or its active presence on social media; rather, it complemented them by relieving pressure on overwhelmed phone lines and allowing staff to focus on complex cases requiring judgment (*Taipei Times* 2020).

Results and Operational Challenges

The chatbot handled thousands of queries during the height of the pandemic, particularly from non-Mandarin speakers who previously had limited access to real-time information. Anecdotal evidence from foreign residents suggested it reduced panic by providing clear, consistent answers to common concerns. The bilingual capacity proved especially valuable in a context where English-language information often lagged behind Mandarin announcements by hours or days.

Yet the system's fragility became apparent quickly. Because COVID-19 policies evolved daily—sometimes hourly—the knowledge base required constant maintenance. Any delay in updating the chatbot risked spreading outdated guidance, which could have been as harmful as spreading misinformation. Public health officials worked evening shifts to review and update content, a labor-intensive process that underscored the hidden costs of seemingly "automated" crisis systems. When the acute phase of the pandemic subsided, the chatbot was retired, a reminder that crisis tools designed for speed may not be sustainable for long-term use.

The Taiwan case demonstrates that AI can enhance crisis communication, but only when institutions accept its limitations and invest in the human infrastructure—updates, oversight, escalation—that makes automation credible. The chatbot was a success not because it was sophisticated but because it was appropriately scoped, rigorously maintained, and transparently positioned as a tool, not a replacement, for human engagement.

Canada's Rapid Response Mechanism: Coordinated Campaign Detection in Crisis

While Taiwan's chatbot addressed information provision during a health crisis, Canada's *Rapid Response Mechanism* (RRM) demonstrates AI's role in detecting and exposing adversarial manipulation campaigns that threaten democratic institutions. Established as part of the G7 RRM initiative, Canada's system uses network analysis and anomaly detection to identify coordinated inauthentic behavior targeting Canadian officials, journalists, and public discourse.

Spamouflage Campaigns: October 2023 and March 2025

The RRM gained prominence through two high-profile advisories documenting "Spamouflage" operations—coordinated networks using AI-generated or bot-amplified content to target Canadian politicians and Chinese-language journalists. The first advisory, issued October 23, 2023, exposed a campaign targeting Members of Parliament with fabricated social media posts and synthetic personas designed to appear as concerned citizens (Global Affairs Canada 2023). The operation sought to influence Canadian debate on foreign policy issues through seemingly organic grassroots activity.

The second advisory, released March 6, 2025, documented a more sophisticated variant targeting Chinese-language journalists and media outlets in Canada. The campaign used AI-generated content to spread false narratives about these journalists' credibility, apparently aiming to suppress independent reporting on issues sensitive to foreign interests (Global Affairs Canada 2025). Network analysis revealed coordination patterns—simultaneous posting across multiple platforms, identical phrasing, and amplification by accounts with suspicious activity histories—that human analysts alone would have struggled to detect at scale.

Detection Methodology and AI Integration

The RRM combines AI-enabled anomaly detection with human expertise. Machine learning systems flag unusual patterns in social media activity: sudden surges in posts about specific politicians, coordinated use of hashtags, or networks of accounts exhibiting non-human behavior. These signals are then investigated by analysts with expertise in both digital forensics and the political context of targeted narratives. The system does not automatically label content as disinformation; rather, it identifies patterns requiring human evaluation.

This hybrid approach proved essential. In the October 2023 case, AI detected the coordination but human analysts determined the political intent and assessed the campaign's potential impact on parliamentary proceedings. In the March 2025 case, understanding required cultural and linguistic expertise that algorithms could not provide—recognizing how narratives would be interpreted within Chinese-Canadian communities and why targeting specific journalists served foreign influence objectives.

Public Advisories as Crisis Communication

What distinguished Canada's approach was its decision to issue public advisories rather than respond quietly. By documenting the campaigns and making findings public, Canada achieved several objectives: it inoculated publics against the manipulation (awareness itself can reduce effectiveness), it demonstrated transparency in defending democratic institutions, and it provided evidence for Canada's Foreign Interference Commission inquiry (Foreign Interference Commission 2025). This transparency carried risks—adversaries learned about detection capabilities—but Canada judged that democratic accountability required openness.

The advisories themselves became a form of crisis communication. They acknowledged the threat without overstating it, provided evidence without revealing all intelligence sources, and framed foreign interference as a challenge requiring societal resilience rather than panic. The RRM demonstrated that crisis communication in the context of adversarial manipulation is not just about responding to specific incidents but about building long-term credibility through transparency and restraint.

The Canadian model illustrates that AI-enabled crisis communication extends beyond responding to organic emergencies (like pandemics) to detecting and exposing adversarial operations designed to manufacture crises. In this context, transparency and public education become forms of crisis prevention, building societal resilience before manipulation can take hold.

WHO EARS in Crisis: Rumor Tracking during the COVID-19 Infodemic

The World Health Organization's *EARS* platform, introduced in Chapter 1 and revisited in Chapter 5 as an evaluation tool, also functioned as a crisis communication system during the COVID-19 pandemic. Originally developed for infodemic management, EARS tracked rumors about vaccines, treatments, and preventive measures across countries and languages. By measuring how quickly specific falsehoods spread and decayed, WHO was able to adjust its communications more responsively (Purnat et al. 2021). In effect, EARS turned rumor surveillance into a form of real-time evaluation, helping authorities focus on which interventions mattered most.

What made EARS particularly valuable in crisis contexts was its ability to reveal geographic and temporal patterns in misinformation spread. A rumor about hydroxychloroquine might gain traction in Latin America before appearing in Asia, giving WHO early warning to prepare responses for affected regions. The system tracked the appearance and evolution of false claims over time, offering a basis for assessing whether corrective communication was gaining traction. This dynamic feedback loop allowed WHO to test which communication strategies worked: validator amplification, translated fact sheets, or social media debunks.

Yet EARS also revealed the limits of automated crisis monitoring. Sarcasm, irony, and culturally specific humor often confused the natural language processing systems, sometimes misclassifying satirical posts as genuine misinformation. Cultural context proved essential: a phrase that signaled panic in one country might be a common expression in another. Human analysts remained indispensable for interpreting what algorithms detected, a reminder that even sophisticated AI systems require judgment to function credibly in crises.

NATO StratCom: The Golden Quarter-Hour

NATO's Strategic Communications Centre of Excellence has used simulations to test how quickly disinformation can dominate an information space during crises. These exercises revealed what many practitioners now call the "golden quarter-hour"—the 15-minute window before hostile narratives establish themselves as the frame through which events are understood (NATO StratCom COE 2024, n.d.). AI monitoring systems play a key role in these exercises, detecting anomalies in real time, but NATO's findings emphasize that technology alone cannot guarantee success. Preparedness and rehearsed workflows are just as important. Institutions must be ready to decide not only how to respond but whether to respond at all.

Israel: Validator Networks under Conflict Pressure

Israel's reliance on validator networks during conflict illustrates yet another dimension of AI-assisted crisis communication. AI tools helped identify suspicious narratives in Arabic and Persian media, but credibility came from validators—journalists, civil society leaders, and diaspora figures—who could echo corrections in their own voices. By combining automated detection with human amplification, Israel sought to counter rumors before they metastasized into widespread belief.

Synthetic Narratives in Action: "All Eyes on Rafah" (2024)

In May 2024, a striking image began spreading across Instagram and TikTok: neat rows of tents arranged to spell the words "All Eyes on Rafah." The visual was stylized, almost too clean to be real, but that did not matter. It became a global rallying cry, shared by celebrities and millions of ordinary users, drawing attention to the humanitarian crisis in Rafah, Gaza. What made the image powerful was not its accuracy as a photograph—it was AI-generated—but its ability to condense a complex crisis into a single emblematic frame.

The picture was legible across languages and cultures, requiring no captions to communicate its message. As a result, it outperformed traditional news photography in virality, setting the tone for online conversations about the conflict. The Rafah image demonstrates both the promise and peril of synthetic media in crises. On the one hand, it mobilized global awareness and solidarity. On the other, it risked oversimplifying a humanitarian tragedy into a meme, potentially displacing nuanced reporting with aesthetic symbolism.

For those studying public diplomacy, the case shows how crisis communication in the AI era requires grappling with visuals that may be more effective as advocacy than as evidence. The challenge lies in balancing empathy-driven engagement with fidelity to reality (Al Jazeera 2024b; Subzwari 2024).

RAPID TRANSLATION AND MULTILINGUAL CRISIS RESPONSE

One of AI's most valuable contributions to crisis communication is its ability to provide instant multilingual translation, ensuring that urgent information reaches diverse publics simultaneously. In moments of emergency—natural disasters, security incidents, public health crises—the ability to communicate clearly in multiple languages can be the difference between panic and calm, between confusion and coordinated response.

The Translation Challenge in Crises

Traditional translation workflows, even when expedited, introduce delays that crises cannot afford. A press release drafted in English may take hours to translate into

Spanish, Arabic, Mandarin, and French through human translators, by which time rumors have already filled the information vacuum. Crises affecting multicultural societies or international populations—embassies serving diverse expatriate communities, UN missions in multilingual regions, international organizations responding to global emergencies—face the impossible choice between speed and linguistic inclusivity.

Neural machine translation (NMT) systems have matured to the point where they can provide near-instant translation across dozens of languages with accuracy sufficient for crisis communication. The European Commission's eTranslation service, operational since 2017, demonstrates this capability by providing translation across 24 official EU languages within seconds (European Commission 2017). During COVID-19, the system handled surges in translation demand as member states rushed to communicate changing health guidance to diverse populations.

Taiwan's Bilingual Model Revisited

Taiwan's CECC chatbot illustrated this in practice. By providing simultaneous Chinese and English responses, it ensured that foreign residents—who constituted a significant minority in Taiwan and often lacked access to real-time health information—received guidance as quickly as Mandarin speakers. This eliminated the two-tier information system that typically develops during crises, where native speakers receive updates first and minority language communities lag behind, breeding resentment and mistrust.

The bilingual design also served diplomatic purposes. International media monitoring Taiwan's COVID-19 response could access official information directly in English, reducing the risk of mistranslation or mischaracterization. This proved valuable as Taiwan sought to share its public health successes globally despite limited formal diplomatic recognition.

Operational Considerations for Multilingual Crisis Systems

Deploying AI translation in crisis contexts requires careful attention to quality, cultural appropriateness, and workflow integration:

Post-editing remains essential for high-stakes content While NMT can provide immediate drafts, critical statements—especially those addressing fatalities, security threats, or policy changes—should be reviewed by human translators before release. The European Commission's model combines AI speed with human oversight: machine translation for routine content, human post-editing for sensitive material.

Cultural adaptation goes beyond literal translation A crisis message that works in English may be culturally inappropriate or ambiguous when translated literally into Arabic, Mandarin, or Swahili. The UN's eLUNa system, which integrates translation with terminology databases, helps ensure that not just words but concepts are conveyed appropriately across cultures (United Nations 2022).

Training data quality determines crisis performance NMT systems trained primarily on formal documents may struggle with the colloquial language and rapid evolution of crisis terminology. Systems deployed for crisis use should be trained or fine-tuned on emergency communication corpora to handle phrases like "shelter in place," "community transmission," or "coordinated inauthentic behavior."

Minority languages require deliberate investment Commercial translation systems perform well for major languages but may be inadequate for minority languages or regional dialects that matter most in specific crises. The African Union's emphasis on linguistic inclusivity is particularly relevant here: crisis systems that function only in dominant languages exclude precisely those communities that may be most vulnerable (African Union 2024).

Verification and correction pathways must be clear Even excellent translation systems make errors. Crises require mechanisms for quickly correcting mistranslations that reach publics, whether through updated advisories or validator amplification. The Taiwan model—daily knowledge base updates—demonstrates this principle applied to content maintenance.

The International Telecommunication Union Model

The International Telecommunication Union's (ITU) deployment of its own neural machine translation system illustrates how AI can enhance multilingual inclusivity within international governance. ITU Translate provides immediate automated translation for documents and web content across the organization's six official languages (Arabic, Chinese, English, French, Russian, and Spanish). While it does not replace human interpretation for high-level negotiations, it significantly accelerates the flow of technical information. In the context of telecommunications policy, the system ensures that complex guidelines—such as those regarding spectrum management and disaster relief protocols—are accessible to experts globally, regardless of their primary working language (ITU 2022; 2023; 2024).

The system's value lies in informational equity. Developing countries participating in ITU regulatory processes can access critical technical documentation in their languages immediately, rather than waiting days or weeks for manual translation. This democratization of access strengthens international cooperation by ensuring that language barriers do not delay the dissemination of vital telecommunications standards.

Future Directions: Real-Time Interpretation and Multimodal Translation

Emerging AI capabilities point toward even more ambitious multilingual crisis tools. Real-time speech-to-speech translation could allow live press briefings to be interpreted simultaneously into multiple languages, expanding reach without the logistics of human interpretation booths. Multimodal systems that translate not just text but also images (signs, infographics, and social media posts) could help missions monitor crisis information in languages they do not have staff to cover.

Yet these advances carry risks. Real-time systems operating without human review may introduce errors that spread before correction is possible. The temptation to over-rely on automation could lead missions to neglect building human language capacity, creating long-term vulnerabilities. And as always, the question of who is included—which languages receive investment in translation systems—remains a matter of power and equity, not just technology.

Rapid translation is not a luxury in crisis communication; it is an equity and credibility imperative. Publics who cannot access timely information in their languages are more vulnerable to misinformation and less likely to trust official sources. The European Commission, UN, ITU, and Taiwan examples demonstrate that rapid multilingual response is achievable, but it requires institutional commitment: preparing for multilingual crisis communication means investing in translation infrastructure before emergencies occur, not improvising when they arrive.

PRACTITIONER GUIDANCE

For practitioners, crises are the moments when public diplomacy is judged most harshly. Messages that might be forgiven in routine circumstances are scrutinized word by word, and publics often remember not only what was said but how it was said. Artificial intelligence offers diplomats new tools to respond at speed, but without disciplined practice, those tools can expose institutions to reputational damage precisely when credibility is most fragile.

The AI Mindset for Crisis Response

In a crisis, diplomats lose the two things they most rely on: time and certainty. Unlike routine messaging, where deliberation and review are possible, crises compress decision-making into minutes. Rumors spread faster than facts, publics demand immediate reassurance, and adversaries exploit hesitation. In such an environment, artificial intelligence offers diplomats the gift of time—flagging anomalies, drafting statements, and detecting manipulated media before human analysts could possibly react. Yet the speed AI provides can be a double-edged sword. Without the right mindset, haste can undermine credibility as quickly as delay.

The first principle is balancing speed with accuracy. NATO StratCom's simulations remind us that hostile narratives can dominate within a quarter of an hour if uncontested. But a rapid denial issued without validation risks amplifying a falsehood or misidentifying legitimate debate as disinformation. AI can detect anomalies, but it cannot decide when a response will help and when it will do harm. Diplomats must cultivate disciplined agility: moving quickly to investigate, preparing drafts in advance, but acting publicly only when proportionate and credible.

The second principle is empathy over efficiency. In crises, publics are not just information-seeking; they are fearful, grieving, or angry. Chatbots and AI assistants can answer questions, but they cannot provide reassurance. Taiwan's COVID-19 chatbot relieved pressure on hotlines, but only human officials could convey compassion in press briefings. In crisis communication, credibility depends as much on tone as on speed. AI can scale facts, but empathy must come from people.

Transparency is the third principle, and in crisis it becomes a shield against suspicion. If publics discover they were interacting with AI without disclosure, they may see automation as concealment at a moment when honesty is most needed. The EU's *AI Act* (2024) requires disclosure for precisely this reason. By labeling AI outputs clearly and emphasizing human oversight, institutions can transform automation from a liability into a demonstration of accountability. In crises, when publics are prone to doubt, transparency is not optional—it is strategic.

Finally, crisis communication requires proportionality. Not every rumor deserves immediate rebuttal, and not every anomaly flagged by AI should trigger public statements. The paradox of amplification is particularly acute in emergencies, when government denials can spread fringe narratives to wider audiences. WHO's practice of categorizing rumors by severity illustrates how triage can help avoid this trap (Purnat et al. 2021). Diplomats must learn when to respond loudly, when to counter quietly through validators, and when to let falsehoods die on their own.

Taken together, these principles define an AI mindset for crisis communication. In moments of crisis, when every word is parsed for sincerity, the measure of success is not how quickly institutions respond but whether publics believe them when they do.

Crisis Communication Workflows

Mindset provides the compass, but in a crisis, workflows are what keep institutions from losing their way. Rumors can spread in minutes, synthetic media can reach millions before breakfast, and publics demand clarity even when facts are still emerging. In such conditions, crisis communication requires structured routines that integrate AI detection with human judgment, ensuring that speed does not come at the expense of credibility.

The workflow begins with detection. AI systems are now capable of scanning social media and messaging platforms for sudden spikes in keywords, hashtags, or images that deviate from baseline patterns. A surge in mentions of an ambassador's name, a video spreading unusually fast, or a new phrase appearing across multiple platforms can all be signs of a brewing crisis. But detection is only the first step. As the Zelenskyy deepfake episode in Ukraine demonstrated, anomalies must be examined critically: is the signal genuine, manipulated, or even a decoy planted to distract from something else?

Validation follows quickly. Locally employed staff, with their cultural and linguistic knowledge, are indispensable in interpreting whether anomalies reflect genuine sentiment or engineered amplification. Trusted validator networks—journalists, academics, and civil society actors—provide external confirmation, helping missions avoid the trap of treating every spike as urgent. In practice, missions that keep "misread logs" during crises build valuable institutional memory, documenting how systems have erred in the past and refining their responses accordingly.

Once anomalies are validated, the next stage is triage. Not every rumor requires a full public rebuttal, and not every manipulated video warrants a press conference. Crisis communication teams must assess scale, velocity, potential harm, and offline consequences before deciding how to act. The World Health Organization's use of rumor categorization during COVID-19 offers a model: minor falsehoods may be monitored quietly, while narratives with significant potential to endanger public safety demand immediate correction. The key is proportionate response, avoiding both paralysis and overreaction.

Authenticity checks are increasingly integrated into these workflows. AI-enabled forensic tools can identify telltale signs of synthetic media—lip-sync errors, mismatched metadata, or improbable shadows in images. Emerging provenance standards, such as those developed by the Coalition for Content Provenance and Authenticity (C2PA), embed metadata into files that can verify whether a video or image has been altered. In crises where trust is thin, being able to demonstrate why a piece of content is manipulated can make corrections more persuasive.

The final stage is coordinated response. Drafts prepared by generative AI can accelerate the release of multilingual statements, but human officers must refine them for tone and context. Some crises call for quiet corrections delivered through validators, others for official clarifications on social media, and the most severe for visible interventions such as live press conferences. Reporting chains must be clear, ensuring that responses are approved and disseminated before the crisis narrative hardens. NATO StratCom's exercises show that institutions that rehearse these workflows in advance respond faster and with fewer errors when the real thing arrives.

Together, these workflows transform AI from a reactive tool into an integral part of crisis preparedness. In the chaos of a crisis, they provide the discipline that turns minutes saved into credibility preserved.

Risks, Ethics, and Compliance

No setting punishes an AI misstep faster than a crisis. Speed, scale, and reach are what make these systems useful under pressure and, in the same instant, what turn a single error into a widely amplified one before anyone can catch it. In moments of heightened tension, publics scrutinize every message for signs of sincerity, adversaries actively manipulate the information space, and institutions are under immense pressure to act quickly. In such circumstances, the ethical stakes of AI-assisted crisis response are especially high.

The most obvious dilemma is the balance between speed and accuracy. NATO StratCom's simulations have shown that hostile narratives can dominate an information space in as little as 15 minutes, leaving little time for deliberation. Yet haste can be costly. A premature denial, issued before facts are validated, may inadvertently lend legitimacy to a falsehood or, worse, discredit the institution if the claim later proves true. The paradox is that both delay and error can damage credibility. AI can help buy time, but ultimately it is human judgment that determines when a response is ready to be released.

Amplification is a second risk. By reacting too quickly or too publicly, governments may give fringe rumors more visibility than they would otherwise have achieved. Research on misinformation has shown that repeating a falsehood, even in the act of debunking, can reinforce it in public memory (Lewandowsky et al. 2020). The World Health Organization's decision to categorize rumors by severity during COVID-19 reflected this concern: some narratives were monitored quietly, while only the most harmful were publicly corrected (Purnat et al. 2021). The ethical challenge for diplomats is knowing when silence is prudent and when intervention is necessary.

A third risk lies in adversarial manipulation. Just as AI is used to detect disinformation, it is also used to generate it. Deepfakes, synthetic personas, and coordinated bot networks are designed to overwhelm dashboards, forcing institutions into overreaction or confusion. Ukraine's deepfake crisis in 2022 illustrated how adversaries deploy synthetic media to provoke hasty denials or sow doubt about official voices. AI detection tools can help, but they are not foolproof, and adversaries often evolve faster than systems can adapt. This asymmetry means that human resilience—through rehearsed workflows and trusted validator networks—remains essential.

Public perception presents another layer of risk. In crises, publics may already be skeptical of official communication. Discovering that they are receiving AI-generated responses without disclosure can reinforce suspicion that institutions are hiding something. The EU's *AI Act* (2024) directly addresses this by requiring that users be informed when they interact with AI systems, while UNESCO's *Recommendation on the Ethics of Artificial Intelligence* (2021) emphasizes proportionality and accountability. For diplomats, this means that transparency is not only a regulatory requirement but a strategic necessity in preserving trust.

These risks make compliance with governance frameworks more than a formality. The OECD's *AI Principles* (2024) stress explainability, reminding practitioners that decisions must be justified even under time pressure. The African Union's *Continental AI Strategy* (2024) highlights inclusivity as a safeguard, warning against systems that exclude minority languages during emergencies. The G7's *Hiroshima Code of Conduct* (2023) commits democratic states to transparency in AI use, including in crisis communication. These frameworks converge on a simple but demanding standard: crises require speed, but not at the expense of fairness, accountability, or legitimacy.

The paradox of AI in crisis communication is clear. It gives diplomats tools to act faster than ever, but it also tempts them to sacrifice the very qualities—accuracy, empathy, and transparency—that publics look for in moments of fear. The challenge is not to resist AI but to use it with discipline, embedding ethical safeguards into workflows so that credibility is preserved even when time is short.

Metrics and Evaluation

Measuring the effectiveness of crisis communication has always been difficult. Success is rarely about the number of statements issued or the volume of information shared. What matters is whether publics trust the response, whether rumors lose traction, and whether the institution emerges from the crisis with credibility intact. Artificial intelligence introduces new ways of measuring these outcomes, but it also demands caution: metrics can illuminate patterns, yet they can also tempt diplomats to confuse speed or volume with legitimacy.

One of the most important indicators in crisis contexts is detection-to-response time. NATO StratCom's exercises showed that adversarial narratives could dominate within 15 minutes if left uncontested (Pamment 2022). AI monitoring tools can detect anomalies quickly, but the real question is how long it takes institutions to validate them and issue a proportionate response. Tracking detection-to-response times allows missions to assess whether workflows are agile enough to meet the tempo of digital crises. A delay of hours can be catastrophic; a delay of minutes may be the difference between containment and escalation (NATO StratCom COE 2024, n.d.).

Rumor half-life, first popularized by WHO during COVID-19, offers another valuable measure. By monitoring how long misinformation persists after correction, diplomats can evaluate the effectiveness of their interventions (Purnat et al. 2021). A shortening half-life suggests resilience—that publics are absorbing corrections and validators are amplifying them effectively. A persistent rumor, by contrast, indicates either weak messaging or insufficient trust in the messenger. In crises, tracking rumor half-life helps institutions distinguish between narratives that fade quickly and those that require sustained attention.

Validator amplification provides a third critical metric. AI can map which validators—journalists, civil society leaders, or alumni—pick up crisis responses and how widely their networks carry them. The success of Ukraine's response to the Zelenskyy deepfake depended not only on official denial but on validators echoing the debunk across multiple platforms. Evaluating who amplifies corrections, how quickly, and with what effect provides insight into which partnerships matter most under pressure.

Finally, provenance adoption is emerging as a measure of credibility in crises shaped by synthetic media. As standards like the Coalition for Content Provenance and Authenticity (C2PA) gain traction, diplomats will be able to track how often content is accompanied by authenticity metadata and whether publics recognize and trust these signals. Over time, provenance metrics may become as important as traditional communication indicators, providing a new layer of evaluation in environments where deepfakes are common.

Together, these metrics reframe evaluation for crises: they emphasize outcomes rather than outputs, focusing on whether publics believe the response and whether misinformation loses ground.

Reflection and Strategic Questions

Before crises occur, missions must address hard questions. How quickly can our detection-to-response workflow move from anomaly to public statement? Which validators are ready to amplify corrections credibly? When should we disclose that AI tools are part of our crisis response, and how do we ensure publics see this as a strength rather than a liability? And perhaps most importantly, what are the thresholds for silence—moments when restraint is the wiser choice?

FRONTIER AND NEAR-TERM PILOTS

While crisis communication with AI is already being tested in contexts like health emergencies and armed conflict, the next generation of tools points toward more ambitious and experimental practices. These frontier initiatives are still emerging, but they suggest how institutions might prepare for crises that are faster, more complex, and more contested than ever before.

One promising area is crisis simulation and narrative wargaming. Borrowing from military exercises, some governments and think tanks are exploring how AI can simulate adversarial information campaigns to stress-test institutional responses. RAND and Carnegie researchers have argued that narrative wargaming can expose vulnerabilities before a real crisis hits, allowing communicators to rehearse counter-messaging strategies (Mazarr et al. 2019). NATO StratCom has already demonstrated how quickly hostile narratives can dominate if left unchecked; AI-driven simulations take this further by modeling multiple "what if" scenarios. The promise is better preparedness, but the risk is false confidence. Simulations can only predict based on past data, and real-world crises often unfold in ways models cannot anticipate.

A second frontier involves AI-driven triage systems for rumor detection. Instead of flagging every anomaly equally, these systems would assess narratives based on scale, velocity, potential harm, and offline consequences, automatically categorizing them for response. A minor rumor might be logged and monitored, while a high-velocity deepfake targeting national leaders would trigger immediate alerts and escalation protocols. Such triage could prevent diplomats from being overwhelmed in moments when thousands of signals compete for attention. The ethical challenge, however, is ensuring that triage systems do not systematically deprioritize minority voices or unconventional platforms, reinforcing the very exclusions AI is meant to overcome.

A third area of experimentation lies in multimodal authenticity verification. Emerging tools are being developed to assess images, video, and audio simultaneously, using metadata and forensic analysis to flag synthetic content. The Coalition for Content Provenance and Authenticity (C2PA) has begun developing standards to embed origin data directly into files, and platforms like YouTube and TikTok are piloting labels for AI-generated media. For diplomats, widespread adoption of provenance standards could provide a new line of defense in crises, allowing them to debunk manipulated content with evidence that publics can verify for themselves. Yet provenance systems will only be effective if publics trust the labels. In polarized environments, even authenticating tags may be dismissed as propaganda.

Together, these frontier initiatives suggest a future in which crisis communication is less reactive and more anticipatory. AI simulations could help institutions rehearse their responses, triage systems could prioritize which rumors deserve immediate attention, and multimodal authenticity checks could provide new tools for debunking synthetic media. But these innovations also carry risks of overconfidence, exclusion, and mistrust. The lesson for diplomats is that technology can enhance preparedness, but it cannot replace the qualities publics most value in crises: honesty, proportionality, and human presence.

CONCLUSION

By now you've worked through what diplomacy looks like when there is no time to deliberate. Crisis is not a separate function alongside listening, messaging, monitoring, and engagement. It is the moment when all of those functions compress into minutes, and the question is no longer what you plan to say but what you do before the facts are in. Ambassador Grant's deepfake crisis put this on the table: 40,000 shares by morning, opposition calling for expulsion, forensic confirmation hours away. His decision—a calm public appearance, no mention of the video, while validators worked the evidence separately—turned on what may be the chapter's central insight: "We are not the most credible voice on our own credibility. We never are. Our job is to give the people who are credible the information they need."

The cases show that AI in a crisis does one thing very well and many things not at all. It buys you time: spikes in conversation get flagged before your team would notice, forensic anomalies in synthetic video surface within minutes, your message gets pushed into six languages before a human translator finishes the first. What it does not do is decide. Ukraine debunked the Zelenskyy deepfake because validators amplified the correction before the narrative hardened. Taiwan's chatbot worked because public health staff updated it every day. Canada's Spamouflage advisories worked because the government chose transparency over operational secrecy. AI saw what humans could not see fast enough; what to do with what it saw stayed with the humans. The "All Eyes on Rafah" image complicates the picture. An AI-generated visual mobilized millions in genuine solidarity while oversimplifying a humanitarian tragedy in the same gesture, more effective as advocacy than as evidence.

Where the previous chapter focused on continuous evaluation of programs that unfold over months, this chapter focused on response under conditions that unfold in minutes. The principle that runs through every stage of the crisis workflow: speed without judgment is just noise. The missions that come out of crises with credibility intact are not the ones that responded fastest. They are the ones that invested in validator networks, rehearsed proportionate responses, and built translation infrastructure before the emergency arrived. Lina's line at the debrief is the one to carry forward: "Crisis communication isn't one playbook—it's knowing which one applies."

Crisis exposes more than operational demands. It surfaces the ethical questions present in every AI deployment but harder to set aside when the clock is running: how much you tell publics about what AI is doing on your behalf, how loudly you respond to fringe rumors before amplification becomes the bigger problem, where the line falls between monitoring and surveillance, and who decides what counts as a manipulated narrative. The next chapter takes those up. The argument it builds is that ethics is not a constraint on innovation but the condition of its credibility.

7 Ethics, Trust, and Responsible AI in Public Diplomacy

"No machine should ever choose to take the life of a human being."

—Pope Francis, Address at the G7 Session on Artificial Intelligence (2024)

"That new tools are coded in old biases is surprising only if we equate technological innovation with social progress."

—Ruha Benjamin, *Race After Technology* (2019)

"If you have a face, you have a place in the conversation about AI."

—Joy Buolamwini, quoted in NPR (2023)

Opening Vignette: When Listening Looked Like Surveillance

The social listening system had been running for months without incident. Aisha Rahman, the mission's audience research and insights officer, monitored the dashboards each morning, tracking how narratives about U.S. programs were circulating across Zorani media—flagging spikes, clustering themes, and scoring sentiment shifts in near real time. The system drew only from publicly available posts, and the embassy had designed it with privacy safeguards recommended by headquarters. David Kim, the public affairs officer, considered it one of the mission's most valuable tools—a way to hear what publics were actually saying rather than relying on the filtered accounts that reached the embassy through official channels.

Then a Zorani investigative journalist published a story. She had noticed that the embassy's social media responses sometimes appeared unusually well-timed—addressing concerns within hours of their first appearance in local forums. Her article, headlined "Is the American Embassy Watching Us?" did not accuse the mission of breaking any law. It simply asked the question. That was enough. Within days, the story had reshaped the public conversation. Civil society groups demanded to know what data the embassy was collecting. Opposition politicians accused the mission of digital espionage. A university

DOI: 10.1201/9781003612377-9

professor who had participated in an embassy-sponsored exchange program publicly withdrew, saying she could not be associated with an institution that monitored its own audiences. On the dashboard Aisha watched every morning, the sentiment indicators shifted sharply—not because of any foreign adversary, but because the embassy's own tool had become the story.

David convened the public affairs team. Lina Perez, the digital communications officer, argued for a transparent response—publish the system's parameters, explain what it tracked and what it did not, and invite independent review. Farid Tessam, a locally employed cultural affairs assistant with deep ties to Zorani communities, cautioned that in Zorani political culture, any official explanation would be read as defensive. "The more technical detail you release," he said, "the more it sounds like you are justifying something that needs justifying." Ambassador Grant asked the question that framed the dilemma: "If we explain the system, we risk legitimizing the accusation. If we stay silent, we confirm it. What does responsible transparency look like when the act of explaining feels like an admission?" There was no clean answer.

The embassy chose a middle path—a brief public statement affirming its commitment to privacy, paired with quiet outreach through trusted validators who could speak credibly about the difference between public monitoring and private surveillance. Some critics were satisfied. Others were not. The journalist published a follow-up noting that the embassy had responded—but had not invited the independent audit she had called for.

At the debrief, Aisha raised the question the team had been circling: "The system did nothing wrong. But the perception of the system did real damage. How do we reconcile those two things?" David nodded. "That's the question we haven't solved yet. The system works. The perception of the system doesn't. And in diplomacy, perception is what we're paid to manage." Lina said quietly what everyone was thinking. "The window for explaining this on our own terms closed the day we launched it without saying so.

FRAMING THE CHAPTER

Ethics has always been implicit in diplomacy, even if rarely named outright. Publics judge not only what states say, but how they say it; not only what policies promise, but whether they are carried out with fairness and respect. In the age of artificial intelligence, this implicit dimension has become explicit. AI can accelerate listening, messaging, monitoring, engagement, and evaluation, but each of these functions carries risks that, if ignored, can erode trust. The question is no longer whether diplomats will use AI, but whether they will use it responsibly—and whether publics will believe that they are doing so.

Artificial intelligence makes the stakes higher because its outputs often feel authoritative while concealing hidden biases. A dashboard may produce elegant charts of public sentiment, but if those charts exclude minority voices, the system reflects not neutrality but omission. A chatbot may answer queries in seconds, but if it fails to disclose its automated nature, publics may later feel deceived. A provenance system may label a video as manipulated, but if publics suspect censorship, the correction may be seen as propaganda. In each case, the technology itself is less decisive than the trust—or suspicion—with which it is received.

Within the framework of this book, ethics cuts across all five strategic domains. Narrative intelligence requires proportionality and respect for privacy. Messaging demands authenticity and transparency. Monitoring disinformation must balance vigilance with freedom of expression. Engagement requires inclusivity and empathy. Evaluation must reflect fairness rather than superficial metrics. Likewise, ethics spans all six categories of real-world deployment: from early warning systems to digital engagement platforms, from disinformation defense to co-pilot tools for communicators. Ethics is not a separate domain but the connective tissue that sustains credibility across them all.

Having examined AI's applications in practice—from listening to crisis response—the book now pauses to address the foundation on which all these practices rest. Ethics in AI-enabled diplomacy is not just about compliance with international frameworks; it is about credibility as a form of soft power. States that use AI transparently, inclusively, and proportionately project responsibility and strengthen legitimacy. Those that ignore ethics risk being seen as manipulative, coercive, or indifferent to publics.

RESEARCH AND POLICY FOUNDATIONS

Ethics in artificial intelligence is essential for diplomacy, as AI systems often hide biases and power imbalances behind apparent objectivity. Kate Crawford (2021) calls AI an "infrastructure of extraction," embedding inequalities through invisible labor and datasets. In public diplomacy, these biases can marginalize minority languages or underserved groups. Trust matters more than technical accuracy; publics value sincerity, consistency, and respect (Zaharna 2010; Coombs 2014). Kissinger, Schmidt, and Huttenlocher (2021) argue AI provides persuasive data without understanding, highlighting the need for human judgment in diplomatic situations.

Global frameworks are addressing these concerns: UNESCO's *Recommendation on the Ethics of Artificial Intelligence* (2021) promotes transparency and accountability, the EU's *AI Act* (2024) introduces legal requirements like content labeling, and the African Union's *Continental AI Strategy* (2024) stresses inclusivity as sovereignty. The OECD (2024) and ASEAN (2025) emphasize fairness and contextual adaptation. Security is also a focus, with the G7's *Hiroshima Code of Conduct* (2023) encouraging transparency and restraint among democratic states. Responsible use of AI enhances public trust and strengthens soft power. Ultimately, ethics is not optional in AI-enabled diplomacy: transparency, inclusivity, and proportionality build legitimacy, sustaining trust as governance evolves.

GLOBAL GOVERNANCE FRAMEWORKS

While scholarly debates provide important context, the practical guardrails for responsible AI in diplomacy are increasingly set by international frameworks. These documents do more than establish ethical aspirations; they function as reference points that shape public expectations and diplomatic credibility. When governments align their use of AI with these norms, they project responsibility. When they ignore them, they invite suspicion.

UNESCO Recommendation on the Ethics of AI

UNESCO's *Recommendation on the Ethics of Artificial Intelligence* (2021) is perhaps the most widely cited, adopted by nearly 200 member states. It emphasizes transparency, accountability, and proportionality, requiring governments to disclose when AI systems are being used and to ensure that decisions affecting publics remain subject to human oversight. For diplomats, this framework is especially salient in contexts such as social listening or chatbot deployment, where publics may otherwise feel they are being monitored or misled. UNESCO's language makes clear that legitimacy requires not only technical safeguards but visible transparency.

The European Union AI Act

The European Union's *AI Act* (2024) represents the most comprehensive legal regime to date, with direct implications for public communication. It classifies certain applications as "high risk" and mandates labeling of AI-generated content, bans manipulative design practices, and requires explainability for systems used in governance. For EU institutions and member states, this means that crisis chatbots, monitoring dashboards, and even AI-assisted translations must be deployed with clear disclosure and audit trails. The Act is not only regulatory; it is normative.

By embedding these requirements into law, the EU signals that democratic practice demands accountability in the use of AI. One implication deserves particular emphasis for public diplomacy practitioners, because it is easy to assume the reverse. The Act carves out systems developed or used exclusively for military purposes, which means that some of the actors most active in the information space—defense establishments and, by extension, alliance structures such as NATO—operate outside its civilian requirements (Bergmanis-Korāts et al. 2024). Public diplomacy enjoys no such exemption. An embassy's monitoring dashboard, crisis chatbot, or audience-analysis tool is a civilian system, fully subject to the AI Act's transparency and high-risk provisions and to the data-protection regime of the GDPR. The counterintuitive result is that the civilian communicator, whose work is openly attributable and non-coercive, is often more tightly bound by AI law than the military actor operating in the same environment—an asymmetry practitioners should plan around rather than discover mid-crisis.

The African Union Continental AI Strategy

The African Union's *Continental AI Strategy* (2024) reframes the ethical debate through the lens of sovereignty. It warns that when AI systems exclude African languages or are trained exclusively on Western datasets, they perpetuate what some call "AI colonialism." For public diplomacy, the AU framework highlights the centrality of inclusivity. Programs that fail to represent diverse publics are not only incomplete—they are illegitimate. By making inclusivity a matter of sovereignty, the AU raises the stakes: equity in AI design is not optional but fundamental to international credibility.

OECD AI Principles

The OECD's updated *AI Principles* (2024) reinforce this emphasis on fairness and inclusivity, calling for purpose-driven AI that serves the public interest. The OECD principles highlight the dangers of quantification bias—celebrating outputs that are easy to measure while overlooking deeper relational outcomes like trust. For diplomats, the OECD framework underscores that efficiency is not success if publics feel excluded or manipulated.

ASEAN Guide on AI Governance and Ethics

ASEAN's *Expanded Guide on AI Governance and Ethics* (2025) adds another layer by emphasizing contextual adaptation. It recognizes that what counts as transparency in one setting may be seen as inadequate—or even inappropriate—in another. For example, labeling every chatbot interaction as AI-generated may build trust in some societies, while in others it may trigger suspicion if publics perceive automation as impersonality. ASEAN's guidance pushes practitioners to calibrate ethics to local expectations, reminding them that cultural sensitivity applies to digital tools as much as to traditional diplomacy.

The G7 Hiroshima Code of Conduct

Finally, the G7's *Hiroshima Code of Conduct on Artificial Intelligence* (2023) reflects a collective democratic commitment to transparency and restraint. It explicitly ties the responsible use of AI to the defense of democratic values, insisting that states model the accountability they demand from others. For public diplomacy, this is not just about compliance but about influence: governments that visibly adhere to such standards enhance their credibility in multilateral arenas.

Together, these frameworks form a patchwork of ethical guardrails, each addressing different dimensions of responsible AI. UNESCO establishes global principles, the EU enforces legal obligations, the AU reframes inclusivity as sovereignty, the OECD emphasizes fairness, ASEAN insists on cultural adaptation, and the G7 positions transparency as a democratic commitment. For practitioners, the message is clear: ethical AI is not only a matter of compliance but of credibility. Aligning with these frameworks is both a protective measure and a strategic asset in projecting trust.

What these frameworks establish as principle, the practitioner is asked to translate into operational discipline. In remarks before the U.S. Advisory Commission on Public Diplomacy in May 2026, I proposed an operational rule that the frameworks above converge on without naming explicitly:

AI must not be used to create or disseminate official government messaging that is intentionally false, misleading, or deceptive.

In other words: "*advocate, don't fabricate.*"

The rule does not prohibit AI assistance in drafting, translation, or analysis, nor does it prohibit AI-generated content where the AI nature of the content is clearly disclosed. What it prohibits is the use of AI to manufacture events that did not occur, to put words into the mouths of officials they did not say, or to fabricate the appearance of public opinion that does not exist. Disclosure alone does not exempt the underlying communication from the standard; a label does not excuse engineered deception. The rule names the line that the frameworks defend and the operational standard that gives them meaning at the workflow level (U.S. Advisory Commission on Public Diplomacy 2026).

REAL-WORLD APPLICATIONS

Transparency in AI Deployment: UK Government Co-Pilots

Transparency—the principle that publics should understand when and how AI is being used—is foundational to responsible AI in diplomacy. Yet transparency can be difficult to operationalize. What level of disclosure is sufficient? How technical must explanations be? And does transparency strengthen or undermine trust in institutions that acknowledge their reliance on automation? The United Kingdom's large-scale trials of AI co-pilots in government communication between September and December 2024 provide rare empirical evidence on these questions, demonstrating both the promise and the complexity of transparent AI deployment.

The Copilot Trials: Scale and Findings

The UK Government Digital Service piloted Microsoft Copilot with approximately 20,000 civil servants across multiple departments, including substantial participation from the Government Communication Service (GCS). The trials aimed to assess whether large language model (LLM) assistants could improve efficiency in routine tasks like drafting, summarization, and information retrieval—and crucially, whether such systems could be deployed transparently without eroding public confidence in government communication.

The productivity findings were striking. As discussed in Chapter 5, users saved an average of 26 minutes per day, translating across 20,000 participants to approximately 8,700 hours saved daily (GDS 2025b). For press officers, social media managers, and policy communicators, the efficiency gains were significant—but the trial's ethical value lay less in those numbers than in how they were reported.

Yet the trials also revealed significant transparency challenges. First, hallucinations—instances where Copilot generated plausible but false information—occurred with concerning frequency. In several documented cases, drafts included fabricated statistics, misattributed quotations, or invented policy details that looked credible on first glance but were factually incorrect. The National Audit Office's 2024 report on AI in government specifically flagged this "automation bias"—the tendency to trust machine outputs uncritically—as a systemic risk requiring explicit countermeasures (NAO 2024).

Second, data confidentiality emerged as a major concern. Microsoft Copilot, as a commercial product, processes inputs through Microsoft's infrastructure. While the company provides assurances about data handling, the UK government remained uncomfortable with the prospect of sensitive policy drafts, ministerial communications, or confidential briefing materials being processed by external commercial systems. This security concern prompted parallel development of *GCS Assist*, a domestic alternative built on open-source LLMs hosted on UK government infrastructure and formally rebranded in May 2025 (GCS 2024).

Transparency as an Institutional Strategy

What distinguished the UK approach was not just the deployment of AI but the transparency with which results—including failures and limitations—were documented and shared publicly. The Government Digital Service published detailed evaluations that candidly discussed error rates, user satisfaction variations, and data security concerns. This transparency served multiple functions.

First, it educated publics and civil servants about AI capabilities and limitations. By acknowledging that AI-generated content required verification and that not all staff found the tools equally valuable, the government avoided creating unrealistic expectations. This honest framing reduced the risk that future AI failures would be interpreted as institutional incompetence or deception.

Second, transparency demonstrated accountability. By publishing evaluation methodologies, error logs, and user feedback, the government showed that AI adoption was being approached thoughtfully rather than recklessly. The NAO's oversight role provided additional assurance that independent actors were monitoring risks.

Third, transparency built an evidence base for informed policymaking. Other governments considering similar deployments now have access to quantitative data on productivity gains, error rates, and adoption challenges. The UK's openness transformed a pilot program into a public good, advancing collective understanding of AI in government communication.

Implications for Diplomatic Transparency

The UK trials offer several lessons for diplomatic missions deploying AI tools:

Disclose AI use proactively, not reactively The UK government made it clear from the outset that civil servants were testing AI assistants. This preemptive disclosure prevented the kind of trust-eroding revelations that occur when AI use is discovered accidentally.

Quantify benefits honestly, including caveats The "26 minutes saved per day" finding was powerful precisely because it was accompanied by discussion of error rates and uneven adoption. Transparency about limitations makes claimed successes more credible.

Publish evaluation methodologies and findings The detailed reports from the GDS and NAO provided transparency not just about outcomes but about how those outcomes were measured. This methodological transparency allows others to assess the robustness of findings.

For diplomatic practitioners, the UK model suggests that transparency in AI deployment requires more than simple disclosure statements. It requires ongoing communication about how systems are working, what errors are occurring, and how governance is evolving. It requires honesty about trade-offs between efficiency and risk. And it requires willingness to share lessons—both successes and failures—with other institutions and publics. In an era where suspicion about government technology use is widespread, transparency itself becomes a form of trust-building.

Democratic Defense Ethics: Canada's Rapid Response Mechanism

If transparency is about disclosing AI use to maintain trust, democratic defense ethics concerns how AI is deployed to protect democratic institutions from manipulation while honoring the values of openness and free expression. Canada's *Rapid Response Mechanism* (RRM), particularly its October 2023 and March 2025 advisories on "Spamouflage" disinformation operations, illustrates both the promise and the ethical complexity of using AI to defend democratic discourse.

Detection and Public Advisories

Established as part of the G7 RRM initiative, Canada's system uses network analysis and anomaly detection to identify coordinated inauthentic behavior targeting Canadian officials, journalists, and public discourse. Unlike many counter-disinformation programs that operate behind closed doors, Canada made a strategic choice to publish public advisories when it identified manipulation campaigns—a decision that transformed detection into a form of democratic defense.

The October 23, 2023 advisory exposed a coordinated network of inauthentic accounts spreading disinformation targeting Canadian Members of Parliament. The campaign employed bot network tactics: accounts created in batches, posting at synchronized intervals, amplifying identical content across multiple platforms. What made the operation particularly insidious was its targeting strategy—the false narratives were designed to inflame existing political divisions, making them more likely to be organically shared by genuine users (Global Affairs Canada 2023).

The March 6, 2025 advisory documented a more sophisticated variant targeting Chinese-language journalists in Canada. This campaign used AI-generated content and a mix of hijacked legitimate accounts with newly created personas, apparently aiming to suppress independent reporting on issues sensitive to foreign interests (Global Affairs Canada 2025). Network analysis revealed coordination patterns—simultaneous posting, identical phrasing, amplification by accounts with suspicious activity histories—that human analysts alone would have struggled to detect at scale.

Ethical Dimensions of Transparent Attribution

Canada's decision to publish these advisories publicly rather than respond quietly raised fundamental ethical questions about the use of AI in defending democratic institutions:

Attribution and Evidence Standards How certain must governments be before publicly attributing disinformation campaigns to foreign actors? The RRM faced criticism that behavioral evidence—suspicious posting patterns, coordination signatures—was circumstantial rather than definitive proof of state sponsorship. Yet waiting for perfect attribution risked allowing manipulation to continue unchallenged. Canada chose transparency with appropriate caveats, framing findings as high-confidence assessments based on available evidence rather than absolute certainties.

Balancing Vigilance and Openness Counter-disinformation efforts risk chilling legitimate dissent if publics perceive governments as policing political speech. The RRM addressed this by focusing narrowly on coordinated inauthentic behavior—networks of fake accounts, bot amplification, and systematic manipulation—rather than the content of political messages themselves. This distinction preserved space for contentious political debate while exposing artificial manipulation tactics.

Transparency about Methods Publishing advisories educates adversaries about detection capabilities, potentially allowing them to adapt tactics. Yet Canada judged that democratic accountability required openness. The advisories acknowledged this trade-off explicitly, reasoning that public awareness of manipulation techniques builds societal resilience that outweighs operational security concerns.

Protection without Paternalism By making findings public rather than quietly suppressing disinformation, Canada treated citizens as partners in democratic defense rather than passive subjects to be protected. This approach respects public agency: informed citizens can decide for themselves how to interpret information, rather than relying solely on government determinations of what is true or false.

Accountability through Transparency The advisories became evidence in Canada's Foreign Interference Commission inquiry, demonstrating how RRM's work connected to broader democratic security concerns (Foreign Interference Commission 2025). This integration of AI-enabled detection into formal accountability mechanisms showed that technological vigilance was subject to democratic oversight, not operating in a black box.

Implications for Diplomatic Ethics

Canada's approach demonstrates that AI-enabled defense of democratic institutions can be conducted ethically, but only with careful attention to transparency, proportionality, and respect for open discourse. Several principles emerge:

- *Narrow the scope to behavior, not speech* Focus AI detection on coordinated manipulation tactics (bot networks, account hijacking, platform manipulation) rather than attempting to adjudicate political content. This preserves democratic pluralism while exposing artificial amplification.
- *Subject AI vigilance to democratic oversight* Integrate counter-disinformation work into formal accountability structures (parliamentary inquiries, independent audits, civil society consultation). This ensures that technological capabilities do not outpace democratic governance.
- *Respect public agency* Treat citizens as capable of critical judgment rather than passive consumers needing protection. Provide information and context, but trust publics to draw their own conclusions.

For diplomatic practitioners, Canada's RRM demonstrates that defending democratic discourse with AI is not incompatible with democratic values—but only if the defense itself is conducted democratically. Transparency, proportionality, and accountability are not constraints on effectiveness but preconditions for legitimacy.

Youth and Vulnerable Populations: UNICEF U-Report

The ethical challenges of AI in public diplomacy intensify when systems engage vulnerable populations, particularly youth. UNICEF's *U-Report* platform—which has grown to 37 million registered users across 102 countries as of 2025—demonstrates both the transformative potential and the distinctive ethical obligations that arise when AI-powered engagement tools target minors and marginalized communities (UNICEF 2025).

Scale and Impact

Launched in 2011 and scaled dramatically during the COVID-19 pandemic (2020–2022), U-Report uses chatbot technology with natural language processing to conduct polls, gather feedback, and provide information on issues ranging from education to climate change. The platform operates via SMS, WhatsApp, Facebook Messenger, and other channels accessible to youth in diverse contexts, including low-connectivity environments. By mid-2025, U-Report was active in over 90 countries, making it one of the world's largest AI-enabled youth engagement initiatives (UNICEF 2020; 2022; 2025).

The platform's reach represents a remarkable achievement in inclusive participation. Youth who previously had no formal channel to influence policy discussions can now share their views directly with UN country offices and national governments. During the pandemic, U-Report provided real-time data on youth concerns about mental health, education disruption, and economic impacts, informing UNICEF's programming and advocacy. In climate diplomacy contexts, the platform has enabled young people to voice priorities for COP negotiations and sustainable development goals.

Distinctive Ethical Challenges

Yet this success brings ethical obligations that exceed those of adult-facing AI systems. Several challenges are distinctive to youth engagement:

Informed Consent in Low-Literacy Contexts Many U-Report users are in their early teens, and some participate from communities with limited digital literacy. Ensuring that young users genuinely understand what data is being collected, how it will be used, and who will have access requires age-appropriate communication that goes beyond standard privacy policies. UNICEF has developed simplified consent processes with visual aids and multiple-language support, but ensuring meaningful consent remains an ongoing challenge, particularly when users access the platform via family members' devices.

Data Protection across Diverse Regulatory Environments Operating in 102 countries means navigating vastly different legal frameworks for child data protection. Some countries have strict regulations (the EU's GDPR includes heightened protections for minors), while others have minimal safeguards. UNICEF must apply the highest standard globally, but implementation varies with local capacity and technical infrastructure. Data residency requirements in some countries create additional complexity: where should data be stored, and who has jurisdiction over it?

Power Imbalances in Participation While U-Report aims to amplify youth voices, there is risk that participation patterns reproduce existing inequalities. Urban, educated youth with reliable device access may dominate the conversation, while rural, disabled, or conflict-affected youth remain unheard despite platform availability. Equity audits have revealed underrepresentation of certain groups, prompting UNICEF to invest in targeted outreach and accessibility features, but achieving genuinely inclusive participation remains a work in progress.

Vulnerability to Misuse Youth engagement platforms can attract predatory actors. Safeguarding protocols must prevent chatbots from being exploited for inappropriate communication, data harvesting, or targeting vulnerable users. UNICEF has implemented content filters, human oversight of flagged interactions, and reporting mechanisms, but the scale of the platform makes comprehensive monitoring resource-intensive.

Balancing Empowerment and Protection Perhaps the most fundamental ethical tension: how to empower youth participation without exposing them to risks they may not fully understand. Paternalistic approaches that overly restrict participation undermine the platform's purpose. Yet insufficient safeguards endanger young users. Finding the right balance requires continuous consultation with youth themselves, treating them as partners in platform governance rather than passive beneficiaries.

UNICEF's Ethical Framework

UNICEF has developed a multi-layered ethical framework for U-Report that offers lessons for any diplomatic initiative engaging vulnerable populations:

Privacy by Design Data minimization is the default: the platform collects only information necessary for programmatic purposes. Personal identifying information is separated from survey responses. Data retention periods are clearly defined and enforced. Third-party access is strictly controlled.

Transparency and Youth Participation in Governance U-Report's design evolution includes input from youth advisory boards. Young users have contributed to decisions about data policies, acceptable use guidelines, and platform features. This participatory governance treats youth as rights-holders rather than mere subjects of protection.

Continuous Safeguarding Review Regular audits by child protection specialists assess emerging risks. The platform's chatbot interactions are monitored for red flags indicating distress, abuse, or exploitation. Staff are trained to recognize when AI-mediated engagement requires human intervention.

Cultural Adaptation U-Report does not assume a universal model of youth engagement. The platform adapts to local cultural norms about appropriate youth participation, consultation with elders, and sensitivity to topics considered taboo in some contexts. This cultural humility prevents AI systems from imposing Western-centric assumptions about youth agency.

Public Accountability UNICEF publishes regular reports on U-Report's reach, impact, and safeguarding incidents. This transparency allows external actors—civil society organizations, child rights advocates, researchers—to assess whether ethical commitments are being honored.

Implications for Diplomatic Youth Engagement

For diplomatic practitioners considering AI-enabled youth engagement, U-Report's experience yields two principles beyond the framework itself:

- *Scale amplifies both benefit and risk* Reaching millions of young people creates unprecedented opportunity for inclusion, but also exponentially increases exposure if systems fail or are misused.
- *Participation rights must be balanced with protection rights* Youth have the right to be heard in decisions affecting them (UN Convention on the Rights of the Child), but also the right to safety and privacy. Neither right should be sacrificed to the other.

U-Report's journey from a pilot in Uganda to a global platform demonstrates that AI can genuinely amplify marginalized voices—but only when ethical considerations are embedded from inception, continuously reviewed, and adapted as systems scale. For diplomacy, where engaging future generations is both strategic priority and ethical obligation, UNICEF's experience provides a crucial template for responsible AI deployment with vulnerable populations.

Synthetic Narratives in Action: Taylor Swift Deepfake Harassment (2024)

In January 2024, one of the world's most recognizable cultural figures, Taylor Swift, became the target of a deluge of non-consensual, AI-generated explicit images. The deepfakes appeared on forums like 4chan before exploding onto mainstream platforms such as X (formerly Twitter). At the height of the incident, searches for Swift's name had to be temporarily disabled as the platform scrambled to contain the spread.

The case illustrates the ethical stakes of synthetic media in stark terms. Unlike political satire or advocacy campaigns, these images carried no public interest value; they were designed solely to humiliate and exploit. Their viral spread revealed the vulnerability of even the most powerful individuals to reputational damage, while also exposing the lag of social media platforms in responding to synthetic harassment. For the millions of ordinary women without Swift's influence or resources, the risks are even higher.

Beyond personal harm, the incident has broader implications for public diplomacy and trust. When deepfakes can be weaponized so easily against cultural icons, they threaten the credibility of the information space itself. Governments and institutions that rely on celebrity partnerships for campaigns—whether on health, human rights, or climate—must now reckon with the possibility that those figures could be undermined by synthetic attacks. The Swift case is not only a lesson in individual violation but also a warning about the fragility of trust in an AI-mediated public sphere (Associated Press 2024b; 2024c).

RISKS AND DILEMMAS

Even when ethics is embedded in mindsets and workflows, the use of AI in diplomacy brings dilemmas that cannot be eliminated, only managed. These risks are not merely technical flaws but political and relational challenges, shaping whether publics view institutions as credible or coercive.

One of the most sensitive dilemmas concerns surveillance perceptions. Social listening tools, even when drawing only on public data, can feel invasive if publics believe they are being monitored. In societies with histories of state surveillance, such systems can quickly be interpreted as spying rather than stewardship. The difference lies not in the data collected but in the perception of intent. Missions that are transparent about how and why they use AI, emphasizing that monitoring is designed to protect publics from manipulation rather than to police them, are more likely to maintain trust. Without this openness, surveillance fears can overshadow the value of early warning systems.

A second dilemma is truth arbitration. AI tools used to detect disinformation risk crossing into the territory of defining what counts as true. The U.S. Department of Defense's pilot with Primer in 2020, which attempted to score the credibility of online narratives, illustrated this risk: systems trained on particular assumptions about credibility may systematically disadvantage voices from outside dominant information ecosystems. The dilemma runs in both directions. Where AI detection tools risk overreaching by labeling legitimate content as false, government-produced AI content can itself become a source of confusion. The February 2025 release of an AI-generated video depicting a glamorized "TRUMP GAZA" resort—circulated by figures associated with the administration—demonstrated how synthetic media originating from official or semi-official sources can blur the boundary between policy communication and fabrication, complicating the task of any institution attempting to model truthful public communication (Goggin 2025; McCammon and Al-Shalchi 2025).

The Trump Gaza incident was not isolated. By mid-2025, a pattern had emerged in which state actors and political leaders were using AI not merely to defend against disinformation but to generate it. In July 2025, unknown actors used AI voice-cloning to impersonate U.S. Secretary of State Marco Rubio, contacting at least three foreign ministers, a U.S. governor, and a member of Congress through SMS, Signal, and voicemail. The communications were sophisticated enough to appear authentic, and the State Department and FBI were forced to issue public warnings before the impersonation was detected across all targets (Foreign Affairs 2025). The episode demonstrated that AI could fabricate not just public narratives but the private channels of diplomacy itself.

State-sponsored AI propaganda has also grown more systematic. China's state broadcaster CGTN produced AI-generated music videos and deployed deepfake news anchors through fictitious outlets to push anti-Western narratives across social media platforms (The Diplomat 2025). In El Salvador, President Nayib Bukele integrated AI-powered bot networks into an already sophisticated state propaganda apparatus, amplifying favorable narratives at a scale that outpaced organic public discourse (Foreign Affairs 2025). More subtly, Chinese AI models such as DeepSeek and Alibaba's Qwen family were found to embed content controls that extended well beyond domestic censorship. Estonia's Foreign Intelligence Service reported in 2026 that DeepSeek concealed security-relevant information and inserted Chinese propaganda into its responses, while a Swedish-funded study found that Alibaba's models carried these embedded biases into thousands of downstream applications worldwide, often without developers or users realizing the manipulation (CEPA 2026).

These cases reveal a dilemma more unsettling than external disinformation. When leaders and states use AI to deceive at scale—whether through fabricated diplomatic communications, synthetic state media, weaponized bot networks, or AI models that quietly embed propaganda into everyday tools—the ethical framework that public diplomacy depends on is challenged from within. Practitioners who advocate for transparency and authenticity must now contend with the possibility that their own governments, or their allies, may be among those undermining trust in the information environment.

Personalization presents a third dilemma. Generative AI makes it possible to tailor messages with extraordinary precision, framing the same policy differently for different publics. Done responsibly, this can clarify communication; done recklessly, it can fragment credibility if publics discover contradictory framings. In polarized environments, adversaries may exploit such inconsistencies to portray institutions as duplicitous. The ethical line lies in ensuring that personalization highlights complementary aspects of a consistent policy rather than constructing divergent realities.

Bias and exclusion remain enduring risks. AI systems trained on dominant languages or digital elites risk erasing minority voices. The vignette in this chapter illustrated a related dynamic: a social listening system designed with legitimate safeguards was perceived as surveillance once its existence became public, eroding trust among the very communities it was meant to serve. Such exclusions are not merely technical oversights; they carry political consequences, reinforcing perceptions of inequality. For diplomacy, where legitimacy depends on inclusivity, failing to correct for bias risks undermining the very purpose of engagement.

The European Union's efforts to counter disinformation provide another example of ethical tensions in practice. Through the European Digital Media Observatory (EDMO) and the European External Action Service's Foreign Information Manipulation and Interference (FIMI) reports, the EU has made its monitoring of hostile campaigns more transparent, publishing daily bulletins and periodic threat assessments (European Commission 2025b; EEAS 2025). Yet these same reports have sometimes drawn criticism, with opponents claiming that labeling narratives as "disinformation" risks policing legitimate debate. The EU case highlights a recurring dilemma: transparency builds resilience, but without careful explanation of criteria, it can also fuel perceptions of censorship. Ethical monitoring requires not only vigilance but openness about where the line is drawn.

Finally, opacity is an overarching dilemma. Many AI systems operate as "black boxes," producing outputs that even their designers struggle to explain. For diplomacy, this is dangerous. When publics ask why a message was flagged, a translation chosen, or a rumor amplified, institutions must be able to provide an answer. Without explainability, even accurate outputs may be dismissed as arbitrary or manipulative. Frameworks such as the EU's *AI Act* (2024) and the OECD's *AI Principles* (2024) highlight explainability as a requirement precisely because opacity erodes accountability.

The Ethical Mindset for AI in Diplomacy

Ethics in AI is not simply a checklist of compliance requirements. It is a mindset—a way of approaching technology that shapes whether publics perceive its use as legitimate or manipulative. For diplomats, this mindset must be grounded in values that are as old as diplomacy itself: humility, transparency, inclusivity, proportionality, and accountability. Each principle provides a compass point for navigating the uncertainties of AI in global communication.

Humility is the first and perhaps most important principle. AI systems can process vast datasets and produce striking outputs, but they cannot explain meaning or anticipate cultural nuance. Dashboards may show that a message is trending positively, but they cannot discern whether the tone is sincere, ironic, or hostile. In public diplomacy, where meaning is relational, treating AI as an oracle is a recipe for error. Humility means recognizing that machine outputs are provisional and must be validated by human judgment.

Transparency follows closely. Publics are increasingly aware that governments deploy AI, and they are quick to perceive concealment as deception. Labeling AI-assisted outputs, clarifying when a chatbot is automated, or disclosing the role of AI in translation signals honesty. Far from weakening credibility, such openness can strengthen it by demonstrating that institutions have nothing to hide. In this sense, transparency is not just a safeguard but a form of soft power.

Inclusivity anchors the mindset in fairness. AI systems trained on dominant languages or urban users risk excluding rural communities and minority voices, reinforcing inequities that diplomacy should work to reduce. The African Union's insistence that inclusivity is sovereignty reflects the stakes: publics who feel erased in digital systems are unlikely to trust the institutions deploying them. Inclusivity means designing AI that reflects diverse voices and correcting for structural biases in data.

Proportionality ensures that AI is used with restraint. In listening, this means monitoring only what is necessary to protect publics rather than surveilling them indiscriminately. In disinformation defense, it means focusing on harmful manipulation while allowing legitimate dissent to flourish. In crisis communication, it means calibrating responses to the severity of rumors rather than amplifying every anomaly. Proportionality is the discipline that prevents AI from becoming a blunt instrument.

Finally, accountability is what ties the mindset together. AI outputs may be automated, but responsibility cannot be outsourced. Publics hold institutions accountable for the consequences of their tools, whether a mistranslation that offends, a chatbot that misleads, or a provenance label that fails to persuade. Building accountability into AI workflows—through algorithmic impact assessments, error logs, and independent audits—signals that governments are prepared to own their choices.

Taken together, these five commitments form a mindset that is both principled and pragmatic. In the end, ethics in AI is less about machines than about the values humans bring to them.

Workflows for Responsible AI

If mindset provides the compass, workflows are what translate ethical commitments into daily practice. Diplomats cannot rely on good intentions alone; they need routines and structures that ensure AI is used responsibly, even under pressure. Embedding ethics into workflows means operationalizing principles such as transparency, inclusivity, and accountability so that they become part of how missions function, not afterthoughts once mistakes are made.

One critical workflow is the use of algorithmic impact assessments. Canada's approach provides a strong model: before deploying an AI system, agencies must document its purpose, risks, and safeguards, scoring its impact on criteria such as transparency and fairness (Government of Canada 2019). For embassies, this could mean evaluating a chatbot not just for efficiency but for inclusivity—does it cover minority languages? Will users understand when they are engaging with AI? By forcing these questions into the design stage, impact assessments prevent ethical concerns from being sidelined in the pursuit of speed.

Disclosure protocols are another essential routine. Missions that clearly label when outputs are AI-assisted avoid the perception of concealment. This can be as simple as adding a line at the start of a chatbot interaction—"You are speaking with the Embassy's AI assistant, supervised by staff"—or noting that a press release was machine-translated and human-edited. Such disclosures may feel minor to practitioners, but to publics they signal accountability and respect. The EU's *AI Act* (2024) makes such labeling a legal requirement; in diplomacy, it should be seen as a credibility requirement.

Equity audits provide a third workflow, ensuring that AI systems do not reproduce bias by amplifying dominant voices. These audits examine who is represented in datasets and who is missing, comparing participation across languages, demographics, and geographies. For platforms like UNICEF's U-Report, this means checking whether rural youth are represented alongside urban elites. For embassies, it might mean verifying whether alumni networks include marginalized groups. Equity audits turn inclusivity into a measurable standard rather than a rhetorical aspiration.

Provenance checks are becoming a fourth standard. In this context, provenance refers to information that documents where a piece of digital content came from, how it was created, and whether it has been modified. As synthetic media proliferates, missions must develop routines for authenticating content before responding to it. The Coalition for Content Provenance and Authenticity (C2PA) offers one emerging model, embedding metadata into files that reveal their origin and editing history. Embedding provenance checks into crisis communication workflows ensures that responses are grounded in evidence, not speculation. Just as importantly, sharing the verification process with publics demonstrates transparency in action.

Finally, error logs and learning loops ensure that when mistakes occur, they become opportunities for improvement rather than sources of repeated failure. Whether it is a chatbot mistranslation, a monitoring dashboard misclassifying satire, or a provenance tool mislabeling an image, documenting these missteps allows missions to refine their systems. Transparency about lessons learned—both internally and, when possible, with publics—reinforces the perception of accountability.

Taken together, these workflows make ethics tangible. In an age where publics scrutinize every technological misstep, they are not optional; they are the scaffolding of credibility.

Metrics and Evaluation

Ethics may seem difficult to measure, but diplomacy cannot afford to treat it as intangible. If credibility is the currency of public diplomacy, then institutions need ways to know whether their AI practices are building or eroding trust. Evaluation in this domain is less about counting activity than about tracking signals of responsibility—whether publics feel included, informed, and respected in their interactions with institutions.

Transparency is one dimension that can be evaluated directly. Missions can track whether AI-assisted outputs are labeled and whether publics recognize those disclosures. User surveys or focus groups can reveal whether citizens feel more confident when they know they are engaging with an AI system. Over time, patterns emerge: if disclosure correlates with higher trust, the case for transparency becomes not only ethical but strategic.

Inclusivity provides another evaluative lens. Equity audits, already used in some organizations, measure participation across languages, demographics, and regions. For example, if alumni engagement platforms or youth surveys show underrepresentation of rural communities or minority-language speakers, the evaluation highlights a gap to be addressed. The African Union's emphasis on inclusivity as sovereignty underscores why such audits matter: publics who feel erased from evaluation are unlikely to see themselves as valued in diplomacy.

Accountability can also be tracked. Canada's algorithmic impact assessments provide one model, requiring agencies to document risks and safeguards before deployment. In practice, missions can adopt similar scorecards, logging not only system performance but ethical considerations such as privacy protection and proportionality. By reviewing these records regularly—and making them available when possible—institutions demonstrate that accountability is more than rhetoric.

Finally, validator trust offers an indirect but powerful metric. When journalists, civil society actors, or alumni amplify a correction or endorse a communication, it signals that publics view the institution as credible. Tracking validator amplification rates in contexts where AI tools are disclosed can reveal whether transparency enhances or undermines trust. If validators echo corrections more readily when AI detection is explained, the link between ethics and credibility becomes measurable.

These metrics—transparency rates, inclusivity audits, accountability scorecards, and validator trust—do not eliminate the complexity of ethics, but they make it visible. They allow institutions to test whether their principles are being realized in practice and to adjust when they fall short. In the end, the true measure of ethical AI in diplomacy is not technical compliance but public confidence. Metrics can guide that process, but trust remains the standard by which success is judged.

Reflection and Strategic Questions

These habits raise questions that practitioners should reflect on regularly. Are our AI tools amplifying the voices already loudest, or are they making space for those previously unheard? Do our publics understand when they are interacting with AI, and do they feel respected when they do? How do we ensure that vigilance against disinformation does not shade into censorship? And how do we balance the demand for efficiency with the imperative of empathy?

FRONTIER PILOTS

As governance frameworks mature, institutions are beginning to experiment with new ways of embedding ethics directly into the design and oversight of AI systems. These frontier initiatives are not yet standard practice, but they hint at how responsible AI in diplomacy might evolve in the years ahead.

One promising development is the adoption of provenance standards. The Coalition for Content Provenance and Authenticity (C2PA), a consortium of technology firms and media organizations, is creating methods to embed metadata into images, video, and audio files that record their origin and editing history. In the context of diplomacy, this could allow missions to provide verifiable evidence when debunking a manipulated video or synthetic audio clip. The EU's *AI Act* (2024) requires labeling of synthetic media in high-risk contexts, and platforms such as YouTube and TikTok are beginning to pilot disclosure policies. The frontier challenge is not technical feasibility but public recognition: provenance systems will only strengthen trust if publics accept them as reliable rather than dismissing them as another layer of government spin.

A second area of innovation lies in explainable AI. Many AI systems operate as "black boxes," producing outputs without clear reasoning. Diplomats using these systems in monitoring or evaluation risk eroding credibility if they cannot explain why a narrative was flagged or a sentiment classified. Research in explainable AI seeks to provide human-readable rationales for machine decisions, from highlighting the features of a dataset that led to a classification to visualizing how an algorithm weighted competing factors. In diplomacy, explainability is more than a technical safeguard; it is a communicative necessity. Publics are unlikely to trust outputs that institutions cannot themselves explain.

A third frontier involves participatory ethics boards within multilateral organizations. Building on traditions of stakeholder consultation, some international bodies are exploring whether publics, civil society groups, and independent experts could be formally included in the oversight of AI systems. Such boards would not only review technical safeguards but also ensure that cultural and contextual sensitivities are considered before deployment. For example, a participatory ethics board in an education-focused agency could evaluate whether an AI translation system adequately supports minority languages. While such initiatives are still in early discussion stages, they signal a recognition that legitimacy cannot be engineered solely from within institutions—it must be shared with the publics they serve.

These frontier experiments reveal a shift from reactive ethics to proactive design. Provenance standards, explainable AI, and participatory oversight all attempt to build responsibility into systems before crises arise. Each comes with limitations—skepticism about provenance, the technical difficulty of explainability, the complexity of managing participatory boards—but all reflect an emerging consensus: trust in AI will not come from efficiency alone but from visible accountability. For diplomacy, this means that ethical leadership may become a form of soft power in its own right, as publics and partners look to those who model responsibility in the digital age.

CONCLUSION

As you reflect on this chapter, remember that ethics is not a barrier to innovation in public diplomacy—it is the foundation of credibility. The real challenge lies not just in technical compliance but in managing perceptions and building public trust. Cases like the Republic of Z vignette show that even when AI systems operate within established guidelines, public concerns and unintended consequences can arise. In diplomacy, how people interpret and respond to these systems matters as much as how they function.

As you move forward in the book, keep in mind that the ethical framework supporting public diplomacy is evolving—and facing new pressures not just from adversaries, but also from allies, governments, and the AI models themselves. Stewardship is the central principle: practitioners are responsible for the information environment, ensuring it is trustworthy and resilient. The next chapter will expand on these foundations, exploring how AI is transforming cultural and educational diplomacy. Consider how scaling access and efficiency must balance with preserving cultural authenticity—the true source of meaning in these programs.

PART III

Expanding Impact

The final challenge is making AI serve diplomacy's longest horizons and broadest coalitions. These chapters address cultural and educational exchange across generations, coordination among multilateral partners, and the institutional transformation required to move from scattered pilots to sustainable systems that enhance credibility, inclusivity, and resilience.

DOI: 10.1201/9781003612377-10

8 AI for Cultural and Educational Diplomacy

"The consequence of the single story is this: It robs people of dignity. It makes our recognition of our equal humanity difficult. It emphasizes how we are different rather than how we are similar."

—Chimamanda Ngozi Adichie, "The Danger of a Single Story," TED Talk (2009)

"Language as culture is the collective memory bank of a people's experience in history."

—Ngũgĩ wa Thiong'o, *Decolonising the Mind* (1986)

"We need to let people who are harmed by technology imagine the future that they want."

—Timnit Gebru, quoted in TIME (2022)

Opening Vignette: When a Poem Lost Its Soul

Miriam Diallo, the embassy's cultural affairs officer, had spent weeks organizing the event. An evening of poetry and music at the national cultural center, showcasing the literary traditions of both countries—classic Zorani poems translated into English alongside American works rendered into Zorani. Local poets had agreed to perform. The Zorani press had confirmed attendance. It was the kind of programming Miriam believed in most deeply—not policy messaging, not strategic outreach, but the slower work of building mutual respect through art. David Kim, the public affairs officer, had approved the programming, given that the poets and the audiences they drew included opinion leaders whose trust the mission would need on harder days—and a country seen honoring Zorani heritage is harder to caricature as an outsider that arrives with promises and leaves with photographs.

The timeline, however, was unforgiving. With dozens of poems to translate in both directions, Miriam made the decision to extend the mission's AI-assisted

DOI: 10.1201/9781003612377-11

translation system to literary work for the first time. The tool was remarkably fast—translations that would have taken a contracted literary translator several weeks were produced in a single afternoon. The printed programs looked polished. The phrasing was fluent. Miriam reviewed the outputs for obvious errors and, finding none, approved them for printing. It was the kind of check that had once caught a single loaded word in a press release before it went out. Poems bury their dangers deeper. The trouble surfaced during the performance itself. In one Zorani poem, the AI had translated a phrase meaning "the river that carries memory" into the flat and literal "water transport." Another rendered a sacred metaphor for resilience—a word rooted in generations of survival through drought and displacement—as "stubbornness." The audience laughed in places meant to evoke reverence. Murmurs spread through the hall. By the second half of the program, several poets were visibly uncomfortable.

Farid Tessam, a locally employed cultural affairs assistant who knew many of the poets personally, heard the reaction in the lobby during the intermission. "They are not angry at the translation," he told Miriam quietly. "They are hurt by what it reveals. They feel their work was treated as text to be processed rather than meaning to be understood." By the next morning, a local newspaper ran an editorial accusing the embassy of "outsourcing culture to machines" and treating Zorani heritage as disposable. What had been intended as a celebration of shared values had become a small diplomatic wound. In the days that followed, Miriam contacted the poets directly. She did not send a press release or issue a formal apology. She sat with them, listened to their frustrations, and asked them to help retranslate the texts. The poets emphasized that their objection was not to technology itself but to the assumption that their art could be flattened into literal equivalents without consequence. For them, the failure was not linguistic but relational. It suggested a lack of care, however unintentional, for the layers of meaning their words carried.

Miriam arranged a second event the following month—this time with the poets themselves reviewing every translation, line by line. The evening was smaller, quieter, and far more powerful. One poet, who had been among the most critical, thanked the embassy afterward. "This time," he said, "the words sounded like ours." At the debrief, Miriam was direct. "I made the call to use the system, and I should have built in a review step that I did not. The AI gave us speed, and I mistook speed for readiness. A poem can be translated by a machine, but its soul has to be carried by someone who understands what it means to the people who wrote it."

FRAMING THE CHAPTER

Cultural and educational diplomacy has always been the long game of international relations. Unlike crisis communication, which is judged in minutes, or disinformation defense, which unfolds over days, cultural exchange and education operate on the scale of years and generations. A single exchange program can shape the worldview of an alumna or alumnus for life. A cultural performance can leave an impression that no press release could match. These efforts form the bedrock of soft power: the capacity to attract and persuade through respect, resonance, and shared values.

Artificial intelligence is increasingly woven into these long-term practices in three broad directions: translation systems that sustain multilingual access across exchange programs and multilateral organizations; heritage technologies that digitize endangered manuscripts and reconstruct damaged artifacts; and education platforms that personalize learning and gather youth perspectives at a scale unimaginable a decade ago. The institutions developing this work—the EU and the UN in translation, UNESCO in heritage, UNICEF in youth engagement—are examined in later sections. Together these tools expand reach, accelerate access, and democratize participation.

Yet the very features that make AI attractive—speed, scale, and efficiency—also carry risks. Translation can flatten cultural nuance into literal meaning, as the vignette illustrated. Heritage digitization can reproduce Western biases in what is preserved and how it is framed. Personalized learning can raise questions about privacy and the safeguarding of minors. Cultural diplomacy succeeds when publics feel seen and respected; it falters when they feel reduced to data points or when traditions are treated as raw material for algorithms.

Within the framework of this book, cultural and educational diplomacy belongs primarily to the domain of content creation and knowledge management, the fifth of the book's strategic domains. Of the six categories of deployment, it aligns most directly with multilingual communication and knowledge management, while also intersecting with public engagement and digital diplomacy. Unlike earlier chapters, which focused on immediate credibility under pressure, this chapter explores how AI shapes the slower, deeper work of building trust across cultures.

Having examined listening, messaging, monitoring, engagement, evaluation, and crisis communication, the book now turns to the sphere where AI has the power not just to inform or defend but to shape memory and identity. Cultural and educational diplomacy asks a different question: not how AI can help diplomats win the moment, but how it can help institutions sustain credibility for the long term.

This chapter develops that theme in three ways. Conceptually, it situates AI within the traditions of cultural diplomacy and soft power, showing how technology both extends and complicates them. Practically, it highlights how AI is being deployed in translation, education, and heritage preservation. Strategically, it addresses the risks of cultural flattening, bias, and exclusion, asking how ethics can be embedded so that efficiency does not come at the expense of authenticity. In cultural diplomacy, credibility depends on more than access; it depends on respect. AI can expand access, but respect must still be carried by humans.

RESEARCH AND POLICY FOUNDATIONS

Cultural and educational diplomacy rests on the premise that relationships, not transactions, are the foundation of influence. Joseph Nye (2004) famously defined soft power as the ability to attract and persuade rather than coerce, and scholars since have shown that culture and education are among its most durable sources (Cull 2008; Zaharna 2010). Exchanges, language programs, artistic collaborations, and heritage preservation all signal respect, creating reservoirs of goodwill that outlast immediate political disputes. AI now enters this landscape as both a multiplier and a disruptor, amplifying what cultural diplomacy can achieve while raising questions about authenticity, ownership, and fairness.

Yet scholars caution that efficiency and scale come with risks. Kate Crawford (2021) warns that AI systems are not neutral but carry the imprint of their training data, often privileging dominant languages and perspectives. This dynamic, sometimes described as "AI colonialism," risks reproducing inequalities by erasing minority voices in the very act of expanding access. In cultural diplomacy, where the perception of respect is as important as the act of engagement itself, such exclusions can be fatal to credibility. Likewise, in education, Mustafa Suleyman (2023) highlights the fragility of AI infrastructures: systems may deliver personalized learning at scale, but they can also fail in ways that disproportionately harm vulnerable publics.

As we have mentioned throughout the book, policy frameworks are addressing digital challenges with a focus on inclusion and cultural integrity. UNESCO emphasizes that innovation should promote diversity, not uniformity. The EU's AI Act (2024) mandates transparency in AI-generated content to protect authenticity. The African Union's Continental AI Strategy (2024) views linguistic inclusivity as essential to sovereignty and cultural autonomy. OECD's AI Principles (2024) prioritize fairness, while ASEAN's Expanded Guide on AI Governance and Ethics (2025) underscores the importance of adapting to local cultural contexts.

TECHNICAL CAPABILITIES

Neural Machine Translation for Cultural Content

AI's contributions are visible in several domains. In language, neural machine translation has lowered barriers to participation in international programs. Studies show that tools such as eTranslation increase productivity and accessibility in multilingual institutions, though human post-editing remains essential to preserve nuance (Gaspari et al. 2014). In education, AI-driven personalization promises to tailor learning to individual students' needs, expanding access across borders. Massive open online courses (MOOCs) and platforms like UNICEF's U-Report demonstrate how AI can engage learners at scale, reaching millions who would otherwise be excluded from traditional classrooms. In heritage preservation, machine vision and deep learning models are being used to digitize manuscripts, reconstruct damaged artifacts, and archive oral traditions, raising hopes that AI can preserve cultural memory for future generations.

Deep Learning for Heritage Digitization and Preservation

UNESCO has turned to AI for heritage preservation, digitizing endangered manuscripts, reconstructing damaged artifacts, and archiving oral traditions. Deep-learning tools are now able to infer missing fragments of texts or reconstruct sculptures from partial remains. These initiatives offer a glimpse of how AI might serve as a cultural lifeline, preserving traditions that might otherwise be lost. Yet they also raise questions of authorship and authenticity. When a damaged manuscript is reconstructed by an algorithm, is the result a faithful representation of the past or a new creation shaped by the biases of its training data? For cultural diplomacy, where trust depends on authenticity, such questions are not merely academic—they are political.

AI-Powered Educational Personalization

In education, AI has enabled programs to expand dramatically beyond the reach of traditional classrooms. Massive open online courses have made university-level instruction accessible to millions, while AI-driven personalization adapts content to individual learners' progress. Yet for all their promise, MOOCs face persistent challenges of completion rates and equitable access: learners in low-bandwidth regions or without devices remain excluded, reminding practitioners that democratizing education requires infrastructure as much as algorithms.

Translation at Institutional Scale

Beyond commercial tools, dedicated institutional translation platforms now operate at a scale that allows entire multilateral systems to sustain linguistic parity across dozens of languages simultaneously. These platforms illustrate both the democratic promise of neural machine translation—ensuring equal access across diverse publics—and its fragility when accuracy is measured only by literal meaning. The case studies that follow examine how this tension is being managed in practice.

REAL-WORLD APPLICATIONS

AI is no longer confined to pilot projects in cultural and educational diplomacy. Around the world, institutions are already deploying it to sustain multilingualism, expand access to learning, and preserve cultural heritage. These initiatives illustrate both the opportunities of scale and the need for constant human oversight to ensure that efficiency does not overwhelm authenticity.

At the United Nations, AI has become an indispensable tool for maintaining multilingualism. The Department for General Assembly and Conference Management has relied on *eLUNa* since 2015, a computer-assisted translation platform that integrates machine translation with translation memory to manage the UN's six official languages (DGACM 2015; United Nations 2022). The International Telecommunication Union supplements this with *ITU Translate*, launched in the early 2020s to handle the highly technical vocabularies of global telecommunications (ITU 2022; 2023). These systems allow vast volumes of documentation to be processed more quickly, sustaining the principle of linguistic parity that underpins multilateral legitimacy. Yet they also illustrate the limits of automation: sensitive negotiations still require human translators to preserve nuance and political tone.

Multilingual Cultural Access: The EU's eTranslation

The principle of linguistic equality has long defined multilateral diplomacy, but sustaining it across dozens of languages has traditionally required vast human resources. The European Union's *eTranslation* platform represents one of the most ambitious attempts to use AI to maintain linguistic parity at scale, with direct implications for cultural and educational diplomacy.

From Concept to Deployment

Chapter 2 examined eTranslation's general architecture and operational history in detail—the November 2017 launch, the 24 official EU languages, the EU-controlled infrastructure, and the deliberate decision to serve civil society and educational institutions alongside EU bodies (European Commission 2017). What concerns Chapter 8 is the platform's evolving role in cultural and educational diplomacy specifically. Erasmus+, the EU's flagship student mobility program, relies on eTranslation to make program materials accessible to students regardless of their native language. Cultural institutions across member states use it to translate exhibition materials, event descriptions, and educational resources, extending their reach beyond linguistically dominant populations. By 2025, cultural and educational content represented a growing share of eTranslation's millions of pages of annual workload (European Commission 2025a).

Cultural Diplomacy Implications

The democratic promise of eTranslation is profound: linguistic minorities within the EU gain access to cultural programming that was previously available only to speakers of dominant languages. A student in rural Slovakia can access Erasmus+ opportunities in their native language. A Greek cultural organization can share its programming with potential partners across the Union without waiting weeks for professional translation. This linguistic parity reinforces the EU's foundational commitment to unity in diversity, making cultural diplomacy truly multilateral rather than dependent on linguistic hegemonies.

Yet the system also reveals AI's limitations in cultural communication. Academic research confirms that while eTranslation handles factual and administrative content competently, it struggles with culturally embedded language—idioms, metaphors, humor, and references that carry meaning beyond their literal translation (Gaspari et al. 2014). A cultural event description that reads as "vibrant and welcoming" in one language may emerge in another as "loud and accessible," subtly altering the tone in ways that affect public reception.

The EU has addressed this through hybrid workflows: eTranslation provides initial translations rapidly, but culturally significant materials undergo human post-editing before publication. Cultural institutions are trained to flag content where nuance matters most—exhibition labels, artistic statements, educational materials for youth—ensuring that efficiency does not override authenticity. This model acknowledges that AI can extend reach but cannot replace cultural literacy.

Lessons for Diplomatic Practice

The eTranslation experience offers insights for diplomatic missions deploying AI in cultural programming:

Linguistic parity requires ongoing investment Not all language pairs perform equally well. Low-resource languages—those with less training data—produce less reliable translations, risking the very exclusion eTranslation aims to prevent. The EU continuously invests in improving performance for these pairs, recognizing that true linguistic equality requires sustained attention to languages often marginalized in commercial systems.

Transparency builds trust The EU clearly labels machine-translated content and distinguishes it from officially translated materials. This honesty prevents misunderstandings: publics know when they are reading a preliminary translation and can request human-translated versions when precision matters. This transparency itself becomes a form of respect.

For diplomatic practitioners, eTranslation demonstrates that AI can genuinely democratize access to cultural programming across linguistic boundaries—but only when paired with human cultural expertise, ongoing quality improvement for marginalized languages, and transparent communication about where machines end and human judgment begins.

Youth Empowerment: The UNICEF U-Report Platform

Chapter 7 examined U-Report's safeguarding architecture as a model for ethical AI engagement with minors. Here the focus shifts to its educational diplomacy contribution: how the platform amplifies voices traditionally excluded from policy conversations, and what its radical localization tells us about scaling cultural exchange across 102 countries without imposing a uniform model.

Origins and Evolution

U-Report began in 2011 as an SMS polling system in Uganda and has grown into one of the world's largest digital youth engagement platforms, with approximately 37 million registered users by mid-2025 (UNICEF 2025). Chapter 10 traces the platform's four developmental phases in detail. What matters here is its current operational shape: U-Report runs across SMS, WhatsApp, Facebook Messenger, Telegram, and Viber, ensuring accessibility even in low-connectivity environments where data costs limit internet access. Users receive periodic polls on topics ranging from education and health to climate and gender; natural language processing categorizes open-ended responses and flags priorities for policymakers. In many countries, U-Report findings inform UNICEF programming, advocacy briefs, and government policy.

Cultural Adaptation at Global Scale

What makes U-Report distinctive in cultural and educational diplomacy is its radical localization. The platform does not impose a universal model but adapts to local cultural contexts, linguistic realities, and communication norms. In some countries, polls address sexual and reproductive health—topics that might be taboo elsewhere. In others, questions focus on traditional practices, agricultural education, or conflict-affected schooling. UNICEF country offices work with youth advisory boards to ensure that questions are culturally appropriate, linguistically accurate, and relevant to local priorities.

This cultural humility distinguishes U-Report from top-down educational surveys. Rather than asking predetermined questions designed in headquarters, the platform treats youth as partners in question design. Young people themselves often propose poll topics, review translations, and interpret findings. This participatory approach ensures that AI-enabled engagement feels empowering rather than extractive: youth are not just data sources but co-creators of the knowledge that informs educational policy.

The multilingual dimension is equally significant. U-Report operates in dozens of languages, including many that commercial AI systems neglect. In countries with multiple official languages or significant linguistic minorities, polls are often conducted in three or more languages simultaneously, ensuring that linguistic barriers do not exclude youth from participation. This commitment to linguistic inclusion reflects UNICEF's understanding that educational diplomacy must reach all young people, not just those privileged by linguistic dominance.

Educational Diplomacy Impact

U-Report's influence on educational diplomacy operates at multiple levels. At the programmatic level, UNICEF uses poll data to refine education initiatives, ensuring that interventions address problems youth actually experience rather than those adults assume they face. At the advocacy level, U-Report findings provide evidence for policy recommendations to governments, demonstrating youth priorities with quantitative backing that policymakers find compelling. At the normative level, the platform models youth participation as a right rather than a concession, gradually shifting how governments conceive of young people's roles in educational policymaking.

The COVID-19 experience exemplifies this impact. When schools closed across much of the world, U-Report documented in real-time how remote learning was failing: students lacked devices, internet access was unreliable, and mental health was deteriorating. UNICEF compiled these findings into advocacy briefs that influenced policy responses in dozens of countries. In some contexts, governments adjusted education policies based directly on U-Report data—reopening schools earlier in areas where remote learning was demonstrably ineffective, or providing device subsidies where digital access was the primary barrier (UNICEF 2022).

Ethical Challenges and Safeguarding

Chapter 7 examined U-Report's safeguarding architecture in detail—informed consent across literacy levels, data protection across 102 jurisdictions, and the tension between empowering youth participation and protecting young users from risks they may not fully understand. UNICEF's approach to each is documented there. The challenge most distinctive to Chapter 8's frame is representational equity, because it determines whether the cultural exchange U-Report enables is actually exchange or only the appearance of it. While the platform aims to amplify marginalized youth voices, participation patterns risk reproducing existing inequalities: urban, educated youth with reliable device access may dominate the conversation, while rural, disabled, or conflict-affected youth remain underheard despite platform availability. UNICEF conducts equity audits to identify underrepresentation and invests in targeted outreach, but achieving genuinely inclusive participation remains a work in progress—and the audit findings themselves illustrate that scale and inclusion do not automatically align.

Lessons for Educational Diplomacy

U-Report's journey offers principles that apply specifically to diplomatic missions integrating AI into cultural exchange and educational programming, beyond the general scaling and safeguarding lessons drawn elsewhere in the book.

Localization is the design, not an adjustment. U-Report works because country offices co-design polls with youth advisory boards, conduct them in the linguistic varieties young people actually use, and treat headquarters templates as starting points rather than mandates. Educational diplomacy that imports content from a central authority and translates outward replicates the exact dynamic publics resent.

Linguistic inclusion is a cultural commitment, not a coverage metric. The platform's operation in dozens of languages, including many that commercial AI systems neglect, signals that minority-language speakers belong in the conversation. The reverse signal—youth being asked to participate in a dominant language not their own—reads as exclusion even when access is technically provided.

Participation must be visibly consequential. U-Report's credibility with youth participants depends on demonstrated examples of polling data shaping UNICEF programming and government policy. Cultural and educational platforms that collect input without showing what changed because of it train participants to disengage. The metric that matters is not response volume but whether respondents return.

Cultural authority over questions matters as much as cultural authority over answers. Letting youth propose poll topics, review translations, and interpret findings transfers a small but meaningful piece of editorial authority. For cultural diplomacy, this is the difference between extractive engagement (asking publics what they think and walking away with the data) and reciprocal engagement (treating their interpretations as part of the output).

For diplomatic missions, U-Report's contribution to cultural and educational diplomacy is not its scale but its discipline about whose questions count. AI can democratize youth participation in policy conversations, but only when missions accept that real participation reshapes the conversation itself—not just its reach.

Synthetic Narratives in Action: Swift's Synthetic Endorsement (2024)

In August 2024, a series of AI-generated images began circulating online showing Taylor Swift and her fans enthusiastically endorsing then former U.S. President Donald Trump. Some images depicted crowds of "Swifties" in Trump merchandise, while others appeared to show the singer herself expressing support. Just 7 months after Swift faced a barrage of non-consensual deepfake imagery (see Chapter 7), her likeness was weaponized again—this time not for personal exploitation but for political co-optation. Trump amplified the content by resharing it on his own platform, ensuring that the fake endorsements reached millions of viewers.

The images were quickly identified as synthetic, yet their effect did not rely on credibility alone. By co-opting the likeness of one of the world's most influential cultural icons, the creators hijacked the symbolic capital of Swift's fandom. Even if many recognized the images as fakes, their circulation blurred the boundaries between satire, propaganda, and wishful thinking. For supporters, the visuals could serve as rallying memes; for detractors, they became further evidence of political manipulation.

This episode demonstrates how cultural figures, whose influence extends well beyond politics, are increasingly drawn into synthetic narratives. For international communication, the lesson is clear: cultural icons are not just entertainers but symbols with global resonance. When their images are manipulated by AI, the stakes extend into diplomacy, education, and cultural exchange. As with other forms of propaganda, the danger lies less in total persuasion than in sowing confusion, mobilizing attention, and shaping perception through repetition (Le and Levine 2024; Robins-Early 2024; Swenson 2024).

AI-ASSISTED CULTURAL PROGRAMMING SELECTION AND AUDIENCE MATCHING

Beyond translation and preservation, AI is beginning to reshape how diplomatic missions select cultural programming and match it to audiences—a process that has traditionally relied heavily on staff intuition, personal networks, and trial-and-error. While these human elements remain essential, AI tools can now augment program selection by analyzing audience interests, predicting resonance, and identifying opportunities for cultural connection that might otherwise be overlooked.

Audience Analysis for Cultural Programming

Traditional cultural programming selection often operates with limited data about what actually resonates with local audiences. A mission might host a jazz concert because jazz represents American culture, but without systematic knowledge of whether local publics appreciate jazz, attend concerts, or view the genre as relevant to contemporary diplomacy. AI-enabled audience analysis can complement human judgment by surfacing patterns in cultural consumption, social media engagement, and attendance data that reveal what types of programming genuinely attract and engage target audiences.

For instance, sentiment analysis of social media conversations can identify which cultural topics are trending in a host country—perhaps a surge of interest in graphic novels, documentary film, or contemporary dance. Natural language processing can analyze how audiences discuss previous cultural events, revealing not just attendance numbers but qualitative reactions: did they find the event accessible or elitist, authentic or performative, relevant or dated? These signals help missions calibrate future programming to meet audiences where their interests actually lie, rather than where programming assumptions suggest they should be.

Similarly, AI can identify underserved audiences whose cultural interests have been overlooked. A mission might discover through data analysis that suburban youth are actively interested in hip-hop culture but have never been reached by embassy programming, which has focused on urban centers. Or analysis might reveal that diaspora communities are seeking connections to heritage traditions but find official cultural programming too mainstream to reflect their experiences. AI surfaces these gaps, but human judgment must determine how to address them authentically rather than opportunistically.

Cultural Exchange Alumni Network Optimization

Many diplomatic missions struggle to maintain engagement with cultural exchange alumni over time. An initial Fulbright scholarship or International Visitor Leadership Program creates a connection, but without systematic follow-up, alumni drift away from the institutional relationship. AI-enabled alumni network management can help missions sustain these connections by identifying natural affinity groups, suggesting programming aligned with alumni career development, and facilitating peer connections that might not occur through traditional alumni databases.

Machine learning can cluster alumni by shared interests, geographic proximity, professional sectors, or life stages, revealing opportunities for targeted programming. For example, AI might identify a cohort of Fulbright alumni now working in renewable energy across three countries who could benefit from a virtual symposium on climate policy. Or it might surface that alumni in a particular city have expressed interest in mentoring current exchange participants, enabling the mission to facilitate these connections.

Natural language processing of alumni communications—emails, survey responses, social media interactions—can also identify signals of disengagement before they become permanent. If alumni who were once active contributors suddenly stop responding, sentiment analysis might reveal frustration with programming that no longer matches their evolved interests. Early identification allows missions to course-correct, perhaps by offering more advanced professional development opportunities or creating leadership roles that re-engage experienced alumni.

However, these capabilities carry risks. Alumni may perceive AI-enabled analysis of their communications as surveillance rather than service, particularly if they were unaware their data was being analyzed. Missions must be transparent about how alumni data is used, provide opt-in rather than opt-out mechanisms, and ensure that network optimization serves alumni interests rather than purely institutional objectives. The goal is to sustain authentic relationships, not to manipulate alumni into continued engagement.

Artist and Speaker Selection

Selecting artists, speakers, and cultural practitioners for diplomatic programming has traditionally relied on personal networks, agent recommendations, and institutional relationships. While these channels remain valuable, they can also reproduce biases toward well-known figures while overlooking emerging voices who might resonate more authentically with contemporary audiences. AI can augment selection processes by identifying rising cultural practitioners whose work aligns with mission themes but who lack the established networks that typically bring them to diplomatic attention.

For example, social media analysis can identify visual artists, musicians, or writers whose work is generating authentic grassroots engagement in a host country, even if they lack gallery representation or major label contracts. Sentiment analysis can assess whether their work is perceived as culturally authentic or as appropriative, helping missions avoid the embarrassment of featuring practitioners whose legitimacy is contested. Network analysis can reveal how cultural practitioners are connected to communities the mission seeks to engage, identifying individuals who serve as cultural bridges rather than distant celebrities.

AI can also help missions assess cultural sensitivities before selecting programming. Natural language processing of local media and social media can flag topics, artistic styles, or cultural figures that are currently contentious, allowing missions to navigate sensitivities proactively. For instance, if analysis reveals that a particular artistic genre is embroiled in debates about cultural appropriation, the mission can either avoid the controversy or engage it deliberately with appropriate framing and local partner consultation.

However, algorithmic selection risks reducing cultural practitioners to engagement metrics, privileging virality over depth and mainstream appeal over challenging art. Missions must resist the temptation to let algorithms dictate programming purely based on predicted reach. The goal of cultural diplomacy is not always to attract the largest audience but sometimes to introduce challenging perspectives, support underrepresented voices, or create space for difficult conversations. Human cultural judgment must remain central, with AI serving as one input among many.

Timing and Context Optimization

Even excellent cultural programming can fail if poorly timed. A celebration of American film might resonate powerfully one month but feel tone-deaf the next if local political developments have soured public attitudes. AI-enabled context monitoring can help missions calibrate timing by tracking shifts in public mood, identifying windows of opportunity for particular themes, and flagging moments when cultural programming might be inadvertently offensive.

Sentiment analysis of news coverage and social media can reveal when publics are receptive to particular cultural themes. For example, if analysis shows growing public conversation about gender equality following local policy changes, a mission might accelerate programming featuring women artists or educational exchanges focused on women's leadership. Conversely, if analysis detects rising sensitivity about foreign influence, the mission might delay programming that could be perceived as heavy-handed and instead emphasize collaborative rather than presentational formats.

Event scheduling can also benefit from data analysis. Machine learning can identify patterns in attendance rates correlated with factors like weather, competing local events, religious holidays, school calendars, or public transportation schedules. While human staff typically know major holidays, AI can surface subtler patterns: perhaps attendance drops during university exam periods, or weekend events consistently underperform compared to weekday evenings in particular neighborhoods. These insights allow missions to optimize logistics for maximum accessibility.

Ethical Boundaries in AI-Assisted Cultural Programming

Yet all these capabilities must be bounded by ethical constraints. The line between understanding audiences and manipulating them is uncomfortably thin. AI that helps missions meet audiences where their interests lie can serve genuine cultural exchange. AI that attempts to engineer cultural preferences or exploit psychological vulnerabilities crosses into manipulation.

Several principles should guide responsible use:

Transparency about data use Audiences, alumni, and cultural practitioners should understand when and how their data informs programming decisions. Covert analysis breeds distrust; transparent processes build confidence.

Human judgment remains central AI surfaces patterns and possibilities; humans decide whether pursuing them serves authentic cultural exchange or merely optimizes metrics.

Respect for cultural autonomy Programming should respond to local cultural interests, not attempt to reshape them. The goal is dialogue, not conversion.

Protection of vulnerable populations When programming involves youth, data collection and analysis must include heightened safeguards beyond those appropriate for adult audiences.

Resistance to filter bubbles AI tends to reinforce existing preferences. Missions must consciously use these tools to expand rather than narrow cultural exposure, introducing audiences to perspectives they would not algorithmically encounter.

For diplomatic practitioners, AI-assisted cultural programming selection offers genuine value—but only when wielded with humility, transparency, and constant attention to the ethical boundaries between service and manipulation. The goal is to make cultural diplomacy more responsive and inclusive, not more manipulative or commercially optimized.

PRACTITIONER GUIDANCE

For practitioners, cultural and educational diplomacy is often the most rewarding but also the most delicate part of their work. These are the spaces where publics encounter a foreign institution not in the heat of political debate or crisis, but in the slower rhythms of art, learning, and heritage. They are also the spaces where missteps can linger longest. An insensitive translation, an exclusionary education program, or a poorly framed heritage initiative can cast shadows over relationships for years. AI can expand reach and efficiency in these fields, but it must be used with extraordinary care—and with the recognition that technology is never neutral. It amplifies the values embedded in its design and deployment, which is why the practitioner's judgment, not the system's capability, sets the ceiling on what cultural diplomacy can achieve.

The first lesson is to balance efficiency with authenticity. Translation systems may allow a speech or poem to be rendered into dozens of languages in hours, but speed should never come at the expense of cultural nuance. Human validators, especially local artists, educators, and scholars, must remain central to the process. Their role is not only to correct errors but to preserve tone, metaphor, and resonance—the elements that make cultural diplomacy meaningful.

A second lesson is to treat inclusivity as a design principle, not a patch applied later. AI systems are only as inclusive as the data they are trained on. If minority languages or rural voices are absent from the training set, they will be absent from the outputs. Missions that interrogate training data before deployment, proactively commission translations into smaller languages, design surveys accessible on low-bandwidth devices, and consult validators from underrepresented communities signal that inclusivity is not symbolic but substantive.

Safeguarding emerges as a third priority, particularly in educational contexts. AI-enabled platforms that collect data from youth participants or personalize learning experiences must embed strict protections for privacy. Publics will not trust programs that put children at risk, no matter how innovative they appear. Missions should be prepared to articulate what data is collected, how it is used, and how it is protected—a transparency that builds confidence rather than suspicion.

Finally, practitioners should remember that cultural and educational diplomacy is about relationships, not content delivery. AI may generate translations, digitize manuscripts, or recommend learning modules, but publics will judge whether those outputs feel respectful and authentic. The credibility of a cultural initiative rests less on the technology behind it than on whether publics believe they are being taken seriously.

WORKFLOWS FOR CULTURAL AND EDUCATIONAL AI

Practitioner guidance establishes what to attend to; workflows determine whether those commitments hold up under daily operational pressure. Cultural and educational diplomacy requires structured routines that embed diversity, authenticity, inclusivity, and safeguarding into practice—because AI tools expand capacity, but without disciplined routines they produce misunderstandings that erode credibility rather than strengthen it.

Translation workflows are the most visible. Whichever platform a mission uses, the lesson recurring across institutional deployments is the same: machine translation produces draft fluency, but cultural fidelity requires human post-editing by validators who can catch what algorithms miss—idioms, metaphors, register, and the rhetorical structures that carry meaning beyond the literal. Glossaries curated by local experts and updated with validator feedback prevent the same misstep from recurring. The discipline is straightforward; what is hard is institutionalizing it before the speed of the tool overrides the judgment of the person reviewing it.

Heritage preservation workflows extend institutional capacity dramatically but carry safeguards for authenticity that translation work does not require. The operative discipline is provenance documentation: every AI-reconstructed artifact should travel with a record of what portions are original and what was inferred. Transparency at that level lets publics appreciate the role of technology while still judging the cultural integrity of what is presented to them. Heritage workflows, in other words, must balance innovation with accountability.

Education workflows turn on safeguarding. The personalization that makes AI valuable in learning depends on data collection that carries real risk when the learners are minors. Responsible workflows therefore include strict data-retention limits, plain-language disclosure of how information is used, and protocols built specifically for youth contexts rather than imported from adult-facing tools. Missions that fold ethics reviews into education partnerships—with schools, parents, and civil society at the table—signal that participation is designed to empower rather than expose.

Finally, narrative archiving is emerging as a workflow that connects culture, education, and institutional memory. AI systems can catalog decades of speeches, cultural programs, and educational exchanges, making them retrievable for diplomats, educators, and publics alike. This preserves continuity across political transitions and ensures that lessons are not lost when staff rotate. But here too, workflows must be designed with care. Archives must respect privacy, distinguish between public and sensitive material, and involve curators who can contextualize rather than simply store outputs.

Together, these workflows demonstrate how cultural and educational diplomacy can integrate AI responsibly. When designed thoughtfully, these routines allow AI to amplify cultural and educational diplomacy rather than diminish it, expanding access while preserving the respect on which soft power ultimately depends.

Risks and Ethics

If cultural and educational diplomacy is where trust is built most slowly, it is also where it can be lost surprisingly quickly. AI offers diplomats powerful tools to expand access, but in doing so it raises ethical risks that strike at the heart of credibility: cultural flattening, digital colonialism, contested authenticity, and the safeguarding of vulnerable publics.

Cultural flattening is perhaps the most immediate danger. Machine translation systems may capture the literal sense of words but miss their cultural resonance. A metaphor meant to convey resilience may be rendered as obstinacy, or a sacred phrase may be stripped of its spiritual weight. As the vignette in this chapter illustrated, what reads as harmless efficiency from the perspective of programmers can come across as disrespect when publics see their traditions reduced to clumsy literalism. Cultural diplomacy succeeds only when audiences feel their identities are honored. AI that flattens nuance risks turning celebration into alienation.

Digital colonialism presents a second risk. AI systems are overwhelmingly trained on data from high-resource languages and dominant cultural contexts. When these systems are deployed in Africa, Asia, or Latin America, they risk imposing Western cultural norms under the guise of technical neutrality. As the African Union's *Continental AI Strategy* (2024) warns, this is not accidental exclusion but structural bias that perpetuates inequalities. For diplomats, the lesson is clear: cultural and educational AI that fails to represent minority languages or non-Western traditions will be perceived not as expansion but as erasure.

Contested authenticity emerges as a third concern. When AI reconstructs a damaged artifact or translates a sacred text, questions arise about whether the result is faithful to the original or a new creation shaped by algorithmic inference. In heritage preservation, publics may reasonably ask: whose past is being preserved, and by whose standards? Transparency about where human expertise ends and machine inference begins is essential. Without it, even well-intentioned preservation efforts can become sites of distrust, with communities questioning whether their heritage is being honored or appropriated.

Safeguarding vulnerable publics, particularly youth, is the fourth ethical imperative. Platforms that collect data from minors, personalize content based on behavior, or facilitate peer interaction all carry risks of exploitation, privacy breaches, or exposure to harmful content. The principle that emerges from the case study earlier in the chapter is that safeguards must scale with reach: protocols adequate for a national pilot are not adequate for a global platform, and the gap between the two cannot be closed by goodwill alone. Yet even with extensive protections, trade-offs remain. Overly restrictive safeguards may exclude youth from participation; insufficient protections may endanger them. The ethical challenge is to empower without exposing.

These risks underscore a paradox: AI can make culture and education more accessible, but it can also make them more vulnerable. Cultural flattening, digital colonialism, contested authenticity, and safeguarding failures are not side effects but central challenges of applying AI in this domain. For diplomats, the task is not to reject AI but to confront these dilemmas directly, embedding transparency, inclusivity, and respect into every cultural and educational initiative. Without such safeguards, publics may see AI not as a bridge across cultures but as another barrier erected by those who fail to listen.

Metrics and Evaluation

Cultural and educational diplomacy has always been challenging to measure. Unlike public relations campaigns, where impressions and shares provide easy metrics, the impact of exchanges, heritage preservation, or youth engagement often unfolds slowly, across years and generations. AI introduces new possibilities for measurement, but the core question remains the same: are publics not only reached but respected?

Representation is one of the most important indicators. AI platforms can now analyze participation across demographics, regions, and languages, making it possible to track whether minority communities are included in cultural programs or educational surveys. An equity audit of an AI translation system, for example, can reveal whether materials are available in all relevant local languages or only the dominant ones. For cultural diplomacy, inclusivity is not simply an efficiency metric but a measure of legitimacy.

Reach offers a second dimension of evaluation. Youth engagement platforms track participation rates across geographies; MOOC systems measure enrollment and completion. Yet reach must be interpreted with care. Large numbers may indicate scale but not resonance, especially when participants suspect that their contributions are not valued—the difference between an audit-friendly headline and a programmatic effect.

Preservation quality is emerging as a third metric in heritage projects. When manuscripts are digitized or artifacts reconstructed with AI, evaluation must go beyond technical accuracy to assess cultural integrity. Provenance logs documenting which portions were machine-inferred allow scholars and publics to judge whether they view the digital object as faithful or synthetic. In this sense, evaluation becomes less about the number of items preserved and more about the trust placed in the preservation process.

Trust itself is perhaps the most critical measure. Surveys, focus groups, and validator feedback can reveal whether publics feel cultural and educational AI systems empower them or erase them. A translation program may deliver access, but if students or artists believe their culture is being flattened, the initiative will have failed in its primary purpose. Similarly, a youth engagement platform may gather millions of responses, but if young participants doubt that their input influences policy, trust will wither.

Together, these metrics shift evaluation away from activity counts toward outcomes that matter for credibility. In cultural and educational diplomacy, the true metric of success is whether publics experience AI as a bridge across cultures or as a barrier that distorts them.

Reflection and Strategic Questions

These lessons lead to reflective questions that practitioners might ask themselves. Are our AI tools preserving cultural nuance or flattening it into literalism? Do our education platforms empower youth, or do they reduce them to data points in an algorithm? Have we considered whose voices are excluded from our datasets, and what message that exclusion sends? And are we using AI to sustain genuine exchange, or are we slipping into one-way projection dressed up as participation?

FRONTIER PILOTS

While many AI applications in cultural and educational diplomacy are already deployed, a new wave of experiments is beginning to shape what the next decade may look like. These frontier initiatives remain tentative, but they reveal both the potential and the dilemmas of embedding AI into the preservation and projection of cultural identity.

One frontier lies in heritage restoration. Deep-learning models are being used to reconstruct damaged manuscripts, rebuild fragmented sculptures, and even colorize historical photographs. In Syria and Iraq, researchers have experimented with AI to recreate monuments destroyed during conflict, offering digital surrogates for sites that can no longer be visited. The promise is powerful: cultural heritage that would otherwise be lost can be reimagined and made accessible to global audiences. Yet the risks are equally profound. When an algorithm infers what a monument "should" look like, does it preserve authenticity or invent a past that never existed? Without transparency about where human expertise ends and machine inference begins, publics may question the legitimacy of what is being presented in the name of preservation.

A second area of experimentation is cross-cultural framing beyond translation. Rather than rendering words literally from one language into another, some research groups are training models to adapt metaphors, idioms, and rhetorical structures so that messages resonate more deeply across cultures. For example, a campaign about climate change might be framed through agricultural metaphors in one society and spiritual stewardship in another. Such tools could dramatically expand the reach of cultural diplomacy by making communication feel more locally authentic. Yet they also carry the risk of manipulation. If publics suspect that algorithms are being used to "play" them with customized framings, trust could collapse. The ethical line lies in adaptation for clarity, not for covert persuasion.

A third frontier involves institutional narrative memory. Diplomatic institutions produce vast archives of cultural programming, speeches, and educational materials, much of which becomes inaccessible after staff rotations or leadership transitions. AI systems are now being tested to catalog and retrieve decades of this content, making it easier to maintain continuity across generations of cultural diplomacy. A diplomat preparing a speech about educational exchanges, for instance, could instantly access past addresses, program evaluations, and alumni testimonials. The potential is to preserve institutional wisdom and prevent the constant reinvention that has long plagued public diplomacy. But here too, dilemmas emerge: which narratives are preserved, which are excluded, and who decides? Narrative memory is never neutral—it reflects choices about what to remember and what to forget.

These frontier pilots illustrate both opportunity and fragility. Heritage restoration promises preservation but risks contested authenticity. Cross-cultural framing offers resonance but risks manipulation. Institutional memory enables continuity but raises questions about bias in curation. For diplomats, the lesson is clear: frontier tools must be approached with humility, transparency, and restraint. AI can expand the reach of cultural and educational diplomacy, but only human care can ensure that what is preserved and shared is received as authentic and respectful.

CONCLUSION

As you reflect on this chapter, consider the transformative—but double-edged—role of artificial intelligence in cultural and educational diplomacy. The lesson is clear: technology enables scale, but only human care ensures meaning.The next chapter explores how these principles shape multilateral collaboration, showing that the trust sustaining global coalitions relies on the same commitment to transparency and respect that underpins every successful cultural exchange.

9 Collaborative Diplomacy

AI for Multilateral Campaigns

"Ideas, cultures, and histories cannot seriously be understood or studied without their force, or more precisely their configurations of power, also being studied."

—Edward W. Said, *Orientalism* (1978)

"Today's real borders are not between nations, but between powerful and powerless, free and fettered, privileged and humiliated."

—Kofi Annan, Nobel Lecture (2001)

"No country can stop a pandemic alone. No army can halt rising temperatures. No algorithm can rebuild trust once it is broken."

—António Guterres, Address to the 80th Session of the UN General Assembly (2025)

Opening Vignette: When the Election Became Everyone's Problem

The first signs appeared in Country A, a small parliamentary democracy preparing for national elections. Overnight, a series of slick videos began circulating on social media, claiming that international observers had already declared the vote fraudulent—two weeks before polling stations were even due to open. The videos carried the logos of respected monitoring organizations, their voices synthesized to sound authentic. By morning, a hashtag calling the election rigged before it had started was trending in three languages.

Country A's own monitoring unit flagged the anomaly but quickly realized the challenge was bigger than any single government could manage alone. Within hours, similar content appeared in Country B, this time tailored to inflame tensions between migrant and host communities. In Country C, memes recycled the same narrative but localized it to accuse specific ethnic minorities of plotting election violence. The campaign was multilingual, multi-platform, and clearly coordinated across borders. A regional digital media observatory

DOI: 10.1201/9781003612377-12

convened its member hubs, pooling data from across the continent. Natural language processing clustered narratives that looked different on the surface but shared identical metadata signatures—matching creation timestamps, image hashes, and coordination patterns. An allied strategic communications center issued a parallel alert, warning that the disinformation surge matched the pattern of adversarial simulations it had modeled months earlier. A joint monitoring task force added context, noting that the narratives echoed earlier influence operations linked to a hostile state actor.

In one corner of this coalition response, the embassy in the Republic of Z contributed a detection flag of its own. Its monitoring system—the same dashboard that had tracked the water contamination narrative months earlier—had picked up early crossover: Zorani-language accounts were beginning to amplify the Country A hashtag, adapting the "rigged election" frame to local grievances. The flag was small, but it added a data point that helped analysts see how quickly the campaign was spreading beyond its original targets. The question facing the coalition was not whether the campaign was coordinated—it clearly was—but how to respond. Should the regional body issue a continent-wide rebuttal, risking accusations of interfering in national debates? Should national governments lead, even if their resources and credibility varied? Should platforms be pressured to act more aggressively, or would that feed narratives of censorship?

In the end, the response was collaborative but uneven. Some member states moved quickly, amplifying the observatory's bulletins through local validators and independent fact-checkers. Others hesitated, fearing that drawing attention to the content would only accelerate its spread. Coordination was strongest where relationships between national monitors and the regional hub had been built before the crisis—and weakest where governments were engaging the coalition for the first time under pressure. By the time Election Day arrived, the narrative had lost some of its momentum, but not before trust in the electoral process had been shaken across borders. The episode underscored a dilemma that no technology could resolve on its own. Detection had been fast because data was shared across institutions and languages. But decisions about action were slow because sovereignty mattered—every government weighed its own political risks before joining a collective response.

AI had given the coalition the ability to see the campaign in near real time. It could not answer the harder questions: who should lead, how fast to move, and what publics in each country would perceive as legitimate. Collaborative diplomacy, the episode revealed, is as much about managing trust among allies as it is about defending credibility against adversaries.

FRAMING THE CHAPTER

Diplomacy has always involved collaboration, but in the digital age, no state can defend credibility alone. Disinformation campaigns spill across borders, crises ripple through regions, and narratives seeded in one language are quickly translated and amplified in another. Artificial intelligence magnifies both the scale of the challenge and the possibilities for collective response. What one embassy cannot see, a network of allies might detect. What one government cannot rebut credibly, a coalition of partners might disarm by acting together. Yet collaboration also introduces dilemmas: whose standards apply, whose voices lead, and how to balance sovereignty with the need for speed.

AI alters the equation by enabling shared monitoring, forecasting, and narrative defense at a scale unthinkable a decade ago. Natural language processing allows multinational institutions like the EU to detect cross-border narratives in dozens of languages. Anomaly detection can reveal suspicious surges across platforms simultaneously in different countries. Provenance standards are beginning to provide tools for verifying content, while simulation exercises model how adversarial narratives might unfold. Properly harnessed, these systems give coalitions an anticipatory capacity: the ability not just to react to disinformation but to forecast and prepare for it.

RESEARCH AND POLICY FOUNDATIONS

Multilateralism has always been a cornerstone of diplomacy, but in the information age it has taken on new urgency. Narratives no longer respect borders, and the ability of states to defend their credibility depends increasingly on their ability to act together. Scholars of public diplomacy have long argued that coalitions amplify credibility: when multiple states speak with one voice, publics are more likely to perceive messages as legitimate (Bjola and Manor 2018; Bjola, Cassidy, and Manor 2019). In the AI era, this principle extends beyond rhetoric to infrastructure. Collective forecasting, monitoring, and simulation are becoming tools of shared resilience, allowing alliances to anticipate adversarial moves and coordinate responses before narratives harden.

Research on disinformation confirms the scale of the challenge. Studies show that falsehoods spread more quickly and widely than factual corrections, especially in polarized environments (Vosoughi, Roy, and Aral 2018). Disinformation campaigns are rarely confined to a single state; instead, they exploit cross-border linguistic and cultural overlaps. This is why organizations such as the European Union and NATO have invested in AI-enabled hubs and simulation exercises. By pooling data across multiple countries, they can detect patterns that no single government would see in isolation. RAND and Carnegie analysts have described this as a move from *reactive communication* to *anticipatory governance*, where simulations help coalitions prepare counter-narratives before they are needed (Mazarr et al. 2019).

Yet forecasting carries risks as well as promise. Mustafa Suleyman (2023) warns that predictive models often create a false sense of certainty, encouraging decision-makers to overestimate their foresight. Forecasting based on past data may miss new tactics or cultural nuances, and overconfidence in simulations can produce blind spots. Scholars of technology and international relations emphasize that models must be treated as provisional signals, not verdicts. The danger of "narrative determinism"—the belief that simulations can map the future of public opinion with precision—remains ever present.

Global governance frameworks have begun to set expectations for how AI forecasting and collaborative monitoring should be deployed. UNESCO's *Recommendation on the Ethics of Artificial Intelligence* (2021) stresses proportionality and transparency, principles especially vital in multilateral contexts where publics may be skeptical of surveillance. The European Union's *AI Act* (2024) requires labeling of synthetic media and explainability for high-risk systems, creating a regulatory baseline that influences global practice. The OECD's updated *AI Principles* (2024) emphasize fairness and inclusivity, ensuring that shared systems reflect diverse voices rather than privileging dominant states. The African Union's *Continental AI Strategy* (2024) warns that coalitions must not marginalize smaller or less digitally connected members. ASEAN's *Expanded Guide on AI Governance and Ethics* (2025) highlights contextual adaptation, reminding practitioners that even in multilateral settings, cultural nuance must remain central. The G7's *Hiroshima Code of Conduct on AI* (2023) ties these principles explicitly to democratic values, committing member states to transparency, restraint, and accountability in the use of AI for governance and security.

These research and policy foundations highlight both the promise and the fragility of collaborative AI in diplomacy. Forecasting and simulation can provide coalitions with valuable foresight, but credibility depends on whether partners share not only tools but also values, thresholds, and trust. Maillart et al. (2024) offer a constructive model through the concept of computational diplomacy—the use of data-driven tools and participatory methods, including collaborative hackathons, to build shared analytical capacity across multilateral institutions. Their work suggests that the challenge is not only technical but political: building the habits of transparency and reciprocity that make collective action legitimate.

REAL-WORLD APPLICATIONS

The practical value of AI in collaborative diplomacy is already visible in the work of multilateral institutions. From the European Union's disinformation monitoring hubs to NATO's simulation exercises and the G7's coordinated response mechanisms, governments have begun to experiment with shared systems that detect, forecast, and defend against hostile narratives. These cases reveal both the promise of pooled capacity and the frictions that arise when sovereignty, legitimacy, and speed must be balanced.

EDMO and EEAS: The EU's Coordinated Response Architecture

The European Union's approach to collaborative AI in information defense represents one of the most sophisticated multilateral systems in operation. The European Digital Media Observatory (EDMO) and the European External Action Service (EEAS)'s work on Foreign Information Manipulation and Interference (FIMI) provide a detailed case study in how coalitions can build shared detection capacity while navigating the sovereignty sensitivities inherent in coordinated responses.

The European Union has been a pioneer in collective disinformation defense. *EUvsDisinfo*, launched in 2015 under the East StratCom Task Force, began as a database of false narratives but has evolved into a multilingual monitoring effort supported by natural language processing tools. By cataloging disinformation in dozens of languages, the platform allows member states to identify common patterns and coordinate responses. During the 2024 European Parliament elections, this effort was supplemented by the European Digital Media Observatory (EDMO), which established regional hubs across the Union. These hubs pooled AI-driven analysis to produce daily bulletins, highlighting anomalies that no single state could have spotted alone (European Commission 2025b). The EEAS added another layer with its *Foreign Information Manipulation and Interference* (FIMI) reports, the third of which, released in March 2025, documented the growing role of synthetic media in hostile campaigns (EEAS 2025). The EU model demonstrates how coalitions can build shared situational awareness—but it also illustrates the challenge of legitimacy, as critics have accused the Union of overstepping by labeling narratives as disinformation.

EDMO's 2024 European Parliament Elections Deployment

The June 2024 European Parliament elections provided a stress test for EDMO's regional hub model. Established in 2020 with initial funding from the European Commission, EDMO had by 2024 built a network of independent fact-checking organizations and research institutions across all 27 member states. These hubs employed natural language processing to monitor disinformation in real time across 24 official EU languages, producing daily situation reports that aggregated threats at the Union level (European Commission 2025b).

During the three-month election period (April–June 2024), EDMO documented over 750 distinct disinformation narratives that crossed at least two member state borders. Machine learning algorithms clustered these narratives into thematic groups: election fraud allegations, anti-immigrant rhetoric, climate change denial, and economic scaremongering. What made EDMO's analysis distinctive was its ability to track narrative mutation—how a claim seeded in one language would be adapted and localized as it spread into other linguistic communities.

For example, a false narrative about electronic voting machines being "pre-programmed" originated in Polish-language social media in early May 2024. Within 48 hours, EDMO detected variants in Czech, Slovak, and Hungarian, each adapted to local electoral systems and political contexts. The cross-border tracking allowed the Commission to alert member states before the narrative gained traction in their domestic debates. In this case, coordinated fact-checking responses were prepared across four countries simultaneously, significantly reducing the narrative's half-life.

However, the 2024 elections also exposed coordination challenges. While EDMO could detect cross-border narratives rapidly, response times varied dramatically across member states. Some countries with well-developed validator networks (Belgium, Netherlands, and Sweden) amplified corrections within hours. Others with more fragmented media ecosystems or political sensitivities about EU involvement (Hungary, Italy) delayed or declined to participate in coordinated responses. This asymmetry created windows where narratives dominated in some countries while being contained in others—a pattern adversaries could exploit.

EEAS FIMI Reports: Synthetic Media Threat Documentation

Complementing EDMO's real-time monitoring, the European External Action Service's Foreign Information Manipulation and Interference (FIMI) reports provide strategic analysis of hostile information operations targeting the Union. The third FIMI report, released March 6, 2025, marked a watershed in documenting the role of generative AI in influence campaigns (EEAS 2025).

The March 2025 report documented a marked rise in the use of generative AI in influence operations targeting EU institutions and member states. Examples included:

- AI-generated "spokesperson" videos purporting to represent EU officials announcing non-existent policies
- Deepfake audio of national leaders making inflammatory statements about migration or security
- Synthetic images showing fabricated protests, violence, or EU symbols in compromising contexts
- AI-generated news articles with fabricated quotes attributed to real journalists and officials

What distinguished the EEAS approach was its attribution methodology. Rather than simply cataloging incidents, the report employed network analysis to link operations back to infrastructure, linguistic patterns, and operational behaviors characteristic of specific state actors. By early 2025, the EEAS had identified three primary sources: Russian state-affiliated actors, Chinese state media ecosystems, and commercial disinformation-for-hire operations based in Eastern Europe and Southeast Asia.

The report's key finding: synthetic media was being deployed not primarily to deceive about specific facts but to create ambient distrust in all information environments. When publics cannot distinguish authentic from fabricated content, the strategic goal—undermining confidence in democratic institutions—succeeds whether individual deepfakes are believed or not.

Coordination Mechanisms and Lessons

The EU's experience with EDMO and EEAS coordination reveals both strengths and persistent challenges:

Strengths:

- *Multi-lingual detection at scale* AI's ability to monitor 24 languages simultaneously provides situational awareness impossible for any single member state
- *Pattern recognition across borders* Machine learning identifies narrative clusters that national-level analysts would miss
- *Shared evidence base* Common documentation allows coordinated rather than contradictory responses
- *Early warning with lead time* Detection 24-72 hours before narratives peak gives states time to prepare validators and messaging

Persistent Challenges:

- *Sovereignty tensions* Member states remain reluctant to cede narrative control, even when evidence suggests coordination would be more effective
- *Response asymmetry* Variations in domestic media ecosystems mean coordinated detection doesn't guarantee coordinated action
- *Legitimacy concerns* Labeling content as "manipulation" or "interference" remains politically sensitive, especially when narratives touch on legitimate domestic policy debates
- *Attribution disputes* Even with strong technical evidence, member states may disagree on whether to publicly attribute operations to specific state actors
- *Platform cooperation gaps* Social media platforms' willingness to act on EU requests varies, with some moving quickly and others citing free expression concerns

Implications for Other Coalitions

The EU's EDMO/EEAS model offers lessons for other multilateral groupings. The African Union, ASEAN, and the Organization of American States have all expressed interest in similar regional hub architectures. However, the EU's relative institutional maturity and resource depth make replication challenging. Smaller or less digitally connected member states within these organizations may lack the technical infrastructure or validator networks needed to participate effectively in shared monitoring.

The EU experience suggests that successful coalition AI depends less on technical sophistication than on pre-existing trust, clear governance structures, and willingness to subordinate some national flexibility to collective action. For diplomatic practitioners, the lesson is that AI can provide the infrastructure for coordination, but political cohesion must precede technological deployment—not follow from it.

Canada's G7 Rapid Response Mechanism

If the EU's approach emphasizes comprehensive cross-border monitoring, Canada's leadership in the G7 Rapid Response Mechanism (RRM) demonstrates a different model: using AI-enabled detection paired with radical transparency to build both coalition coordination and public trust simultaneously.

Origins and Evolution

The G7 RRM was established at the June 2018 Charlevoix Summit in Canada, emerging from recognition that hostile information operations were targeting all seven democracies with coordinated campaigns. Canada volunteered to serve as the mechanism's coordinating node, leveraging expertise in both signals intelligence and open-source analysis.

By 2023, the RRM had evolved from primarily human-analyst-driven work to incorporating AI-enabled anomaly detection and network analysis. Global Affairs

Canada's Rapid Response Mechanism team deployed natural language processing to monitor social media, news ecosystems, and online platforms across G7 member states, looking for coordinated inauthentic behavior patterns that suggested state-sponsored operations.

The Spamouflage Operations

Canada's October 23, 2023 advisory on "Spamouflage" operations targeting Canadian Members of Parliament exemplifies the RRM's transparency-focused approach (Global Affairs Canada 2023). The advisory publicly documented a coordinated information operation that used thousands of fake social media accounts to amplify anti-Canadian narratives and target specific politicians with harassment campaigns.

The technical analysis was sophisticated: network mapping revealed that accounts were operated in clusters, posting during specific time windows consistent with work hours in a particular geographic region. Linguistic analysis showed unnatural phrasing patterns characteristic of machine-assisted translation. Behavioral analysis flagged coordination—accounts would go dormant simultaneously, then resume activity in synchronized bursts.

What made Canada's approach distinctive was the decision to publish these findings publicly rather than limiting them to classified intelligence sharing. The advisory included:

- Specific examples of fabricated content
- Network diagrams showing coordination patterns
- Technical indicators observers could use to identify similar operations
- Attribution assessment (with appropriate caveats about confidence levels)
- Recommendations for platforms, civil society, and individual users

The March 6, 2025 advisory on operations targeting Chinese-language journalists in Canada followed a similar pattern, documenting how diaspora media were being targeted with coordinated harassment, doxing, and synthetic media designed to discredit their reporting (Global Affairs Canada 2025). Again, Canada published technical analysis publicly, demonstrating both to domestic audiences and to adversaries that such operations would be exposed.

Strategic Logic: Transparency as Inoculation

Canada's transparency approach rests on a strategic theory: that public exposure of operations reduces their effectiveness even if individual pieces of disinformation continue to circulate. When citizens understand the mechanics of manipulation, they become more resilient to future attempts. When platforms see documented coordination patterns, they have public justification for enforcement action. When adversaries know their operations will be exposed, the cost-benefit calculation of conducting them shifts.

This "inoculation through exposure" model contrasts with more secretive approaches to counter-disinformation. Some coalition members argued that publicizing operations might teach adversaries which detection methods to evade. Canada's counter-argument: adversaries already know detection methods are improving, and transparency builds democratic resilience in ways secrecy cannot.

The RRM's AI tools played a critical role in making transparency feasible. Network analysis algorithms could process millions of accounts to identify coordination patterns that human analysts would miss. Natural language processing could detect linguistic anomalies across multiple languages. Behavioral modeling could distinguish between organic engagement and artificial amplification with statistical confidence.

However, AI alone couldn't make the attribution assessments or decide what to publish. Those remained human judgments balancing available evidence, intelligence protection, and strategic communication goals.

Coordination Challenges at G7 Scale

Despite Canada's transparency successes, the G7 RRM faces persistent coordination challenges. With seven member states (Canada, France, Germany, Italy, Japan, UK, and USA), plus the EU as an institutional member, consensus on what constitutes an "actionable" operation remains elusive.

The 2024 French National Assembly election illustrated these tensions. Canadian and British RRM analysts detected coordinated amplification of anti-Macron narratives that bore hallmarks of state-sponsored operations. However, French authorities were reluctant to have G7 partners issue advisories about their domestic election, viewing it as potential interference. By the time French agencies independently confirmed and publicized the operation, several weeks had passed—and the narrative's impact had already occurred.

This sovereignty-speed trade-off is inherent in multilateral coordination. The G7's strength—representing diverse democracies—is also its constraint: what seems like clear manipulation to one member may appear like legitimate domestic criticism to another. Cultural and political contexts shape threat perception, and AI detection systems, however sophisticated, cannot resolve these inherently political disagreements.

Lessons for Coalition Information Defense

Canada's RRM experience offers several principles for other coalitions:

Transparency builds multi-directional trust Public advisories demonstrate accountability both to citizens and to coalition partners. When detection methods and evidence are shared openly (within security constraints), publics can assess credibility for themselves.

Speed requires pre-delegated authority The RRM works best when Canada can issue advisories without requiring real-time consensus from all seven members. Pre-agreed frameworks for what constitutes sufficient evidence allow faster action, with members retaining sovereignty over whether to amplify.

AI is necessary but not sufficient Detection algorithms can identify patterns humans would miss, but attribution, strategic assessment, and communication decisions remain irreducibly human. Over-automating these judgments risks both false positives and loss of political legitimacy.

Adversaries adapt, requiring continuous evolution Spamouflage-type operations evident in 2023 had largely shifted tactics by 2025, incorporating more sophisticated linguistic models and avoiding the behavioral tells that earlier campaigns exhibited. Coalition detection must evolve continuously, which requires sustained investment beyond initial system deployment.

Coalition coordination does not require operational uniformity G7 members respond to RRM findings differently based on domestic legal frameworks, cultural norms, and political contexts. Rather than demanding uniform responses, the RRM succeeds by providing shared evidence that members can adapt to their specific circumstances.

For diplomatic practitioners in other multilateral settings, the RRM model suggests that AI-enabled transparency can serve coalition coordination even when members retain significant operational independence. The key is building trust through consistent evidence-sharing while respecting sovereignty constraints that no technology can overcome.

NATO StratCom Simulations

NATO has approached the problem through preparedness (NATO 2024). Its Strategic Communications Centre of Excellence in Riga has developed simulations that model how adversarial disinformation might spread in crisis scenarios (NATO StratCom COE 2024, n.d.). These exercises incorporate AI-driven anomaly detection and sentiment analysis, training member states to recognize how quickly a hostile narrative can dominate the information environment (Bergmanis-Korāts et al. 2024). The "golden quarter-hour" lesson introduced in Chapter 3 has become a touchstone for crisis response planning. NATO's work underscores that detection is only part of the equation; without rehearsed workflows and shared protocols, even the best monitoring tools cannot translate into effective collective action.

WHO EARS: Multilateral Early Warning

Even outside the Euro-Atlantic space, collaborative AI systems are emerging. The World Health Organization's *EARS* platform, first piloted in 2021, applies natural language processing to track rumors across dozens of countries and languages. Originally designed for pandemic response, EARS has since expanded into broader health communication, offering a model of how international organizations can provide early warning to multiple governments simultaneously (Purnat et al. 2021; WHO 2023). The platform illustrates both the strength and the fragility of coalition tools: it provides shared situational awareness, but interpretation of its outputs depends on national authorities who may act with varying levels of speed and transparency.

Taken together, these cases highlight the spectrum of AI-enabled collaboration in diplomacy. The EU demonstrates how pooled monitoring can create cross-border situational awareness; NATO shows the importance of simulation and preparedness;

the G7 emphasizes transparency as a collective defense; and the WHO illustrates how early warning can be scaled globally.

Synthetic Narratives in Action: Olympics Deepfake Campaign (Paris 2024)

In the months leading up to the 2024 Paris Olympics, cybersecurity researchers at Microsoft and other firms uncovered a coordinated campaign using AI-generated videos to undermine confidence in the Games. Among the most notorious examples was a deepfake impersonation of actor Tom Cruise, who appeared in slickly produced clips criticizing the event and spreading false claims about security and corruption. Analysts attributed the campaign to Russian-aligned influence networks seeking to embarrass France and weaken Western unity.

The Olympics are more than a sporting event; they are a stage for cultural diplomacy and global soft power. By targeting them with synthetic disinformation, adversaries sought to disrupt not just the reputation of the Games but also the credibility of the host nation and its allies. The choice of a Hollywood celebrity as the vehicle for the message underscored how easily deepfakes can hijack symbols of trust and recognition.

For students of public diplomacy, the Olympic campaign highlights the importance of multilateral defense against disinformation. France alone could not contain the synthetic narratives; international platforms, allied governments, and independent watchdogs had to collaborate to expose and counter the content. This episode demonstrates that the integrity of shared global events depends increasingly on collective vigilance in the face of synthetic threats (Milmo 2024; Watts 2024).

JOINT MESSAGING AND STRATEGIC FORECASTING: COORDINATING NARRATIVE RESPONSES

Beyond detection and defense, coalitions are beginning to use AI for proactive narrative coordination—developing joint messaging strategies that anticipate adversarial framings and prepare coordinated responses before crises fully emerge. This shift from reactive to anticipatory coalition communication represents a frontier in collaborative diplomacy.

Anticipatory Messaging Frameworks

Traditional coalition communication has been reactive: waiting for a hostile narrative to emerge, then scrambling to coordinate a response across multiple governments with different political priorities and communication styles. By the time consensus is reached, narratives have often already hardened in public consciousness.

AI-enabled strategic forecasting changes this dynamic by allowing coalitions to model likely narrative trajectories before they fully materialize. Natural language processing can analyze how similar issues have been framed in the past, identifying patterns in how adversaries exploit policy announcements, international incidents, or domestic political events. Machine learning can predict which aspects of a planned policy initiative are most vulnerable to hostile framing, allowing coalitions to prepare counter-narratives proactively.

For example, when the G7 was preparing joint climate finance commitments in late 2024, strategic forecasting models analyzed how previous climate pledges had been attacked. The analysis revealed consistent patterns: adversaries would frame commitments as "Western imperialism," claim they unfairly burdened developing nations, and amplify any apparent hypocrisy in member states' domestic policies. Armed with this foresight, G7 communication teams prepared coordinated responses before the announcement, emphasizing partnership with Global South nations, highlighting developing country voices in the commitment design process, and proactively addressing implementation credibility concerns.

When the predicted attacks materialized, coalition responses were already prepared, translated, and positioned for rapid deployment. The result: narrative half-life of adversarial framings was significantly shorter than in previous climate announcements, and public polling showed higher trust in the commitments' sincerity.

Scenario-Based Messaging Preparation

NATO's experience with StratCom simulations has demonstrated that practicing coordination before crises improves real-world performance (NATO StratCom COE 2024). This principle is now being extended to joint messaging: coalitions conduct scenario exercises where they develop coordinated responses to hypothetical crises, building muscle memory for rapid coordination.

These simulations typically involve:

- *Scenario design* AI analyzes current geopolitical tensions and media environments to generate plausible crisis scenarios (e.g., contested elections, border incidents, major policy failures, humanitarian crises)
- *Narrative war-gaming* Teams model how adversaries might frame the scenario, using historical data on their messaging patterns and current platform algorithms to predict how narratives would spread
- *Response development* Coalition members practice developing joint messaging, testing whether they can achieve consensus on framing, attribution, and tone before response windows close
- *Validator engagement* Simulations include practice coordination with non-governmental validators (journalists, civil society, and academic experts) to test whether coalition messages would be amplified authentically
- *Platform coordination* Exercises include scenarios where platforms must be engaged to counter coordination or manipulation, practicing how to present evidence and requests consistently across member states

The value isn't primarily in the specific messages developed—scenarios are hypothetical and actual crises always differ. Rather, the value lies in identifying coordination friction points: which topics trigger sovereignty concerns, where linguistic or cultural differences create misunderstandings, which member states consistently have slower decision cycles, and which communication channels reach which audiences most effectively.

Challenges in Joint Forecasting

Despite promise, strategic forecasting for joint messaging faces significant challenges:

Over-confidence risks Forecasting models can create false certainty, tempting coalitions to over-prepare for scenarios that don't materialize while missing unexpected crises. The danger of "fighting the last war" is particularly acute when models rely heavily on historical data.

Sovereignty sensitivities Pre-coordinating messages on sensitive topics (domestic politics, cultural issues, security matters) can feel like pre-empting national decision-making. Coalition members may resist preparing joint responses to scenarios that implicate their domestic governance.

Linguistic and cultural translation Messages that work well in one cultural context can backfire in another. AI translation captures literal meaning but often misses connotation, idiom, and cultural reference. Joint messaging requires human cultural expertise to ensure coalition responses resonate authentically across diverse publics.

Validator authenticity When coalitions coordinate extensively with validators before crises emerge, there's risk that responses will feel scripted rather than authentic. Civil society actors value independence; if they perceive they're being instrumentalized for coalition messaging, their credibility suffers—and with it, the coalition's.

Adversarial learning If adversaries discover coalition forecasting models, they can deliberately employ tactics the models aren't trained to expect. Publishing forecasting insights builds public resilience but also educates adversaries about detection methods.

Lessons for Multilateral Strategic Communication

For coalitions developing joint messaging capabilities with AI assistance:

Use forecasting for preparation, not prescription Scenarios should drive readiness (developing shared terminology, clarifying decision authorities, pre-positioning validators) rather than prescribing exact messages.

Build flexibility into joint responses Rather than scripting precise language, coalitions should agree on framing principles and values, allowing members to adapt messaging to domestic contexts while maintaining thematic consistency.

Test coordination under pressure Simulations work best when they include realistic time pressures, information ambiguity, and sovereignty tensions. Practicing in comfort produces capabilities that collapse under stress.

Balance efficiency with authenticity AI can accelerate message development, but coalition responses must sound like they come from real governments addressing real concerns, not from algorithms generating optimal talking points.

Invest in cultural expertise alongside technical capability The most sophisticated forecasting models cannot replace human understanding of how messages will resonate across diverse cultural contexts. Coalitions need linguists, cultural advisors, and regional experts working alongside data scientists.

MULTILATERAL PLATFORM COORDINATION: BEYOND EURO-ATLANTIC COALITIONS

While much attention focuses on EU, NATO, and G7 AI collaboration, multilateral coordination extends far beyond Euro-Atlantic structures. International organizations operating globally—particularly the United Nations, ITU, UNICEF, and WHO—are developing shared approaches to AI deployment that offer lessons for how diverse coalitions can coordinate despite less institutional cohesion than regional blocs.

UN System-Wide AI Adoption

The United Nations' approach to AI coordination differs fundamentally from regional organizations. With 193 member states spanning vastly different political systems, development levels, and strategic interests, the UN cannot impose uniform standards. Instead, UN agencies have developed a federative approach: shared principles and interoperable tools, with implementation adapted to local contexts and agency mandates.

The UN Secretary-General's *Roadmap for Digital Cooperatio*n (2020) established basic AI governance principles across the UN system: transparency, accountability, inclusivity, and human rights compliance. Individual agencies have since developed specialized applications while adhering to these common frameworks.

For example, *eLUNa* (the UN's computer-assisted translation system deployed in 2015) and *ITU Translate* (launched in the early 2020s for telecommunications terminology) share underlying architectural principles but serve different needs. Both employ neural machine translation, both incorporate translation memory, and both require human post-editing for official documents. However, ITU Translate specializes in highly technical vocabularies (spectrum allocation, network protocols, satellite coordination) that general-purpose systems handle poorly, while eLUNa prioritizes the six official UN languages and political/diplomatic terminology.

This specialized-but-interoperable model allows UN agencies to benefit from shared research and development while adapting to their operational realities. When agencies need to coordinate communications—as during the COVID-19 pandemic, when WHO, UNICEF, UNESCO, and multiple others needed aligned messaging—they can do so because underlying systems share common data formats and quality standards.

WHO and UNICEF: Coordination at Scale

The World Health Organization's EARS (Early AI-supported Response with Social listening) platform, discussed earlier, demonstrates how AI enables coordination among countries with minimal pre-existing trust infrastructure. During COVID-19, EARS tracked health misinformation across dozens of countries simultaneously, providing early warning when dangerous rumors (e.g., false cures, vaccine conspiracy theories) emerged.

What made EARS effective was its role as information provider rather than enforcement authority. WHO didn't tell countries what actions to take; it provided real-time data on what rumors were circulating, how they were spreading, and which populations were most exposed. National health authorities could then respond according to their own priorities, capacities, and cultural contexts. Some countries used EARS data for targeted public health messaging. Others shared it with local fact-checking networks. Some simply monitored trends without direct response.

This "shared awareness without mandated action" model reduces sovereignty concerns that plague more prescriptive coalition approaches. Countries retain full decision authority but benefit from collective intelligence that none could develop individually.

UNICEF's U-Report platform offers a parallel model for youth engagement coordination. As discussed in Chapter 8, U-Report operates in 102 countries with 37 million users, using AI to aggregate youth perspectives on education, health, and social issues. While UNICEF provides the technical infrastructure and some analytical capacity, country offices control how data is used, which questions are asked, and how findings inform policy.

This decentralized coordination allows radical adaptation to local contexts while maintaining global standards on safeguarding, data protection, and ethical engagement. A question about sexual health education might be appropriate in some countries but culturally sensitive in others. Rather than imposing universal survey instruments, U-Report's federated architecture allows country teams to design engagement appropriate to their contexts while contributing to global learning about youth priorities and AI engagement ethics.

Lessons from Global Coordination Models

The UN/WHO/UNICEF experience with AI coordination offers principles applicable beyond health and humanitarian contexts:

Shared infrastructure with local autonomy Provide common tools and platforms, but allow members full control over how they're used. This reduces sovereignty friction while building collective capacity.

Information sharing over enforcement Focus on providing situational awareness rather than demanding specific actions. Members respond according to their capabilities and priorities, but informed by collective intelligence.

Interoperability over uniformity Systems should be able to exchange data and insights, but need not operate identically. Different contexts require different implementations; coordination requires shared standards, not shared systems.

Specialized adaptation with common principles Sectoral needs (health, education, and telecommunications) require specialized AI applications, but underlying ethical and governance principles should be consistent across UN agencies and international organizations.

Progressive implementation Not all members need to adopt AI systems simultaneously. Early adopters demonstrate value, others learn from their experience, and laggards eventually join as capacity and trust develop. Coordination happens at multiple speeds.

Continuous learning across diverse implementations When 50+ countries implement AI tools for related purposes, the diversity of approaches generates learning that no single country could achieve. Coordination structures should facilitate sharing lessons, not enforcing uniformity.

For diplomatic practitioners, these global coordination models suggest that effective AI collaboration doesn't require the institutional cohesion of the EU or NATO. Even loosely coupled coalitions can coordinate AI deployment if they focus on shared principles and information rather than demanding operational uniformity.

PRACTITIONER GUIDANCE

For diplomats working in multilateral settings, the challenge of AI is not only technical but relational. Collaborative systems can provide speed and foresight, but coalitions succeed or fail on the trust they inspire—among partners and with the publics they serve. The credibility of one state can bolster the collective, but it can also imperil it if action is seen as heavy-handed or exclusionary. Responsible collaboration requires habits of practice that turn AI from a source of suspicion into a foundation for resilience.

The first habit is clarity about thresholds. Coalitions must agree in advance on what constitutes actionable manipulation, rather than debating case by case in the heat of crisis. Shared dashboards are only useful if members have a common understanding of what to do when anomalies appear. Without agreed thresholds, multilateral tools risk producing more friction than foresight.

The second habit is radical transparency. Publics are far more likely to trust coalition action when they see not only the conclusions but also the reasoning. Canada's practice of publishing RRM advisories illustrates this principle: by showing how conclusions were reached, the coalition demonstrates accountability rather than secrecy. In multilateral settings, transparency must extend across borders as well, ensuring that publics in smaller states feel as informed as those in larger ones.

A third habit is inclusivity in design and interpretation. Coalitions that privilege the languages, datasets, or perspectives of powerful states risk alienating less resourced members. Inclusivity means ensuring that smaller states, minority communities, and diverse publics see themselves reflected in the data and in the responses it drives. This requires deliberate investment in translation, regional validators, and culturally specific interpretation. Inclusivity is not simply fairness; it is the glue that holds coalitions together.

Finally, practitioners must practice humility in forecasting. AI simulations and predictive models can help coalitions prepare, but they must be treated as possibilities, not certainties. Overconfidence in forecasts risks creating groupthink, where coalitions act on assumed inevitabilities rather than lived realities. Humility requires building flexibility into workflows, allowing coalitions to adapt when publics respond in unexpected ways.

The AI Mindset for Collaborative Diplomacy

Coalition work runs on trust, and shared AI systems test it in a new way. When members pool their monitoring and forecasting into a single dashboard, they gain foresight none could reach alone—and simultaneously hand a measure of interpretive control to the group. For AI to strengthen multilateral diplomacy, practitioners must adopt a mindset shaped by shared responsibility, humility, inclusivity, and proportionality.

Shared responsibility is the starting point. Disinformation campaigns and hostile narratives are rarely confined within borders, and no single government can manage them alone. Coalitions succeed when members see AI tools not as national assets to be hoarded but as collective infrastructure to be maintained together. The European Union's EDMO hubs illustrate this principle: regional monitoring centers share data across states, creating situational awareness that no single country could achieve independently. Responsibility, in this sense, is not diluted by sharing; it is multiplied.

Humility is equally important, particularly in forecasting. Predictive models and narrative simulations can create the illusion of certainty, tempting decision-makers to act as if they know in advance how publics will respond. But forecasting is always provisional, shaped by past data that may not capture future tactics or cultural nuance. NATO's StratCom simulations teach this lesson repeatedly: models can illuminate vulnerabilities, but they cannot guarantee how a real crisis will unfold. A humble mindset treats forecasts as signals for preparation, not verdicts about the future.

Inclusivity across partners anchors the legitimacy of collaborative AI. Smaller states and less digitally resourced members often fear being sidelined in multilateral systems dominated by larger powers. The African Union's insistence that inclusivity is sovereignty applies here as well: coalitions that privilege the data of powerful states risk eroding trust among the very members they seek to protect. Ensuring that shared systems incorporate diverse languages, contexts, and validators is not just a technical safeguard but a political necessity for sustaining cohesion.

Finally, proportionality must guide joint responses. Multilateral institutions can move more forcefully than individual states, but the risk of overreach is greater as well. Labeling narratives as hostile manipulation or issuing cross-border corrections carries legitimacy costs if publics perceive the response as censorship. The G7's Rapid Response Mechanism demonstrates the balance: advisories are issued transparently, but responsibility for action remains with national governments. Proportionality ensures that coalition responses protect credibility without undermining the democratic values they are meant to defend.

Workflows for Collaborative AI

Coalitions are only as strong as the routines that hold them together. Artificial intelligence can provide shared foresight, but unless multilateral institutions embed it into structured workflows, the promise of collaboration quickly unravels into hesitation and mistrust. Effective collective diplomacy requires habits of practice that translate data into action across borders: shared dashboards for early warning, provenance standards for authenticity, validator networks for amplification, and simulations for preparedness.

Shared dashboards form the backbone of collective monitoring. EDMO's regional hubs in the European Union illustrate how natural language processing and anomaly detection can be pooled to track narratives across dozens of languages and platforms. By aggregating signals from multiple states, dashboards reveal patterns that no single mission could see alone—for example, how a rumor seeded in one country migrates into another's political discourse within hours. But dashboards are not neutral. Coalitions must agree on thresholds: when does a spike become a threat, and when does silence serve better than escalation? Without consensus, shared data risks producing divergent interpretations rather than coordinated action.

Provenance standards are emerging as another critical workflow. The Coalition for Content Provenance and Authenticity (C2PA) is developing ways to embed metadata into images, video, and audio files that can verify origin and editing history. Applied at scale in multilateral contexts, such standards could allow the EU, NATO, or the G7 to debunk manipulated media with shared evidence rather than fragmented denials. The EU's *AI Act* already requires labeling of synthetic media in high-risk contexts; extending such norms across alliances would give coalitions a common language for authenticity. But provenance only works if publics recognize and trust it, which means coalitions must invest not just in technology but in public education about what verification means.

Validator amplification extends this process beyond institutions. NATO's simulations and Ukraine's deepfake response both revealed the same lesson: detection is useless without trusted voices to carry corrections. Coalitions can coordinate validator networks across borders, ensuring that corrections are not only issued by official channels but echoed by journalists, civil society actors, and alumni in multiple languages. This turns corrections from institutional statements into transnational narratives of credibility. Yet building such networks requires trust and reciprocity: validators will only echo coalition outputs if they see them as transparent and proportionate.

Simulations close the loop by ensuring preparedness before crises erupt. NATO's StratCom Centre in Riga has pioneered exercises that model adversarial disinformation campaigns, allowing states to practice coordination under pressure. Expanding such simulations across multilateral institutions could help identify weak points in workflows: where coordination slows, where sovereignty concerns create hesitation, and where publics might interpret coalition action as censorship. By rehearsing these scenarios, coalitions can shorten detection-to-response times and avoid paralysis when crises strike.

Taken together, these workflows turn AI from a fragmented tool into collective infrastructure. Coalitions that embed these routines demonstrate not only technical sophistication but also the discipline of trust—among themselves and with the publics they seek to serve.

Risks and Ethics

Collaboration strengthens diplomacy, but it also magnifies risks. When states act together, their credibility is shared: one misstep, one poorly judged response, can undermine the legitimacy of the whole coalition. Artificial intelligence compounds these vulnerabilities by accelerating detection, dramatizing anomalies, and promising foresight that may prove fragile. For multilateral campaigns, the central risks lie in sovereignty concerns, legitimacy gaps, coordination delays, bias, and overconfidence in predictive models.

Sovereignty is the first challenge. AI monitoring systems rely on shared data, but not all governments are equally comfortable with ceding control over information flows. Smaller states often worry that their perspectives will be subsumed by larger powers, while more powerful states may resist subjecting their narratives to collective review. The dilemma is political as much as technical: who defines what counts as disinformation, and whose cultural and linguistic contexts shape the thresholds for action? Without clear agreements, sovereignty disputes can slow or derail coalition efforts.

Legitimacy gaps form the second risk. When a coalition labels a narrative as hostile manipulation, publics may view it not as protection but as censorship. The European Union's experience with *EUvsDisinfo* illustrates this tension. While the project catalogues disinformation across member states, critics sometimes frame its judgments as an attempt to police legitimate debate. In multilateral contexts, where messaging carries the weight of multiple governments, accusations of overreach can be even more damaging. Credibility in collective campaigns requires transparency about criteria and humility about limitations.

Coordination delays present a third risk. More actors mean more voices to consult, and more time before consensus emerges. In crises, minutes matter. NATO's StratCom simulations have shown that hostile narratives can dominate within a quarter of an hour if left unchallenged. Yet in practice, coalitions often spend hours or days debating who should speak, how forcefully, and through which channels. AI may detect anomalies instantly, but without streamlined decision-making, foresight turns to frustration.

Bias within AI systems also poses dangers. Multilateral datasets often privilege the languages and perspectives of member states with more resources, sidelining smaller or less digitally connected publics. The African Union's *Continental AI Strategy* warns against precisely this dynamic. If shared systems fail to represent the diversity of voices within a coalition, they risk reinforcing inequality and eroding trust among the very publics they aim to defend.

Finally, overconfidence in forecasting is a persistent danger. Predictive models can simulate how narratives might spread, but they remain speculative. Mustafa Suleyman (2023) cautions that such systems create a seductive illusion of control, encouraging policymakers to mistake probabilities for certainties. When coalitions act on forecasts too aggressively, they risk misjudging publics and amplifying the very narratives they seek to contain. In diplomacy, where credibility is hard won and easily lost, humility in forecasting is essential.

Together, these risks highlight the paradox of collaborative AI in diplomacy. Collective foresight can be powerful, but it also concentrates responsibility. Publics may forgive a single embassy's misstep; they are less forgiving when multiple governments act together and get it wrong. For coalitions, the ethical challenge is to embed transparency, inclusivity, and proportionality into every stage of AI-enabled collaboration. Only then can foresight become a source of resilience rather than suspicion.

Metrics and Evaluation

Evaluating collaborative AI in diplomacy requires different benchmarks than those used at the mission or national level. Success cannot be measured by how many anomalies are detected or how many advisories are issued. Instead, the central question is whether coalitions act quickly, credibly, and inclusively enough to defend legitimacy across borders. AI enables new forms of measurement, but interpretation must remain anchored in political judgment and trust among partners.

This book treats detection-to-response time as one of the most important metrics for multilateral campaigns (Pamment 2022). NATO's StratCom simulations highlight the "golden quarter-hour.". In practice, coalitions must measure not only how fast anomalies are flagged by AI systems but how quickly partners can validate and respond. A shared dashboard that detects a spike in one country is only useful if others act in time to prevent its spread. Tracking average detection-to-response times across members helps identify where bottlenecks—political or technical—are slowing coalition action.

Cross-border rumor half-life provides another useful measure. Borrowed from epidemiology and first applied in WHO's EARS platform, the concept captures how long it takes for a falsehood to lose traction after correction (Purnat et al. 2021). In collaborative diplomacy, rumor half-life can be tracked across languages and states. If a correction spreads quickly in one country but lingers in another, the discrepancy highlights where validators are strong and where coalition communication needs reinforcement.

This book uses the term validator amplification to describe a third indicator. Coalitions are most effective when corrections and clarifications are not only issued by governments but echoed by trusted validators in multiple contexts. AI tools can track which validators pick up coalition messages, how far those messages travel across platforms and borders, and whether the tone remains consistent. Amplification rates reveal not only the reach of a message but its resonance—whether publics accept it as credible because it is carried by voices they already trust.

Finally, this book treats provenance adoption as a critical measure in an era of synthetic media. Coalitions can evaluate how often provenance tools are used across member states, how consistently labels are applied, and how publics respond to them. Do citizens recognize provenance tags as trustworthy signals, or do they dismiss them as government spin? Tracking adoption rates and public confidence in provenance systems will determine whether these tools function as effective bulwarks against deepfakes in multilateral settings.

Together, these metrics move the evaluation of collaborative AI beyond activity counts to the outcomes that matter for legitimacy. The effectiveness of multilateral AI systems will always be judged by publics not only on speed or reach but on whether responses feel transparent, inclusive, and respectful.

Reflection and Strategic Questions

These lessons point to reflective questions for practitioners. Are thresholds for coalition action clear, and do they respect the sovereignty of all members? When advisories are issued, do publics understand the evidence, or do they suspect censorship? Whose voices are privileged in shared datasets, and whose are excluded? And how can coalitions ensure that forecasting sharpens preparedness without becoming a substitute for judgment?

FRONTIER PILOTS

If collaborative AI in diplomacy today is still focused on monitoring and coordinated response, the next wave of experiments is turning toward prediction and preparedness. These frontier pilots are uneven and experimental, but they suggest how coalitions may use AI not only to defend credibility but to anticipate threats before they materialize.

One area of innovation is multilateral narrative wargaming. Building on NATO's simulations of disinformation campaigns, researchers at RAND and Carnegie have proposed more advanced AI-driven exercises where coalitions test how adversarial narratives might unfold across multiple states simultaneously (Mazarr et al. 2019). These systems model not only the spread of falsehoods but also the likely responses of publics, platforms, and governments. The promise is foresight: helping coalitions rehearse counter-messaging strategies before crises hit. Yet the risks are significant. Overconfidence in simulated outcomes can create blind spots, while publics who discover they are the subject of "narrative wargames" may perceive the practice as manipulative.

A second frontier involves coalition forecasting platforms. Inspired by tools already in use in economics and epidemiology, these systems aim to predict how policies—such as climate pledges, sanctions, or migration initiatives—are likely to be framed across different regions and actors. By combining historic data with real-time monitoring, coalitions could anticipate which narratives adversaries might exploit and prepare responses in advance. The advantage is agility; the danger lies in mistaking probabilistic forecasts for certainty. As Suleyman (2023) cautions, AI forecasting often creates the illusion of inevitability, tempting decision-makers to treat predictions as facts rather than possibilities.

A third area of experimentation lies in global provenance frameworks. Building on the EU's requirements for labeling AI-generated content, multilateral organizations are exploring standards that extend beyond Europe to encompass the G7, AU, ASEAN, and UN agencies. Such frameworks would allow coalitions to coordinate authenticity verification globally, ensuring that provenance labels applied in one region are recognized in another. If successful, this could provide a transnational bulwark against deepfakes and synthetic media. But provenance will only function if publics trust the labels. In polarized environments, even verified tags may be dismissed as propaganda, making credibility as important as technology.

These frontier pilots show how collaborative AI is shifting from reaction to anticipation. Narrative wargaming, forecasting platforms, and provenance frameworks promise to strengthen resilience before crises erupt. But they also highlight the fragility of collective trust: coalitions that appear overconfident, manipulative, or opaque risk undermining the very credibility they seek to defend. For practitioners, the lesson is humility. AI can extend foresight, but legitimacy still depends on openness, proportionality, and respect for publics across borders.

CONCLUSION

By now you've seen that in an era of borderless influence operations and synthetic media deployed at industrial scale, defending democratic credibility is no longer a sovereign function but a coalition imperative—and that the central tension of collaborative AI is not technical but political. The Republic of Z vignette dramatized that asymmetry: detection was fast because data was shared; action was slow because sovereignty mattered. AI can give coalitions the ability to see a campaign in near real time, but it cannot answer the harder questions of who should lead, how fast to move, and what publics in each country will perceive as legitimate.

The institutions this chapter examined—EU/EDMO, the EEAS, Canada's G7 Rapid Response Mechanism, NATO StratCom, WHO's EARS, and the federative model the UN, WHO, and UNICEF have developed—coordinated despite enormous variation in institutional cohesion, resource depth, and political trust. What they share is not a common detection technology but a common discovery: coordinated detection does not guarantee coordinated action when domestic media ecosystems and political sensitivities vary. AI provides the cross-border visibility. Whether that visibility converts to action turns on relationships built before the crisis, not on the dashboards that surface it.

What you now have is a workflows architecture for collaborative diplomacy that links cross-border visibility to rehearsed preparedness. None of its elements is sufficient alone; together they form the collective infrastructure that lets coalitions act faster than adversaries and more credibly than any single state. The guiding principle is resilience—not the resilience of any single institution but the collective resilience that emerges when coalitions build habits of transparency, inclusivity, and proportionate action before emergencies demand them.

The multilateral coordination examined here, however, remains largely experimental—coalition campaigns, shared pilots, and voluntary frameworks that depend on political will and institutional momentum. The next chapter takes up the decisive challenge: how to move from scattered innovation to institutional integration, embedding AI into the governance, training, and daily workflows of diplomatic institutions so that the capabilities you've encountered across this book become permanent, sustainable, and accountable rather than dependent on the enthusiasm of individual champions or the pressure of individual crises.

10 From Innovation to Integration

A Roadmap for AI-Ready Public Diplomacy

"Technology is central to how the future will unfold — that's undoubtedly true—but technology is not the point of the future, or what's really at stake. We are."

—Mustafa Suleyman, *The Coming Wave* (2023)

"Democratic leaders can—and must—resist the influence of corporate lobbying and reinvent themselves as dynamic, flexible guardians of our digital world."

—Marietje Schaake, *The Tech Coup* (2024)

"Progress depends on the choices we make about technology. New ways of organizing production and communication can either serve the narrow interests of an elite or become the foundation for widespread prosperity."

—Daron Acemoglu and Simon Johnson, *Power and Progress* (2023)

Opening Vignette: Innovation Without Integration

The Ministry of Foreign Affairs in the Republic of Z had earned a reputation as an innovator. Over the previous 3 years, under the direction of Amara Osei, the ministry's director of digital strategy, it had launched a dozen AI pilots: a listening dashboard to track online sentiment, a neural machine translation system to accelerate press releases, a chatbot for consular inquiries, and a large language model co-pilot to help speechwriters draft talking points. Each project had been celebrated as a milestone—proof that the ministry was keeping pace with the digital age. Osei had presented the portfolio at two international conferences, and delegations from neighboring countries had visited to study the ministry's approach.

But none of the systems spoke to each other. Each was owned by a different department, built by a different vendor, trained on a different dataset, and reporting through a different chain. The listening dashboard fed

DOI: 10.1201/9781003612377-13

into the strategic communications unit. The translation system served the press office. The chatbot reported to the consular division. The co-pilot sat on the minister's floor. On an ordinary day, the fragmentation was invisible. Each tool performed its function adequately in isolation. The fracture lines became visible when a crisis hit. A protest movement erupted in a major partner country after a trade dispute escalated. The listening dashboard flagged rising hostility online, but the translation system lagged behind, producing statements in the wrong register for local idioms. The chatbot, drawing from an outdated knowledge base, reassured citizens that travel remained safe even as demonstrations filled the streets. Meanwhile, the co-pilot in the minister's office drafted remarks that contradicted the embassy's field reports, producing confusion about whether the government was escalating or calming tensions. The result was visible to anyone paying attention. Journalists accused the ministry of sending mixed signals. Protesters mocked the chatbot's outdated advice, turning screenshots into viral memes. Allied governments privately complained that the ministry seemed disorganized. Within days, the government's credibility in the crisis was weakened—not because any single AI system had failed, but because the systems had never been designed to work together.

In the aftermath, Osei was candid in her assessment. "We built twelve pilots and celebrated each one," she told her team. "But we never connected them—no shared data layer, no agentic workflow to let one system hand off to another. We had adopted AI agents without hiring agent wranglers. We innovated in pieces and assumed coherence would follow. It did not." Across town, David Kim, the public affairs officer at the U.S. embassy, watched the ministry's struggle with recognition rather than satisfaction. The embassy's own tools—the narrative dashboard, the translation workflows, the chatbot Lina had rebuilt after its early stumble—operated in much the same way: useful individually, connected by habit and improvisation rather than by design. What had happened to the ministry could happen to any mission that mistook a collection of pilots for an integrated strategy.

At the next country team meeting, David raised the question with Ambassador Grant. "We have good tools. What we do not have is a system. If a crisis hits us the way it hit the ministry, are we confident our tools will talk to each other?" The ambassador's answer was brief. "Then that is the next problem we solve." The episode clarified something that no single pilot could have revealed on its own. Innovation was necessary but insufficient. The test was not whether an institution could adopt AI, but whether it could weave separate tools into something coherent—transparent to publics, consistent across functions, and resilient under pressure. The ministry had learned that lesson the hard way. The question for every diplomatic institution was whether it would learn it before the next crisis arrived.

FRAMING THE CHAPTER

For much of the past decade, AI in diplomacy has been defined by pilots. Embassies experimented with chatbots for consular inquiries. Multilateral institutions trialed translation systems to keep pace with multilingual demands. Crisis teams tested dashboards to track rumors in real time. These initiatives proved that AI could accelerate listening, amplify messaging, detect manipulation, and even preserve heritage. But they also revealed a persistent weakness: fragmentation. Projects were siloed, duplicated across agencies, or launched without common standards. When crises struck, the lack of integration made institutions look inconsistent, reactive, and unprepared.

The next stage of AI in diplomacy is therefore not more innovation but smarter integration. Moving from pilots to permanence requires weaving AI into the fabric of institutions: across ministries, between missions, and within multilateral organizations. Integration means connecting listening, messaging, monitoring, engagement, evaluation, and crisis communication so that insights flow smoothly rather than stopping at bureaucratic borders. It also means embedding ethical safeguards—transparency, inclusivity, accountability—into workflows from the start, rather than bolting them on afterward.

Having explored each function of diplomacy through AI—listening, messaging, monitoring, engagement, evaluation, crisis response, ethics, culture, and collaboration—this chapter addresses the systemic challenge: how to build AI-ready institutions. The question is no longer whether AI can support diplomacy, but how governments and multilateral organizations can embed it responsibly, consistently, and inclusively. This chapter argues that the future of credibility in diplomacy depends on integration. Innovation brought the tools; integration will determine whether they endure.

RESEARCH AND POLICY FOUNDATIONS

Innovation in diplomacy is rarely the problem; institutionalization is. History shows that ministries and multilateral organizations are often quick to test new tools but slow to integrate them into lasting practice. Nicholas Cull (2019) has observed that public diplomacy has too often been treated as a "boutique" function, with projects that flourish briefly but fail to embed themselves in the organizational DNA. The same pattern risks repeating with AI: promising pilots are launched, celebrated, and then left to languish without sustainable funding, training, or governance. The challenge now is to convert experimentation into enduring capability.

Scholars of digital governance emphasize that integration requires more than technology. Helen Margetts and Patrick Dunleavy (2013) argue that "digital-by-design" institutions differ fundamentally from those that layer new tools onto old bureaucratic processes. Digital transformation succeeds when workflows, accountability structures, and staff training are redesigned around technology, not when machines are patched into legacy systems. In diplomacy, this means that AI cannot simply be added to consular services or public affairs divisions; it must be woven into the ministry as a whole, from strategy and planning to crisis response and evaluation.

AI also introduces governance dilemmas that institutionalization must address directly. Kate Crawford (2021) reminds us that AI systems are never neutral: they carry the biases of their training data and the power dynamics of their design. Corneliu Bjola and Markus Kornprobst (2023) argue that ethics must therefore be embedded at the structural level—through transparency, inclusivity, and proportionality—rather than treated as optional safeguards. Mustafa Suleyman (2023) warns of "fragile infrastructures" in AI, where systems that appear robust can fail dramatically under pressure. For diplomacy, these insights underline that integration must be paired with resilience: not just adopting AI but ensuring it is trustworthy when publics are watching most closely.

Policy frameworks are beginning to push institutions in this direction. Canada's Directive on Automated Decision-Making requires algorithmic impact assessments before AI systems are deployed, setting a precedent for governance embedded into workflows rather than applied retrospectively. The OECD's AI Principles (2024) and the EU's AI Act (2024) similarly push toward accountability by design. The U.S. Department of State's Enterprise Data and Artificial Intelligence Strategy (2025) identifies integration as a core institutional imperative, calling for AI to be embedded across diplomatic functions while maintaining human oversight and ethical accountability. UNESCO's Recommendation on the Ethics of Artificial Intelligence (2021) adds proportionality and cultural sensitivity as integration requirements, reminding institutions that the how of embedding AI matters as much as the what.

These research and policy foundations converge on the same insight: the real test of AI in diplomacy is not innovation but adoption. Institutions that embed AI responsibly, redesign workflows around it, and invest in staff capacity will enhance credibility; those that treat it as a series of disconnected pilots risk appearing fragmented and unprepared. For diplomacy, credibility in the AI era depends less on the brilliance of individual projects than on whether institutions can make them cohere into a trusted system.

REAL-WORLD APPLICATIONS

If pilots demonstrate possibility, integration shows permanence. A handful of governments and international organizations have already begun to embed AI into their institutional fabric, offering glimpses of how diplomacy might evolve when technology is not an experiment but a routine. These cases illustrate both progress and pitfalls: how AI can become part of daily workflows, and what happens when governance and training do not keep pace.

The UK Copilot Experience: Scaling AI across Government

The United Kingdom's deployment of AI co-pilots across the civil service between 2024 and 2025—examined from different angles in Chapters 2, 4, and 5—represents one of the most ambitious attempts to move from pilot to institutional integration at scale. The experience offers detailed lessons about what works, what fails, and what governance structures must accompany widespread adoption.

Phase 1: The 20,000-User Pilot

In September 2024, the UK Government Digital Service launched a 4-month trial of Microsoft 365 Copilot across 20,000 civil servants representing multiple departments. The scale was unprecedented for government AI adoption: this was not a boutique innovation project in a single ministry but a whole-of-government experiment designed to generate data on real-world impact.

The pilot's design was methodical. Users received standardized training on Copilot's capabilities: drafting documents, summarizing lengthy reports, generating meeting notes, and answering queries about internal knowledge bases. Departments were selected to represent diverse functions: policy analysis, communications, legal services, operational delivery, and corporate services. The Government Digital Service deployed analytics to track time savings, adoption rates, and user satisfaction, creating a dataset that could inform expansion decisions.

The results were striking in their efficiency metrics. As established in Chapter 5, the official evaluation released in January 2025 documented average time savings of 26 minutes per user per day—approximately 5% of an 8-hour workday (GDS 2025b). Across 20,000 users over 4 months, this translated to roughly 433,000 hours of reclaimed time, with an estimated value of £15–20 million in productivity gains. Users reported particular value in three applications: drafting initial versions of routine correspondence, summarizing multi-page briefing documents into executive summaries, and extracting key points from lengthy meeting transcripts.

However, the evaluation also documented significant challenges. Adoption was highly uneven: while some departments reported 70–80% of staff using Copilot regularly, others saw adoption rates below 30%. The variance correlated with three factors: quality of departmental training, managerial encouragement, and perceived relevance to daily tasks. Communications and policy teams became heavy users; operational and technical teams were more skeptical.

Quality concerns emerged quickly. Users reported "hallucinations"—instances where Copilot generated plausible-sounding but factually incorrect information. In one documented case, a draft briefing on trade policy included citations to non-existent reports with fabricated statistics. While the error was caught before publication, it highlighted the necessity of human review. The National Audit Office's concurrent assessment (NAO 2024) emphasized that efficiency gains could not justify reduced oversight, warning that co-pilot outputs required the same verification as human drafts.

Data security posed another challenge. Microsoft 365 Copilot operates within Microsoft's cloud infrastructure, raising questions about where sensitive government data was processed and stored. While Microsoft provided assurances about UK data sovereignty, oversight bodies recommended that highly classified or diplomatically sensitive materials remain outside Copilot workflows until stricter controls could be verified.

Phase 2: GCS Assist and Secure Alternatives

Recognizing the need for a secure, government-controlled alternative, the Government Communication Service began developing *GCS Assist* in parallel with the Copilot trial. Launched in beta in late 2024 and expanding through 2025, GCS Assist was purpose-built for government communicators with three distinguishing features.

First, data sovereignty: GCS Assist operates on UK government infrastructure, ensuring that sensitive communications never leave controlled environments. This addressed the primary concern preventing Foreign, Commonwealth, and Development Office (FCDO) and Ministry of Defence communications teams from fully embracing commercial co-pilots.

Second, specialized training: Rather than using general large language models, GCS Assist was fine-tuned on government communication products—press releases, ministerial statements, briefing documents, and crisis responses. This specialization improved both the relevance of outputs and their adherence to government style and tone guidelines.

Third, transparency features: GCS Assist includes built-in explainability, showing users which training data informed specific outputs. This audit trail serves both quality control and accountability functions, allowing supervisors to verify that drafts don't inadvertently reproduce inappropriate source material.

By mid-2025, approximately 5,000 government communicators across central departments had access to GCS Assist. Early evaluations (GCS 2024; 2025) reported similar efficiency gains to the Copilot pilot—20–30 minutes saved daily—but with higher user confidence because of the security architecture. Significantly, adoption rates were more uniform: when security concerns were addressed, skeptical teams became more willing users.

Change Management Lessons

The UK experience surfaced five critical change management lessons for institutions attempting AI integration at scale:

Lesson 1: Training must be job-specific, not generic The most successful departments didn't simply train staff on Copilot's features; they demonstrated how co-pilots could accelerate specific tasks users performed daily. Generic "here's what AI can do" training showed poor correlation with adoption. Task-specific "here's how to draft your monthly report 40% faster" training drove sustained use.

Lesson 2: Middle management buy-in is decisive Senior leadership enthusiasm and front-line user interest matter, but middle managers control the adoption valve. When team leaders actively encouraged AI use, modeled it in their own work, and adjusted performance expectations to account for AI assistance, adoption flourished. When middle managers remained skeptical or passive, adoption languished regardless of top-down mandates.

Lesson 3: Metrics-driven expansion prevents premature scaling The Government Digital Service's decision to deploy to 20,000 users before full rollout, while seemingly large, was actually conservative compared to "go big" alternatives. The pilot generated quantitative data on efficiency, adoption patterns, and failure modes that would have been invisible in a smaller test. This evidence base proved essential for justifying continued investment and designing better training for full expansion.

Lesson 4: Security architecture determines adoption in sensitive functions For government communications, foreign affairs, and defense functions, efficiency gains are meaningless if security is compromised. The development of GCS Assist demonstrated that purpose-built, sovereignty-respecting alternatives can unlock adoption in functions where commercial tools face insurmountable trust barriers.

Lesson 5: Human oversight cannot be casualty of efficiency The most dangerous assumption would be that 26-minute time savings means 26 fewer minutes of work required. The UK explicitly framed efficiency gains as time reallocation: staff spend less time on mechanical drafting, more on strategic thinking and quality review. Institutions that treated AI as a headcount reduction opportunity rather than a capability enhancement created perverse incentives that increased error risk.

Implications for Diplomatic Integration

For foreign ministries and multilateral organizations considering similar integration, the UK Copilot experience offers a roadmap:

Start with controlled pilots at meaningful scale (thousands, not dozens) to generate robust data. Prioritize data sovereignty for diplomatically sensitive applications, even if it means developing purpose-built tools rather than adopting commercial solutions. Invest heavily in change management—particularly middle manager engagement—as much as in technology procurement. Establish clear metrics before deployment so expansion decisions are evidence-based rather than enthusiasm-driven. And crucially, treat efficiency gains as capacity reallocation rather than headcount reduction, preserving human oversight while accelerating workflows.

The UK's journey from 20,000-user commercial pilot to purpose-built government co-pilot demonstrates that integration at scale is achievable—but only with institutional commitment extending far beyond technology acquisition.

UNICEF U-Report: 14 Years from Pilot to Global Platform

If the UK Copilot experience illustrates rapid scaling within a single government, UNICEF's U-Report platform demonstrates sustained, incremental integration across 102 countries over 14 years. The contrast is instructive: where the UK pursued deliberate, metrics-driven expansion over months, U-Report evolved through patient iteration, learning from failures, and adapting to radically diverse contexts from 2011 to 2025.

Origins: The Uganda Pilot (2011–2013)

U-Report began in 2011 as a straightforward SMS polling system in Uganda, designed to let young people share views on health, education, and governance issues. The initial concept was simple: UNICEF would send periodic poll questions via text message; youth would reply; responses would be aggregated and shared with government partners. No sophisticated AI, no natural language processing, just basic SMS infrastructure and manual analysis.

The Uganda pilot succeeded because it addressed a genuine gap: young people, particularly in rural areas, had no reliable way to communicate priorities to decision-makers. Traditional surveys were expensive, slow, and urban-biased. U-Report offered real-time, low-cost, geographically distributed data. By 2013, 300,000 Ugandan youth had registered—a scale that proved the concept's viability.

However, the pilot also revealed limitations. Manual analysis of open-ended SMS responses was labor-intensive, slow, and couldn't handle the volume generated by 300,000 users. The system could ask simple yes/no questions but struggled with nuanced topics requiring more sophisticated analysis. And expanding beyond Uganda would require adapting to different languages, mobile networks, and cultural contexts.

Phase 2: Multi-Country Expansion (2014–2019)

Between 2014 and 2019, UNICEF began deploying U-Report in additional countries: Zambia (2013), Liberia (2014), Democratic Republic of Congo (2015), and gradually across Africa, Asia, Latin America, and the Middle East. By 2019, U-Report operated in 60 countries with approximately 10 million users.

This expansion phase coincided with UNICEF's integration of basic natural language processing. Rather than manually categorizing thousands of open-ended responses, U-Report began using NLP to identify themes, cluster similar responses, and flag priority concerns. This didn't replace human analysis but accelerated it dramatically: what once took days now took hours.

The multi-country expansion also forced radical localization. U-Report couldn't impose uniform question sets across diverse contexts. A poll on sexual health appropriate in Uganda might be culturally inappropriate in conservative Middle Eastern contexts. Questions about school attendance had different meanings in contexts with formal education systems versus those with primarily informal or religious education.

UNICEF country offices gained autonomy to design questions, interpret results, and determine how findings informed programming. This decentralization was essential for cultural appropriateness but created coordination challenges: each office was effectively running a separate platform sharing only underlying technology infrastructure.

Phase 3: COVID-19 Scaling (2020–2022)

The COVID-19 pandemic proved a decisive moment. As schools closed and youth faced unprecedented disruptions, U-Report became a critical tool for understanding their experiences in real time. Between 2020 and 2022, U-Report's user base exploded from 10 million to 30 million, and country deployments expanded from 60 to 90+.

The pandemic scaling also drove AI sophistication. With tens of millions of users generating responses about rapidly evolving situations, more advanced NLP became essential. UNICEF integrated sentiment analysis to gauge youth anxiety levels, multilingual processing to handle responses in dozens of languages simultaneously, and predictive clustering to identify emerging concerns before they became crises.

One documented case: in mid-2021, U-Report polling in multiple African countries detected sharp increases in youth reporting food insecurity, mental health struggles, and inability to access remote learning. This data, aggregated across countries, informed UNICEF's advocacy for expanded youth support services and provided evidence for government policy adjustments. In several countries, education ministries modified school reopening plans based directly on U-Report findings about youth readiness and safety concerns.

The pandemic also exposed U-Report's limitations. The platform's reach remained constrained by mobile phone access: youth without devices or reliable connectivity were systematically excluded, risking that policy decisions informed by U-Report data reflected experiences of relatively privileged, connected youth while missing the most vulnerable.

Phase 4: Institutional Permanence (2023–2025)

By 2023, U-Report had transitioned from innovative pilot to permanent UNICEF infrastructure. The platform operated in 102 countries with 37 million users by 2025, integrated into UNICEF's standard operating procedures for youth engagement, program design, and emergency response.

This institutionalization involved several structural changes. First, dedicated U-Report units were established at UNICEF headquarters and in regional offices, ensuring sustained technical support, training for country offices, and continuous platform improvement. Second, U-Report findings were formally incorporated into UNICEF's annual reporting, making youth voice data a standard component of organizational accountability. Third, partnerships with governments, NGOs, and academic institutions created ecosystems around U-Report, with multiple actors using the platform for complementary purposes.

The platform's AI capabilities also matured significantly. By 2025, U-Report employed:

- Advanced multilingual NLP handling 70+ languages
- Sentiment analysis calibrated for youth communication styles
- Demographic pattern recognition identifying underrepresented populations
- Real-time dashboard aggregation for rapid response
- Safeguarding algorithms flagging concerning content (potential self-harm, abuse reports) for immediate human review

Lessons from 14 Years of Scaling

U-Report's journey offers five principles for institutions pursuing sustained AI integration across diverse contexts:

Principle 1: Start simple, add complexity incrementally The 2011 Uganda pilot succeeded because it solved a clear problem with minimal technology. Adding AI sophistication gradually—as actual usage patterns revealed where automation would help—proved far more sustainable than attempting comprehensive AI deployment from the outset.

Principle 2: Decentralize implementation while centralizing infrastructure U-Report's success across 102 countries depended on allowing massive local adaptation while maintaining common technical standards. Country offices that feel empowered to adapt tools to their contexts become champions; those forced into rigid, one-size-fits-all implementations become grudging users.

Principle 3: Crises accelerate adoption but sustainability requires institutionalization COVID-19 drove explosive growth, but U-Report endured because UNICEF committed to permanent support structures rather than treating it as a pandemic-specific initiative. Pilots that scale during emergencies often collapse afterward unless deliberately institutionalized.

Principle 4: Integration succeeds when diverse stakeholders see value U-Report works because youth find it empowering, country offices find it informative, governments find it useful for policy design, and UNICEF finds it valuable for program accountability. Multi-stakeholder value creates resilience against budget cuts, leadership changes, or shifting priorities.

Principle 5: Equity requires proactive intervention, not just platform availability Making U-Report accessible in 102 countries didn't automatically ensure equitable voice. Continuous work to reach rural youth, disabled youth, and those without device access proved essential. Integration that prioritizes efficiency over equity risks becoming another mechanism for privileged voices to dominate.

Relevance to Diplomatic Integration

For foreign ministries and multilateral organizations, U-Report's 14-year evolution demonstrates that sustainable integration operates on different timelines than pilot-to-scale efforts like UK Copilot. Both approaches have merit: rapid evidence-based scaling works when institutional context is relatively uniform (UK civil service), while patient, iterative adaptation works when contexts are radically diverse (102 countries with vastly different political systems, cultures, and infrastructure).

Diplomatic institutions pursuing AI integration can learn from both models. For functions where context is relatively consistent—internal communications, document processing, routine consular services—rapid scaling with strong change management may be appropriate. For functions requiring deep cultural adaptation—public engagement, educational programming, strategic messaging—U-Report's patient, locally empowered approach offers better lessons.

The most important insight: integration is not a destination but a continuous process. U-Report at 14 years is more sophisticated, widely deployed, and institutionally embedded than at year one, but UNICEF continues refining, adapting, and learning. Institutions that treat integration as a finite project with completion dates will fail; those that embrace it as ongoing organizational evolution will endure.

Canada's Governance-First Model

Canada has taken a different path, focusing on governance rather than efficiency. Its *Directive on Automated Decision-Making* requires federal agencies to conduct algorithmic impact assessments before deploying AI systems. This means that ethical safeguards are built into the process of adoption, forcing ministries to consider transparency, fairness, and privacy before pilots can move forward (Government of Canada 2019). Global Affairs Canada has applied this approach to its evaluation dashboards and disinformation monitoring systems, ensuring that integration is paired with accountability. Canada's example demonstrates that institutional adoption is not only about embedding tools but also about embedding trust.

EU and UN Translation Systems as Invisible Infrastructure

Multilingual institutions like the EU and UN offer another model of integration. The EU's *eTranslation* system, first launched in 2017, has become a permanent fixture across 24 official languages. It now underpins cultural programs like Erasmus+ and provides translation services for NGOs, SMEs, and public administrations (European Commission 2017; 2018; 2025a). At the United Nations, *eLUNa* and *ITU Translate* have been institutionalized to handle immense volumes of documentation and highly technical vocabularies. These systems illustrate how AI can become invisible infrastructure—so embedded in daily workflows that it ceases to be noticed, functioning like electricity or water. But they also highlight persistent limits: human post-editing remains essential to preserve nuance, and confidentiality concerns continue to restrict automation for sensitive diplomatic texts.

WHO EARS: From Pandemic Pilot to Permanent Capability

The World Health Organization's *EARS* platform provides a final example of pilot-to-permanence. Launched in 2021 as an experimental rumor-tracking tool, it has since been absorbed into WHO's broader infodemic management system (WHO 2023). What began as a pandemic-specific initiative has become a standing capability for global health communication, with applications in climate, migration, and humanitarian contexts. EARS demonstrates how a system designed for one crisis can evolve into institutional infrastructure when its value is proven and sustained.

Taken together, these cases illustrate a spectrum of integration. The UK shows how co-pilots can be scaled across a government workforce; Canada shows how governance frameworks can be institutionalized; the EU and UN show how multilingual AI can become permanent infrastructure; and WHO shows how pilots can mature into global programs.

CHANGE MANAGEMENT AND CAPACITY BUILDING

Technology integration fails far more often from organizational resistance than from technical inadequacy. For AI in diplomacy, the challenge is not whether language models can draft speeches or dashboards can track sentiment—these capabilities are proven. The challenge is whether institutions can change workflows, retrain staff, and manage resistance from those who see AI as threat rather than tool.

The Change Management Triad: Leadership, Champions, and Skeptics

Successful AI integration requires navigating three constituencies simultaneously:

Senior leadership provides mandate, budget, and institutional legitimacy. Without executive support, pilots remain experiments that die when priorities shift. But leadership enthusiasm alone is insufficient and can even backfire. When executives mandate AI adoption without addressing practical implementation challenges, they create performative compliance: staff use tools minimally to satisfy mandates while actual work continues through traditional channels.

Mid-level champions are practitioners who see AI's value and voluntarily adopt it, becoming organic advocates within their teams. These individuals are integration's accelerant. They discover practical applications leaders didn't imagine, troubleshoot problems before they become institutional complaints, and demonstrate value to skeptical peers through results rather than mandates. Identifying, empowering, and connecting champions across departments creates networks that diffuse adoption more effectively than top-down directives.

Skeptics and resisters are often dismissed as obstacles, but their concerns frequently contain essential insights. A speechwriter worried that AI will "sound like everyone else" is raising valid questions about authenticity and voice. A regional desk officer skeptical that dashboards capture cultural nuance is highlighting real limitations in algorithmic understanding. Treating skepticism as problem to overcome rather than input to incorporate alienates precisely those whose expertise matters most for responsible integration.

Effective change management creates forums where leadership commitment, champion enthusiasm, and skeptic concern can interact productively. This might involve working groups with mixed perspectives piloting tools together, feedback mechanisms where concerns inform iterative improvement, and transparency about what AI can and cannot do.

Capacity Building: Beyond Technical Training

Most AI training programs fail because they focus narrowly on technical skills—how to use a dashboard, write a prompt, or interpret an output—without addressing the contextual judgment required for responsible use. Comprehensive capacity building for AI-ready diplomacy requires four levels:

Technical literacy Basic proficiency with tools. This is necessary but insufficient. Diplomats must know how to operate AI systems, but technical skill without contextual understanding produces dangerous overconfidence.

Limitation awareness Understanding what AI cannot do. This includes recognizing when outputs are plausible but wrong (hallucinations), when training data biases skew results, when cultural contexts require human judgment AI lacks. Training that emphasizes limitations as much as capabilities produces more responsible users.

Ethical literacy Knowing when disclosure, transparency, or human override are required. This involves understanding policy frameworks (like the EU AI Act's disclosure requirements), recognizing when AI use might undermine trust if revealed or concealed, and applying institutional values to technology decisions.

Strategic judgment Determining when AI use advances diplomatic objectives and when it undermines them. A co-pilot might draft a condolence message efficiently, but should sensitivity drive hand-crafting? A dashboard might detect sentiment shifts, but should response be immediate or contemplative? Strategic literacy means treating AI as one input among many, not as decision-making substitute.

Building capacity across these four levels requires sustained investment far exceeding typical "half-day workshop" approaches. Diplomatic academies integrating AI literacy into core curricula over months, not hours, are creating the sustained competency integration demands.

Addressing the Replacement Anxiety Barrier

The elephant in every integration conversation: will AI take jobs? This anxiety, whether expressed overtly or as passive resistance, undermines adoption more than any technical limitation.

Honest institutions acknowledge that AI will change roles without pretending it won't. Some functions will become automated, reallocating staff to higher-value work. But evidence from early integrations suggests expansion rather than replacement: UK civil servants using Copilot redeploy time savings into more strategic analysis, not toward fewer positions. UNICEF's U-Report expanded youth engagement capacity without reducing staff, because AI handled scale while humans handled complexity.

The key is framing integration as capability enhancement, not efficiency extraction. When institutions treat AI adoption as opportunity for headcount reduction, staff rationally resist tools threatening their livelihoods. When integration genuinely means "do more, better" rather than "do the same with fewer people," resistance diminishes.

Transparent communication about how efficiency gains will be used matters immensely. Will time savings become 10% headcount cuts or 10% more capacity for strategic priorities? The answer determines whether staff become integration partners or obstacles.

Lessons from Failed Integrations

Just as success stories like UK Copilot and U-Report teach valuable lessons, examining failures illuminates what not to do. Three patterns characterize failed AI integration in government and multilateral organizations:

Pattern 1: The "deploy and pray" failure Organizations acquire AI tools, provide minimal training, and assume adoption will follow from availability. When usage remains low, they blame user resistance rather than inadequate change management. This pattern treats integration as technology procurement rather than organizational transformation.

Pattern 2: The "executive pet project" failure A senior leader becomes AI enthusiast, mandating adoption across the institution without understanding practical implementation challenges. Staff comply minimally to satisfy mandates while actual work continues unchanged. When the champion leaves, the initiative collapses immediately.

Pattern 3: The "pilot purgatory" failure Organizations launch pilot after pilot, celebrating each as innovation milestone, but never committing to sustained investment required for full integration. Tools remain perpetually in "testing" phase, never quite trusted for real-world stakes. This pattern avoids the hard work of institutionalization while maintaining appearance of modernization.

Avoiding these patterns requires treating integration as multi-year organizational change initiative, not as technology acquisition project. It demands executive commitment, mid-level champion networks, capacity building investment, and honest engagement with skeptics' concerns. Technology is the easy part; transformation is the challenge.

PHASED INTEGRATION: FROM PILOT TO SCALE

Integration is not binary—fully adopted or completely absent—but proceeds through recognizable phases. Understanding this progression helps institutions assess where they are, what risks each phase presents, and what capabilities the next phase requires.

Phase 1: Experimental Pilots (Months 1–12)

Characteristics: Small-scale tests (dozens to hundreds of users), departmental rather than institutional, minimal governance, enthusiast-driven, success measured by proof-of-concept.

Typical tools: A consular chatbot serving one embassy. A listening dashboard monitored by a single social media team. A translation pilot for one language pair.

This phase is valuable for learning what's possible, but staying here permanently creates fragmentation. Pilots succeed or fail quietly without institutional stakes. The key transition question: has the pilot proven sufficient value to justify investment in broader deployment?

Phase 2: Structured Scaling (Year 2–3)

Characteristics: Multi-departmental deployment (thousands of users), emerging governance structures, formal training programs, success measured by adoption rates and efficiency metrics.

Typical tools: A co-pilot system deployed across multiple departments with standardized training. An EDMO-style monitoring hub serving multiple member states. A translation platform handling multiple language pairs with quality controls.

This phase is where most integration initiatives currently exist. It's also where failures become visible: uneven adoption across departments, quality issues at scale, and security concerns in production environments. The UK Copilot pilot exemplifies structured scaling—large enough to generate meaningful data, structured enough to inform expansion decisions, but still short of permanent institutionalization.

The key challenge: can the organization maintain momentum through the "trough of disillusionment" when initial enthusiasm wanes, problems emerge, and continued investment competes with other priorities?

Phase 3: Institutional Embedding (Years 3–5)

Characteristics: Whole-of-institution deployment, AI integrated into standard operating procedures, robust governance frameworks, success measured by system reliability and public trust.

Typical tools: The EU eTranslation system serving all 27 member states across 24 languages. WHO EARS transitioning from pandemic pilot to permanent infodemic infrastructure. GCS Assist becoming default drafting tool across UK government communications.

This phase represents true integration: AI is no longer experimental or exceptional but routine. New staff are trained on AI tools as standard onboarding. Budget lines are permanent, not project-based. Governance structures are formalized through policy frameworks, not ad hoc oversight.

The key risk: institutional complacency. Systems that become "invisible infrastructure" may receive insufficient maintenance, update investment, or ethical review. Embedding requires continuous improvement, not static permanence.

Synthetic Narratives in Action: Biden AI Robocalls (2024)

In January 2024, just ahead of New Hampshire's presidential primary, thousands of voters received phone calls with a startling message. The voice on the line sounded like President Joe Biden, and it urged recipients not to vote in the upcoming election. Within days, investigators confirmed that the calls were generated using AI voice-cloning technology and traced to a political consultant working with outside operatives. The Federal Communications Commission (FCC) responded by declaring AI-generated voices in robocalls illegal under the Telephone Consumer Protection Act and later imposed a multimillion-dollar fine on the consultant responsible.

The Biden robocalls marked a turning point in the governance of synthetic media. Unlike earlier deepfakes that circulated primarily online, this case brought AI deception directly into the mechanics of electoral participation. The goal was not persuasion through argument but disruption through confusion—suppressing turnout by impersonating the very figure whose legitimacy depended on it. The speed of the FCC's response showed how regulatory bodies can adapt existing legal frameworks to new technological threats, offering a model for how institutions might integrate safeguards against AI misuse.

For international observers, the episode underscored both the vulnerabilities and the resilience of democratic systems. It demonstrated how cheaply synthetic media can be deployed to interfere with elections, but also how swiftly governments can respond when legal authority and political will align. The broader lesson is that AI is no longer confined to experiments and pilot projects. It is embedded in the daily realities of governance and diplomacy, requiring institutions to integrate technological awareness and ethical safeguards into their operations. The Biden robocalls were not merely a story of deception; they were a wake-up call for building AI-ready systems of public trust (Federal Communications Commission 2024a; 2024b; 2024c; Ramer and Swenson 2024).

Phase 4: Adaptive Maturation (Years 5+)

Characteristics: Systems that evolve with changing needs, continuous improvement cycles, expansion to new functions, success measured by adaptability, and sustained relevance.

Typical tools: UNICEF U-Report at 14 years, continuously adding features, languages, and countries while refining core functionality. UN eLUNa progressively improving translation quality while maintaining 6-language coverage.

This phase distinguishes integration that endures from integration that ossifies. Technologies evolve, threats change, public expectations shift. Systems deployed in 2020 must adapt to 2025 contexts. Organizations reaching this phase treat AI as permanent capability requiring sustained investment, not as completed project.

PRACTITIONER GUIDANCE

For diplomats and policymakers, the challenge of AI is no longer whether to experiment but how to institutionalize. Pilots have shown what is possible, but publics will not measure governments by their innovations alone. They will measure them by whether those innovations cohere into systems that are transparent, inclusive, and resilient. Integration is therefore not a technical upgrade but a credibility project.

The first lesson is that integration must be intentional. AI will not weave itself into the fabric of diplomacy by accident. Ministries and multilateral organizations need deliberate strategies that connect listening dashboards, engagement platforms, evaluation tools, and co-pilots into shared infrastructures. Fragmentation is the natural state of bureaucracy; integration is the result of leadership.

The second lesson is that ethics cannot be bolted on later. Pilots sometimes treat transparency, inclusivity, and accountability as add-ons, but integration requires them at the core. Algorithmic impact assessments, provenance standards, and error logs must be built into workflows before systems are scaled. Without such safeguards, institutions risk embedding fragility into their infrastructure, making errors more visible and less forgivable once AI is part of daily operations.

Third, integration must be equitable. Large, well-resourced states and institutions will always find it easier to adopt AI. Smaller states or underfunded missions risk being left behind, excluded from coalitions that increasingly rely on shared dashboards and provenance frameworks. For collaborative diplomacy to be credible, integration must include provisions for capacity-building, ensuring that all partners can contribute and benefit. Inclusivity is not only about publics; it is also about allies.

Finally, integration requires humility. AI systems can appear seamless once embedded, but they remain vulnerable to failure. Forecasts will sometimes be wrong, provenance labels may be doubted, and co-pilot drafts will occasionally miss the mark. The most credible institutions are those that admit these limits openly, showing publics that they are prepared to correct and learn rather than to conceal. Humility is not weakness; it is resilience.

The AI Mindset for Integration

Most AI pilots stall for reasons that have nothing to do with the technology. An enthusiast can launch a promising tool alone; making it stick requires leaders, staff, and publics who share a common view of what the technology is for and how far it should reach. For AI, that vision must be grounded in whole-of-institution adoption, ethics by design, inclusivity across contexts, and a clear recognition of the enduring role of human judgment.

The first principle is whole-of-institution adoption. Fragmentation occurs when individual departments experiment with AI in isolation, producing a patchwork of tools that cannot communicate with one another. Integration requires ministries and multilateral organizations to think holistically: linking listening dashboards to translation systems, connecting engagement platforms to evaluation tools, and ensuring that provenance standards apply across the entire information cycle. AI becomes an institutional capability, not a departmental experiment.

Ethics by design is the second principle. As earlier chapters have shown, publics are quick to detect concealment or exclusion. If transparency, accountability, and inclusivity are added as afterthoughts, trust will always lag. Integration means embedding ethical safeguards at the beginning—through algorithmic impact assessments, disclosure protocols, and data governance standards—so that every system is built with credibility in mind. Canada's insistence on impact assessments before deployment illustrates this shift: ethics is not compliance after the fact but a precondition for adoption.

The third principle is inclusivity, both within and across institutions. Internally, integration means ensuring that smaller missions and less resourced agencies are not left behind. A co-pilot tool that functions only in headquarters while field posts rely on outdated processes will deepen inequality rather than efficiency. Externally, inclusivity means designing systems that reflect the diversity of publics. Multilingual translation must extend to minority languages, and evaluation dashboards must capture rural and marginalized voices, not just the digitally visible. Integration succeeds only when it is inclusive by design.

Finally, human judgment must remain central. The danger of integration is overreliance—treating AI as a substitute rather than a supplement. A co-pilot may draft a statement, but only diplomats can judge tone; a simulation may forecast narrative spread, but only practitioners can decide whether publics will perceive intervention as censorship. Integration requires a disciplined humility: using AI to accelerate workflows while preserving space for human interpretation, empathy, and accountability.

Taken together, these principles share a common thread: each treats AI adoption as an institutional commitment rather than a personal enthusiasm. That distinction is what integration ultimately tests. Pilots survive only as long as their champions do; a mindset embedded across the institution survives leadership changes, budget cycles, and the fading of novelty.

Workflows for AI-Ready Diplomacy

Mindset provides direction, but integration ultimately succeeds or fails in the daily routines of institutions. For AI to become a trusted part of diplomacy, it must be embedded in workflows that connect pilots into a coherent system, sustain transparency, and preserve continuity across leadership changes and staff rotations. Training, dashboards, provenance standards, institutional memory, and governance routines are the cornerstones of this architecture.

Training and literacy form the foundation. AI-ready institutions cannot rely on a handful of digital enthusiasts; they must ensure that diplomats and communicators at every level understand both the capabilities and the limitations of AI tools. Training goes beyond technical skills to include ethical literacy: knowing when to disclose AI use, how to interpret machine outputs critically, and how to safeguard data. Diplomatic academies that weave AI literacy into their core curriculum are preparing officers not just to use technology, but to evaluate it responsibly and explain it credibly to publics.

Integrated dashboards represent the next layer. Instead of operating separate systems for listening, monitoring, engagement, and evaluation, ministries can build unified platforms where signals flow seamlessly across functions. A rumor flagged by monitoring can be linked to messaging drafts, multilingual translations, and engagement strategies, creating coherence rather than fragmentation. Dashboards that combine these functions reduce duplication and ensure that institutions respond to crises with one voice.

Provenance standards are a third essential workflow. In an age of synthetic media, credibility requires the ability to authenticate content quickly and visibly. Embedding provenance protocols—such as the standards developed by the Coalition for Content Provenance and Authenticity (C2PA)—into institutional workflows ensures that manipulated images, videos, or texts can be identified and debunked with evidence. For coalitions, this means adopting common standards across borders, so that a provenance tag recognized in Brussels is trusted in Nairobi, Ottawa, and Tokyo as well.

Institutional narrative memory is another critical innovation. Diplomatic institutions generate immense archives of speeches, cultural programs, and exchange records, yet much of this knowledge is lost with staff rotations. AI systems can catalog and retrieve decades of content, allowing diplomats to build on continuity rather than reinventing from scratch. Properly designed, such systems become more than repositories: they serve as engines of institutional learning, ensuring that lessons from past crises, campaigns, and cultural exchanges remain accessible across generations.

Finally, governance routines provide the scaffolding that keeps AI trustworthy. Algorithmic impact assessments, equity audits, and error logs should be standard practice. These tools ensure that AI systems are reviewed for bias, inclusivity, and accuracy, and that mistakes are documented rather than buried. Transparency reports, shared with publics where possible, reinforce accountability by showing not only successes but also lessons learned.

With these workflows in place, AI ceases to be an experiment on the margins and becomes part of the everyday discipline of diplomacy.

Risks and Ethics

Integration is often presented as a technical challenge, but in diplomacy it is also a political and ethical one. Bringing AI into the institutional core raises risks that go beyond pilot errors or one-off failures. Inertia, fragmentation, overreliance, inequity, and data governance all threaten to undermine credibility if they are not confronted directly.

Institutional inertia is the first obstacle. Pilots thrive on enthusiasm, but embedding them into permanent systems requires budget lines, governance structures, and training programs. Many ministries celebrate pilot successes only to let them fade when priorities shift or champions move on. Without leadership commitment, AI risks being trapped in a cycle of perpetual experimentation, never crossing into integration.

Fragmentation is a related danger. When departments or missions adopt AI in isolation, the result is a patchwork of systems that cannot communicate with one another. The vignette at the start of this chapter dramatized the cost of this problem: listening, translation, chatbots, and co-pilots all functioning separately, undermining coherence when coherence mattered most. Integration requires not just more tools but common standards and connective infrastructure.

Overreliance is the third risk. Once AI is institutionalized, there is a temptation to trust it too much. Dashboards may be treated as definitive, provenance labels as unquestionable, or co-pilot drafts as authoritative. But as Suleyman (2023) reminds us, AI infrastructures are fragile; they can fail suddenly and dramatically. Institutions that embed AI without maintaining strong habits of human oversight risk replacing inefficiency with automation bias.

Equity gaps present another challenge, and integration is the stage where they harden. Pilots are cheap; the infrastructure, training, and sustained budgets that institutionalization demands are not, so wealthier ministries pull ahead while smaller or less digitally advanced partners fall behind. The remedy runs through this book's own cases: pooled infrastructure. eTranslation gives every EU member state translation capacity that no small ministry could build alone, and U-Report gives more than a hundred countries a participation platform that none of them had to engineer. Pooling, it should be said, is not dependence: the difference between shared infrastructure and borrowed sovereignty lies in governance, in whether smaller members hold real voice in how a system is built and run. For less-resourced ministries, the practical path is joining and shaping such systems, not renting someone else's.

Finally, data governance is a persistent concern. Integration requires institutions to pool sensitive information across functions, departments, and sometimes borders. Without robust safeguards, these systems could expose confidential communications, diplomatic cables, or personal data. A breach in one part of an integrated system can cascade across the whole, damaging not only security but also credibility.

These risks highlight a paradox. Integration is essential if AI is to move from pilots to permanence, but integration also amplifies vulnerabilities by making systems more interconnected and less forgiving of error. For diplomacy, the answer is not to resist integration but to approach it with humility, discipline, and transparency. Institutions must be candid about the risks they face, proactive in designing safeguards, and prepared to explain their choices to publics. Only then can integration become a source of resilience rather than fragility.

Metrics and Evaluation

If pilots can be judged by novelty, integration must be judged by consistency. The question is no longer whether AI can work but whether it is embedded responsibly across the institution. Measuring "AI readiness" requires indicators that capture not just adoption but inclusivity, transparency, and trust. Numbers alone will not suffice; evaluation must focus on whether institutions have built systems that publics and practitioners alike can depend on.

Adoption across functions is the most basic measure. An institution that uses AI only in a single pilot or department is not AI-ready. Readiness implies that listening, messaging, monitoring, engagement, evaluation, and crisis communication are all supported by integrated systems rather than isolated tools. Tracking adoption across the full cycle provides a clear picture of whether AI is becoming part of the institutional fabric or remaining a patchwork of experiments.

Inclusivity audits provide a second layer of evaluation. AI systems must reflect the diversity of publics they serve. Multilingual translation tools should include minority languages, not just those of majority populations. Engagement platforms should reach rural and marginalized communities, not only the digitally fluent. Evaluations that compare usage patterns against demographic realities can reveal whether integration is widening participation or reinforcing existing gaps. In this sense, inclusivity is not a soft metric but a hard test of legitimacy.

Error logs and transparency reports are a third measure. Pilots often fail quietly, with mistakes noted but not systematically recorded. Integrated systems must do better. Institutions that maintain logs of AI errors—whether a mistranslation, a chatbot misstep, or a flawed forecast—can identify recurring problems and adapt. Public-facing transparency reports, modeled on Canada's algorithmic impact assessments or the EU's explainability requirements, reinforce accountability by showing that errors are not hidden but addressed.

Staff literacy is another key indicator. AI readiness cannot rest with technical teams alone. Diplomats and communicators across the institution must understand how AI systems work, what their limits are, and how to explain them to publics. Measuring literacy—through training completion, scenario exercises, or demonstrated ability to question AI outputs—provides a practical gauge of whether integration is sustainable.

Finally, validator trust offers a vital external measure. AI integration will only be credible if validators—journalists, civil society actors, and alumni networks—echo and reinforce the institution's outputs. Tracking amplification and endorsement rates in contexts where AI is disclosed reveals whether transparency strengthens trust or leaves publics skeptical.

Together, these metrics provide a framework for evaluating AI readiness. True readiness lies in whether publics experience AI as a sign of modernization or as another reason to doubt.

Reflection and Strategic Questions

These lessons raise reflective questions for practitioners. Are our AI tools integrated into a coherent system, or are they still scattered pilots? Have we embedded ethical safeguards before scaling, or are we hoping to retrofit them later? Are smaller partners and marginalized publics included in our systems, or are we privileging the already powerful? And when AI fails—as it inevitably will—are we prepared to acknowledge mistakes openly and transparently?

FRONTIER PILOTS

While many governments and organizations are still consolidating pilots, a handful of frontier initiatives suggest what the next stage of integration could look like. At the U.S. Department of State, officials have signaled readiness to move beyond assistive AI toward agentic systems—tools capable of executing multi-step tasks autonomously, such as drafting and routing cables, coordinating responses across bureaus, or monitoring multiple information streams simultaneously (Bracken 2026). These experiments point toward systems that are not only embedded within single institutions but connected across ministries, coalitions, and multilateral organizations—suggesting that the next horizon of AI in diplomacy is not just institutional but systemic.

One frontier is the development of institutional narrative memory. Ministries of foreign affairs and multilateral organizations generate immense archives of speeches, cultural programs, evaluations, and crisis responses, yet much of this material is effectively lost with staff turnover or leadership change. AI systems are now being tested to catalog and retrieve decades of such content, providing continuity across generations of diplomats. A speechwriter preparing remarks on climate policy, for example, could instantly access how the issue has been framed in past decades, across different administrations and cultural contexts. If implemented responsibly—with strong data governance and clear provenance—narrative memory could preserve institutional wisdom while avoiding the cycle of reinvention that has long characterized public diplomacy.

Another frontier lies in global provenance frameworks. Building on the EU's requirement for labeling AI-generated content, coalitions such as the G7 and regional bodies like ASEAN and the AU are beginning to explore common standards for verifying authenticity. If provenance tags applied in Brussels were recognized in Ottawa, Nairobi, or Jakarta, coalitions could coordinate corrections and counter-disinformation campaigns with greater efficiency. Such frameworks would allow publics across regions to trust that a verified image or statement carries shared standards of authenticity. Yet their effectiveness depends on whether publics believe in the labels. Without broad trust, provenance could be dismissed as another layer of government branding rather than a neutral signal of truth.

A third frontier is AI literacy in diplomatic academies. Training programs are beginning to include modules not only on how to use AI tools but on how to question them. Courses now ask diplomats to practice drafting with co-pilots, interpreting outputs critically, and explaining to publics how automation is supervised by humans. This literacy shift is not just technical but ethical, preparing a generation of officers to embed transparency and inclusivity into their daily work. If sustained, it could normalize responsible AI as part of the culture of diplomacy itself.

Finally, integrated coalition dashboards are being imagined as the next step beyond national systems. These platforms would connect the monitoring hubs of multiple states, allowing coalitions to track cross-border narratives, coordinate validators, and share provenance evidence in real time. The vision is ambitious: a NATO member detecting a deepfake in one language could instantly share verification across the alliance, or a WHO hub tracking health rumors could link seamlessly to regional partners. Yet integration at this scale raises sovereignty concerns. Who owns the data, who sets thresholds for action, and how do coalitions prevent larger members from dominating the interpretation of shared signals? These questions remain unresolved but are central to the future of collective resilience.

Perhaps the most vivid signal of AI's trajectory in diplomacy arrived not from a policy document but from a red carpet. On March 25, 2026, First Lady Melania Trump walked into the White House East Room alongside Figure 03, a humanoid robot built by the California-based startup Figure AI, to open the second day of her Fostering the Future Together Global Coalition Summit. The robot greeted first spouses from 45 nations in 11 languages before retracing its steps down the carpet. Trump called it "my first American-made humanoid guest in the White House" and suggested that humanoid educators could soon become fixtures in classrooms worldwide (Associated Press 2026). The moment was part spectacle, part harbinger. It demonstrated that AI is no longer confined to dashboards and chatbots; it is entering the physical spaces where diplomacy happens—embodied, multilingual, and visible to global audiences. For practitioners planning integration roadmaps, the implication is clear: the next generation of AI tools may not just process language—they may walk into the room.

Together, these frontier pilots point to the contours of an AI-ready future. Each remains experimental, fragile, and politically contested, but taken together they suggest how integration could move beyond national adoption to a global architecture of responsible AI in diplomacy.

CONCLUSION

The Republic of Z vignette made the integration question concrete. Amara Osei's ministry had launched 12 AI pilots and celebrated each one, but when a crisis struck, the listening dashboard, the translation system, the chatbot, and the co-pilot produced contradictory outputs because none had been designed to communicate with the others. "We innovated in pieces and assumed coherence would follow," Osei reflected. "It did not." Across town, David Kim recognized the same vulnerability in the embassy's own tools—useful individually, connected by habit and improvisation rather than by design—and Ambassador Grant's response was characteristically direct: "Then that is the next problem we solve." Whether institutions can weave separate capabilities into something coherent enough to sustain credibility across leadership transitions and staff rotations is the work that now defines AI-readiness in diplomacy.

By now you've seen that rapid scaling and patient iteration are both viable paths to integration, and that each depends on the same discipline. The UK, UNICEF, Canada, the EU and UN, and the WHO have reached integration through different timelines and architectures, but what distinguishes them is not the size of the deployment or the sophistication of the technology. It is the willingness to treat AI as institutional capability rather than departmental experiment. Where pilots celebrate individual successes, integration weaves them into something that survives the departure of any champion—and that is the test publics will apply when crises arrive.

The signal of where this is heading arrived on March 25, 2026, in the White House East Room: a humanoid robot greeting first spouses from 45 nations in 11 languages. The Biden voice-cloned robocalls of 2024 already showed that AI is no longer confined to dashboards and chatbots; Figure 03 was a reminder that the next generation of AI tools may not just process language but walk into the room where diplomacy happens. The guiding principle through all of it is continuity—integration as ongoing discipline, not destination. The tools will change. The principles will not. What remains is for practitioners, policymakers, and publics to decide whether AI will be wielded with the judgment, transparency, and care that credibility demands, or whether the speed of the technology will outpace the wisdom of those who deploy it.

Conclusion

When I entered the Foreign Service in 2003, the tools of public diplomacy still belonged to another era. Cables arrived after narratives had already hardened. Real-time public diplomacy dashboards did not exist. And the idea that a shaky video posted after dark could, by morning, bring a crowd to the embassy gates would have seemed improbable. That world is gone. The Republic of Z vignette that opened this book—the deepfake, the scrambling team, the fragile line between credibility preserved and credibility lost—is not a thought experiment. It is Tuesday.

Having walked through the three parts of this book—the core cycle of understanding and engaging publics, the practices that strengthen credibility under pressure, and the expansion of diplomatic reach through cultural exchange and coalition-building—I want to return to that opening moment with sharper vision. What once felt like an unmanageable flood of inputs becomes navigable when institutions build workflows informed by principles that emerged throughout these chapters.

The chapters of this book have traced not a series of isolated techniques, but a cycle of practice. Listening informs messaging; messaging requires monitoring; monitoring enables effective engagement; engagement must be evaluated; evaluation prepares institutions for crises; crises expose the need for ethics; ethics sustain cultural exchange; cultural exchange strengthens coalitions; and coalitions depend on integration. Break any link in this cycle, and credibility frays. Maintain the cycle consistently, and credibility can be strengthened even under pressure.

The speed of AI may tempt some to focus on outputs—how many posts, how many translations, how many dashboards. But credibility rests not on volume but on coherence: a system in which each function supports the others and all are aligned with a core commitment to trust.

Consider how this coherence plays out in practice. During COVID-19, the World Health Organization's Early AI-supported Response with Social Listening tool (EARS), discussed in Chapter 6, demonstrated how early listening could inform both messaging and crisis response. Ukraine's rapid exposure of the March 2022 deepfake of President Zelenskyy, examined in Chapter 3, revealed how authenticity, ethical judgment, and coordinated response converge when reputational security is at stake. Singapore's Virtual Intelligent Chat Assistant (VICA), featured in Chapter 4, showed that even routine public interactions require more than efficiency: they depend on

 DOI: 10.1201/9781003612377-14

responsiveness, clarity, and sensitivity to the people being served. The African Union's rapid development and 2024 endorsement of a continental AI strategy, referenced in Chapter 7, underscored how integration and coalition-building can be accelerated by political will and shared technological tools. Each case illustrates the same point: AI does not transform diplomacy by itself. It magnifies whatever systems, habits, and principles institutions already embody.

Several lessons emerge clearly. AI is neither panacea nor existential threat—it is a dual-use technology, equally available for authentic engagement or manipulation, for transparency or deception. Its impact depends less on the brilliance of algorithms than on the integrity of those who wield them. The adoption of AI is not about keeping pace with fashion; it is about institutional survival in an environment where publics judge credibility by how quickly, inclusively, and transparently institutions respond. And the work of public diplomacy remains irreducibly human. No dashboard can replicate the judgment of a seasoned officer who knows when silence speaks louder than a press release, or when cultural nuance transforms a standard exchange into a relationship of trust.

This book has also been honest about limitations. AI is prone to hallucination, bias, and opacity. It can flatten cultural nuance, obscure accountability, and erode privacy if used carelessly. Detection of deepfakes will never be perfect; provenance systems may be gamed; personalization may edge into manipulation. Readers should leave not with the illusion that technical solutions resolve ethical dilemmas, but with clarity about where tools help, where they risk harm, and how steady oversight makes the difference.

Looking forward, several frontiers demand attention. Multimodal AI is increasingly merging text, voice, and video more seamlessly, intensifying the challenge of distinguishing authentic from synthetic. The governance landscape remains fragmented: the EU AI Act, shifting U.S. executive-branch AI policy, the African Union Continental AI Strategy, and ASEAN's AI governance guides continue to evolve in different directions. Compute inequality risks deepening what Chapter 7 identified as "AI colonialism" unless inclusive approaches are adopted. The rise of autonomous, agentic AI systems will test the very boundaries of oversight, demanding new red lines about which decisions must always remain human. These developments will not resolve the ethical dilemmas this book has raised; they will intensify them.

And yet there is reason for confidence. Institutions that commit to transparency, provenance, and inclusion will be better positioned not only to survive but to lead. Public diplomacy officers already know that trust is hard to build and easy to lose. Embassies that disclose AI assistance rather than hiding it, that use AI to amplify local voices rather than erase them, and that invest in staff training rather than outsourcing judgment will find that publics reward those choices.

For students, the takeaway is clear: literacy matters. Understanding AI's capabilities and limits is no longer optional for careers in international affairs. For practitioners, the message—developed most fully in Chapter 10's integration roadmap—is to start small but act deliberately. Adopt workflows you can maintain, measure what builds trust, and capture lessons in ways that survive rotations. For policymakers, the imperative is to align governance with practice, ensuring that compliance becomes a credibility enhancer, not merely a burden. For stakeholders outside government, the challenge is to recognize your role in shaping an information environment that belongs to no single actor.

Diplomacy has always depended on credibility. AI changes only the speed at which that credibility is tested. The final counsel of this book is therefore not to chase novelty, but to cultivate coherence. In every embassy, every ministry, every coalition, the advantage will belong to those who can listen widely, speak honestly, act proportionately, and disclose openly.

If technology magnifies human choices, then the surest strategy is to make credibility the default.

This, then, is the promise AI holds for public diplomacy: not to replace the art of human connection, but to extend its reach, sharpen its timing, and sustain its trust. The Republic of Z may be fictional, but the challenges it dramatized across these ten chapters are real. The way they are resolved will depend on choices made by diplomats, policymakers, technologists, and publics. May those choices be guided by judgment, humility, and the enduring truth that in the end, diplomacy is about people—and people, not machines, will always be the measure of credibility.

Epilogue

The horizon I have tried to map throughout this book is defined not by technology alone but by a dangerous convergence: AI is arriving precisely when democratic institutions are most fragile, when truth itself is contested, and when corporate entities wield unprecedented control over the information systems that shape public understanding. I believe this convergence creates the most consequential challenge public diplomacy has ever confronted.

What I have witnessed throughout my career is a dual transformation that threatens the very foundations of democratic discourse. Leaders with weak attachments to democratic principles embrace authoritarian methods while technology corporations command influence over public conversation that rivals nation-states themselves. Public diplomacy practitioners may find themselves caught between these forces, tasked with building trust and credibility using tools controlled by entities whose primary allegiance lies with profit rather than democratic values.

This is not a distant concern but an immediate operational reality. Credibility, which once could be built slowly through cultural exchanges and institutional presence, can now be destroyed in minutes by deepfakes spreading through coordinated networks of AI-generated content. State-sponsored disinformation campaigns leverage artificial intelligence not merely to create false content but to optimize its distribution with machine efficiency across platforms whose algorithms prioritize engagement over truth. What once required sophisticated state resources can now be executed by any actor with basic technical skills.

The asymmetry is profound and growing. While democratic institutions struggle with deliberative processes and accountability mechanisms, authoritarian actors and profit-driven platforms operate at machine speed. They flood information spaces with noise designed to overwhelm publics into cynical disengagement. They exploit algorithmic systems that fragment societies into isolated echo chambers, systematically eroding the common ground essential for democratic dialogue.

Yet I remain convinced that within this crisis lies unprecedented opportunity for those willing to act decisively. AI can detect and counter disinformation faster than any previous tool. It can amplify previously marginalized voices and provide diplomatic practitioners with real-time understanding of global sentiment and emerging narratives. Most importantly, it can strengthen authentic democratic storytelling by

DOI: 10.1201/9781003612377-15

enabling more responsive, culturally sensitive, and personally relevant communication with diverse global audiences.

Based on what I have observed and argued throughout this book, seizing this potential requires fundamentally reimagining traditional approaches to public diplomacy. We must build new forms of coalition that transcend state-to-state relationships, working directly with civil society organizations, academic institutions, and technology companies to establish governance frameworks that prioritize human flourishing over engagement metrics. This demands diplomatic practitioners develop fluency not only in AI technologies but also in the ethical and political implications of algorithmic governance systems that increasingly mediate human communication.

The path forward requires four fundamental commitments. First, we must use AI transparently, establishing precedents for responsible deployment that other actors cannot exploit. Second, we must invest in verification and authentication systems rather than manipulation tools, building infrastructure that strengthens truth rather than obscures it. Third, we must balance personalization with unity, tailoring messages to cultural contexts while reinforcing shared democratic values. Fourth, we must move with unprecedented urgency, recognizing that every day of delay allows authoritarian and commercial actors to further entrench their advantages.

The stakes could not be higher. The information space may prove the most consequential terrain of international competition for generations to come. Success or failure in this domain will determine whether democratic values can survive in an age of artificial intelligence, whether global publics retain the capacity to distinguish truth from fabrication, and whether diplomatic institutions can maintain their essential role as bridges between peoples and nations.

We stand at a crossroads where the decisions made today will echo through history. The question before us is stark: Will we allow algorithmic systems optimized for profit and authoritarian control to define the future of human communication, or will we act swiftly and decisively to ensure these powerful tools serve democracy's highest aspirations?

Appendix A
100 AI Use Cases in Public Diplomacy and Strategic Communication

This appendix offers 100 practical AI use cases in public diplomacy and strategic communication. Each example includes a concise description of what the tool does in practice, assuming it is feasible and operational.

I. NARRATIVE INTELLIGENCE AND RESEARCH

(Audience insight, listening, and early warning—Chapter 1)

1. **Scan multilingual media for trending narratives**—Continuously monitors global media in dozens of languages to highlight the most-discussed topics related to your policy area.
2. **Detect early warning signals of protests**—Clusters online chatter to identify sudden spikes in grievance or mobilization language that may precede street activity.
3. **Map sentiment shifts after announcements**—Tracks whether public opinion around a policy, speech, or initiative becomes more positive, negative, or polarized in the hours and days after.
4. **Monitor diaspora conversations**—Surfaces how diaspora communities abroad discuss homeland or host-country policies across social media platforms.
5. **Benchmark attitudes against historical baselines**—Compares today's discourse on an issue with past data to highlight trends over time.
6. **Identify demographics driving narrative spread**—Pinpoints which age groups, regions, or interest communities are fueling specific storylines.
7. **Distinguish satire and memes from disinformation**—Flags when viral humor is benign versus when it risks being weaponized as false information.
8. **Compare narrative framing across countries**—Analyzes how the same story is framed differently in local vs international contexts.
9. **Detect cross-border spillover of narratives**—Identifies when a narrative originating in one country starts influencing conversations in another.
10. **Flag youth-driven narratives**—Alerts communicators to issues disproportionately discussed by younger publics, which may gain traction rapidly.

II. MESSAGING AND CONTENT CREATION

(Crafting impactful, culturally adapted content—Chapter 2)

11. **Draft press releases in multiple languages**—Generates high-quality press releases instantly translated into dozens of official languages.
12. **Generate culturally adapted statements**—Adjusts phrasing, tone, and idioms so messages resonate locally while staying consistent globally.
13. **Turn speeches into tweet threads or clips**—Condenses long speeches into engaging social media content optimized for different platforms.
14. **Produce audience-specific talking points**—Creates tailored bullet points for journalists, NGOs, or diplomats with different emphasis for each.
15. **Localize visuals, colors, and symbols**—Suggests culturally appropriate design elements for campaign graphics and videos.
16. **Run A/B testing of message framings**—Generates multiple message variants and predicts which will resonate better with target audiences.
17. **Create infographics from reports**—Converts dense policy documents into easy-to-understand visual summaries.
18. **Generate subtitles for videos**—Produces accurate multilingual captions to broaden accessibility and reach.
19. **Draft FAQs for policy rollouts**—Prepares likely questions from publics and supplies clear answers in advance.
20. **Standardize tone and terminology**—Ensures consistency of language and branding across all offices worldwide.

III. ENGAGEMENT AND DIALOGUE

(Interactive diplomacy, alumni, and youth platforms—Chapters 4 and 8)

21. **Deploy chatbots for consular inquiries**—Provides automated answers to common visa, travel, and consular questions 24/7.
22. **Host virtual town halls with AI moderation**—Runs interactive online sessions with real-time summarization and question clustering.
23. **Run youth consultations with AI-analyzed polling**—Collects youth perspectives through surveys and automatically categorizes responses into themes.
24. **Personalize newsletters to subscribers**—Uses AI to send tailored updates aligned with recipients' interests and engagement history.
25. **Match alumni with mentors**—Recommends mentor-mentee pairings based on career data, interests, and prior program participation.
26. **Provide 24/7 multilingual "front desk" service**—An AI concierge answers public inquiries in local languages around the clock.
27. **Summarize citizen submissions**—Converts thousands of messages into concise thematic reports for staff review.
28. **Detect recurring concerns in public inquiries**—Highlights patterns in embassy emails or call logs to inform communication strategies.

29. **Translate questions live during dialogues**—Offers instant multilingual translation for real-time Q&A sessions.
30. **Archive citizen engagement**—Stores and indexes feedback for institutional memory and long-term analysis.

IV. COUNTER-DISINFORMATION AND AUTHENTICITY

(Detection, provenance, and defense—Chapters 3 and 7)

31. **Detect deepfake videos**—Scans and flags AI-generated video content before it goes viral.
32. **Verify provenance of images**—Checks metadata to confirm whether a photo has been altered or manipulated.
33. **Map disinformation networks**—Reveals clusters of accounts and websites working together to spread falsehoods.
34. **Identify bot clusters**—Detects groups of automated accounts amplifying hashtags or posts inorganically.
35. **Generate daily threat briefs**—Produces up-to-date disinformation reports for embassy staff and policymakers.
36. **Flag fake news websites**—Identifies AI-generated news portals posing as legitimate outlets.
37. **Benchmark adversary narratives**—Compares hostile narratives against allied messaging to expose distortions.
38. **Simulate exploitation of new policies**—Forecasts how adversaries might twist upcoming announcements.
39. **Pre-bunk anticipated distortions**—Creates proactive counter-narratives to inoculate publics before false claims spread.
40. **Rank disinformation risks**—Scores potential narratives by reach, virality, and likelihood of causing harm.

V. CRISIS COMMUNICATION

(Rapid response and rumor management—Chapter 6)

41. **Auto-draft holding statements**—Generates quick public statements within minutes of a crisis event.
42. **Provide multilingual SMS alerts**—Sends accurate emergency information simultaneously in multiple languages.
43. **Flag rumors about closures**—Detects and alerts when false claims about embassy operations circulate.
44. **Translate evacuation instructions**—Produces instant, accurate instructions in local languages during emergencies.
45. **Generate rumor dashboards**—Provides real-time overviews of crisis-related rumors and their spread.

46. **Summarize hotline calls**—Analyzes public inquiries into daily situational reports for staff.
47. **Draft crisis FAQs**—Prepares plain-language Q&A documents to calm publics during uncertainty.
48. **Identify trusted validators**—Highlights credible local voices to amplify corrections.
49. **Detect aid-related misinformation**—Flags false narratives around humanitarian aid delivery.
50. **Map crisis sentiment in real time**—Tracks evolving public emotions to guide tone of communication.

VI. METRICS AND EVALUATION

(Quantitative monitoring, benchmarking—Chapter 5)

51. **Measure reach vs resonance**—Evaluates not just how far content spreads, but how strongly it resonates.
52. **Compare outcomes against peers**—Benchmarks one's office or campaign's results against others.
53. **Automate annual reports**—Compiles program data and produces polished reports automatically.
54. **Provide real-time dashboards**—Visualizes communication performance for managers in near-real time.
55. **Benchmark performance across missions**—Compares outcomes across embassies for best practices.
56. **Visualize network amplification**—Maps how messages spread through online and offline networks.
57. **Track machine translation accuracy**—Monitors error rates in AI translations for ongoing quality improvement.
58. **Identify weak communication channels**—Detects platforms where reach is low relative to effort.
59. **Generate KPIs automatically**—Produces standard indicators to track performance over time.
60. **Forecast reputational outcomes**—Predicts how policy actions might affect reputation scores.

VII. PROGRAM LEARNING AND ADAPTATION

(Feedback loops, inclusivity, and adaptation—Chapter 5)

61. **Cluster alumni survey responses**—Groups open-text responses into clear categories for reporting.
62. **Detect gender disparities**—Identifies whether men and women are participating equally in programs.
63. **Measure rumor half-life**—Calculates how long falsehoods persist after being corrected.

64. **Summarize focus group transcripts**—Extracts key insights from qualitative program feedback.
65. **Identify missing demographics**—Detects which communities are absent from feedback surveys.
66. **Flag underrepresented groups**—Highlights segments underserved by current programming.
67. **Recommend program adjustments**—Suggests concrete adaptations to improve inclusivity and impact.
68. **Rank programs by diversity metrics**—Scores initiatives on how well they represent different publics.
69. **Identify recurring engagement barriers**—Surfaces consistent reasons why groups opt out.
70. **Suggest pilots for marginalized groups**—Proposes targeted new initiatives to reach overlooked communities.

VIII. CULTURE AND EDUCATION

(Heritage preservation, cultural diplomacy, education—Chapter 8)

71. **Translate literature with nuance**—Provides side-by-side literal and adapted versions of texts.
72. **Digitize manuscripts with OCR**—Converts fragile documents into searchable digital archives.
73. **Reconstruct heritage sites virtually**—Builds 3D models of destroyed or damaged cultural landmarks.
74. **Provide real-time interpretation at events**—Offers simultaneous translation in multiple languages.
75. **Adapt educational materials**—Adjusts textbooks or training content for cultural sensitivity.
76. **Personalize MOOC learning pathways**—Suggests tailored study tracks for exchange participants.
77. **Transcribe oral traditions**—Records and indexes oral histories for preservation and research.
78. **Summarize exchange student reflections**—Extracts common themes from program feedback.
79. **Suggest exchange pairings**—Matches participants and hosts based on shared interests.
80. **Deploy bilingual outreach chatbots**—Provides cultural and educational information interactively.

IX. COLLABORATION AND FORECASTING (MULTILATERAL)

(Coalitions, alliances, foresight—Chapter 9)

81. **Share monitoring dashboards**—Provides coalition members with a unified view of narrative trends.

82. **Forecast narrative uptake**—Predicts how policies will be received across different countries.
83. **Run disinformation simulations**—Tests how adversarial narratives might spread during crises.
84. **Develop provenance standards**—Creates coalition-wide rules for authenticating content.
85. **Harmonize labeling of synthetic media**—Ensures consistency across member states in identifying AI-generated content.
86. **Benchmark adversary narratives**—Compares how hostile messaging differs across regions.
87. **Forecast backlash to policies**—Models potential negative reactions before policy rollout.
88. **Maintain best practice libraries**—Shares case studies and templates across alliances.
89. **Coordinate validator amplification**—Synchronizes trusted voices across borders to rebut falsehoods.
90. **Operate shared rumor databases**—Stores collective intelligence on recurring disinformation themes.

X. INTERNAL GOVERNANCE AND CO-PILOTS

(Institutional memory, drafting, compliance—Chapter 10)

91. **Summarize decades of speeches**—Creates concise historical syntheses for quick reference.
92. **Retrieve past talking points instantly**—Searches archives to pull up relevant briefing lines.
93. **Draft memos and briefs**—Produces first drafts of policy notes in standard formats.
94. **Flag inconsistencies across drafts**—Checks whether documents contradict each other.
95. **Generate training manuals**—Automates production of onboarding materials for new staff.
96. **Auto-format reports**—Prepares documents in templates for interagency sharing.
97. **Suggest precedents for negotiations**—Identifies comparable cases from archives.
98. **Draft transparency reports**—Produces disclosures on AI system use and safeguards.
99. **Capture lessons from crises**—Stores and tags “lessons learned” into searchable databases.
100. **Conduct algorithmic impact assessments**—Guides teams through structured risk and ethics reviews.

Appendix B
20 Specialized AI Assistant Concepts for Public Affairs and Strategic Communication

These specialized AI assistant concepts translate the book's analysis into practical tools. Depending on the platform, similar capabilities may be called custom GPTs, AI assistants, agents, Gems, copilots, skills, bots, or reusable AI workflows. Organized by primary function, each concept includes three example prompts or task requests showing how practitioners might use it. This list is only a starting point; the possible assistant concepts are limited chiefly by practitioners' needs, imagination, and judgment.

CATEGORY 1: NARRATIVE INTELLIGENCE AND LISTENING

1. Narrative Monitoring Assistant

Purpose: Detect and summarize emerging narratives across platforms and languages.

- Prompt 1: "*Summarize the top five narratives trending about [issue] in [country/language].*"
- Prompt 2: "*Identify early warning signals of unrest based on these posts.*"
- Prompt 3: "*Compare sentiment toward [policy] across Twitter, TikTok, and Facebook.*"

2. Validator Mapping Assistant

Purpose: Identify trusted validators amplifying key narratives.

- Prompt 1: "*List the top 10 validators amplifying positive narratives on [topic].*"
- Prompt 2: "*Map validator networks in [region] and their reach.*"
- Prompt 3: "*Highlight validators who could help counter misinformation on [issue].*"

3. Meme and Satire Classifier Assistant

Purpose: Distinguish satire and humor from harmful disinformation.

- Prompt 1: "*Classify these viral posts as satire, parody, or disinformation.*"
- Prompt 2: "*Explain how this meme might be misinterpreted as hostile content.*"
- Prompt 3: "*Suggest whether this narrative requires response or can be ignored.*"

CATEGORY 2: MESSAGING AND ENGAGEMENT

4. Messaging Draft Assistant

Purpose: Generate multilingual, culturally adapted statements.

- Prompt 1: "*Draft a statement about [policy] for [audience] in [language].*"
- Prompt 2: "*Provide three tone variations: empathetic, formal, and informal.*"
- Prompt 3: "*Highlight potential cultural missteps in this draft.*"

5. Visual Adaptation Assistant

Purpose: Suggest culturally sensitive adaptations of visual content.

- Prompt 1: "*Suggest alternative colors and symbols for this graphic to fit [culture].*"
- Prompt 2: "*Identify any imagery in this design that might offend [audience].*"
- Prompt 3: "*Propose three culturally adapted versions of this campaign poster.*"

6. Engagement Chatbot Assistant

Purpose: Provide automated but transparent public-facing responses.

- Prompt 1: "*Draft a chatbot response for FAQs on [policy].*"
- Prompt 2: "*Explain how to disclose clearly that the user is interacting with AI.*"
- Prompt 3: "*Generate empathetic responses for crisis-related queries.*"

CATEGORY 3: COUNTER-DISINFORMATION AND AUTHENTICITY

7. Deepfake Detector Assistant

Purpose: Analyze videos and images for manipulation signs.

- Prompt 1: "*Analyze this video for evidence of deepfake manipulation.*"
- Prompt 2: "*Explain the anomalies that indicate AI-generation in this image.*"
- Prompt 3: "*Provide a confidence rating on authenticity with supporting reasons.*"

8. Pre-bunking Assistant

Purpose: Anticipate adversary distortions and generate pre-bunk messages.

- Prompt 1: "*List likely distortions adversaries could spread about [policy].*"
- Prompt 2: "*Draft a pre-bunk message to inoculate audiences against these distortions.*"
- Prompt 3: "*Suggest validators to amplify the pre-bunk narrative.*"

9. Disinformation Network Assistant

Purpose: Map and analyze coordinated campaigns.

- Prompt 1: "*Identify signs of coordinated bot activity in this dataset.*"
- Prompt 2: "*Visualize connections among accounts spreading [narrative].*"
- Prompt 3: "*Explain how this campaign targets specific demographics.*"

CATEGORY 4: CRISIS COMMUNICATION

10. Crisis Draft Assistant

Purpose: Generate fast, proportional crisis statements.

- Prompt 1: "*Draft a holding statement for [crisis event].*"
- Prompt 2: "*Refine tone for empathy while avoiding speculation.*"
- Prompt 3: "*Shorten this message to SMS length.*"

11. Rumor Triage Assistant

Purpose: Prioritize which rumors to address and which to monitor.

- Prompt 1: "*Rank these rumors by urgency and potential harm.*"
- Prompt 2: "*Explain why some rumors are best ignored.*"
- Prompt 3: "*Suggest proportionate response strategies for each rumor.*"

12. Validator Amplification Assistant

Purpose: Identify trusted voices to amplify corrections.

- Prompt 1: "*List validators trusted in [community] who could rebut rumors.*"
- Prompt 2: "*Suggest how validators could frame corrections authentically.*"
- Prompt 3: "*Map validator networks to maximize amplification of corrections.*"

CATEGORY 5: EVALUATION AND LEARNING

13. Survey Analyzer Assistant

Purpose: Extract themes and insights from survey data.

- Prompt 1: "*Cluster alumni survey responses into 5 themes.*"
- Prompt 2: "*Highlight demographic gaps in these responses.*"
- Prompt 3: "*Summarize recommendations for program adaptation.*"

14. Rumor Half-Life Tracker Assistant

Purpose: Measure how long misinformation persists after correction.

- Prompt 1: "*Track the persistence of this rumor over 7 days post-correction.*"
- Prompt 2: "*Compare rumor decay rates across [country A] and [country B].*"
- Prompt 3: "*Suggest factors influencing longer rumor half-lives.*"

CATEGORY 6: CULTURE AND EDUCATION

15. Cultural Translator Assistant

Purpose: Provide literal and culturally adapted translations.

- Prompt 1: "*Translate this poem literally and provide an adapted version.*"
- Prompt 2: "*Explain metaphors that risk losing meaning in translation.*"
- Prompt 3: "*Suggest culturally sensitive alternatives for ambiguous terms.*"

16. Heritage Archivist Assistant

Purpose: Digitize and contextualize heritage materials.

- Prompt 1: "*Summarize this manuscript into searchable metadata.*"
- Prompt 2: "*Transcribe this oral history recording with annotations.*"
- Prompt 3: "*Propose cultural tags for archiving this artifact.*"

CATEGORY 7: COLLABORATION AND FORECASTING

17. Multilateral Simulation Assistant

Purpose: Forecast how narratives spread across states.

- Prompt 1: "*Simulate reactions in [country A] and [country B] to [policy].*"
- Prompt 2: "*Predict adversarial exploitation opportunities.*"
- Prompt 3: "*Suggest coalition-wide response options.*"

18. Coalition Dashboard Assistant

Purpose: Standardize insights for alliances.

- Prompt 1: "*Summarize narrative monitoring across these five states.*"
- Prompt 2: "*Highlight divergences in sentiment across member countries.*"
- Prompt 3: "*Propose a unified coalition narrative response.*"

CATEGORY 8: INSTITUTIONAL KNOWLEDGE AND GOVERNANCE

19. Diplomatic Memory Assistant

Purpose: Preserve institutional narrative memory.

- Prompt 1: "*Summarize how our ministry has framed [issue] since 2000.*"
- Prompt 2: "*Retrieve comparable past statements on [policy].*"
- Prompt 3: "*Identify lessons learned from previous crises.*"

20. Ethics and Compliance Assistant

Purpose: Guide teams through governance requirements.

- Prompt 1: "*Generate an algorithmic impact assessment for this AI system.*"
- Prompt 2: "*Highlight inclusivity risks if minority languages are excluded.*"
- Prompt 3: "*Draft a disclosure note explaining AI use to the public.*"

Appendix C Glossary of Key Terms in AI, Public Diplomacy, and Strategic Communication

A

Adversarial Examples—Inputs intentionally crafted to fool AI systems (e.g., slight pixel changes causing misclassification); relevant for media forensics and platform safety teams.

Agentic AI—Systems that can plan and execute multi-step tasks (e.g., monitor narratives, draft responses, post to channels) under policies and guardrails.

Algorithmic Impact Assessment (AIA)—A structured review process to evaluate risks, fairness, and transparency before deploying an AI system. *Example:* Canada's federal directive requires AIAs for all government AI tools.

Alignment (e.g., RLHF/RLAIF/Constitutional AI)—Techniques to align model behavior with human or institutional values and policies; critical to "human-in-the-loop" PD workflows.

Artificial Intelligence (AI)—Computer systems that perform tasks normally requiring human intelligence, such as pattern recognition, language processing, or decision-making. *Example:* AI used in WHO's EARS platform for rumor detection.

Attention / Transformer Architecture—Neural network mechanism underlying modern LLMs; enables models to track long-range dependencies in text and multimodal data.

Authenticity Verification—Tools and processes to confirm whether content (video, photo, text) is real or manipulated; often involves provenance metadata.

B

Bayesian Inference—Probabilistic updating central to forecasting and risk/uncertainty communication.

Bias (AI)—Systematic distortion in AI outputs due to skewed training data or flawed design. *Example:* Underperformance on African languages if trained mostly on European data.

Big Data—Extremely large datasets analyzed to reveal patterns, trends, associations. *Example:* Social media data used for narrative intelligence.

Black-Box vs. Glass-Box Models—Degree to which model internals are interpretable for accountability and red-teaming.

Bot Network—Coordinated automated accounts amplifying content. Example: "Spamouflage," a coordinated inauthentic campaign attributed to Chinese state actors and detected across multiple countries, including Canada.

C

C2PA (Content Authenticity)—Open standard to embed tamper-evident provenance into files (image/video/audio/text) to prove origin and edits—vital for countering the "liar's dividend."

Causal Inference (DAGs, Counterfactuals)—Methods to infer cause-effect (beyond correlation) for PD impact claims.

Chatbot—AI conversational agent. *Example:* Taiwan's bilingual COVID-19 bot.

Cognitive Warfare—Information operations shaping perceptions (e.g., deepfakes during conflict).

Concept/Model Drift—When data or behavior changes over time, degrading model performance; requires monitoring in fast-moving information spaces.

Coordinated Inauthentic Behavior (CIB)—Organized deceptive activity on platforms; a takedown category in trust and safety operations.

Crisis Communication—Accurate, timely, empathetic communication during emergencies. *Example:* Embassy evacuation notices with AI translation.

D

Deepfake—AI-generated synthetic media depicting people doing/saying things they never did. *Example:* 2022 Zelenskyy "surrender" video.

Differential Privacy—Techniques adding statistical noise to protect individuals in datasets (useful for survey/PD research under privacy laws).

Diffusion Models—State-of-the-art generative image/video models with escalating policy/compliance implications.

Digital Colonialism—Dominance of tools trained on Western data that marginalize other voices.

Disinformation—False information spread deliberately to deceive/manipulate.

DPIA (Data Protection Impact Assessment)—EU/UK privacy assessment for high-risk data processing (complements AIA).

E

Early Warning System (AI)—Tools that detect narrative shifts before escalation. *Example:* WHO EARS for vaccine rumors.

Embeddings / Vector Search—Numeric representations of text/media supporting semantic search and RAG pipelines in PD knowledge bases.

Engagement Platform—Systems enabling two-way dialogue (chatbots, forums, alumni networks).

Ethics in AI—Fairness, transparency, accountability. *Example:* UNESCO 2021 Recommendation.

EU AI Act (Risk Tiers and Labeling)—European framework with obligations (incl. synthetic-media disclosures) relevant to posts operating in or reaching EU audiences.

Evaluation Metrics—Precision/Recall/F1/ROC-AUC, BLEU (MT), human eval for message quality/credibility.

F

Fake News Site—Outlet mimicking legitimate media to push false/AI-made stories.

Few-Shot and In-Context Learning—Getting models to perform tasks with minimal examples; critical for low-resource language contexts.

Foundation Model—Broad, pre-trained model adapted to multiple tasks; governance and model cards matter.

Forecasting (Narrative)—Predicting audience responses to policies/messages.

Frontier AI—Cutting-edge or emerging capabilities not yet widely deployed.

G

Generative AI—Models that create new text/image/video/audio. *Example:* GPT drafting speeches.

Global Governance of AI—International norms (EU AI Act, G7 Hiroshima Code).

Golden Quarter-Hour—NATO StratCom: hostile narratives can dominate in ~15 minutes if unchallenged.

Guardrails—Policy, prompt, and tool constraints preventing unsafe content/actions (e.g., preventing posting without human approval).

H

Hallucination (AI)—Confident fabrication by AI.

Human Oversight—Humans supervise AI outputs for accountability.

Human-in-the-Loop (HITL)—Operational design ensuring humans review/release sensitive outputs (e.g., crises, policy).

Hybrid Warfare—Conventional tactics blended with disinformation/cyber ops.

I

Impact Forecasting—Predicting diplomatic/economic/reputational consequences of strategies.
Infodemic—Overabundance of (mis)information in crises.
Inoculation Theory—Communication strategy "prebunking" likely false claims to build audience immunity.
Interpretability (SHAP/LIME/Saliency)—Techniques explaining model decisions to build trust and diagnose bias.
Institutional Narrative Memory—AI-enabled archives of campaigns/speeches.

J

Joint Simulation—Multilateral AI-assisted scenario planning (e.g., NATO).
Journalistic Validation—Independent verification of claims, often with AI for authenticity checks.
Justice (AI Ethics)—Ensuring fair, inclusive systems.

K

K-Anonymity—Privacy technique ensuring individuals are indistinguishable within a group in shared datasets.
Key Performance Indicators (KPIs)—Measures of effectiveness (e.g., rumor half-life, validator amplification).
Knowledge Graph—Entity-relationship maps organizing complex data.
Knowledge Management—Systematic capture and retrieval of institutional memory.

L

Language Model—AI trained on text to generate/analyze language (e.g., GPT).
Literacy in AI—Skills for diplomats to use/supervise AI effectively.
Listening Tool (AI)—Monitors public discourse at scale, often multilingual.
LLM Security (Prompt Injection/Jailbreaks)—Attacks that steer models to reveal secrets or violate policy; requires sandboxing, content filters, and clear "channels of record."
Logic Model (PD)—Inputs→Activities→Outputs→Outcomes planning tool central to PD MEL and the PDIP process.

M

Machine Learning (ML)—Systems that learn from data to improve performance.
Media Monitoring—Tracking coverage to analyze narratives and sentiment.
MEL (Monitoring, Evaluation, and Learning)—Practice of measuring outcomes and iterating PD programs; complements logic models/theory of change.
Memetic Warfare—Strategic use/analysis of viral cultural units (memes) in influence operations.
Multilingual Communication—AI translation/interpretation across languages.
Multimodal AI—Models handling text+image+audio/video jointly (useful for authenticity and accessibility).

N

Narrative Intelligence—Detecting/mapping/analyzing circulating narratives.
Narrative Mapping—Visualizing how narratives travel across borders/communities.
Network Analysis (Centrality/Modularity)—Methods to study influence flows and key amplifiers within information networks.
Neural Machine Translation (NMT)—Neural-network-based translation (e.g., EU eTranslation).

O

Off the Record / On Background—Media ground rules affecting sourcing and credibility in official comms (press office best practice).
Opacity (AI Black Box)—Lack of transparency in model decisions.
Open-Source Intelligence (OSINT)—Public data collection/analysis, often AI-augmented.
Outreach Campaign—Coordinated communications optimized with AI insights.
Overfitting/Underfitting—Model generalization failures to watch for in applied PD analytics.

P

Participatory Diplomacy Platform—Systems enabling citizen input (e.g., UNICEF U-Report).
PDIP (Public Diplomacy Implementation Plan)—Section-level plan linking PD initiatives to ICS/FBS objectives and MEL.
Personalization—Tailoring messages to segments/individuals.
PETs (Privacy-Enhancing Technologies)—Techniques (DP, federated learning) enabling analytics with minimized data risk.

Press-Office Ground Rules—"On the record," "on background," "off the record," and disciplined message coordination remain the backbone for credibility in an AI era.

Prompt Injection and Jailbreaking—Malicious inputs steering models off-policy; mitigated by content filters, retrieval isolation, and signed outputs.

Provenance—Embedded metadata verifying origin/authenticity.

Q

Q&A (Question and Answer)—Evaluation of LLM retrieval accuracy, grounding, and citation fidelity for policy briefs.

Qualitative Analysis (AI)—Clustering and interpreting open-text feedback.

Quantification Bias—Over-reliance on easy-to-measure metrics.

Quick Response System—AI-assisted workflows enabling faster public statements.

R

RAG (Retrieval-Augmented Generation)—Combining LLMs with trusted corpora (e.g., policy repositories) to improve accuracy/transparency.

Red Teaming (AI)—Stress-testing systems via adversarial prompts and misuse scenarios.

Resilience (Communications)—Sustaining credibility under information pressure.

Risk Assessment (Systemic vs. Model Risk)—Distinguishing governance/operational risks from model-level risks for AI deployments in missions.

Rumor Half-Life—How long misinformation persists after correction.

S

Safety Classifiers and Downranking—Platform-side systems that label, reduce reach, or remove harmful/synthetic content; PD must plan for enforcement impacts.

Saliency / Feature-Attribution Maps—Visualizations revealing what inputs drove a model's decision (vision/audio tasks).

Scenario Modeling—Simulating audience responses to policy/crisis.

Sentiment Analysis—Classifying attitudes (positive/negative/neutral).

Speech-Act Theory—How utterances perform actions (e.g., promises, warnings)—useful in crafting diplomatic language.

StateChat / Northstar / FAM Search—Internal AI tools supporting drafting, media monitoring/disinfo detection, and policy lookup at the U.S. Department of State; "AI intern" model with strict human review.

Synthetic Narratives—Narratives generated or amplified artificially, often by AI.

T

Targeted Engagement—Audience segmentation for tailored messages.

Threat Modeling (InfoOps/Cyber)—Anticipating attacker goals (impersonation, prompt injection, data poisoning) and mapping mitigations.

Tokenization—Breaking text into tokens for model processing; affects multilingual performance.

Transformers / Transfer Learning—Foundation of modern LLMs and efficient domain adaptation.

Transparency (AI)—Openness about how/when AI is used.

Trusted Validators—Third-party voices who credibly amplify official messages.

U

U-Report (UNICEF)—Global youth engagement platform using AI.

U.S. EO 14110 (2023)—U.S. federal direction on safe, secure, trustworthy AI including watermarking/provenance for federal communications. Revoked January 2025; noted here for its influence on federal AI governance norms during 2023–2024.

UNESCO Recommendation on AI Ethics (2021)—Global framework emphasizing proportionality, accountability, inclusivity.

Uncertainty Calibration—Techniques to quantify model confidence for operational decision-making.

User Safeguarding—Privacy/security for vulnerable groups, especially minors.

V

Validator Network—Coalition of trusted voices for amplification.

Viral Amplification—Rapid online spread; monitored/simulated with AI.

Virtual Diplomat—AI-enabled agents representing institutions in basic engagements.

Voice Cloning—Synthetic voice generation; use in accessibility/translation but also impersonation risks; pair with channels of record and takedown playbooks.

W

Wargaming (Narrative)—AI-assisted simulation of narrative strategies.

Watermarking—Invisible/visible signals indicating synthetic origin; combine with C2PA provenance for defense-in-depth.

Weak Supervision—Using noisy/indirect labels to build classifiers when gold data is scarce.

Web Scraping (AI)—Automated collection of online data for analysis.
WHO EARS—WHO's AI-powered rumor detection platform.

X

Explainability (XAI)—Systems designed to show how decisions are made.
Cross-border Narrative Tracking (X-Narratives)—Detecting narrative movement across borders.
XML (Extensible Markup Language)—Data format for structuring multilingual/provenance metadata.
XGBoost—Strong baseline ML method (non-deep-learning) often used for tabular policy/PD datasets.

Y

Youth Engagement Platforms—AI systems like U-Report that give youth a voice in diplomacy.
YouTube Labeling (AI Policy)—Emerging practice of labeling synthetic content and rolling out likeness-protection tools to combat impersonation.
Yield Analysis (Communications)—Measuring which messages generated the most meaningful engagement.
Youth Digital Safety—Age-appropriate design, content controls, and crisis messaging adapted for minors.

Z

Zero-Day Narrative—False narrative seeded suddenly to catch institutions off-guard.
Zero-Shot Learning—Handling tasks/languages without explicit prior training.
Zelenskyy Deepfake (2022)—Canonical wartime deepfake example targeting credibility.
Zero-Knowledge Proofs (ZKPs)—Cryptographic method to verify claims without revealing underlying data; emerging use for privacy-preserving verification.

Statement of Independence and Compliance

This book, *AI Use Cases for Public Diplomacy: Applying AI to Public Affairs and Strategic Communication*, was authored in a personal capacity and is not affiliated with, nor does it represent the views of, the U.S. Department of State or the U.S. government. The content was prepared in full compliance with all relevant legal, ethical, and regulatory requirements for current and former federal employees. In accordance with 11 FAM 614.5 and 5 C.F.R. § 2635, the author is permitted to receive compensation for this work as it does not relate to official duties past or present or in substantial part. The author did not receive any government funding, grants, or contractual support for this book. Any financial proceeds from its publication are entirely personal and unrelated to any government employment, duties, or obligations.

As a former U.S. government official, the author draws upon their professional experience to provide context and analysis. That experience informs the perspectives presented in this work; however, the book does not describe internal government systems, operational procedures, or nonpublic government practices. Discussions of workflows, decision environments, and administrative processes are presented at a conceptual and analytical level for educational purposes and should not be interpreted as descriptions of specific internal systems or operational procedures. Any discussion of technological capabilities, security processes, or decision-support tools does not disclose operational techniques, system configurations, vulnerabilities, safeguards, or implementation details used by any government or private organization.

The author's prior role in consular affairs informs the analytical framework of this book; however, none of the AI applications, use cases, or technological initiatives discussed were matters in which the author was personally or directly involved during their government service. The book is based on general AI principles and forward-looking analyses, with no direct reference to current or anticipated government programs or operations beyond what the Department has already shared publicly. Artificial intelligence is a rapidly evolving field, and its applications in diplomacy are subject to ongoing technological, ethical, and policy developments. The content of this book reflects the state of knowledge and public discourse at the time of writing and may not fully align with future advancements, regulations, or interpretations.

The author has taken all necessary steps to ensure there is no conflict of interest in the publication of this book, consistent with applicable post-employment restrictions governing former federal officials, including 18 U.S.C. § 207. No nonpublic, classified, or privileged information obtained through the author's prior government service has been used in this manuscript. The book is based on publicly available information, academic research, and generally accepted industry standards. The author has taken all reasonable steps to ensure that no copyrighted material has been used without appropriate permissions or attributions, and that all references, quotations, and ideas are properly cited to respect intellectual property rights and avoid inadvertent plagiarism. Care has been taken to ensure that the synthesis or aggregation of publicly available information does not reconstruct, infer, or reveal internal government systems, classified insights, or nonpublic operational frameworks.

This book was written by a former U.S. government employee and is intended for informational and academic purposes only. Readers from other jurisdictions should be aware that legal, ethical, and diplomatic considerations regarding AI may vary by country and are subject to different regulatory and policy frameworks. The author's prior affiliation with the U.S. Department of State is noted solely for biographical purposes and in compliance with 5 C.F.R. §§ 2635.702-705. The mention of the author's prior title does not imply any official endorsement of the views or content expressed in this book, which are entirely the author's own.

All case studies and scenarios discussed are either historically documented in publicly available work or they are hypothetical, designed for educational purposes, and do not reflect any current real-world policies, programs, or operations of the U.S. government. Any resemblance between the hypothetical case studies, scenarios, or analyses in this book and actual persons, policies, or events—past or present—is purely coincidental and unintentional. The analyses are speculative, forward-looking, and not tied to any specific diplomatic initiatives. While the author has made every effort to ensure the accuracy of the content, no responsibility is assumed for how the information may be interpreted or applied. The author and publisher disclaim any liability for damages, direct or indirect, resulting from the use or application of this book's content. Readers assume full responsibility for any actions taken based on the information provided, and they are encouraged to consult subject matter experts before making decisions influenced by the material herein.

The AI use cases in diplomacy project was submitted for pre-publication review by the Bureau of Global Public Affairs (GPA) and approved on October 1, 2024, in accordance with 11 FAM 614.5 and the pre-publication review requirements outlined in 11 FAM 600. The author has adhered to all applicable guidelines, including those outlined in 5 C.F.R. § 2635, and has taken care to avoid any misuse of prior official position or appearance of endorsement consistent with 5 C.F.R. §§ 2635.702–705. This work was completed using personal time and resources, without any use of government facilities or resources.

Descriptions of potential applications of artificial intelligence or digital systems in government contexts are analytical and exploratory in nature and should not be interpreted as operational guidance, legal advice, procurement specifications, security recommendations, or government policy directives. Readers should not rely on this work as a substitute for official government guidance, operational manuals, legal counsel, or regulatory directives.

About the Author

Don Kilburg is a retired U.S. diplomat, global strategist, and psychologist with a Ph.D. in Experimental Psychology from DePaul University, where he was also a Japanese Government Monbusho Research Fellow. For more than 30 years, he has applied behavioral science and emerging technology to complex challenges in international governance and public engagement, living and working across five continents, with postings in Latin America, Asia, Europe, the former Soviet Union, and Washington, D.C., in four languages.

A U.S. Foreign Service Officer from 2003 to 2025, Dr. Kilburg specialized in public diplomacy, strategic communication, and the application of emerging technology to diplomatic practice. He retired as a Public Affairs Officer in the Bureau of Global Public Affairs, the State Department's principal office for public diplomacy and strategic communication. He served as Spokesperson for the Bureau of Energy Resources and Press Attaché at the U.S. Embassy in Beijing, contributed intelligence reports to the President's Daily Brief, and briefed secretaries of state and ambassadors on public affairs and communications strategy. In 2024, he pioneered the "ChatGPT Diplomacy" project, helping thousands of U.S. diplomats adopt AI tools responsibly. His innovations earned him multiple Superior and Meritorious Honor Awards from the U.S. Department of State.

A U.S. Army veteran, former professor of psychology at Eastern Washington University, and author of *AI Use Cases for Diplomats* (Routledge, 2025), Dr. Kilburg is now Founder and CEO of Mind Leap Institute, LLC, where he helps leaders and organizations build the human capabilities needed to flourish in the age of AI. He is a frequent speaker at international AI and governance forums and an active thought leader mentoring the next generation of professionals at the intersection of technology, science, and diplomacy.

Bibliography

Acemoglu, Daron, and Simon Johnson. 2023. *Power and Progress: Our Thousand-Year Struggle Over Technology and Prosperity*. New York: Public Affairs.

Adichie, Chimamanda Ngozi. 2009. "The Danger of a Single Story." TED Talk, July. www.ted.com/talks/chimamanda_ngozi_adichie_the_danger_of_a_single_story.

African Union. 2024. *Continental Artificial Intelligence Strategy.* Addis Ababa: African Union Commission. https://au.int/sites/default/files/documents/44004-doc-EN-_Continental_AI_Strategy_July_2024.pdf.

Al Jazeera. 2024a. "Deepfake Democracy: Behind the AI Trickery Shaping India's 2024 Elections." *Al Jazeera*, February 20. www.aljazeera.com/news/2024/2/20/deepfake-democracy-behind-the-ai-trickery-shaping-indias-2024-elections.

Al Jazeera. 2024b. "What Is 'All Eyes on Rafah'? Decoding the Latest Viral Social Trend." *Al Jazeera*, May 29. www.aljazeera.com/news/2024/5/29/what-is-all-eyes-on-rafah-decoding-the-latest-viral-social-trend.

Alder, Madison. 2024. "From Translation to Email Drafting, State Department Turns to AI to Assist Workforce." *FedScoop*, December 11, 2024. https://fedscoop.com/state-department-ai-chatbot-email-drafting-northstar-famsearch/.

Allyn, Bobby. 2022. "Deepfake Video of Zelenskyy Could Be 'Tip of the Iceberg' for Info War, Experts Warn." NPR, March 16. www.npr.org/2022/03/16/1087062648/deepfake-video-zelenskyy-experts-war-manipulation-ukraine-russia.

Anlen, Shirin, and Mahsa Alimardani. 2026. *How AI Content Detection Is Being Weaponized in the Iran War.* Tech Policy Press, March 17, 2026. www.techpolicy.press/how-ai-content-detection-is-being-weaponized-in-the-iran-war/

Annan, Kofi. 2001. Nobel Lecture. Oslo, December 10. www.nobelprize.org/prizes/peace/2001/annan/lecture/.

Annan, Kofi. 2006. "Final Speech as UN Secretary-General." Harry S. Truman Presidential Library, Independence, MO, December 11. https://archive.globalpolicy.org/us-un-and-international-law-8-24/general-analysis-on-us-un-and-international-law/27069.html.

Arendt, Hannah. 1967. "Truth and Politics." *The New Yorker*, February 25. Reprinted in *Between Past and Future*, rev. ed. New York: Penguin, 1968.

ASEAN. 2025. *Expanded ASEAN Guide on AI Governance and Ethics — Generative AI.* Jakarta: ASEAN Secretariat. https://asean.org/wp-content/uploads/2025/01/Expanded-ASEAN-Guide-on-AI-Governance-and-Ethics-Generative-AI.pdf.

Associated Press. 2024a. "Pope Francis Addresses G7 Summit on AI Ethics, Becomes First Pope to Attend G7." AP News, June 14, 2024. https://apnews.com/article/pope-francis-ai-g7-italy-610b8f16aac4d36aa8a56c88de2ca09f

Associated Press. 2024b. "Deepfake Explicit Images of Taylor Swift Spread on Social Media. Her Fans Are Fighting Back." *AP News*, January 26, 2024. https://apnews.com/article/taylor-swift-ai-images-protecttaylorswift-nonconsensual-d5eb3f98084bcbb670a185f7aeec78b1.

Associated Press. 2024c. "X Pauses Some Taylor Swift Searches as Deepfake Explicit Images Spread." *AP News*, January 29, 2024. https://apnews.com/article/taylor-swift-deepfake-images-x-protecttaylorswift-6e5f9d086d1923a1cf5f5cde39fc890a.

Associated Press. 2025. "Moldova Detains 74 People over an Alleged Russia-Backed Unrest Plot around Key Election." *AP News*, September 22, 2025. https://apnews.com/article/moldova-russia-arrests-plot-election-293ee902e878ce1efcca339759eb06d0.

Associated Press. 2026. "Melania Trump Shares the Spotlight with a Robot at an Education and Technology Event." *NPR*, March 26, 2026. www.npr.org/2026/03/26/nx-s1-5761898/melania-trump-robot-education-technology-ai

Australian Government Department of Finance. 2024. *National Framework for the Assurance of Artificial Intelligence in Government: Implementing Australia's AI Ethics Principles in Government*. Canberra: Australian Government. www.finance.gov.au/government/public-data/data-and-digital-ministers-meeting/national-framework-assurance-artificial-intelligence-government/implementing-australias-ai-ethics-principles-government.

Ayon, Abir, and Tarek Hosen. 2026. "AI Fakes and Recycled Footage Fuel Disinformation Surge in US-Israel War on Iran." *The Daily Star*, March 20, 2026. https://www.thedailystar.net/fact-check/news/us-israel-war-iran-click-over-credibility-4132991.

Benjamin, Ruha. 2019. *Race After Technology: Abolitionist Tools for the New Jim Code*. Medford, MA: Polity.

Bergmanis-Korāts, Gundars, Giorgio Bertolin, Adele Pužule, and Yukai Zeng. 2024. *AI in Support of StratCom Capabilities*. Riga: NATO Strategic Communications Centre of Excellence. https://stratcomcoe.org/publications/ai-in-support-of-stratcom-capabilities/296.

Bhuiyan, Johana. 2025. "As Iran and Israel Fought, People Turned to AI for Facts. They Didn't Find Many." *NPR*, June 26, 2025. www.npr.org/2025/06/26/nx-s1-5442682/ai-chatbots-fact-check-videos-images-israel-iran

Bjola, Corneliu, and Ilan Manor, eds. 2024. *The Oxford Handbook of Digital Diplomacy*. Oxford: Oxford University Press. https://doi.org/10.1093/oxfordhb/9780192859198.001.0001.

Bjola, Corneliu, and Ilan Manor. 2018. "Revisiting Putnam's Two-Level Game Theory in the Digital Age: Domestic Digital Diplomacy and the Iran Nuclear Deal." *Cambridge Review of International Affairs* 31 (3): 3–32. https://doi.org/10.1080/09557571.2018.1476836

Bjola, Corneliu, and Ilan Manor. 2022. "The Rise of Hybrid Diplomacy: From Digital Adaptation to Digital Adoption." *International Affairs* 98 (2): 471–491. https://doi.org/10.1093/ia/iiac005.

Bjola, Corneliu, and Ilan Manor. 2025. "Digital Diplomacy in the Age of Technological Acceleration: Three Impact Scenarios of Generative Artificial Intelligence." *Place Branding and Public Diplomacy* 21: 303–308. https://doi.org/10.1057/s41254-023-00323-4.

Bjola, Corneliu, and Marcus Holmes, eds. 2015. *Digital Diplomacy: Theory and Practice*. London and New York: Routledge. https://doi.org/10.4324/9781315730844

Bjola, Corneliu, and Markus Kornprobst, eds. 2023. *Digital International Relations: Technology, Agency and Order*. London: Routledge. https://doi.org/10.4324/9781003437963.

Bjola, Corneliu, Jennifer Cassidy, and Ilan Manor. 2019. "Public Diplomacy in the Digital Age." *The Hague Journal of Diplomacy* 14 (1–2): 83–101. https://brill.com/view/journals/hjd/14/1-2/article-p83_7.xml.

Bjola, Corneliu. 2018. "Diplomacy in the Digital Age." Real Instituto Elcano ARI 113/2018, October 11. https://media.realinstitutoelcano.org/wp-content/uploads/2018/10/ari113-2018-bjola-diplomacy-digital-age.pdf.

Bjola, Corneliu. 2019. "Diplomacy in the Age of Artificial Intelligence." CPD Blog. USC Center on Public Diplomacy, October 31, 2019. https://uscpublicdiplomacy.org/blog/diplomacy-age-artificial-intelligence.

boyd, danah. 2016. "Data, Algorithms, Fairness, Accountability." Talk at U.S. Department of Commerce, Data Advisory Council, Washington, DC, October 28. www.danah.org/papers/talks/2016/CDAC.html.

Bracken, Matt. 2026. "State Department Is Gearing Up to 'Roll Out Agentic AI.'" *FedScoop*, February 13, 2026. https://fedscoop.com/state-department-agentic-ai-statechat-chatbots/

Buolamwini, Joy. 2023. Interview by NPR. "'Unmasking AI' Author Joy Buolamwini Says Prejudice Is Baked into Technology." NPR, November 28. www.npr.org/2023/11/28/1215529902/unmasking-ai-facial-recognition-technology-joy-buolamwini.

Calmis, Daniela, Victoria Olari, and Givi Gigitashvili. 2024. "Malign Interference in Moldova Ahead of Presidential Election and European Referendum." *Digital Forensic Research Lab (DFRLab)*, October 18, 2024. https://dfrlab.org/2024/10/18/malign-interference-moldova/.

Carnegie Endowment for International Peace. 2025. "Iran-Israel AI War Propaganda Is a Warning to the World." By Sam Gregory. Carnegie Endowment for International Peace, July 2025. https://carnegieendowment.org/research/2025/07/iran-israel-ai-war-propaganda-is-a-warning-to-the-world

CEPA. 2026. "Chinese AI Models Spread Propaganda Globally." Center for European Policy Analysis, February 2026. https://cepa.org/article/chinese-ai-models-spread-propaganda-globally/

Chenrose, Ali, and Max Rizzuto. 2025. "The Evolving Role of AI-Generated Media in Shaping Disinformation Campaigns." *Digital Forensic Research Lab (DFRLab)*. May 1, 2025. https://dfrlab.org/2025/05/01/the-evolving-role-of-ai-generated-media-in-shaping-disinformation-campaigns/

Chesney, Robert, and Danielle Citron. 2019. "Deepfakes and the New Disinformation War: The Coming Age of Post-Truth Geopolitics." *Foreign Affairs* 98 (1): 147–155.

Christopher, Nilesh, and Varsha Bansal. 2024. "Indian Voters Are Being Bombarded With Millions of Deepfakes. Political Candidates Approve." *Wired*, May 20, 2024. www.wired.com/story/indian-elections-ai-deepfakes/.

Coalition for Content Provenance and Authenticity (C2PA). 2024. *C2PA Technical Specification, Version 2.3*. https://c2pa.org/specifications/specifications/2.3/

Coombs, W. Timothy. 2014. *Ongoing Crisis Communication: Planning, Managing, and Responding*. 4th ed. Thousand Oaks, CA: SAGE Publications.

Council of Europe. 2024. *Framework Convention on Artificial Intelligence and Human Rights*. Strasbourg: Council of Europe.

Crawford, Kate. 2021. *Atlas of AI: Power, Politics, and the Planetary Costs of Artificial Intelligence*. New Haven: Yale University Press.

Cull, Nicholas J. 2008. *The Cold War and the United States Information Agency: American Propaganda and Public Diplomacy, 1945–1989*. Cambridge: Cambridge University Press.

Cull, Nicholas J. 2019. *Public Diplomacy: Foundations for Global Engagement in the Digital Age*. Cambridge: Polity.

Cull, Nicholas J. 2023. "The War for Ukraine: Reputational Security and Media Disruption." *Place Branding and Public Diplomacy* 19 (2): 195–199. https://doi.org/10.1057/s41254-022-00281-3.

Department for Business and Trade. 2025. *Microsoft 365 Copilot Pilot: DBT Evaluation Report*. London: Department for Business and Trade, August 28, 2025. www.gov.uk/government/publications/microsoft-365-copilot-pilot-dbt-evaluation-report.

Devlin, Sean. 2025. "The Prompt Engineering Guide for Comms Pros." Ragan Communications, June 26. www.ragan.com/ai-prompt-engineering-comms/.

DGACM (UN Department for General Assembly and Conference Management). 2015. *eLUNa Machine Translation System: Implementation Report*. New York: United Nations.

DiResta, Renée. 2024. *Invisible Rulers: The People Who Turn Lies into Reality*. New York: Public Affairs.

Doubleday, Justin. 2024. "With New AI Tools Available, State Department Encourages Experimentation." *Federal News Network*, June 28, 2024. https://federalnewsnetwork.com/artificial-intelligence/2024/06/with-new-ai-tools-available-state-department-encourages-experimentation/

Eco, Umberto. 2003. *Mouse or Rat?: Translation as Negotiation*. London: Weidenfeld and Nicolson.

EDMO. 2025. "The First AI War: How the Iran-Israel Conflict Became a Battlefield for Generative Misinformation." European Digital Media Observatory. https://edmo.eu/publications/the-first-ai-war-how-the-iran-israel-conflict-became-a-battlefield-for-generative-misinformation/

Eubanks, Virginia. 2018. *Automating Inequality: How High-Tech Tools Profile, Police, and Punish the Poor*. New York: St. Martin's Press.

European Commission. 2017. *eTranslation: Building Europe's Multilingual Machine Translation Service*. Brussels: European Commission.

European Commission. 2018. *CEF eTranslation: Building Europe's Multilingual Digital Service*. Brussels: European Commission. https://ec.europa.eu/digital-building-blocks/sites/pages/viewpage.action?pageId=533365621

European Commission. 2025a. *Annual Activity Report 2024—Translation*. Brussels: Directorate-General for Translation. https://commission.europa.eu/publications/annual-activity-report-2024-translation_en

European Commission. 2025b. "Report on the 2024 elections to the European Parliament." COM(2025) 287 final, June 6, 2025. Brussels: European Commission.

European External Action Service (EEAS). 2025. "3rd EEAS Report on Foreign Information Manipulation and Interference Threats: Exposing the Architecture of FIMI Operations." March 2025. www.eeas.europa.eu/sites/default/files/documents/2025/EEAS-3nd-ThreatReport-March-2025-05-Digital-HD.pdf.

European Union. 2024. *Artificial Intelligence Act*. Brussels: European Union.

Europeana Foundation. 2024. *Common European Data Space for Cultural Heritage Report*. The Hague: Europeana Foundation.

Federal Communications Commission. 2024a. "FCC Proposes $6 Million Fine for Illegal Robocalls That Used Biden Deepfake Generative AI Voice Message." Press Release, May 23. www.fcc.gov/document/fcc-proposes-6m-fine-nh-robocalls.

Federal Communications Commission. 2024b. "FCC Settles Case Against Provider That Transmitted Spoofed AI-Generated Robocalls for Election Interference in New Hampshire." Press Release, August 21, 2024. https://docs.fcc.gov/public/attachments/DOC-404951A1.pdf.

Federal Communications Commission. 2024c. "FCC Issues $6 Million Fine Against Steve Kramer for AI-Generated Biden Robocalls." Press Release, September 26. www.fcc.gov/document/fcc-issues-6m-fine-nh-robocalls.

Financial Times. 2025. "UK Civil Servants Who Used AI Saved Two Weeks a Year, Government Study Finds." *Financial Times*, May 29, 2025. www.ft.com/content/7c2aa19d-4c92-490d-bb35-f329a246fe5b

Foreign Affairs. 2025. "AI Is Supercharging Disinformation Warfare." By David R. Shedd and Ivana Stradner. *Foreign Affairs*, December 2025. www.foreignaffairs.com/united-states/artificial-intelligence-supercharging-disinformation-warfare

Foreign Interference Commission. 2025. *Public Inquiry into Foreign Interference in Federal Electoral Processes and Democratic Institutions: Final Report*. January 28, 2025. https://foreigninterferencecommission.ca/fileadmin/report_volume_1.pdf

Francis, Pope. 2024. "Address at the G7 Session on Artificial Intelligence." Borgo Egnazia, Italy, June 14. www.vatican.va/content/francesco/en/speeches/2024/june/documents/20240614-g7-intelligenza-artificiale.html.

G7 Rapid Response Mechanism. 2023. G7 Rapid Response Mechanism Annual Report 2023. Ottawa: Global Affairs Canada. https://international.canada.ca/en/global-affairs/corporate/reports/rapid-response-mechanism/annual-report-2023.

G7. 2023. "Hiroshima Process International Code of Conduct for Organizations Developing Advanced AI Systems." *Hiroshima AI Process*. October 30, 2023. www.mofa.go.jp/files/100573473.pdf.

Gaspari, Federico, Antonio Toral, Sudip Kumar Naskar, Declan Groves, and Andy Way. 2014. "Perception vs. Reality: Measuring Machine Translation Post-Editing Productivity." In Proceedings of the 11th Conference of the Association for Machine Translation in the Americas, 60–72. Vancouver, Canada: Association for Machine Translation in the Americas. https://aclanthology.org/2014.amta-wptp.5/

Gebru, Timnit. 2022. Interview by Billy Perrigo. "Why Timnit Gebru Isn't Waiting for Big Tech to Fix AI's Problems." *TIME*, January 18. https://time.com/6132399/timnit-gebru-ai-google/.

Geller, Eric. 2024. "The Tech Crash Course That Trains US Diplomats to Spot Threats." *WIRED*, July 2, 2024. www.wired.com/story/us-state-department-diplomacy-school/

Global Affairs Canada. 2023. "Rapid Response Mechanism Canada detects Spamouflage campaign targeting Members of Parliament." Statement, October 23, 2023. Ottawa: Global Affairs Canada.

Global Affairs Canada. 2025. Rapid Response Mechanism Canada Detects Second 'Spamouflage' Campaign Targeting Canada-Based Chinese-Language Commentators and Their Families. Ottawa: Global Affairs Canada.

Goggin, Ben. 2025. " 'Trump Gaza' AI Video Creators Say They Don't Want to Be the President's 'Propaganda Machine.' " NBC News, February 28, 2025. www.nbcnews.com/tech/internet/trump-gaza-ai-video-propaganda-machine-rcna194097.

Goldstein, Josh A., and Andrew Lohn. 2024. "Deepfakes, Elections, and Shrinking the Liar's Dividend." *Brennan Center for Justice*, January 23. www.brennancenter.org/our-work/research-reports/deepfakes-elections-and-shrinking-liars-dividend.

Government Communication Service (GCS). 2024. *Innovating with Impact Strategy.* London: Cabinet Office. www.communications.gov.uk/publications/gcs-innovating-with-impact-strategy/

Government Communication Service. 2025. "GCS Assist." *AI Knowledge Hub*. UK Government. https://ai.gov.uk/knowledge-hub/tools/gcs-assist/.

Government Digital Service (GDS). 2025a. *Artificial Intelligence Playbook for the UK Government.* London: Government Digital Service. www.gov.uk/government/publications/ai-playbook-for-the-uk-government/artificial-intelligence-playbook-for-the-uk-government-html

Government Digital Service (GDS). 2025b. *Microsoft 365 Copilot Experiment: Cross-Government Findings Report.* London: Government Digital Service, June 2025. www.gov.uk/government/publications/microsoft-365-copilot-experiment-cross-government-findings-report

Government of Canada. 2019. *Directive on Automated Decision-Making.* Ottawa: Treasury Board of Canada Secretariat.

Government of Canada. 2023. *Algorithmic Impact Assessment Tool: 2023 Update.* Ottawa: Treasury Board of Canada Secretariat.

Government Technology Agency of Singapore. 2025. "VICA: Features & Roadmap." Singapore Government Developer Portal. Last updated March 7, 2025. https://www.developer.tech.gov.sg/products/categories/platform/vica/features-roadmap.

GovTech Singapore. 2023. *VICA (Virtual Intelligent Chat Assistant): Design and Implementation.* Singapore: Government Technology Agency.

Graviss, Matthew. 2023. "Decision Advantage: Empowering Diplomacy through Responsible AI." *State Magazine*, December 2023. https://statemag.state.gov/2023/12/1223feat02/

Guterres, António. 2025. Address to the 80th Session of the UN General Assembly. New York, September 25. www.america-times.com/speech-delivered-by-his-excellency-antonio-guterres-secretary-general-of-the-united-nations-at-the-80th-session-of-the-un-general-assembly/.

Hao, Karen. 2022. Artificial Intelligence Is Creating a New Colonial World Order. MIT Technology Review, April 19, 2022. https://www.technologyreview.com/2022/04/19/1049592/artificial-intelligence-colonialism/.

Hoffman, Reid. 2023. *Impromptu: Amplifying Our Humanity Through AI.* Written with GPT-4. Dallepedia LLC.

International Telecommunication Union. 2022. "ITU Translate: Neural Machine Translation for ITU Documents and Websites." Geneva: International Telecommunication Union. www.itu.int/hub/news/itu-translate/

International Telecommunication Union. 2023. "AI for Good Global Summit." https://aiforgood.itu.int

International Telecommunication Union. 2024. *Global Connectivity Report 2024.* Geneva: International Telecommunication Union.

James. 2022. A Capability Definition and Assessment Framework for Countering Disinformation, Information Influence, and Foreign Interference. Riga: NATO Strategic Communications Centre of Excellence. https://stratcomcoe.org/publications/a-capability-definition-and-assessment-framework-for-countering-disinformation-information-influence-and-foreign-interference/255.

Jensen, Benjamin, Christopher Whyte, and Scott Cuomo. 2020. "Algorithms at War: The Promise, Peril, and Limits of Artificial Intelligence." *International Studies Review* 22 (3): 526–50. https://doi.org/10.1093/isr/viz025.

Jensen, Benjamin, Christopher Whyte, and Scott Cuomo. 2022. *Information in War: Military Innovation, Battle Networks, and the Future of Artificial Intelligence.* Washington, DC: Georgetown University Press.

Jobin, Anna, Marcello Ienca, and Effy Vayena. 2019. "The Global Landscape of AI Ethics Guidelines." *Nature Machine Intelligence* 1: 389–99. https://doi.org/10.1038/s42256-019-0088-2.

Johnson, J. 2019. "Artificial Intelligence and Future Warfare: Implications for International Security." *Defense & Security Analysis* 35 (2): 147–69. https://doi.org/10.1080/14751798.2019.1600800.

Juršėnas, Alfonsas, Kasparas Karlauskas, Eimantas Ledinauskas, Gediminas Maskeliūnas, Donatas Rondomanskas, and Julius Ruseckas. 2022. *The Role of AI in the Battle Against Disinformation*. Riga: NATO Strategic Communications Centre of Excellence. https://stratcomcoe.org/publications/the-role-of-ai-in-the-battle-against-disinformation/238.

Kapoor, Rishi. 2024. "Digital Platforms and AI Are Empowering Individual Investors." *World Economic Forum,* December 20. Accessed January 19, 2025. www.weforum.org/stories/2024/12/digital-platforms-ai-empowering-individual-investors.

Kasparov, Garry. 2021. "AI Should Augment Human Intelligence, Not Replace It." *Harvard Business Review,* March 18. www.kasparov.com/ai-should-augment-human-intelligence-not-replace-it-harvard-business-review-march-18-2021/.

Kasparov, Garry. 2023. "Worry About Human (Not Machine) Intelligence." *Encyclopedia Britannica,* October 31. www.britannica.com/topic/Worry-About-Human-Not-Machine-Intelligence-2119055.

Kello, Lucas. 2024. "Digital Diplomacy and Cyber Defence." In *The Oxford Handbook of Digital Diplomacy,* edited by Corneliu Bjola and Ilan Manor, 121–137. Oxford: Oxford University Press. https://doi.org/10.1093/oxfordhb/9780192859198.013.7.

Keskin, Tugrul, and Ryan Kiggins, eds. 2021. *Towards an International Political Economy of Artificial Intelligence.* Cham: Palgrave Macmillan.

Khalid, Raja Awais. 2021. "Twitter Diplomacy on CPEC: Impact on the Triangular Relationships Between Pakistan, China, and the USA." In *Artificial Intelligence and Digital Diplomacy: Challenges and Opportunities,* edited by Fatima Roumate, 195–207. Cham: Springer. https://doi.org/10.1007/978-3-030-68647-5_13.

Khan, Farakh. 2024. "AI in Action." *State Magazine*, December. U.S. Department of State. https://statemag.state.gov/2024/12/1224feat03/.

Kiggins, Ryan. 2018. "Big Data, Artificial Intelligence, and Autonomous Policy Decision-Making: A Crisis in International Relations Theory?" In *The Political Economy of Robots: Prospects for Prosperity and Peace in the Automated 21st Century,* edited by Ryan Kiggins, 85–111. Cham: Springer. https://doi.org/10.1007/978-3-319-51466-6_10.

Kilburg, Don. 2025. *AI Use Cases for Diplomats: Applying Artificial Intelligence to Diplomacy.* 1st ed. Chapman and Hall/CRC. https://doi.org/10.1201/9781003612308.

Kilburg, Don. 2025a. "AI and Diplomacy: Enhancing Global Engagement in the Age of AI." LinkedIn, May 28, 2025. www.linkedin.com/pulse/ai-diplomacy-enhancing-global-engagement-age-don-kilburg-ph-d--biaxe/

Kilburg, Don. 2025b. "Artificial Intelligence at the U.S. Department of State." LinkedIn, June 9, 2025. www.linkedin.com/pulse/artificial-intelligence-us-department-state-tools-don-kilburg-ph-d--ryxjf/

Kilburg, Don. 2026a. "Synthetic Statecraft: The Deepfake State: How Governments Learned to Love the Deepfake and What Thinking People Can Do About It." *LinkedIn*, March 18, 2026. https://www.linkedin.com/pulse/synthetic-statecraft-deepfake-state-don-kilburg-ph-d--h9yke/.

Kilburg, Don. 2026b. "Remarks on Synthetic Statecraft." In "AI-Powered PD: Navigating the New Frontier," U.S. Advisory Commission on Public Diplomacy official meeting minutes, May 6, 2026. U.S. Department of State. https://www.state.gov/acpd-official-meeting-minutes-may-6-2026

Kimani, C. J., and J. Scott. 2023. *Introduction to International Relations–Diploma Level.* Nairobi: Finstock Evarsity Publishers.

Kissinger, Henry A., Eric Schmidt, and Daniel Huttenlocher. 2019. "The Metamorphosis." *The Atlantic,* August. www.theatlantic.com/magazine/archive/2019/08/henry-kissinger-the-metamorphosis-ai/592771/.

Kissinger, Henry A., Eric Schmidt, and Daniel Huttenlocher. 2021. *The Age of AI: And Our Human Future.* New York: Little, Brown and Company.

Le, Brendan, and Daniel S. Levine. 2024. "Taylor Swift Endorses Kamala Harris in 2024 Presidential Election." *People*, September 10, 2024. https://people.com/taylor-swift-endorses-kamala-harris-2024-presidential-election-8557112.

Lewandowsky, Stephan, John Cook, and Doug Lombardi. 2020. *The Debunking Handbook 2020.* Databrary. https://doi.org/10.17910/b7.1182

Lewis, James Andrew. 2019. "Trust Your Eyes? Deepfakes Policy Brief." Center for Strategic and International Studies. October 23, 2019. www.csis.org/analysis/trust-your-eyes-deepfakes-policy-brief.

Li, Fei-Fei, and Sara Frueh. 2024. "AI Is a Tool, and Its Values Are Human Values." *Issues in Science and Technology* 40, no. 3 (Spring): 26–29. https://doi.org/10.58875/LBZG7966.

Li, Fei-Fei. 2023. Interview by Mike Borruso. "Stanford's Fei-Fei Li on Human-Centered AI." Author Talks, McKinsey Global Publishing, December 11. www.mckinsey.com/featured-insights/mckinsey-on-books/author-talks-dr-fei-fei-li-sees-worlds-of-possibilities-in-a-multidisciplinary-approach-to-ai.

Llana, Sara Miller. 2026. "With Viral 'Lego' Videos, Iran Stakes Claim as a Propaganda Powerhouse." *Christian Science Monitor*, May 20, 2026. www.csmonitor.com/World/Middle-East/2026/0520/iran-ai-slopaganda-propaganda-social-media-trump

Maillart, Thomas, Lucia Gomez, Ewa Lombard, Alexander Nolte, and Francesco Pisano. 2024. "Computational Diplomacy: How 'Hackathons for Good' Feed a Participatory Future for Multilateralism in the Digital Age." *Philosophical Transactions of the Royal Society A* 382 (2285): 20240103. https://doi.org/10.1098/rsta.2024.0103

Manor, Ilan. 2019. *The Digitalization of Public Diplomacy.* Cham: Palgrave Macmillan.

Manor, Ilan. 2023. "The Road Not Taken: Why Digital Diplomacy Must Broaden Its Horizons." *Place Branding and Public Diplomacy* 19 (2): 206–210. https://doi.org/10.1057/s41254-022-00280-4

Marcelo, Philip. 2023. "FACT FOCUS: Fake Image of Pentagon Explosion Briefly Sends Jitters through Stock Market." *AP News*, May 22, 2023. https://apnews.com/article/pentagon-explosion-misinformation-stock-market-ai-96f534c790872fde67012ee81b5ed6a4

Margetts, Helen, and Patrick Dunleavy. 2013. "The Second Wave of Digital-Era Governance: A Quasi-Paradigm for Government on the Web." *Philosophical Transactions of the Royal Society A* 371 (1987): 20120382.

Mazarr, Michael J., Ryan Michael Bauer, Abigail Casey, Sarah Anita Heintz, and Luke J. Matthews. 2019. *The Emerging Risk of Virtual Societal Warfare: Social Manipulation in a Changing Information Environment.* Santa Monica, CA: RAND Corporation.

McCammon, Sarah, and Hadeel Al-Shalchi. 2025. "Trump's AI-Generated Gaza Video Has Glitz, Gold and 'TRUMP GAZA' Resort." NPR, February 26, 2025. www.npr.org/2025/02/26/nx-s1-5309695/trump-gaza-video.

McGrath, Stephen, and Vadim Ghirda. 2024. "Moldovans Cast Votes to Choose President and Decide on EU Path as Russian Interference Claims Spike." *AP News*, October 20, 2024. https://apnews.com/article/moldova-elections-referendum-eu-russia-sandu-9411ab04ffb3230a83a4f8751c4e2414.

McGrath, Stephen. 2025. "Moldova's Election Faces AI-Driven Disinformation from Russia." *AP News*, September 22, 2025. https://apnews.com/article/moldova-election-europe-disinformation-russia-461e9a1c9558ae140c5b7539a5c89fd4.

Milmo, Dan. 2024. "Russia Targets Paris Olympics with Deepfake Tom Cruise Video." *The Guardian*, June 3, 2024. www.theguardian.com/technology/article/2024/jun/03/russia-paris-olympics-deepfake-tom-cruise-video.

Moore, Simon, and Roland Hübscher. 2021. *Strategic Communication and AI: Public Relations with Intelligent User Interfaces.* London: Routledge. https://doi.org/10.4324/9781003111320

National Audit Office (NAO). 2024. *AI in UK Government.* London: NAO.

NATO. 2024. "NATO's Approach to Counter Information Threats." October 18, 2024. https://www.nato.int/en/about-us/official-texts-and-resources/official-texts/2024/10/18/natos-approach-to-counter-information-threats.

NATO Strategic Communications Centre of Excellence. 2024. "Military Training Taken to Another Level—NATO StratCom COE Introduces a Simulated Information Environment Training Platform." April 16, 2024. https://stratcomcoe.org/news/military-training-taken-to-another-level-nato-stratcom-coe-introduces-a-simulated-information-environment-training-platform/164.

NATO Strategic Communications Centre of Excellence. n.d. "Information Environment Simulation Platform 'InfoRange.'" Accessed July 4, 2026. https://stratcomcoe.org/projects/information-environment-simulation-platform-inforange/3.

NATO Strategic Centre of Excellence. 201

Newsweek. 2026. "Trump Shares Map of US Including Greenland, Canada, Venezuela." Newsweek, January 20, 2026. www.newsweek.com/trump-shares-map-of-us-including-greenland-canada-venezuela-11384438.

Nextgov. 2020. "Air Force Turns to Machine Learning to Fight COVID-19 Disinformation." By Brandi Vincent. *Nextgov*, November 10. www.nextgov.com/emerging-tech/2020/11/air-force-turns-machine-learning-fight-covid-19-disinformation/169900/

Ngũgĩ wa Thiong'o. 1986. *Decolonising the Mind: The Politics of Language in African Literature*. London: James Currey.

NIST (National Institute of Standards and Technology). 2023. *AI Risk Management Framework*. Gaithersburg, MD: NIST.

Nye, Joseph S. 2004. *Soft Power: The Means to Success in World Politics*. New York: PublicAffairs.

Nye, Joseph S. 2011. *The Future of Power*. New York: PublicAffairs.

Nye, Joseph S. 2017. "Soft Power: The Origins and Political Progress of a Concept." *Palgrave Communications* 3 (1). https://doi.org/10.1057/palcomms.2017.8.

O'Neil, Cathy. 2017. "The Era of Blind Faith in Big Data Must End." TED Talk, April. www.ted.com/talks/cathy_o_neil_the_era_of_blind_faith_in_big_data_must_end.

OECD. 2024. *OECD Principles on Artificial Intelligence: 2024 Update*. Paris: OECD Publishing.

OECD/UNESCO. 2024. *G7 Toolkit for Artificial Intelligence in the Public Sector*. Paris: OECD Publishing.

Oremus, Will, Drew Harwell, and Teo Armus. 2023. "A Tweet about a Pentagon Explosion Was Fake. It Still Went Viral." *The Washington Post*, May 22. www.washingtonpost.com/technology/2023/05/22/pentagon-explosion-ai-image-hoax/.

Pahlavi, Pierre. 2007. "Evaluating Public Diplomacy Programmes: Lessons from the Canadian Case." *Clingendael Discussion Papers in Diplomacy*. The Hague: Netherlands Institute of International Relations.

Pamment, James. 2022. *A Capability Definition and Assessment Framework for Countering Disinformation, Information Influence, and Foreign Interference*. Riga: NATO Strategic Communications Centre of Excellence. https://stratcomcoe.org/publications/a-capability-definition-and-assessment-framework-for-countering-disinformation-information-influence-and-foreign-interference/255.

PR Newswire. 2020. "SOCOM and US Air Force Enlist Primer to Combat Disinformation." PR Newswire, October 1, 2020. www.prnewswire.com/news-releases/socom-and-us-air-force-enlist-primer-to-combat-disinformation-301143716.html

Purnat, Tina Dorothea, Tim Nguyen, Mark Briaud, and Sylvie Briand. 2021. "Infodemic Signal Detection During the COVID-19 Pandemic: Development of a Methodology for Identifying Potential Information Voids in Online Conversations." *JMIR Infodemiology* 1 (1): e30971. https://doi.org/10.2196/30971

Ramer, Holly, and Ali Swenson. 2024. "Political Consultant Behind Fake Biden Robocalls Faces $6 Million Fine and Criminal Charges." *AP News*, May 23, 2024. https://apnews.com/article/biden-robocalls-ai-new-hampshire-charges-fines-9e9cc63a71eb9c78b9bb0d1ec2aa6e9c.

Reuters. 2023. "Pakistan's Jailed Imran Khan Uses AI-Crafted Speech to Call for Votes." *Reuters*, December 18, 2023. www.reuters.com/world/asia-pacific/pakistans-jailed-imran-khan-uses-ai-crafted-speech-call-votes-2023-12-18/

Robins-Early, Nick. 2024. "Trump Posts Deepfakes of Swift, Harris and Musk in Effort to Shore Up Support." *The Guardian*, August 19, 2024. www.theguardian.com/us-news/article/2024/aug/19/trump-ai-swift-harris-musk-deepfake-images.

Roumate, Fatima, ed. 2021. *Artificial Intelligence and Digital Diplomacy: Challenges and Opportunities*. Cham: Springer.

Said, Edward W. 1978. *Orientalism*. New York: Pantheon Books.

Satter, Raphael, and Courtney Rozen. 2026. "State Department Switches to OpenAI as US Agencies Start Phasing Out Anthropic." Reuters, March 2, 2026.

Schaake, Marietje. 2024. *The Tech Coup: How to Save Democracy from Silicon Valley*. Princeton: Princeton University Press.

Shirky, Clay. 2008. *Here Comes Everybody: The Power of Organizing Without Organizations*. New York: Penguin Press.

Shirky, Clay. 2011. "The Political Power of Social Media." *Foreign Affairs* 90 (1): 28–41.

Snyder, Timothy. 2017. *On Tyranny: Twenty Lessons from the Twentieth Century*. New York: Tim Duggan Books.

Subzwari, Verda. 2024. "One Image, Seen by Millions: A Social Media Effort to Draw Attention to Rafah Surges." *AP News*, June 6, 2024. https://apnews.com/article/eyes-on-rafa-gaza-israel-hamas-fae6f49887637aaf4cbf548ce236dcb9.

Suleyman, Mustafa. 2023. *The Coming Wave: Technology, Power, and the Twenty-First Century's Greatest Dilemma*. New York: Crown.

Sullivan, Marguerite H. 2001. *A Responsible Press Office: An Insider's Guide*. Washington, DC: U.S. Department of State.

Sutherland, Kate E. 2025. "AI and the Future of Strategic Communication." In Artificial Intelligence for Strategic Communication. Singapore: Palgrave Macmillan. https://doi.org/10.1007/978-981-96-2575-8_12

Swenson, Ali. 2024. "Trump's Post of Fake Taylor Swift Endorsement Is His Latest Embrace of AI." *AP News*, August 20, 2024. https://apnews.com/article/trump-taylor-swift-fake-endorsement-ai-fec99c412d960932839e3eab8d49fd5f.

Taipei Times. 2020. "Taiwan's COVID-19 Response: Digital Tools and Communication Strategy." *Taipei Times*, April 15.

Taiwan Centers for Disease Control. 2020. "Public Can Use Chatbot to Gain Latest Information on COVID-19 Prevention." Press release, May 22, 2020. https://www.cdc.gov.tw/En/Bulletin/Detail/9_I4QsfPWwp9lSQLfK2nSg?typeid=158.

Tang, Audrey. 2020. "The Key to Taiwan's Pandemic Success: Fast, Fair … and Fun." *Global Asia* 15, no. 3 (September). https://globalasia.org/v15no3/cover/the-key-to-taiwans-pandemic-success-fast-fair-and-fun_audrey-tang.

The Diplomat. 2025. "AI Propaganda and the China-US Race for Influence." *The Diplomat*, September 2025. https://thediplomat.com/2025/09/ai-propaganda-and-the-china-us-race-for-influence/

Thompson, Stuart A., and Alexander Cardia. 2026. "Cascade of A.I. Fakes About War With Iran Causes Chaos Online." *The New York Times*, March 13, 2026.

Trotman, Andy. 2017. "AI Must Be Built with Empathy, Microsoft CEO Satya Nadella Says during UK Release of Book Hit Refresh." Microsoft UK Stories, October 6. https://ukstories.microsoft.com/features/ai-must-be-built-with-empathy-microsoft-ceo-satya-nadella-says-during-uk-release-of-book-hit-refresh/.

Trudeau, Elizabeth Kennedy. 2026. "How the World Sees the US Matters." Video, February 23, 2026. Public Diplomacy Council of America. www.youtube.com/watch?v=C2PEAeBGYdE

Tucker, Patrick. 2019. "The Newest AI-Enabled Weapon: 'Deep-Faking' Photos of the Earth." *Defense One*, March 31, 2019. www.defenseone.com/technology/2019/03/next-phase-ai-deep-faking-whole-world-and-china-ahead/155944/?>.

Tucker, Patrick. 2020. "Can AI Detect Disinformation? A New Special Operations Program May Find Out." Defense One, October 2, 2020. www.defenseone.com/technology/2020/10/can-ai-detect-disinformation-new-special-operations-program-may-find-out/168972/?>.

Tufekci, Zeynep. 2017. *Twitter and Tear Gas: The Power and Fragility of Networked Protest.* New Haven: Yale University Press.

Tuquero, Loreben. 2025. “Trump’s White House Is Testing the Limits of AI-Driven Political Messaging.” Poynter, October 28, 2025. www.poynter.org/fact-checking/2025/trump-white-house-ai-political-messaging/.

Tuquero, Loreben. 2026. "No, Netanyahu Didn't Have Six Fingers During His Press Conference." *PolitiFact*, March 13, 2026. https://www.politifact.com/factchecks/2026/mar/13/social-media/netanyahu-dead-video-artificial-intelligence/.

Turkle, Sherry. 2011. *Alone Together: Why We Expect More from Technology and Less from Each Other.* New York: Basic Books.

Turkle, Sherry. 2015. *Reclaiming Conversation: The Power of Talk in a Digital Age.* New York: Penguin Press.

Tuset Varela, Damián. 2024. “Diplomacy in the Age of AI: Challenges and Opportunities.” *Journal of Artificial Intelligence General Science* 2 (1): 101–128. https://jaigs.org/index.php/JAIGS/article/view/28

U.S. Advisory Commission on Public Diplomacy. 2026. *AI-Powered PD: Navigating the New Frontier — Public Meeting Transcript, May 6, 2026.* Washington, DC: U.S. Department of State. https://www.state.gov/summary-of-may-2026-meeting-ai-powered-pd/.

U.S. Department of State. 2022. *Public Diplomacy Foundations: Public Diplomacy in Practice.* Washington, DC: Office of Policy, Planning, and Resources (R/PPR).

U.S. Department of State. 2025. *Enterprise Data and Artificial Intelligence Strategy: Empowering Diplomacy through Responsible AI.* Washington, DC: U.S. Department of State.

UN Department for General Assembly and Conference Management (DGACM). 2015. *eLUNa Machine Translation System: Implementation Report.* New York: United Nations.

UNESCO. 2005. *Convention on the Protection and Promotion of the Diversity of Cultural Expressions.* Paris: UNESCO. www.unesco.org/en/legal-affairs/convention-protection-and-promotion-diversity-cultural-expressions

UNESCO. 2021. *Recommendation on the Ethics of Artificial Intelligence.* Paris: UNESCO. https://unesdoc.unesco.org/ark:/48223/pf0000381137.

UNESCO. 2023. *Guidelines for the Governance of Digital Platforms: Safeguarding Freedom of Expression and Access to Information through a Multi-Stakeholder Approach.* Paris: UNESCO. https://unesdoc.unesco.org/ark:/48223/pf0000387339.

UNESCO. 2024. *AI and the Holocaust: Rewriting History? The Impact of Artificial Intelligence on Understanding the Holocaust.* Paris: UNESCO. https://unesdoc.unesco.org/ark:/48223/pf0000390211.

UNICEF. 2020. *U-Report: COVID-19 Outbreak Response.* New York: UNICEF. www.unicef.org/innovation/ureportCOVID19

202 UNICEF. 2022. Information and Communication Technology Division: 2021 Annual Report. New York: UNICEF. https://www.unicef.org/media/125646/file/Annual%20Report%202021%20.pdf.

UNICEF. 2025. *U-Report Impact Assessment 2024.* New York: UNICEF.

United Nations Secretary-General. 2020. *Roadmap for Digital Cooperation.* Report No. A/74/821. New York: United Nations. Available at: www.un.org/en/content/digital-cooperation-roadmap/

United Nations. 2022. *State of Broadband Report.* Geneva: ITU/UNESCO.

United Nations. 2023. *Our Common Agenda: Policy Brief 5—A Global Digital Compact: An Open, Free and Secure Digital Future for All.* New York: United Nations. https://digitallibrary.un.org/record/4011891/files/%5EEOSG_2023_5%5E--EOSG_2023_5-EN.pdf.

United Nations. 2024. *Governing AI for Humanity: Final Report.* New York: United Nations. www.un.org/sites/un2.un.org/files/governing_ai_for_humanity_final_report_en.pdf.

USAID. 2015. *Collaborating, Learning, and Adapting (CLA) Framework.* Washington, DC: U.S. Agency for International Development.

USC Center on Public Diplomacy. 2023. "Integrating Artificial Intelligence into an Embassy's Public Diplomacy Workflows." Event page, October 18, 2023. https://uscpublicdiplomacy.org/event/integrating-artificial-intelligence-embassy%E2%80%99s-public-diplomacy-workflows

Vosoughi, Soroush, Deb Roy, and Sinan Aral. 2018. "The Spread of True and False News Online." *Science* 359 (6380): 1146–51.

Vota, Wayan. 2024. "How US State Department Uses AI Strategically in Modern Diplomacy." ICTworks, August 23, 2024. www.ictworks.org/state-department-uses-ai-strategically/.

Wardle, Claire. 2019. "Understanding Information Disorder." First Draft. https://firstdraftnews.org/long-form-article/understanding-information-disorder/.

Watts, Clint. 2024. "How Russia Is Trying to Disrupt the 2024 Paris Olympic Games." *Microsoft On the Issues* (blog), June 2, 2024. https://blogs.microsoft.com/on-the-issues/2024/06/02/russia-cyber-bots-disinformation-2024-paris-olympics/.

White, B. K., Anna L. Funk, Timothy M. Uyeki, and David L. Heymann. 2023. "Using Machine Learning to Support Infodemic Management: Lessons from COVID-19." *JMIR Infodemiology* 3 (1): e45311. https://doi.org/10.2196/45311.

World Economic Forum. 2025. *Industries in the Intelligent Age Report.* Geneva: WEF.

World Health Organization. 2021a. *Ethics and Governance of Artificial Intelligence for Health: WHO Guidance*. Geneva: World Health Organization. www.who.int/publications/i/item/9789240029200

World Health Organization. 2021b. *Infodemic Management: A Key Component of the COVID-19 Global Response*. Geneva: World Health Organization. www.who.int/publications/i/item/9789240010314.

World Health Organization. 2021c. "WHO Launches Pilot of AI-Powered Public-Access Social Listening Tool." *World Health Organization*, January 29, 2021. www.who.int/news-room/feature-stories/detail/who-launches-pilot-of-ai-powered-public-access-social-listening-tool

World Health Organization. 2022. *Infodemic Insights: Global Lessons from COVID-19.* Geneva: World Health Organization. www.who.int/publications/i/item/9789240052390.

World Health Organization. 2023. *An Overview of Infodemic Management during COVID-19 Pandemic, January 2020–July 2022*. Geneva: World Health Organization. https://iris.who.int/handle/10665/370860.

Yousif, Nadine. 2025. "Imposter Used AI to Pose as Marco Rubio and Contact Foreign Ministers." *BBC*, July 8, 2025. www.bbc.com/news/articles/crrqkyyjewno.

Zaharna, R. S. 2010. *Battles to Bridges: U.S. Strategic Communication and Public Diplomacy after 9/11*. New York: Palgrave Macmillan.

Index

D

www.ingramcontent.com/pod-product-compliance
Lightning Source LLC
LaVergne TN
LVHW010949010926
846999LV00031B/341
* 9 7 8 1 0 4 1 0 0 8 3 7 8 *